SPECIAL STUDIES

# Air Warfare
# and
# Air Base Air Defense
# 1914–1973

John F. Kreis

Office of Air Force History
United States Air Force
Washington, D. C. 1988

# Library of Congress Cataloging-in-Publication Data

Kreis, John F., 1940–
    Air warfare and air base defense 1914–1973 / John F. Kreis.
    407 p. cm. — (Special studies)
    Bibliography: p. 387
    Includes index.
    ISBN 0–912799–55–2
    1. Air defenses, Military.   2. Air bases—Defense measures.
3. Air warfare.  I. Title.  II. Series: Special studies (United
States. Air Force. Office of Air Force History)
UG730.K7 1988                88–19692
358.4'17—dc19              CIP

For sale by the Superintendent of Documents, U.S. Government Printing Office
Washington, D.C. 20402

# Foreword

While the projection of air power in contemporary warfare is among the most complex endeavors facing a military commander, few of the activities required to support and sustain air forces in battle have been explored in depth in historical literature. Even less studied has been the defense of air bases.

Since the introduction of airplanes to warfare, it was obvious that bases must be kept functioning at peak efficiency to sieze and maintain air superiority over an enemy as well as to carry out close air support and interdiction operations. A number of factors have been critical in actions involving air bases: advancing technology in aircraft and in defensive weapons, command and control systems, detection capabilities, evolving air power doctrine that predisposes air forces to specific courses of action, human endurance and morale, camouflage or concealment, dispersion, the ability to foresee and counter the strategy of a potential enemy, and in many cases pure chance that favors one side over the other.

In response to a request by the Air Force Director of Plans, the Office of Air Force History undertook to condense into one volume the experiences of various nations' air forces in defending air bases against attacks from the air. Maj. John Kreis, an experienced air security officer who spent much of his career providing protection for U. S. Air Force bases, accomplished this task by adopting a case study approach that highlights the interplay of the factors affecting air base defense over half a century. In these pages he has presented examples of the earliest attempts to defend airfields and troops in World War I from aerial assault. He chronicles the development of radar and command organizations that influenced so heavily the Royal Air Force's performance in the Battle of Britain, the ability to marshal defenses and repair crews on the island of Malta, and evolving command arrangements in North Africa that made for success against a capable enemy whose own command arrangements were deficient. Cases were also chosen to investigate failures from which sound lessons could be drawn. Limited conflict in the cold war world has imposed its own logic on base defense and attacks on installations, and the examples of base destruction in the Middle East wars between 1948 and 1973 are also instructive.

This volume has wide application in staff planning for developing base structures, establishing command and security arrangements, positioning of defensive emplacements, providing repair and support services, and training base personnel to react in a host of contingencies. For the Air Force generally, it offers new insights into matters not usually treated in doctrinal literature. The cases elaborated upon here will also have an appeal to a wider public audience interested in military aviation in all of its aspects.

DR. RICHARD H. KOHN
Chief, Office of Air Force History

# The Author

Maj. John F. Kreis completed the research and writing of this volume while serving as a historian in the Special Histories Branch, Office of Air Force History, Bolling Air Force Base, Washington, D.C. He has served in the U.S. Air Force for twenty years as a specialist in air base security and defense. He holds a BA in economics (1962) from Willamette University and an MA in history (1975) from the University of Delaware. Major Kreis is also a graduate of the FBI National Academy, Quantico, Virginia. He is currently preparing a companion volume on the ground defense of airfields.

# Acknowledgments

This book originated in a request from the Directorate of Plans, Deputy Chief of Staff, Plans and Operations, Headquarters, U.S. Air Force, for an analysis of past air base air defense actions to assist in current planning. Once work on the project began, however, it became apparent that its scope had to be widened to include more than the isolated defense of airfields.

Many of the ideas leading to development of this volume came from discussions with Mr. Bernard Nalty and Mr. Jack Neufeld, two of my colleagues in the Special Histories Branch. Both Mr. Neufeld and Mr. Nalty were generous with their time and knowledge of air warfare and both spent many hours reading draft manuscripts and discussing various campaigns in detail.

Dr. Richard H. Kohn, Chief of the Office of Air Force History, read and commented on the manuscript, but I am most indebted to him for encouraging and giving me the freedom to inquire into areas not automatically associated with air base air defense. The present volume owes much to his willingness to explore new areas. He was an enthusiastic supporter of the project from its beginning.

Lt. Col. Vance Mitchell, Dr. Eduard Mark, Lt. Kenneth Schaffel, Dr. Wayne Thompson, Dr. Daniel Mortensen, Dr. George Watson, Dr. Walton Moody, Mr. Warren Trest, Mr. Herman Wolk, and Col. John Shiner of the Office of Air Force History all read and commented on the drafts and offered thoughtful comments during several seminars. Dr. Fred Beck and Ms. Joyce Truett, who so ably edited the volume, are due much appreciation. Mr. William Heimdahl and MSgt. Roger Jernigan of the Reference Services Branch always responded to my requests for help in research, frequently abandoning temporarily other pressing duties. Sgt. Glenn Reynolds, Ms. Kim East, Ms. Jewell Newman, Ms. Elaine Estrada-Aherne, and Sgt. Rosalyn Culbertson provided much help with typing manuscripts; their willing assistance shortened considerably the process of manuscript preparation. Special thanks are due to my friend and editor, Mr. Eugene P. Sagstetter, who sadly did not live to see the work's conclusion, and to Mr. Louis C. Mattison for the time given to interviews and the kind permission to use his diary and other papers from Guadalcanal during late 1942 and early 1943.

Above all, special thanks go to my wife, Thea, who spent many hours helping with research in the National Archives and the Library of Congress. She proofread most of the manuscript, offering many suggestions to bring clarity to these pages.

# Contents

|  |  | *Page* |
|---|---|---|
| Foreword | | iii |
| The Author | | vi |
| Acknowledgments | | vii |
| Introduction | | xv |

## Part One
### The Early Development of Air Base Air Defense

| I | Air Base Defense in World War I | 3 |
|---|---|---|
| | Protecting the Flying Birdcages | 5 |
| | The Americans Arrive | 13 |
| II | Interwar Doctrine and Technology Changes | 23 |
| | American Defense Development | 24 |
| | Germany Prepares | 32 |
| | Japanese Defense | 36 |
| | The Soviet Union | 39 |
| | Great Britain and the Commonwealth | 42 |

## Part Two
### World War II

| III | *Blitzkrieg* and the Battle of Britain | 53 |
|---|---|---|
| | The Attack on Poland | 54 |
| | Fighting in the West | 62 |
| | The Battle of Britain | 76 |
| | Summary | 91 |
| IV | Malaya and Malta: 1941–1942 | 93 |
| | Malaya and Singapore: A Study in Failure | 94 |
| | The Siege of Malta, 1941–1942 | 111 |
| | Comparison of the Campaigns | 133 |
| V | Campaigns in Africa | 137 |
| | War of Movement in the Western Desert | 138 |

The Desert *Luftwaffe* ................................... 153
TORCH and the Drive to Tunis ......................... 159
The Axis Defense of Tunisia ........................... 169
Summary .............................................. 173
VI    The Eastern Front: 1941–1944 ......................... 177
Operation BARBAROSSA ................................ 177
The Russians Regroup ................................. 184
German Air Base Defense .............................. 189
The Struggle on the Steppe: 1942–1943 ................. 193
The Battle for Kursk .................................. 199
The Attack on Poltava Air Base, June 21, 1944 .......... 204
Summary ............................................. 212
VII   The Solomons and New Guinea: 1942–1944 .............. 217
Guadalcanal and Munda ............................... 219
The Fifth Air Force: Port Moresby to Hollandia ......... 236
The Japanese Respond ................................ 248
Summary ............................................. 257

## Part Three
## Postwar Changes

VIII  Two Limited Wars: Korea and Southeast Asia .............. 265
Dominating the Air in Korea .......................... 266
Success and Frustration in Vietnam .................... 278
Comparison of the Campaigns ......................... 296
IX    The Middle East: 1948–1973 .......................... 299
The Six Day War: 1967 ................................ 306
War of Attrition: 1967–1970 .......................... 319
The October War: 1973 ............................... 325
Mid-East Air Warfare in Perspective ................... 338
X     Conclusion ........................................... 343
Appendices .................................................. 354
Glossary .................................................... 359
Notes ....................................................... 363
Bibliographic Note ........................................... 387
Index ....................................................... 395

## Maps

1. World War I, The Western Front ........................... 14
2. Radar and Observer Network; Great Britain, 1940 ............ 46
3. Poland, 1939 .............................................. 58
4. Dutch Air Bases, 1940 ..................................... 68
5. German Attack in the West, 1940; Airfields in France .......... 73

6. British Fighter Force Deployment, 1940 . . . . . . . . . . . . . . . . . . . . . . 87
7. R.A.F. in Malaya, December 1941 . . . . . . . . . . . . . . . . . . . . . . 98
8. British Defenses in Singapore . . . . . . . . . . . . . . . . . . . . . . . 99
9. Malta: Mediterranean Bastion . . . . . . . . . . . . . . . . . . . . . . 114
10. Airfields on Malta . . . . . . . . . . . . . . . . . . . . . . . . . . . . . 116
11. Luqa – Hal Far Airfields, Malta, May 1942. . . . . . . . . . . . . . 126
12. Takali Airfield, Malta, 1942 . . . . . . . . . . . . . . . . . . . . . . . . 127
13. North African Operations, 1941 . . . . . . . . . . . . . . . . . . . . . 139
14. North African Operations, 1942 . . . . . . . . . . . . . . . . . . . . . 152
15. German Invasion of Russia; Operation BARBAROSSA . . . . . . . . . . . 178
16. Eastern Front, 1943; Operation CITADEL . . . . . . . . . . . . . . . . 200
17. Pacific Operations, 1942 . . . . . . . . . . . . . . . . . . . . . . . . . 218
18. Solomon Islands, 1942 (Inset: Henderson Field) . . . . . . . . . . . . 224
19. Port Moresby – New Guinea . . . . . . . . . . . . . . . . . . . . . . . 237
20. Port Moresby Airfields . . . . . . . . . . . . . . . . . . . . . . . . . . 238
21. Buna – Dobodura Airfields . . . . . . . . . . . . . . . . . . . . . . . . 246
22. Western New Guinea . . . . . . . . . . . . . . . . . . . . . . . . . . . . 250
23. East Asia . . . . . . . . . . . . . . . . . . . . . . . . . . . . . . . . . . . 266
24. Korean Airfields . . . . . . . . . . . . . . . . . . . . . . . . . . . . . . 276
25. Air War in North Vietnam . . . . . . . . . . . . . . . . . . . . . . . . . 282
26. The Middle East. . . . . . . . . . . . . . . . . . . . . . . . . . . . . . . 303
27. Israeli and Egyptian Airfields, October 1956. . . . . . . . . . . . . . . 310
28. Syrian Airfields, 1967 . . . . . . . . . . . . . . . . . . . . . . . . . . . 312
29. Egyptian Airfields, 1967 . . . . . . . . . . . . . . . . . . . . . . . . . . 314
30. Israeli and Jordanian Airfields, 1967 . . . . . . . . . . . . . . . . . . . 318
31. Egyptian Airfields, 1973 . . . . . . . . . . . . . . . . . . . . . . . . . . 328
32. Israeli Airfields, 1973 . . . . . . . . . . . . . . . . . . . . . . . . . . . 329
33. Syrian Airfields, 1973. . . . . . . . . . . . . . . . . . . . . . . . . . . . 331

## Tables

1. *Luftwaffe* Order of Battle, September 1939. . . . . . . . . . . . . . . . . 60
2. Strengths and Losses, Polish Air Force, 1939 . . . . . . . . . . . . . . . 61
3. French Air Force, May 1940. . . . . . . . . . . . . . . . . . . . . . . . . 64
4. British Air Forces in France, 1940. . . . . . . . . . . . . . . . . . . . . . 72
5. The *Luftwaffe* in the West, 1940. . . . . . . . . . . . . . . . . . . . . . . 74
6. Comparative Strengths, Battle of Britain. . . . . . . . . . . . . . . . . . 79
7. RAF Strength, Dispositions in Malaya, 1941 . . . . . . . . . . . . . . . 102
8. Antiaircraft Artillery Forces, Malaya . . . . . . . . . . . . . . . . . . . . 103
9. Malayan Air Defenses, December 1941 . . . . . . . . . . . . . . . . . . 104
10. Japanese 3d Army Air Corps. . . . . . . . . . . . . . . . . . . . . . . . . 105
11. Japanese Navy 22d Air Flotilla . . . . . . . . . . . . . . . . . . . . . . . 106
12. RAF Order of Battle, Malta . . . . . . . . . . . . . . . . . . . . . . . . . 120

13. Malta Antiaircraft Defenses ................................. 121
14. *Luftwaffe* Order of Battle, Sicily 1942 ....................... 122
15. Axis Air Forces, Africa, December 1941 ..................... 145
16. RAF in Africa, November 1941 ............................. 146
17. Axis Air Forces, Africa, May 1942 ......................... 157
18. RAF in Africa, May 1942 ................................... 158
19. Axis Air Strength, North Africa, April 1943 .................. 171
20. *Luftwaffe* Strength, Eastern Front, June 1941 ................ 186
21. Soviet Antiaircraft, June 1941 ............................. 187
22. *Luftwaffe* Air Strength, Eastern Front, June 1941 ............. 190
23. Soviet Air Strength, June 1941 ............................. 191
24. U. S. Air Defense Units, Guadalcanal ...................... 226
25. Japanese Navy Air Units, Pacific, 1942 ...................... 227
26. Allied Air Units Used Against Wewak ....................... 253
27. Estimate of Japanese Air Strength, February 1944 .............. 254
28. North Vietnamese Antiaircraft Artillery ..................... 286
29. North Vietnamese Air Threat ............................. 292
30. Egyptian Air Force, 1956 ................................. 304
31. RAF – French Air Force, Middle East, 1956 .................. 305
32. Israeli Air Force, 1967 ................................... 308
33. Israeli Air Force, 1973 ................................... 332
34. Israeli Air Defense Systems, 1973 ......................... 333
35. Syrian Air Defense Systems, 1973 ......................... 335
36. Probable Aircraft Losses, October 1973 ..................... 336
37. Daily Loss Summary, Israeli Air Force, October 1973 ........... 338

## Photographs

1. Royal Flying Corps Field at Beauval ........................  4
2. Flanders Aerodrome, Richthofen Squadron ..................  5
3. Aerial View of Souilly Aerodrome .........................  6
4. Improvised Antiaircraft Emplacements ......................  8
5. Allied Barrage Balloon under German Attack ................ 10
6. 94th Aero Squadron Pilots on Alert ........................ 18
7. Lt. Douglas Campbell Attacks a Pfalz DIII ................. 19
8. Bomb Loading ........................................... 20
9. Lt. William C. Sherman .................................. 26
10. Fort Bragg Maneuvers, 1938 ............................... 28
11. SCR–268 Radar and Searchlight ............................ 29
12. U. S. Army Antiaircraft Guns during World War II ............. 30
13. German Antiaircraft Guns of World War II .................. 35
14. Japanese Antiaircraft of World War II ...................... 37
15. German Würzburg D Radar ................................ 47

16. Polish Aircraft Destroyed at Deblin ......................... 56
17. Okechie Airfield after German Attack ....................... 57
18. British Guns in France, 1940 ............................... 65
19. Wrecked German Ju-52s at Waalhaven ..................... 69
20. British RAF Filter Center and Radar in Operation,
        Winston Churchill Inspecting Rocket Device.............. 80
21. German Aerial Photos of RAF Station Eastchurch ............ 86
22. RAF Leadership, Battle of Britain ......................... 91
23. Grand Harbor, Malta ..................................... 115
24. Scenes from the Siege .................................... 118
25. Bofors Gun Crew near Valetta............................. 124
26. British Serviceman with Siege Rations ..................... 128
27. Maltese Airfield under Attack, 1942........................ 129
28. Maltese Terrain.......................................... 132
29. German Aerials of British Desert Landing Grounds ........... 142
30. American Bomber in Egyptian Sandstorm ................... 148
31. British Air Strike at Tamet, Libya.......................... 151
32. Wrecked American B-17s at Maison Blanche, Algeria ......... 161
33. Algerian Laborers Stack Supply ........................... 162
34. Allied Commanders at Casablanca, 1943.................... 164
35. American Bulldozer Fills Crater ........................... 166
36. British Bofors Crew on Tripoli Beach....................... 168
37. Allied Bombs over Axis Airfield, Tripoli .................... 172
38. Abandoned Russian Aircraft during German Attack........... 179
39. Camouflaged German Radio Vans ......................... 182
40. Field Marshal Albert Kesselring .......................... 183
41. *Luftwaffe* 88-mm Gun Crew in Russia ..................... 192
42. German Airfield Construction in Russia ..................... 194
43. German Aerial of Russian Field at Kirovsk.................. 195
44. German Light Flak Crew in Action ......................... 196
45. German Field at Demyansk ............................... 197
46. German Crew Manning a Predictor ........................ 203
47. American Engineers Lay Out Pierced Steel Plank
        Runways at Poltava.................................... 205
48. German Aerial of American Bombers at Poltava.............. 207
49. German Attack on Poltava................................. 209
50. Yak-9s Defending the Poltava Base ........................ 210
51. Poltava Base Commander General Alexander R. Perminov ...... 210
52. Ju-52s Blaze in Russian Field ............................. 213
53. U. S. Marine 90-mm Guns on Guadalcanal .................. 222
54. F4F Wildcats in Open Revetments, Guadalcanal .............. 223
55. Crew with 20-mm Guns on Henderson Field ................ 225
56. Control Panel of Japanese Radar .......................... 228

57. American SCR–270 Radar Used on Guadalcanal . . . . . . . . . . . . . . . 229
58. Maj. Gen. Roy S. Geiger, USMC . . . . . . . . . . . . . . . . . . . . . . . . . . . 230
59. Japanese Hit on American Hangar, Henderson Field . . . . . . . . . . . 232
60. American Aviation Facilities on New Guinea . . . . . . . . . . . . . . . . . 249
61. Concealed Japanese Guns with Telltale Gardens . . . . . . . . . . . . . . . 251
62. Low Level Operations in New Guinea . . . . . . . . . . . . . . . . . . . . . . . 258
63. American 40–mm Gun in Korea, 1950 . . . . . . . . . . . . . . . . . . . . . . . 268
64. Stripped Yak–9 at Wonsan, Korea, 1950 . . . . . . . . . . . . . . . . . . . . . 270
65. American Bombers Reduce Sunan Airfield, Korea . . . . . . . . . . . . . . 274
66. American Aerial Outlining Dummy Airfield, North Korea . . . . . . . 277
67. American Fighters in Prefabricated Revetments,
        South Vietnam, 1966 . . . . . . . . . . . . . . . . . . . . . . . . . . . . . . . . . . . 280
68. North Vietnamese Surface to Air Missile Battery, 1966 . . . . . . . . . 283
69. Drone Mission Over North Vietnam, 1969 . . . . . . . . . . . . . . . . . . . 284
70. American Bomb Damage at Hoa Loc Airfield, North Vietnam . . 287
71. Phuc Yen Airfield Bomb Damage . . . . . . . . . . . . . . . . . . . . . . . . . . . 289
72. Israeli Gun Crew in the Sinai, 1973 . . . . . . . . . . . . . . . . . . . . . . . . . 326
73. Israeli Strike on Egyptian Airfield, 1973 . . . . . . . . . . . . . . . . . . . . . 340
74. Israeli Bombs over Syrian Field, 1973 . . . . . . . . . . . . . . . . . . . . . . . 341

The experience which I gained during this advance
through Cyrenaica formed the main foundation
for my later operations. I had made heavy demands throughout the action, far more than precedent permitted, and had thus to relearn the fact
that standards set by precedent are based on
something less than average performance, and,
for that reason, one should not submit to them.
— Erwin Rommel, Field Marshal

I have sometimes reflected that it was an advan-
tage to the Royal Air Force that we had no long
Service tradition behind us, no set ways of tack-
ling our job. Improvisation, which saved us in the
Middle East, came the more easily to us, I think,
than to our contemporaries in the Army and the
Royal Navy.
— Arthur William Lord Tedder,
Air Marshal

# Introduction

Some medieval European cartographers, preparing maps based in part on travelers' tales or superstition, occasionally labeled otherwise unknown areas of far continents with the phrase "Here be Dragons," seeking to warn the unwary of dangers in venturing beyond the clearly defined regions of the world. None of these men had ever seen a dragon, and although they had vivid ideas of flying, fire-breathing monsters based on mythological or biblical accounts, no dragon was found on journeys across unknown lands. In the twentieth century, however, a war weapon with some of the dragons' attributes, yet far more lethal, appeared. The new weapon was the airplane, and as airplanes grew in size, complexity, and destructive capability, their need for bases and support systems grew. In the ancient stories, Hercules, Perseus, Jason, and St. George ventured to the dragons' lairs to outwit or destroy the creatures. As with the ancient heroes, modern warriors trying to destroy warplanes often went to airfields to obliterate modern dragons. In the process, they showed that combat aircraft, like the mythical dragon, might be hard to destroy, but they were not invincible.

From virtually the first appearance of aircraft in warfare, their bases have been the targets of enemy attack and the concern of defending friendly forces. Between 1914 and 1973, the concept of air base air defense grew with the technological changes of the 20th Century. In 1914, antiaircraft guns could barely contend with early warplanes. Until World War II an attacker could do little permanent damage to the grass or dirt fields that sustained the light military aircraft and service equipment of the time. Starting on a small scale early in World War II, assaults on air bases grew in intensity as opposing sides realized the impact of airpower. These attacks involved paratroops, glider forces, air raids, and ground assaults. Since that era, faster planes, technologically improved ordnance of increased destructiveness, permanent concrete runways, and the presence of fixed, complex service and support establishments made airfields ever more vulnerable to destruction. By 1973, tactical air base defense used some of the most sophisticated weapon systems and advanced electronic command and control systems yet known. Radar-controlled guns and missiles guided toward an attacker still miles from his target gave new options to defenders. Air base air defense was continually redefined as much by doctrinal prescription as by context: time, place, the technological evolution of control mechanisms, munitions and aircraft, and the interplay of other elements of airpower all contributed to the nature of the individual cases chosen for study here.

Technology had similar, but not simultaneous, effects on both attack and defense. Over time, technological change caused the advantage to swing back and forth. In 1940, during the Battle of Britain, the RAF's radar system greatly assisted the defenders. Subsequently, air commanders in other battles and other theaters learned to overcome, or at least control, air defense systems, thus prompting new air base defense measures in turn. Changes to attack and defense technology over the years necessarily altered the methods whereby commanders sought air superiority or attempted to protect their bases. It was air superiority which weighed heavily in the success or failure of counterair operations, and by the peak of fighting in World War II, air superiority became the crux of air base air defense.

Air superiority normally gives one side such a degree of dominance as to permit it to operate its land, sea, and air forces without prohibitive interference by the opposing air force. In practice, however, air superiority was not permanently attained. Often it was contested anew each day, and it was not based on numerical advantage. Concentration of force, ingenuity of command, and effective use of defense weapons were important aspects of air superiority and air base air defense efforts. During World War I, tactical air superiority was achieved by air-to-air combat. Between the wars, aircraft, especially bombers, became faster and able to carry a much more destructive bomb load. The changes opened the way to new applications of air power so that by 1939 many air commanders viewed air warfare much differently than they had twenty years before. At the beginning of World War II, German Air Force doctrine advocated destruction of enemy aircraft on the ground by surprise strikes. Other nations' air forces saw air warfare and base defense differently depending on the conditions prevailing in their respective combat theaters. The air combat of World War II made clear, however, that air base air defense and air superiority were closely interwoven; one could not exist without the other.

Adequate protection of air bases has been complex and difficult; at times it was greatly underrated or misunderstood, frequently to the detriment of one side or the other. In general, there were four facets of base defense. The first, but not necessarily the most important, was active defense (sometimes called point defense*), and involved the use of antiaircraft

---

* Point air defense is the protection of a specific site, such as an airfield, factory complex, rail yard, or the like. It can be contrasted with the concept of area defense, which is the protection of a region or an entire country.

guns, surface-to-air missiles, or fighter aircraft operating under varying levels of ground or airborne control. Second was passive defense, such as camouflage, the use of revetments, hardening facilities with concrete and steel construction, or the use of decoys and deception, such as dummy airfields. A third, dispersal, involves scattering the aircraft and other vulnerable resources, such as fuel and spare parts, over a wide area of a single base or over many bases to increase an enemy's targeting problems. The fourth aspect was too often unrecognized, but highly important: the ability of an air installation's units to effect repairs and recover from an attack as quickly as possible. To the extent these factors were neglected, bases suffered from the depredations of the opposing air force.

Traditional formulae predicting that ground troops in prepared defenses should be able to defeat a force three times their number do not hold for aerial operations. Air forces cannot make use of terrain features to aid the defense, but air defense systems using all of the advantages at their disposal have in the past held their own against greater than three-to-one odds. The portion of the Battle of Britain fought between August 10 and September 15, 1940, was a struggle for air superiority over England and for control of RAF Fighter Command's main bases in East Anglia, Kent, and Sussex. On August 10, the *Luftwaffe's* fighters outnumbered those of Fighter Command. Not only were the British short of fighters, their pilot-to-plane ratio was well below 2:1, which meant fliers had to endure long, stressful duty shifts day after day, often engaging in combat several times a day. British pilot training rates at that time were less than those of the Germans, and bomber and transport pilots could not be quickly retrained to fly the new, high-performance Spitfires or Hurricanes. But in 1940, the British had an advantage: a radar directed defense system tailored to the needs of its guns and fighters. The result was Fighter Command's ability to detect enemy bomber groups forming over France. British interceptor pilots and antiaircraft guns were thus able to attack the German aircraft, taking a heavy toll.

The Battle of Britain was a seminal air defense experience, influencing tactical air defense doctrine in such diverse theaters as the Mediterranean and North Africa, the Southwest Pacific and the Solomon Islands, as well as the air defense of North America and North Vietnam. Almost two years after the Battle of Britain, the RAF applied the same techniques to defend Malta, at times against odds of ten to one. During April 1942, the weight of bombs dropped on Malta's airfields was thirty-six times the amount that hit Coventry, England, on the night of November 14–15, 1940, and more than fell on London during August, September, and October of 1940. Air operations at Malta, although reduced, did not halt because of enemy action.[1]

The style of defensive air combat employed by the British over Malaya, by the Allies in North Africa and the South and Southwest Pacific all reflected the command and control system first used over England. After World War II, the defenses favored by the Americans during the Korean War and by both sides in Southeast Asia and the Arab-Israeli fighting in the Middle East were based upon the same system. In contrast Germany, Japan, and the Soviet Union did not trace the origins of their doctrine on air defense to the Royal Air Force. The differences in German, Japanese, and Soviet air base protection in World War II become clear in the chapters covering the Eastern Front, the Mediterranean, and the Pacific; all three air forces developed methods of safeguarding their airfields that varied in effectivenss. The influence of these campaigns has been felt to the present day, and the experiences form the basis of much of today's tactical air warfare planning.

Military history has paid little attention to air base defense, though the topic is vital. Most accounts of air campaigns concern planning for and carrying out the flying aspect of the fighting. While flying is the most important aspect of a campaign, the costs of building modern air bases and sophisticated attack aircraft require that we carefully consider ground assets as well. The World War II experience taught the Unites States Army and Army Air Forces many lessons by the end of 1944, and brought them into a close working arrangement that overcame their parochial prewar views. One year later, however, the two services disagreed with each other over the subject of air base air defense more heatedly than they had in 1941. Since that time, the arguments have continued.

The cases selected for study in this volume reflect a wide variety of geographic and operational differences in the sixty years from the beginning of World War I through the Arab-Israeli War of 1973. The Second World War was the first to involve large air forces fighting over long periods of time. All of the cases involve the application of tactical, as opposed to strategic air power. Some campaigns that might interest a reader were excluded. The Japanese attacks on Pearl Harbor and Clark Field have been so frequently analyzed that little would be gained by a repetition here; the United States Army Air Forces' raids on Germany's airfields in 1943 and 1944 were part of a strategic effort, and therefore were purposely omitted. Finally, the Allied operations on the European continent after D-day, June 6, 1944, pitted the British and Americans against a *Luftwaffe* which had been so badly debilitated on the Russian Front, in the Mediterranean Theater, and in its efforts to protect the German homeland from Allied strategic bombers that it was no longer a viable fighting force capable of any sustained operations, let alone air base air defense. Assaults on air bases by paratroops or ground forces will not be discussed except where directly affected by the air operation in question. The forms of attack associated with ground forces require the insertion, supply, reinforcement, and possibly the removal of military units not normally common to an air force; their complexities call for a separate volume to afford them adequate review.

The episodes discussed here depict actions that involved air defense planning and operations in several countries over a long (for aviation history) span of time. Selections of cases do not necessarily imply approval of the tactics or the weapons involved, but were made in the hope that today's air commanders and planners could benefit from the experience of others.

Part 1
The Early Development of Air Base Air Defense

# Chapter I

# Air Base Defense in World War I

When the British Expeditionary Force (BEF) moved to France in the late summer of 1914 virtually all of the Royal Flying Corps' aircraft went along as an integral, if small, part of the BEF. On the Continent, they joined the equally small French air service, the *Aeronautique Militaire,* but neither the Allies nor the Germans had a chance to build substantial aerodromes for some time. In the maneuvering of the first months of the war, airplanes on both sides often flew from a different location each day as ground forces advanced or retreated. Aerodromes were sometimes prepared fields, but usually no more than hastily chosen flat ground where aircraft could land safely. Antiaircraft fire, both small arms and exploding artillery shells, appeared during the first month of fighting, and pilots and mechanics found great sport in shooting at an enemy overhead. As the war progressed, both sides resorted to antiaircraft fire.[1] The Allies and Germany scored significant technical gains in aircraft design and construction, gunnery, and communications during the four years of fighting.

By war's end elaborate air defenses sited near the front for the protection of armies were common. Extensive detection and warning systems appeared everywhere along the trenches. In addition, airfields near the battle lines benefited from their proximity to army antiaircraft (AA) gun positions. Often it was impossible to tell if an army intended its air defenses for the protection of ground or flying units.

Most aerodromes of early World War I were level, open fields. Cows often grazed while aircraft landed and took off. Maintenance shops, hangars, and living quarters were temporary canvas-covered wood-frame structures that could be knocked down and moved on short notice. As the war slowed to a stalemate, these facilities became semipermanent and some airfield improvements, such as grading and crushed rock or cinder surfaces,

**Royal Flying Corps field at Beauval. Tents house flying personnel and ground crews.** U.S. Army Air Defense Museum.

were made. Usually, the aircraft and shops were the only inviting targets. Cratering runways was not worthwhile, as their construction often needed no more than several groups of men walking over a field to compress the soil. The light bombs then in use could not substantially damage the surface.[2]

Shelters of some sort were necessary from the first. The people stationed at the field had to be quartered and supplied; aircraft and equipment needed protection. World War I airplanes deteriorated rapidly in the rain and dampness of Europe. Without a cover to keep the weather at bay, an airplane's wood warped and its canvas loosened, making the craft unflyable in as little as eight days. As the war progressed, many of the bases became a good deal more permanent, even acquiring some basic comforts. Supply and air depot installations, such as those at Orly, Romorantin, and Colombey-les-Belles, became rather elaborate.[3]

By November 1918, the Americans had brought over and set up some 148 steel hangars and had another 266 ready for the builders. The American Expeditionary Force's production center located at Romorantin was projected to have 600,000 square feet of covered hangars for aircraft assembly

**Flanders aerodrome housing the Richthofen squadron. Tents provide shelter on a provisional air field. When conditions required, the entire field could move to a new location within hours.** U.S. Army Air Defense Museum.

and storage. By Armistice Day 371,000 square feet were in use. The changes taking place at the rather informal locations of early air bases could be seen not only in the relatively safe rear area, but also at forward sites. By November 11, the Air Depot at Colombey-les-Belles, near Toul, had 357,363 square feet of building space.[4] These aircraft shelters became obvious targets; opposing airmen's attacks caused the ground crews to install a variety of light defensive weapons.

## Protecting the Flying Birdcages

On the 24th of August 1914 Capt. H. C. Jackson and Lt. E. L. Conran of the Royal Flying Corps were on an observation patrol near Tournai, in Flanders. About noon, they spotted three parked German aircraft on an airfield outside the town of Lessines. Lieutenant Conran banked the plane for a closer look, and as they passed one of them threw a bomb overboard. The attack caused no damage and was notable only because it was one of the first air attacks on an enemy air base.[5] Neither bombardment nor attack was

5

**Aerial view of Souilly Aerodrome in the last two years of the war. Structures and flying field have become more permanent, but are still relatively impervious to damage by air attack.** U.S. Army Air Defense Museum.

the mission of fliers early in World War I. They were observers, sent to report on troop movements, supply and artillery positions, and the like. The most important function of aircraft units during the early years of fighting was to spot for and adjust gun fire. If these early aviators used bombs, they were often nothing more than hand grenades or containers of gasoline thrown from the cockpit. The pilot or observer usually released the first externally mounted bombs by cutting the retaining strings, and their destructive power was quite limited. Not to be outdone by the British, the Germans attacked an airfield near Compiegne on August 29th. Again, there was no damage.[6]

As the war continued into the autumn, it grew in scope. Germany introduced zeppelins to the conflict and with their use gained the ability for both long range reconnaissance and bombardment. In September 1914, the British Admiralty concluded that German zeppelins posed a threat to the British fleet as well as to targets in England. The Royal Naval Air Service's (RNAS) squadron at Dunkirk received orders to attack the zeppelin bases. All the airships within 100 miles were to be destroyed. On September 22, 1914, the RNAS launched the first raid on the zeppelin hangars at Duesseldorf; it failed when the bombs fell short of the target or did not explode. On October 8, two attacks by single aircraft at Cologne were more successful. They destroyed a zeppelin, a zeppelin shed, and a machine shop. The pilots met heavy ground fire from rifles and antiaircraft guns. One airplane was badly damaged, but both pilots returned safely. The destruction at Cologne

6

pleased one man ever on the lookout for new ideas: Winston Churchill, then First Lord of the Admiralty, encouraged more attacks and was, in fact, an early believer in destroying an enemy's air force on the ground at his bases.[7]

These flights of about 200 miles to attack the zeppelins were remarkable not only for their endurance; misty weather introduced much guesswork into the navigation for the mission. More important, the imaginative raids clearly illustrated that the British realized from the start of the war the need for counterair attacks on the enemy's flying fields. At the same time, Germany's antiaircraft defenses demonstrated that they, too, had given the problem considerable thought. The airplane's great potential as a weapon of war was now becoming clear, and the need for counterweapons was recognized.

Antiaircraft (AA) weaponry was not new. An AA gun was first used in the Franco-Prussian War of 1870-1871 and was specifically designed to shoot at balloons leaving the surrounded city of Paris. The original *Ballongeschütz* was a 37-mm wheeled cannon which came from the Krupp Steel Company's Essen works. Although testimony on its accuracy was not recorded, it fired a shell up almost 2,000 feet and seems to have shot down one balloon, damaged others, and discouraged the French from further daylight flights. The first commercially available antiaircraft gun was exhibited in 1906 by the German *Rheinmetall* firm at the Berlin Auto Exhibition. *Rheinmetall*'s weapon was a vehicle mounted 50-mm gun in two designs, one with an armor shield protecting the gunner and having a 60-degree traverse, and one with no armor and a 360-degree traverse. The barrel could be elevated to 70 degrees.[8]

In the complex armament race of the pre-World War I period, companies actively competed for customers and nationality was no bar to purchasing. When Count Zeppelin began to build airships for the Kaiser's government in 1906, commercial possibilities of a counterweapon did not escape notice. The tactic of creating a threat and then a weapon or armor to defend against it was common in the rush to sell. In 1909, Krupp introduced a 65-mm antizeppelin gun based on its 1870 model. It was available for purchase by Britain, France, and Russia, so that by 1914 all of the major powers had access to the design. Nevertheless, sales for AA guns were not especially brisk at first and by July 1914, two Rhine River bridges and the zeppelin hangars at Metz and Friedrichshafen were the only protected locations in Germany. The German Army planned, however, the purchase of movable AA guns for each field army headquarters and infantry division. The basic requirement was to stop reconnaissance and observation craft more than to protect against attack.[9]

By the early summer of 1914, several types of AA guns were being manufactured in small quantities in England. The most popular were the 3-inch gun and the 37-mm pom-pom, a fast firing cannon which the Royal Navy intended placing aboard ships. These weapons were quickly adapted

Improvised antiaircraft machine gun emplacements. (*Left*) American troops use log as pedestal for Lewis gun. Gunner of the French 65th Antiaircraft Autocannon Section aims skyward. *(Below)* German tub emplacement rotated to allow a 360 degree arc of fire. U.S. Army Air Defense Museum.

for air defense. The first shells had impact fuzes that required a direct hit on a target, but ground commanders worried that their men would be hurt when the shells fired at aircraft returned to earth. Moreover, pilots were unaware they were being fired upon and hence AA guns had no deterrent effect upon them. Subsequently engineers developed more responsive fuzes to detonate the projectiles after a few seconds' flight, but their large scale manufacture was intially slow. These crude affairs used a burning powder train that could be set to activate at a chosen altitude, but a true proximity fuze, which would explode upon encountering even a maneuvering airplane, was three decades in the future. Early AA shells were not intended to destroy aircraft by force of a nearby explosion. Rather, gunners attempted to score direct hits with smaller automatic weapons or small arms. Heavier weapons such as the 3-inch or 75-mm relied on the nearly chance effects of shell splinters to damage aircraft parts or hurt the pilot.[10]

The antiaircraft gun, which came into use on both sides in 1914, was not produced in large numbers for some time. As the armies expanded, factories could not meet the need for artillery. The first effective British antiaircraft gun sent to the front was the 3-inch thirteen pounder. Able to fire high explosive or shrapnel shells, the 3-inch gun reached an altitude of 17,000 feet. Faulty ammunition, however, limited the weapon until April 1916 to the use of shrapnel only, which had a greatly reduced killing range. The British intended assigning a 2-gun antiaircraft artillery section to each front-line division in Flanders and northern France, providing a line of AA fire through which intruding enemies were forced to fly. Another 30 heavy guns were to be used for AA protection in rear areas, including airfields. Of the 112 guns needed for this scheme, only 80 were in place by April 1916. By July of that year, 113 guns were distributed among the field armies with another 18 along lines of communication. Eight more were assigned to the BEF's General Headquarters.[11]

The German munitions industry suffered similar production problems, and resorted to two expedient measures. The first campaigns in Russia yielded a great many captured Putilov M1903 field guns with a high angle of fire. Mounted on a pedestal and supplied with captured shrapnel ammunition, they became the first widely used German *Fliegerabwehrkanone,* or flak weapons. In the west, the Germans employed French 75-mm guns captured during their drive to the Marne. Since there was little captured ammunition, German factories in the Ruhr bored out the French guns to accept German 77-mm shells.[12]

Probably the most widely used antiaircraft gun early in the war was the high velocity French 75-mm adapted to high angle fire and mounted on a De Dion Bouton motor chassis. French defenders employed these mobile weapons for area air defense with field armies and for the defense of Paris. Later they were deployed around aerodromes by the U.S. Army. The 75-mm had a

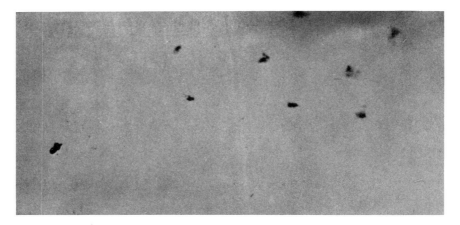

**Allied barrage balloon under German antiaircraft fire. Enemy shells are wide of the mark. Hitting even a stationary target in the sky was a feat at this time.**

high rate of fire and a vertical range of 21,000 feet, the maximum operating altitude of most aircraft. The French depended upon it heavily to make up shortages of fighter aircraft. With the entry of the United States into the war, American antiaircraft gun carriages were fitted with French 75-mm gun barrels. The U.S. Army also purchased 75-mm truck-mounted guns from France to complete the antiaircraft protection for its field armies.[13]

All of the belligerent powers used antiaircraft guns as area defense weapons during the war. In an area defense, guns protected regions such as corps areas rather than small points like transportation junctions or air bases. Area defense use was a rather general application of the new artillery pieces, but reflected the fact that for some time few people knew how to employ an AA gun effectively. Since the weapons were new to combat, there were a number of technical problems that frustrated the gunners.[14]

Firing at targets moving through three dimensions was unique in the history of war to that time. Gun crews needed training and experience; range finding problems seemed almost insurmountable. Until 1916, there was no practical method of predicting an airplane's future position in the sky. The gunners could not see where their fire was going in relation to the small and rapidly moving target and could not easily adjust for range and speed. Estimates of speed and altitude were mostly guesswork; observers directed changes in aim after watching shell bursts, but at best their new targeting information lagged by several seconds by the time it reached the gun crew. British and French designers devised electrical and gear driven deflection meters which reduced the time needed to aim an AA gun. In 1916 the invention of position finders greatly facilitated accurate aiming, and aircraft were forced to fly higher to avoid damage. Even after a method of accurately predicting an aerial target's line of flight was in use, however, gunners had to assume it would continue at the same speed, altitude, and direction when they adjusted sights and fuzes. No sooner had the designers solved the problems of aiming and firing, however, than another difficulty arose. Above 15,000 feet powder train fuzes in the early AA shells did not function well. Lack of oxygen and the projectile's spin made detonation erratic. Changing fuze design and powder composition rectified the newest difficulty, and by war's end, 20,000 feet was the highest altitude at which an antiaircraft shell could be expected to be effective. That, however, was adequate for the aircraft then in use.[15]

The ballistic and aiming limitations of antiaircraft guns and their rather restricted availability often made them unsuitable for point air defense of sites such as aerodromes. As a result, defense of World War I air bases devolved largely upon machine guns and small arms fire plus camouflage, dispersal, deception, as well as fighter interception. By late 1915, the Royal Flying Corps (RFC) aggressively attacked aerodromes in German-held territory. Maj.-Gen. Hugh M. Trenchard, its commander, believed in repeated attacks to curb the German Air Service's growing power. Large raids by the RFC were loosed upon a variety of targets, including airfields. Bombers met strong AA fire, forcing an abandonment of the small unit formation. The RFC found that large groups reaching the objective together reduced the ability of AA guns to score a hit. The Allied policy of attacking repeatedly brought them air superiority by forcing the Germans onto the defensive. By early 1916, on the other hand, the threat to Allied bases was not yet of serious proportions. The Germans preferred to operate over their own territory where they could concentrate force, recover a downed pilot easily, and better contend with the superior numbers of Allied aircraft.[16]

The Germans countered Allied superiority by organizing units called *Jagdstaffeln,* fighter squadrons, that attacked Allied aircraft. Led by experienced combat pilots and equipped with new, fast flying Halberstadt and Albatros D aircraft, the squadrons quickly outmatched the Allies. The German aircraft were fitted with two machine guns firing forward through the propeller arc. The first of the new squadrons went into action in September 1916 and found success against British Martinsyde bombers. The new fighter tactics broke up several Allied raids against German airfields. The new fighter squadrons and superior aircraft employed by the Germans now gave them air superiority in areas where they operated. Neither side, however, could control the air entirely. The Germans massed aircraft in areas they felt were important; the French did the same, but to support specific attack missions. Defensive patrols to counter these thrusts were found ineffectual. A stronger air arm now made possible increased German attacks on Allied areas.[17]

Late in 1916, seeking to control German aerial activity, the British incorporated their army wireless observation stations into the aircraft reporting net. Direction finding stations reported bearings of German airborne radio transmissions to the area army's wing headquarters. Cloth panels laid out on the ground were then used to relay coded information to pilots in the air who attempted interception. Fighters were launched if exceptionally large formations were detected.[18] By 1917, the system included interception stations able to listen in on German air-to-ground radio transmissions. Information was passed quickly by telephone to antiaircraft gun units and, with coded ground panels, to pilots aloft. Various technical problems kept radio reception sets out of the fighters of the time, but the system added greatly to warning capability. The British were not alone in this improvement. Germany adopted a similar system in the summer of 1916, just at the time German air forces also began to use the new aircraft and squadron formations. German aircraft losses in combat with the RFC during the battle of the Somme from July to November were about half those of the British. The new detection, warning, and tactical improvements doubtless contributed to the drop in casualties. [19]

The RFC also used its airplanes to alleviate fear of air attack among Allied ground troops who especially connected the accuracy of enemy artillery with the presence of an enemy observer overhead and were often terrified by strafing. During 1917 the ground war intensified, and the aggressive German Air Service struck supply depots, transport parks, and infantry positions. Ground commanders wanted to see their own aircraft above to protect their men. At the Battle of Ypres, the RFC tried a new tactic intended to keep German aircraft tied up away from the front during the early stages of assault. Ninth Wing, consisting of No. 19, 27, 55, 56, 66, and 70 Squadrons, attacked a number of rear area objectives, including the German airfields at Ingelmunster, Huele, and Marcke. This approach was successful in spite of bad weather, which may have hampered the German detection and warning service. In this instance, the high level Martinsyde bombers were accompanied by RFC fighters each carrying four 25-pound bombs on specially fitted racks. The nearly simultaneous high and low level attacks complicated the task of the defenders who had to divide their attenti'n to engage both.[20]

Expecting retaliation in kind, the British prepared area defenses consisting of 3-inch AA artillery supported by machine guns and searchlights to protect their airfields. They readied dual mount Lewis guns, each with a one man crew, and positioned at least twelve of these weapons on each base. In addition, they located 3-inch or 75-mm guns on some of the more important aerodromes near the front. On their side, the Germans, seeking to prevent further losses of aircraft on the ground, built numerous standbyairfields with hangars and support buildings ready for use on short notice. Multiplying the possible number of airfields they could use was a wise tactic as the British and French were forced to keep all of them under continuous observation. The concentrations of German aircraft near important locations meant that Allied reconnaissance and attack pilots faced a heavy AA fusillade as well as fighter opposition as they approached the target bases.[21]

The Germans also exploited camouflage and deception to protect planes and bases. They painted the upper surfaces of many of their Gotha bombers with a pentagonal pattern of brown, black, green and purple. The color arrangement helped hide the planes on the ground and made them less conspicuous targets from above in the air. After an Allied attack in August 1918 at Boulay aerodrome destroyed five aircraft and damaged ten, they built a dummy field nearby. Most of the next British raid went to the decoy location and subsequent attacks seem not to have destroyed any aircraft.[22]

## The Americans Arrive

In April 1917, a new combatant, the United States, entered the war and began enlarging its military services to build an expeditionary force to be sent to France. The American planners were full of good intentions, but most lacked knowledge of how to conduct war on a large scale. Moreover, American industry was not yet ready to supply the numbers of guns and aircraft needed by the armed forces. The American Expeditionary Force naturally looked to its new Allies for advice and experience that would reduce both the time and the tribulations of mobilization.

British and French tactics and policies were often adopted by the United States' air and antiair* services when they entered the war. Most American units acquired French and British equipment and used all or parts of existing air fields. (*Map 1*) Often the Americans depended on Allied defenses for base protection. What they found on arrival in the way of facilities was indicative of the past defense effort. For example, the 17th Aero Squadron, located at Petit Synth, France, near Dunkirk, with two RFC squadrons, No. 210 and 213, occupied existing wooden buildings revetted with sandbags. The squadron dugout alone was protected by almost 30,000 sandbags, stacked like a stepped pyramid as protection against the frequent attacks by German night bombers. Accuracy by the early bombardiers was poor in the darkness and little damage was inflicted on the field. People soon ceased taking the raids seriously and found an evening's adventure by climbing onto

---

* Because of its experience in firing at rapidly moving surface targets (ships), the U.S. Army's Coast Artillery Corps became responsible for AA defense of the AEF's troops and bases.

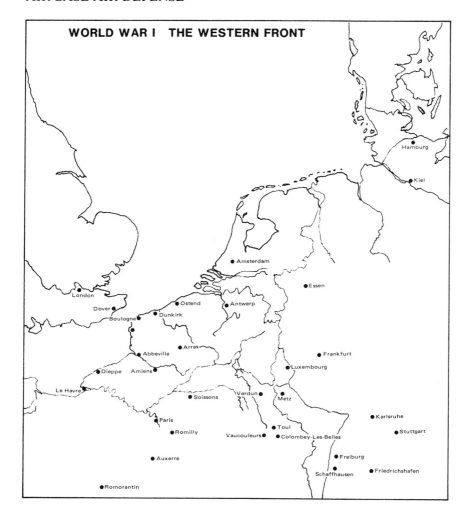

**WORLD WAR I THE WESTERN FRONT**

## Map 1

rooftops to peer up into the dark during the attacks. The 17th Squadron's reports noted that there was heavy but inaccurate British fire. The squadron history recorded neither daytime attacks on the base nor any attackers being shot down or deterred by ground fire. The darkness that protected bombers had been partly overcome by the British use of searchlights, but even so, AA accuracy was not good.[23]

Concerted American planning for air defense on the Western Front began with a report in October 1917 by Brig. Gen. James A. Shipton, Chief of Anti-Aircraft Services, First U.S. Army, AEF. Shipton had formed an American antiaircraft school in France, but lacked weapons and trained people. The American AA school acomplished little until February 1918, when Shipton proposed a plan for organizing the whole of the AEF's Anti-Aircraft Service. On March 5th, an American Army board of officers recommended AA protection for the rear areas, where many air bases were located. The board's report favored a U.S. air defense system closely tied to that of the British and French. It specified places which required immediate protection and noted the need for more dispersal to reduce the vulnerability of the AEF's sites to air attack. Aerodromes, however, were not included in the list of places to be defended. The recommendations were not unanimous, however, and a strong minority report was filed by the Air Service's member, Lt. Col. Carleton V. Chapman.[24]

Colonel Chapman, the only aviator on the board,* recognized the need for air base defense, and objected to giving the preponderance of AA protection to ground units. Chapman bluntly argued that the board's work was inadequate, and that the AEF's previous air defense studies, like that of General Shipton, had little result. Chapman prepared his own recommendations that Air Service officers like Lt. Col. Edgar S. Gorrell and Maj. Harold Fowler, experienced in aerial bombardment, be consulted on questions of air defense. He also wanted more explicit planning for AA weapons deployment, ammunition consumption, and camouflage. Chapman insisted on revisions to the list of American aerodromes needing protection. Issoudon, Tours, and Aulnat headed his list, but little was done.[25]

On June 1, General Shipman requested that the AEF's Headquarters approve air defense artillery for Ourches, Colombey-les-Belles, and Orly airfields, all of which were exposed to aerial bombardment. The AEF's Chief of Staff approved the request on June 8. Shipman's antiaircraft schemes, however, continued to be hampered by shortages of guns, inexperienced staff personnel, and slow training of gunners. As a result, antiaircraft artillery protection could not be organized for locations farther behind the front than Is-sur-Tille, about thirty miles north of Dijon and some eighty miles from the lines. Commanders farther to the rear were advised to use passive defensive measures like camouflage, sandbags, and dispersal. Machine guns could also be used where available but only if improvised mounts could be made.[26]

Base defense was too often hit or miss. Before their own air defense units were available, American airdromes were ordinarily protected from air

---

* The remaining board members were Lt. Col. J. W. Wright, Infantry, and Capt. W. J. Pearmain, Ordnance. The group visited thirteen major locations, only one of which, Colombey-les-Belles, was an air base. Chapman was a pilot who had previously served with Gorrell and Capt. Benjamin D. Foulois as part of the 1st Aero Squadron in Texas and Mexico in 1916.

attack by Allied organizations, other U.S. forces in the area, or by base support troops who had received some machine gun instruction. In the absence of trained AA crews, base commanders resorted to whatever expedient they could devise. Of all the Air Service units in France, only the Balloon Wing and subordinate balloon groups and companies were authorized antiaircraft machine guns; none was specified for pursuit, bombardment, or observation squadrons or groups. The balloonists had first priority because they had to protect their vulnerable, stationary locations. The flying squadrons already drew on armament stocks for their aircraft, and supply officers chaffed at the thought of giving more. Demands for machine guns were so heavy that on May 14 Brig. Gen. C. B. Wheeler, the AEF's Chief Ordnance Officer, prohibited assignment of more than two per air base. Any additional weapons, he said, must be taken from airplanes or other local resources. Many contemporary photographs show a variety of machine gun types mounted on wooden posts and wagon wheels, capable of firing up at various angles.[27]

Shortly after entering the war, the U.S. Army organized 5 antiaircraft machine gun battalions along British lines, only 2 of which arrived in France in time to see service at the front. The 2nd Antiaircraft Machinegun Battalion, commanded by Maj. Orville L. Whitney, had about 600 officers and men divided into 4 companies. The main weapons used by this battalion were 64 Hotchkiss machine guns. The Americans intended to use their antiaircraft units to protect the front line infantry from low-level German attacks and they motorized them so that they could move their weapons to areas where they were most needed. Upon arrival in France, the battalions received AEF antiaircraft training before their assignments to specific sectors. Company B of the 2nd Battalion moved to the large American aerodrome at Colombey-les-Belles. There it joined the 5th, 6th, 7th, and 8th Antiaircraft Batteries, constituting the 10th AA Sector, commanded by Capt. C. C. Robertson.[28]

Problems plagued the American base defenders, however. Machine gun and AA units arrived slowly at Colombey-les-Belles; artillery pieces were not delivered until late July or early August. Allied plans called for a major attack on the St. Mihiel salient, near Verdun, starting on September 12. American forces were to play a prominent part. By August 27, AA guns were not yet unpacked at Colombey, leaving the installation exposed to German raiders. In a fit of frustration, Brig. Gen. Benjamin D. Foulois, the AEF's Assistant Chief of Air Service, pointedly telegraphed General Shipton his insistence that gunners go into action "without delay." Shipton assured Foulois the next day that four batteries of men would be sent to Colombey-les-Belles as soon as they completed training. Another four batteries would go to Ourches shortly afterward. Unfortunately, even Shipton's intervention availed him nothing. The AA artillery units did not arrive until the end of September.[29]

Colombey-les-Belles lay 25 miles from the front lines and was the home of the 1st Air Depot, through which the American Air Service supplied all its units in the Toul sector. Normally, the airfield was a repair site for damaged aircraft and worn engines, but late in August 1918, the Americans began assembling there aircraft for the St. Mihiel offensive. The first recorded attack on the American operation at Colombey on September 2 inflicted no damage or injuries. Intent on protecting their aircraft, the Americans hid them and enforced blackout rules at night. The Germans were unable to bomb the field accurately throughout the five days of fighting at St. Mihiel.[30] By October 28th, the Germans regrouped, and a night raid on Colombey damaged about fifty planes. Most of the loss was superficial, but about six aircraft were destroyed. The Americans reacted hastily. Zigzag trenches were dug for protection of the workers and antiaircraft defenses were strengthened. By October 30 the Americans had sixteen 75-mm guns of the 10th AA Sector and thirty machine guns deployed about the base along with six 60-inch searchlights. That night the Germans returned and a "fierce barrage" of antiaircraft fire was put up. No planes were shot down, but the installation commander attributed the lack of bomb hits to the defenses.

The base defense measures used at Ourches by the 1st Observation Group were also typical of growing American defense practices. There, they camouflaged hangars with nets and hid airplanes among trees along the field. Dugouts ran to thirty or forty feet underground, overbuilt with heavy log roofs, dirt, and sandbags for protection; all windows were curtained to block light at night. Antiaircraft machine guns located at several places around the base defended against low-level attacks.[31]

A rather complex but effective warning and protection system also grew up in the Toul area. The stability of the front lines through most of the war permitted permanent ground observation posts, telephone lines, and a radio net to report on incoming air raids. The warning system's organization long preceded the American arrival, but the U.S. Signal Corps added its own radios. Four of the American stations intercepted enemy radio traffic, all reported air activity to a net command post at Vaucouleurs. Originally of French design, the network protected against German aerial threats to front line troops, and allowed AA gunners to find and fire on photoreconnaissance and artillery spotting aircraft. When the Americans arrived, they used the talents of the forward AA gunners; their own men became as skilled as the French. The ground and radio observers directed their reports to the 1st Pursuit Group at Toul. Information on aircraft type, number, direction of flight, and altitude would all be at the airfield in less than the five minutes necessary to warn personnel and prepare the guns. On April 14, 1918, two

**94th Aero Squadron pilots wait on air defense duty in alert tent at Toul in June 1918.**

American aircraft of the 94th Squadron took off at the first report of intruders and shot down two German planes, which crashed on the Toul aerodrome. Many Americans in the 94th were veterans of French or British flying units who made optimum use of early warning information.[32]

Through the course of the war, attacks on air bases became progressively better organized, more sophisticated, and relatively more destructive. Even so, they were not of major importance during the war because aircraft carried limited bomb loads, bombs lacked destructive power, and bombing accuracy, especially at night, was poor. All the belligerents constantly worked at improving defenses, but at the armistice the art of air base air defense was far from efficient. The Americans tried to absorb all they could from Allied experience, but the confusion inherent in organizing and moving a huge army overseas prevented the efficient use of many AA units. After the war many Air Service commanders discussed the need for better base defense in official reports.

Maj. Maxwell Kirby, commander of the 5th Pursuit Group, favored combining the American air and antiair arms for better coordination. Kirby believed that pursuit aircraft should not be wasted in individual combat, but should protect army corps and bombers while antiaircraft complemented the effort by protecting operational air forces over friendly territory. Al-

**Lt. Douglas Campbell of the 94th attacks a German Pfalz DIII, which crashed on the Toul aerodrome moments later. British aviation artist Frank Wooton commemorated the event in this painting.** Courtesy of T. Hamady.

though the suggestion to combine service arms was not adopted by the U.S. Army, the German *Luftwaffe* and the French Air Force applied the basic idea in their doctrine before World War II.[33]

Maj. Harold E. Hartney, wartime commander of the 1st Pursuit Group, reached conclusions similar to Kirby's. Hartney believed that attacking airfields could force enemy air operations so far to the rear that the tactical situation could be significantly changed by putting aircraft out of reach of the front line. In addition, he speculated on the eventual need for underground hangars and base shops, an idea used by the Germans in World War II, later by the North Koreans, Swiss, and Swedes, and to some extent explored by American planners during the 1930s. While looking at the offensive power of aviation, Hartney did not disregard the need for defense. He realized that his desired attack units had to have secure bases. He believed a generous distribution of antiaircraft guns to be vital. Hartney made the preparation of dummy airdromes and auxiliary fields for intermittent operational support part of his plan for future air defense.[34]

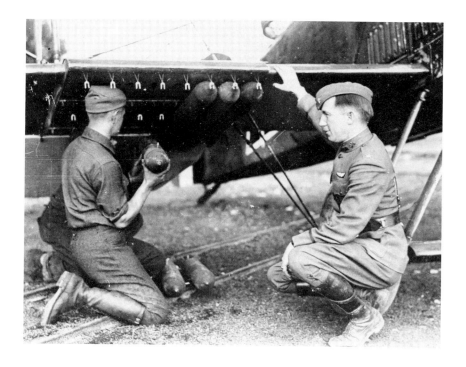

**Loading bombs into early racks. Narrow gauge track running beneath aircraft was laid on the larger aerodromes to service dispersed areas by the end of the war.**

Maj. William C. Sherman, writing several years after the war, noted that bombing methods and bombing equipment had been crude and undeveloped. Most bombing efforts were directed against targets other than airfields.[35] Air doctrine was young and air commanders were under great pressure to protect the ground combat arms. The psychological effect of air attacks upon ground troops served to increase the clamor for cover on all sides. At the same time, there was no significant collection of air experience that could adequately support or deny most arguments and the opposing claims greatly taxed air resources during the war. The shifting balance of air superiority was often the factor which governed frequency and effectiveness of attacks.[36] Airdrome defenses varied from base to base but, in general, benefited from both technical and practical improvements by war's end. Antiaircraft guns became much more accurate and could reach higher elevations. Expanded production allowed increasing gun defenses everywhere on the Western Front. When the American Expeditionary Force arrived in

France, antiaircraft officers trained with the French and, in turn, imparted years of experience to the newly enlarged United States' military. As a result, American gunners achieved an effectiveness per round fired that equalled or surpassed that of the other Allied armies.[37]

Base defenders on both sides met the growing threat from air attack by a variety of means and in conjunction with regional antiaircraft artillery. Machine guns were located about the bases to protect people and equipment; camouflage was used for deception and concealment and dummy installations drew attacks away. The year 1918 saw increasingly heavy attacks on air bases in support of the major campaigns that led to the war's conclusion. During that year, General Hugh M. Trenchard directed more than one third of his Independent Air Force's attacks at German aerodromes in order to suppress German aircraft that might retaliate against Allied columns.[38]

The AEF's First Corps observation base at Ourches, in the Toul sector, developed an extensive defense that used antiaircraft machine guns, camouflage, dispersal of buildings, underground dugouts and nighttime blackouts. The newly assigned Americans adopted the lessons of years of war and advancing technology painfully learned by the other combatants. Nevertheless, many air defense techniques remained crude. The problem of truly long range detection and warning was never adequately solved. Front line observers were limited by the range of sight and hearing. Even binoculars or sound ranging equipment was not effective beyond five miles. Radio intercept and observation stations became common, but the short reception ranges limited their utility too. Frequently, commanders were unsure of the value of defenses. In his report in July 1917, Col. Chauncey B. Baker of the U.S. Army's Quartermaster Corps, who went to France to survey and report on war needs and priorities, was not impressed with French antiaircraft prowess. Noting that gunners scored only 1 hit per 10,000 rounds fired since 1916 he stated that the only practical effect of ground fire was to make the planes fly higher. By 1918 many commanders seemed to share Baker's sentiment. His judgment was, perhaps too harsh. He gauged only artillery and used incomplete statistics, and he failed to understand that forcing planes higher was in itself a success, as it reduced bombing accuracy or reconnaissance ability. Still, he had grounds for skepticism. During 1918 the French Antiaircraft Service shot down 220 airplanes, expending an average of only 7,500 rounds per victory.[39]

By the end of the war, many questions remained about air base air defense, but, at the hands of Trenchard's airmen, the Germans especially had learned many lessons in fending off attacking Allied airplanes. Although they held air superiority in certain areas, often they took aircraft from lesser priority needs to achieve it. The German Army and air arm thus were forced to balance numerical inferiority with a well organized warning and reporting system supported by many guns. German long range air raids on England, though strategic in nature, gave the future RAF a major lesson for fighting tactical air battles: warning and fighter control were essential to the defeat or deflection of an attacker. During the next twenty years of peace, these lessons took root.

# Chapter II

# Interwar Doctrine and Technology Changes

After the 1918 Armistice, the air forces of both the Allied and the Central Powers were rapidly dismantled. The Treaty of Versailles forced a subdued Germany to give up all of her airplanes and most of her antiaircraft weapons, which were seized or destroyed by the Army of Occupation. At the same time, the Allies reduced their air forces to skeleton strength for economic reasons and for several years experimentation and development came to a virtual standstill. Not all of the lessons learned by the airmen were forgotten, however. In Germany the Weimar Republic's small German Army established an air technical office responsible for collecting and studying aeronautical information. British, French, and American air leaders returned to peacetime duties that often involved teaching or developing air doctrine. Japan began adding powerful air arms to its army and navy. Until the early 1920s, Russian fliers contended first with revolution and civil war at home, then war with Poland, but would soon begin to design and build excellent aircraft.

In England and America, smaller budgets and strong pacifist or isolationist political forces after World War I helped prohibit the development of modern air forces able to employ new technical knowledge. During the 1920s, Russia suffered a shortage of skilled designers, but obtained information from Germany in return for supporting secret German design and testing on Russian territory.[1] Japan's insular outlook seems to have retarded her development of radar, defense systems, and antiaircraft weapons. The failure of the League of Nations in 1931 to force Japan to alter her designs on Manchuria did nothing to change her view that she was not very vulnerable to direct air attack from overseas.[2] Finally, the financial turbulence that accompanied the worldwide depression of the 1930s affected development and production of both weapons and technology in all of the major countries.

During the interwar years, the British, Germans, French, Americans, Italians, Japanese, and Soviets designed several types of fighters that would be instrumental in tactical air warfare in World War II. Many of these fighters appeared in several models; some were used for both air base attack and air base defense, others were suited for only a single role. The table in Appendix 1 shows the relative capabilities of each country's aircraft, and the general development of combat aircraft of the various nations. In addition to the design and performance of fighters, other factors such as imaginative leadership, differences in air force organization, and technological improvements of nonflying areas of military and naval services gave certain countries advantages not possessed by others.

## American Defense Development

Many participants in the Great War recorded their experiences and ideas in books published in the 1920s. William Sherman's *Air Warfare,* published in 1926, was a compilation of the subject matter being taught at the Air Corps Tactical School (ACTS). It was a comprehensive restatement of his "Tentative Manual for the Employment of Air Service," written in 1919 for the Final Report of the AEF Air Service rather than a new treatment of the subject. Sherman was a supporter of the air power advocate William Mitchell, and his book became influential among American air force thinkers in the 1920s; it included sections on principles of warfare, characteristics of aircraft, individual aircraft combat and defense, observation, pursuit, attack, bombardment, antiaircraft defense, logistics, and naval aviation. Although it seemed all-encompassing, Sherman's book failed to assess advancing technology or analyze the possible changes in post war aerial fighting based on new equipment. The sections covering antiaircraft defense were very short and reflected both the technical problems of shooting at moving objects in the air and Sherman's fervent belief that military airplanes, especially bombers, would prevail over national defenses if another war began.[3]

A more concise view of the need for and value of defense was prepared several years later by an Air Corps officer, Claire L. Chennault. His short monograph, *The Role of Defensive Pursuit,* was written after the 1932 Joint Antiaircraft–Air Corps Exercises.* Although discussing defense against long-range bombardment, and contemplating area defense (as opposed to base or point air defense) Chennault's ideas had application in the narrower

---

* The exercises, held near Ft. Knox, Kentucky, tested the U.S. Army's antiaircraft and fighter interception tactics against bombers and explored new air defense techniques.

sense of base defense against both high and low altitude attack.[4] He emphatically rejected the thesis of Giulio Douhet and others that an air force, using massive offensive aerial bombardment, could achieve victory in war. He believed strongly that active fighter interception could deflect a bomber formation, and he insisted that an air unit that kept its planes on the ground and awaited assault was sure to be destroyed, as it could not react quickly enough to meet the threat.[5] Chennault sought to build an aggressive air defense, but faced a great many problems because of the practical inability to detect and report approaching aircraft. He proposed adopting the British visual observation system (ground observer posts spaced about seven miles apart) with telephone and telegraph to transmit information to a central authority which would dispatch fighter forces. Citing the successful British experience of World War I, he made central command of warning and interception a key to his system.[6]

Chennault's proposals were not entirely welcome in the Air Corps. He was an irascible, difficult person with many enemies among senior Air Corps leaders who had other ideas on how to defend against an enemy air force. These ideas were bound up with the desire to build an air arm able to carry out an offensive war should the need arise. In September 1933, the Air Corps' Chief, Maj. Gen. Benjamin D. Foulois, told the Army War College that "the real effective air defense will consist of our ability to attack and destroy the hostile aviation on the ground before it takes to the air." Foulois voiced the official position of the Army Air Corps, which was reflected at the Air Corps Tactical School. Chennault's opinions were eclipsed within the service, and he retired late in the 1930s to serve as air adviser to China's leader, Chiang Kai-shek. Nevertheless, the attack-defense dispute continued. During the 1935 Air Corps maneuvers in Florida, 1st Lt. Gordon R. Saville demonstrated central control of fighters to American military officers and established what the British knew and Chennault had argued previously.[7]

While this debate went on in Air Corps circles, the practical application of radar brought the promise of far reaching changes to base attack and defense. Conceived in the early thirties both in England and at the U.S. Naval Research Laboratory, the military use of radio detection was forced by Britain's vulnerable position. By mid-1939, radar stations on England's east coast observed aircraft approaching from the Continent. Small radar units for field application were built in both Britain and the United States by 1940, allowing defenders of tactical air bases a measure of warning. Experimentation was also under way in Germany, the Soviet Union, and to a lesser extent, Japan.[8]

Few countries, however, exploited radar consistently. Despite the advances in its laboratory deployment, its incorporation into military use and doctrine was slow and uneven. The acceptance of radar in the U.S. Army

Lt. Col. William C. Sherman's post-World War I book, *Air Warfare*, influenced American aviation doctrine in the 1920s.

was impeded by secrecy, a shortage of money for more extensive experimentation and purchase, and an apparent unwillingness to fully approve and assimilate the new equipment. A few field sets were in experimental use by the Signal Corps and Coast Artillery in 1940. The Army Air Corps' Tactical School, however, did not mention radar or countermeasures in its attack or light bombardment courses until 1940. The antiaircraft defense course at the Air Corps Tactical School in March 1940 made only an oblique reference to radar in England and none to developments in the United States. In fact, the course taught that ground observers were the main source of information for a defense commander. This was in part due to the secret nature of radar experiments, but also because radar did not belong to the Air Corps. Unlike the Royal Air Force, which was at that time busy teaching its fighter controllers how to use radar, the new medium was little known to American Army air officers. In 1940, with war raging in Europe, the Commander of the New York Air Defense Sector, Brig. Gen. Earle E. Partridge,* found that radar stations on Long Island reported to him. General Partridge later remembered that at the time he "couldn't technically evaluate what they were doing" because he had not been told what radar was, how it worked, and how he should use it to direct his forces. Radar found an easier acceptance in the Navy and Marine Corps, which faced the need to defend forces put ashore in isolated parts of the world. Thus from 1940 plans were made to set up and defend airfields on hostile shores.[9]

---

\* Among later assignments Partridge commanded the U.S. Fifth Air Force during the Korean conflict and, later, the Air Defense Command.

Unlike the U.S. Army's prewar preparations, the Navy Department's base defense planning between 1937 and 1941 was less fragmented. In May 1938, faced with a growing threat from Japan, Congress directed the Secretary of the Navy to study the need for new and enlarged naval bases in America and overseas. The resulting Hepburn Board, named for its chairman, Rear Adm. A. J. Hepburn, selected sites for new bases in the United States, the Carribean, and the Atlantic, and in the Pacific as far as Guam. The Hepburn Board's report was the basis for a rapidly accelerating naval air base construction program. In May 1939, Congress overcame strong isolationist opposition and appropriated $63 million for naval base construction. With the money in hand, the Navy formed an Air Base Construction Board, charged with developing and overseeing the various projects. At about the same time, the Navy Antiaircraft Defense Board studied the best ways to protect the new advanced installations and any other bases that might be needed in war. The upshot of the planning was a clear Navy policy that gave the U.S. Marine Corps responsibility for defending advanced installations "not defended by the Army," presumably the bulk of the new airfields. Shortly thereafter, the Marines organized four Base Defense Battalions for AA and shore defense work. Each battalion varied in composition according to its task, but included AA guns similar to those in the Army, 5-inch coast defense guns, infantry, sound detectors, and searchlights. The overall naval defense posture improved when the Navy took an added interest in the RAF's use of radar in the Battle of Britain and formed a fighter director school in Hawaii that taught the latest fighter radar interception techniques. By 1941, SCR-268 and SCR-270 radar sets were added to the battalions' makeup. The senior Navy officers responsible for this preparation had the support of the President, and were driven by the specter of a fleet at war in the far Pacific or the Atlantic with few bases available for their ships and aircraft. Although the Navy and Marine Corps were not ready to defend all their offshore installations, their approach to the problem was distinctly different from that of the Army, charged mostly with responsibility for continental and Western Hemisphere defense.[10]

Through the interwar period, the emphasis in the antiaircraft course at the Army Air Corps Tactical School was on area, or strategic, defense of the United States, especially the industrial northeast and various territorial possessions such as Hawaii. In March 1940, the school added a section on antiaircraft defense of an air base.[11] Thereafter, the ACTS somewhat hesitantly acknowledged the need to protect an air base in a hostile area with the weapons then in Army service. Heavy machine guns, 37-mm cannon, and artillery were mentioned, but with the qualifier that there were not enough available in the army to protect existing continental United States installations. Weapons were so few that one instructor suggested using machine guns taken from B-17 bombers to augment low level protection if necessary.

**Fort Bragg maneuvers in October 1938. Searchlights blaze in the North Carolina night during joint Army-Air Corps exercises.**

Camouflage and target hardening were discussed, and protection from chemical attack received a lengthy treatment by a chemical warfare officer. It was, however, a beginner's inquiry into base defense, prompted by the collapse of Poland six months before, and it pointed out the many shortcomings in the American ability to defend an air base. Because the United States was neutral and still focused on defending the western hemisphere, there was no discussion of overseas base operation or defense coordination with allied forces. After considering all these matters, the instructor soberly concluded that no United States base had adequate protection.[12]

The air defense command structure taught by the Tactical School was based upon an area protection concept, with an Army ground officer as commander. Subordinate to the area commander were to have been antiaircraft, barrage balloon, bombardment, pursuit units, and the various support agencies such as signal, quartermaster, and medical. The area air defense commander would not necessarily have had expertise in any of the major defense specialities in his organization and, surprisingly enough, there was some question as to whether or not an air officer would be present on his staff. Considerable groping would have been needed to create a functioning command and, with only limited experience being gained in

**SCR–268 radar used to direct accompanying searchlight. Though still an imprecise instrument, the radar was quickly employed as a gun laying mechanism.**

such exercises as the 1935–36 maneuvers in Florida, few people were qualified for the various jobs that would be created.[13]

Improvements were at hand, however. First Army maneuvers during August and September 1940 in New York state pitted a Red and a Blue Army against each other in a series of tactical problems that included air defense. Formed in June to develop air defense doctrine and training, a new Air Defense Command (ADC) had its first chance to organize and test a regional aircraft warning service. The ADC used Signal Corps SCR–270 radar sets with a 50-mile range under optimum conditions. The radar sets augmented a network of civilian American Legion spotters.* The radar worked satisfactorily, but the overall aircraft warning service had too few volunteers for round-the-clock operation. The exercise included practice in area airdefense protection for a field army, but the final report did not discuss the need for point defense of the Blue Army's air bases. There was such a serious shortage of air defense weapons that all vulnerable points of the

---

* The American Legion was a society organized in 1919 and made up of American veterans of World War I. In 1940, the Legionnaires were patriotic volunteers used as ground observers.

**Water cooled 50–cal. machine gun on alert during 1st Division maneuvers in North Carolina, 1941. (*Below*) A gun crew trains on the 40–mm Bofors in the same area in 1943.**

Blue Army's limited forces could not have been protected. Despite its short-comings, the maneuvers were an advance for the growing Army of the United States.[14]

With the increasing possibility of American participation in the war, Congress authorized President Franklin D. Roosevelt in August 1940 to order several National Guard units into federal service in mid-September. Fifteen divisions, nine antiaircraft battalions, and twenty-two antiaircraft regiments were called up, many in varying states of readiness. Late in the 1920s, the U.S. Army had prepared tables of organization for several types of antiaircraft units under the Coast Artillery Corps, which became responsible for all antiaircraft gun and searchlight operations and for AA protection for expeditionary forces (including the Air Corps) sent overseas. In 1940, some National Guard units, like the 200th Coast Artillery (AA) Regiment from New Mexico, had only recently converted from other branches, such as cavalry, and were anything but fully qualified or equipped. The newly converted units were to be equipped with either medium (between 20- to 57-mm bore) or heavy (larger than 57-mm) AA guns. Some of the new units could theoretically be used for air base defense. When fully equipped and trained they would have been the only source of such protection, as the Air Corps had no AA guns of its own. Although the call up of the National Guard improved the operational defensive fire and warning capability of the United States, the size and training of the AA arm was not yet adequate for a global conflict. The total weaponry available equipped sixty-two under-strength AA batteries, usually of three 3-inch guns plus 37-mm and .50 caliber support.[15] In November 1941, a final prewar change came from a board of officers studying the need for a mobile Aircraft Warning Service that noted that each of the Army Air Forces'* pursuit groups needed a warning regiment, but none was available. Each warning regiment had to have signal and support services, and be ready to deploy to areas where pursuit aircraft would operate. The AAF's growing force of fast, durable fighters could have been a superb air base defense tool, but in late 1941, there were still too few fighters, and the warning and command structure was fragmented between the Air Forces, the Coast Artillery Corps, and the Signal Corps. The Pearl Harbor attack intervened before a new warning and control structure was organized, but the groundwork for expansion had been laid.[16]

---

* The term Army Air Forces (AAF) was used beginning in June 1941. The AAF included the Air Corps, which continued through the war, at first supervising technical, logistic, and support services. After the Army reorganization in March 1942, the Air Corps continued as the statutory body of the AAF, but most of its functions were absorbed by new commands and staff offices of the AAF.

In the late thirties the United States Army Coast Artillery Corps had three types of weapons for use against aircraft. The largest was the 3-inch gun with a maximum effective range of 28,000 feet. The intermediate range weapon was the 37-mm cannon, capable of firing 80 rounds per minute, with a maximum effective vertical range of 10,500 feet. The shorter range .50 caliber machine gun could fire short bursts at 500 to 650 rounds per minute to 5,400 feet depending upon the model in use. The prewar .50 caliber machine gun used a cumbersome 500-pound mount which made it difficult to transport and set up. A lighter mount did not appear until 1942. Just before the war the United States began to manufacture 40-mm guns and rushed the design of a 90-mm high velocity antiaircraft gun, which did not appear in significant numbers until 1941. The three main weapons, .50 caliber, 37-mm, and 3-inch guns, were used in conjunction with sound locators, searchlights, and the very early gun laying radar, the SCR–268, for direction finding and aiming.[17]

In general, the type of defensive fire available to the United States was adequate for use against prewar planes, although the speed of potential attacking aircraft imposed distinct limitations in addition to the general shortage of weapons. The widely used sound locator was completely inadequate. Bad weather or ambient noise reduced its detection range to as little as 5,000 yards. As it took time to set a gun for firing, advance warning was crucial. With a 5,000-yard detection capability, antiaircraft crews would have an attacker within range for only seconds. Pursuit fighters and a first rate warning system were the answer to the base defenders' dilemma, but there were too few of them and the command systems were too poorly developed to make them the mainstay of air base air defense. To maintain even limited fighter patrols aloft was costly because of the short fuel capacity of the aircraft. Keeping a full squadron on aerial defense patrol was practically impossible because the Air Corps had not enough planes to guard even a single base in such a fashion.[18]

In 1940, much remained to be done in the area of defense against low level air attack. At that time, only the new 37-mm gun was seen as a possible defense, and very little was known of its combat characteristics. Once production was able to meet demand, there was still no standard fire control system for the gun and only a small pool of trained gunners who could deploy to a threatened area with that weapon.[19]

## Germany Prepares

In 1935, Hitler reorganized his armed forces, creating an independent air force, the *Luftwaffe*. Over the next few years, both offensive and defensive air weapon systems and employment doctrine appeared. *Luftwaffe* Directive 16, first issued in 1936, and revised slightly in 1940, was the basis for air operations and air force cooperation with other services. German air doctrine called for aggressive attack to seize air superiority. Directive 16 viewed "attack, defense, and protection [as] interchangable." In general, German air doctrine called for first strikes on enemy air forces to forestall attacks on the *Luftwaffe*. The German air leaders reasoned that "surprise makes [our] attack less difficult and increases the efficiency of one's own defenses." The *Luftwaffe*'s rules stressed avoiding air to air combat with an enemy air force except in self defense. If strong enemy fighter formations were present, they would be controlled by strikes at their home bases. In Europe, the Germans had the first clear cut strategy calling for air superiority over an enemy's territory as the first step to victory in an air campaign.[20]

The *Luftwaffe* was unique among the aerial combatants of World War II. In many respects it was a separate military department within the *Wehrmacht*, containing not only flying units, but also the nation's antiaircraft defenses, the aircraft warning service, paratroop divisions, an armored division, and in 1942 and 1943, twenty field infantry divisions. As much as anything else the inclusion of the *Flakartillerie* in the service made for a close relationship between attack and defense elements, and promoted useful, coordinated weapon development. Under Directive 16 as revised in 1940, fighters and flak operating in combat zones were part of a unified command. Separate flak units were assigned to the army for protection of its troops. Aerial reconnaissance was divided among the Air Force, the Army, and the Navy, with the *Luftwaffe* responsible for long range operations. Each of the other services used its own reconnaissance squadrons for short range surveillance. For the Army, this was done by *Luftwaffe* air cooperation squadrons assigned to Army field forces.[21] The relatively young German Air Force, although it had an adequate doctrinal base, faced serious but unassayed problems in organizing tactical air defenses as well as joint airground operations. Early German victories masked these problems, which became more stark by the war's second year. In 1939, the *Luftwaffe* had less than five years of organizational experience, and most of its officers transferred from the Army. Few air officers had seen service in ranks between captain and colonel, when one normally commanded flying groups and attended various staff schools. Many of the Army transfers lacked extensive knowledge of flying, air strategy, and technology. The *Luftwaffe*'s rapid growth also returned to the colors men who had served in German aviation in World War I, but who had been inactive for years. Nazi ideology also militated against a wholesale immersion in modern technology, reinforcing vague tendencies among rising German bourgeois classes to aspire to the patterns of wealth of the old land owning Junker class. The result was an air officer corps unprepared to integrate fully the demands of technology into tactical air warfare decisionmaking. Because of their inexperience and the tendency of such senior commanders as General Hans Jeschonnek, Chief of the *Luftwaffe*'s General Staff, toward abject acceptance of Hitler, the leadership made several serious errors of lasting consequence. They neglected to train an adequate reserve of aircrews, overestimated the value of dive bombers, slighted the development of air transport, failed to develop a long range heavy bomber, and did not insure production of adequate numbers of combat planes in the first three years of war.[22] One postwar U.S. Air Force study remarked that the service "lacked completely the decades of formative experience which had created a certain type of [well trained] individual for the Army."[23] Organizationally independent, the *Luftwaffe* nonetheless remained in a real sense a creature of the Army; its main function was, by doctrine, equipment, and Hitler's wishes, army support. Service doctrine stated that until air superiority was established, units intended for protection of specific targets remained in that role. Protection of Army units was usually considered subordinate to airfield defense missions for the AA force, but antiaircraft assigned to the Army was under its operational control and was not withdrawn for air base defense.

The rearmament program of the 1930s saw a rapid increase in the *Luftwaffe*'s air defense artillery. The German government placed high priority on weapon design and built a variety of antiaircraft weapons. The most favored was the 88-mm gun, the early models of which could fire effectively to between 22,960 and 26,240 feet. The "88", or Flak 18, was the best weapon of its type in the world when it was introduced in 1933. By 1939, there were more than 1,000 in the *Flakartillerie,* with better models in production. Lighter weapons such as the 20-mm and 37-mm cannon came into service, and all could be found in stationary or motorized configurations. The light flak guns were prominent in tactical air-defense plans. They could be easily moved as air units advanced from base to base. By the start of war there were almost 1,000,000 active duty and reserve men assigned to this function which increased to 1,250,000 by 1944. A large proportion of these manned the heavy AA as the mainstay of home air defense. In the field, AA units protected the air force's ground installations with a variety of light and medium caliber weapons. German designed 20-mm and 37-mm cannon were the most used low level defense weapons. The 20-mm had a rather short effective range of 1,100 yards, the 37-mm 1,600 yards, so that it was important to bring fire on a target as soon as possible. Both weapons lacked a predictor,* severely restricting use against any but aircraft moving directly towards or away from the gun's position. The Germans also used 7.92-mm machine guns in both single and dual mounts for defense of bases against low level attack. Prior to the war, spotters assigned to AA units provided

---

* A predictor or director was an early mechanical computer which, using information about speed, direction of flight, and altitude permitted a gunner to lead a target and fire into its path.

German antiaircraft pieces used in World War II. The track mounted 20–mm flak gun gave mobile protection against aerial and ground attackers around Luftwaffe installations. The 88–mm piece, (*below*), designed as an antiaircraft weapon, was extensively used as artillery against armor and infantry.

almost all air raid warning. The spotters were usually among the most able people in the unit, and information they developed was entered into a reporting net that ran throughout an operational area.[24]

As the Germans expanded their Air Force during the middle and late 1930s, so too did they increase the number of military airfields in Germany. Some were permanent installations, many were dirt or grass strips on open land in the country or were laid out on sections of highways selected for this purpose. Travelers reported that these tactical airfields and their runways and buildings were well camouflaged. Windows were angled downward so they would not reflect the sun, and hangars and other structures were set among trees or so constructed as to minimize detection from the air. The object was to conceal the true size and operational nature of Germany's Air Force and to protect the airfields from enemy bombardment in wartime. Thus Germany's tactical commanders were well versed in the techniques of camouflage and dispersal.[25]

Radar experiments began in Germany in 1934 but did not progress very rapidly. The German Navy experimented with a gun laying unit and an air and sea search system. The *Luftwaffe* began looking into radar in 1936, but its continually changing specifications and lack of coordination among the three services slowed experimental progress. German radar was more accurate than that of other countries, but the Germans failed to establish a single office to direct the research and development and to prepare a coherent plan for radar use until after the war had begun. Thus, they dissipated their early lead in the field. The *Luftwaffe* finally ordered 1,000 sets in 1939. Failure to understand fully the operational requirements and benefits of radar was to have significant consequences early in the fighting.[26]

## Japanese Defense

By 1939, while many countries were making technological progress in antiaircraft protection, the Japanese lagged badly. An insular nation, protected from air assault by vast oceans and control of Korea and portions of China, Japan did not realize the full importance of modern tactical air defense systems. Most Japanese AA weapons were designed and introduced to service in the 1920s and early 1930s. The newest weapons were a 7.7-mm machine gun, first used in 1939, and two types of 40-mm guns captured from the Dutch and British in 1941 and 1942. There was a variety of 6.5-mm and 7.7-mm machine guns usable only against low level attacks. The machine guns all had maximum ranges of 5,000 to 6,000 feet with effective ranges of 2,000 to 2,400 feet. Their basic heavy weapon was a 75-mm low velocity gun supported by 20-mm and 25-mm cannon. The Japanese also had some mobile 88-mm guns, but both their equipment and control sys-

Japanese 20–mm antiaircraft on traverse mount. The 25–mm triple barrel mount (*below*) was common in the Japanese defense of airfields during the war.

tems were poor. The Japanese fire control system was manually operated, based upon sound detection, and comparable to an American system that became obsolete in 1930. In the field, the Japanese assigned these weapons to armies and corps and deployed them where the situation demanded. Despite the shortcomings of the equipment, the 20-mm and 25-mm weapons and machine guns and small arms threw up a heavy curtain of fire through which low level attackers had to pass to reach a target. For the lightly armored aircraft of the 1930s, this was a formidable obstacle. Allied use of large numbers of aircraft built to protect the crews and vital airplane parts and tactics suited to high speed, heavily armored aircraft created serious problems for Japanese defense planners.[27]

In 1939 Japan was far behind the British, Americans, and Germans in the development of practical radar units. Early warning and fire control radar sets were built in Japan, but the advent of war in 1941 actually retarded continued development. The first Japanese tactical radars were not seen until 1942, and were bulky semipermanent units. Portable radar sets were not in the field until 1943, and were copies made from British and American sets captured in Malaya and the Philippines. Gun laying radar sets appeared in 1943; they too were patterned on captured British sets. Identification Friend or Foe (IFF) experimentation did not yield good results, thus ground control intercept (GCI) development was retarded until well into the war and never attained the levels reached by the British or Americans.[28]

The AA defense of Japanese tactical air bases was well organized and effectively handled under an assigned garrison company of an airfield battalion. Normally, one platoon of the garrison company specialized in air defense and consisted of about 70 men armed with automatic cannon (20-mm and 25-mm), 6.5-mm and 7.7-mm AA machine guns plus other light machine guns. As necessary, the area Army commander could add heavier weapons such as 75-mm guns and move defense forces around to meet the needs of changing situations, adding to or subtracting from existing bases and creating defenses for new bases.[29]

Japan's air strength was divided between the Navy and the Army, with the Navy having both land and carrier based air units. In the years before World War II, both services apparently resisted a single shore based air force, as neither was willing to give up its air service. Japanese pilots, especially those in the Navy, were excellent. Prewar military pilots were an elite class, graduates of a rigorous training program that continued after the men were assigned to operational units. Air combat against China and the Soviet Union in the late 1930s sharpened the skills of these men, so that in 1941, when Japan went to war with Britain and the United States, some Allied observers in the Far East had difficulty believing the previously underrated Japanese were not Germans. The elite status of Japan's pilots, however, threatened to undo Japan's war effort. Prewar naval aviator training programs had such strict standards that as few as 25 men of an original class of 100 completed a year's flying instruction. Relatively few pilots meant that combat losses could not be readily replaced.[30]

The Japanese Army Air Force's (JAAF) flying units were subordinate to Army ground commanders. During fighting in China after 1937, the JAAF was used largely for ground support. With air superiority in China easily attained, the Japanese did not engage in heavy counterair operations until the 1939 border war with the Soviet Union. The JAAF was not then fully prepared to carry out large scale air attack and defense in a concerted bid to seek air superiority. In Siberia and Manchuria, the Japanese were roughly handled by the Red Air Force, in large measure because their aircraft were not armored and were vulnerable in combat. Studies of Russian armor plating led the Japanese to experiment on their own planes, but neither armor nor self sealing fuel tanks were in common use until 1943. When the Zero, or Zeke, fighter appeared in the summer of 1940, the Japanese recognized it for the excellent weapon it was. They came to rely on it too much and failed to pursue aircraft design vigorously. They did not build either an advanced fighter or a long range heavy bomber until late in the war. Consequently, the Japanese were committed to fighting the war with medium bombers lacking armor and self sealing tanks that could not withstand Allied gunfire.[31]

Japanese equipment was not standard among the services, and development proceeded independently in the Army and the Navy. Originally, this was done to foster and gain the benefits of competition. Unfortunately, the divided effort produced a vast array of weapons. Machine guns for fighters in both services were .50 caliber, but had different size chambers. The ammunition was not interchangable, nor were parts for the weapons. The ground forces had yet other designs. The lack of standardization created severe logistics problems. Sometimes, aircraft of one service lacked ammunition, but could not use that of the other service's neighboring unit because it would not fit the guns.[32]

## The Soviet Union

Shortly after Russia's revolutionary leaders established themselves early in the 1920s, they began to look abroad for help in technical areas including military hardware. They found a ready partner in the post-World War I German Republic's military. The German-Russian cooperation on aircraft design and testing in the 1920s was beneficial for both countries. The secret effort allowed Germany to skirt the Versailles Treaty's prohibition on designing and testing of weapons, while Russia too gained vital information.

Controlled by the Bolsheviks after the revolution and civil war, the basic doctrine of Russian air elements after 1920 emphasized tactical support of the Red Army. Early in its history, the Red Air Force faced severe shortages of fuel, parts, and aircraft. Expedient measures to keep the air force flying were often used, and, as a result, the service quickly formed a pragmatic tradition of flying regardless of the problems faced. After 1930, when his political control of the Soviet Union was secure, Joseph Stalin paid much attention to aviation; enormous improvements in flight technology brought Russia many aviation records in the decade before World War II. Long distance aviation received special attention, but the efforts detracted from the design of tactical combat aircraft and impeded development of fighters that could be used in air superiority campaigns. By 1939, Russia's first line fighters were outclassed by those of the other major powers. In addition, Stalin's political purges of the late 1930s severely affected the growth of air doctrine and the development both of aircraft and support equipment.[33]

Joseph Stalin had an enormous impact on the Soviet Union's military doctrine and operation. Throughout his career, he constantly stressed the offensive. Stalin's insistence on offensive actions can be traced to at least 1918, when, as Commissar of Food Supply in Tsaritsyn (later Stalingrad), he severely criticized the area's military leader, A. E. Snesarev, for being "defensist," rather than aggressive. Stalin, at the same time, also had other military leaders removed from office and some shot for displaying similar "defensist" views while fighting the counter-revolutionary White Army.[34]

In the mid-1930s, Stalin began the systematic expulsion from the Communist Party and the government of whomever he believed disloyal. He extended the purge in the late 1930's by large scale removal of military leaders. In 1938, he ordered the Red Air Force's Chief of Staff, Yakov I. Alksnis, shot; Alksnis was soon followed by his deputy and successor, Vasili V. Khripin. Khripin's successor, General Alexandr Loktionov, was shot, too, in a general bloodletting that took some twenty-five percent of the service's senior officers. Many more were sent to labor camps. The replacements for the executed and imprisoned men were young, inexperienced officers, chosen mostly because they would be obligated to Stalin for their careers. The loss of these experienced air commanders retarded training and operational readiness of the Red Air Force and contributed heavily to the collapse of the Soviets in the face of Germany's attack in 1941.[35]

At the end of the political purges in 1940, a new generation of fighter and ground attack aircraft began to appear in the field. Designs were based on lessons the Russians learned in Spain while helping the Republican government in 1938, in the fighting against Japan in Siberia in the following year, and in the Winter War of 1939-1940 with Finland. Excellent new aircraft would put the Soviet Air Force on an even footing in many areas with Germany and the Allies, but not until 1943. In 1940, Stalin appointed a new head of the Aviation Industry Commissariat, A. I. Shakurin. Universal military service began, and the length of service was extended from two to five years. The Air Force received a talented Chief of Staff, General Pavel Rychagov, and the long process of modernization began.[36]

The Soviet Air Force (*Voyenno-Vozdushnyye Sily* or *VVS*) was a highly decentralized flying branch of the Red Army, designed to support the ground forces in areas as divergent as Western Europe and China. The *VVS* was not a unified service; its units were subordinate to Army commands mobilized for war, its staff a division of the Red Army Staff. Decentralizing the air force was done to insure cooperation between the forces. Before the war, air regiments were assigned to the various Military Districts, subordinate to the District Commanders. When the war began, the *VVS*'s units became part of corps, armies, and fronts, commands roughly equal to army groups. The regiments that made up Russia's tactical air force were commonly referred to as the Red Air Force or *VVS* and were required to secure air supremacy, support army ground forces, and perform air reconnaissance. In addition to the *VVS*, there was a national air defense force, the *Protivozodushnaya Oborona Strany* (*PVO Strany*), with fighters, observation units, and AA guns. It was charged with protecting strategic targets such as cities and vulnerable industrial sites. In addition, *PVO* units were assigned to army fronts. The Soviet High Command controlled the Long Range Bomber Force (the *Dahinaya Bombardirovshchik Aviatsiya* or *DBA*), and the Navy had an aviation section with aircraft assigned to each fleet. As part of the 1940 Soviet military reform, air base districts were created. Each district supported the air units within an army front by building, operating, and protecting air bases. Initially, the *VVS* sought to have three airfields for each of its flying regiments: a main field, an alternate or standby, and a field facility or dispersal field. The large number of landing grounds made dispersal easier, but also complicated problems of AA gun allocation and command and control of fighter aircraft. Very few of the forward airfields, built in former Polish territory seized in late 1939, were ready by June 1941, and many of the *VVS*'s aircraft were grouped on a few operational bases.[37]

While aviation underwent changes, so too did air defense artillery. One of the main Russian derivations from the secret partnership with Germany was a 76-mm gun. Later, German success with the 88-mm gun in the Spanish Civil War prompted the Russians to devise an 85-mm gun, first produced in 1939 with an effective range of 27,500 feet. Medium range weapons were primarily 37-mm guns of Swedish, German, or British design; mass production began in Russia in 1939. Prewar Russian training and doctrine placed heavy stress on the use of machine guns such as the 7.62-mm, with an effective range of 2,400 feet, for low-level air defense of the Red Army's forces. The Russian manufactured 12.7-mm machine gun was also employed for air defense in a similar fashion.[38]

The Red Army's AA target plotting and fire control methods before the war were not good. The systems were almost always manual and seem not to have been refined, even with the outbreak of fighting. Soviet technicians began work on electronic aircraft detection early in the 1930's. By the middle of the decade they were developing rudimentary radar sets and making significant strides in solving problems of frequencies to be used. The Russian attempts to create a viable radar capability were hampered by a divided research and development effort, made more difficult because of disputes between research agencies over the value of long and short microwaves and the use of thermal (infrared) detection. In addition, Stalin's aggressive removal of people he deemed unreliable affected technical institutions and resulted in the loss of many skilled scientists to labor camps during 1937. Research continued, however, under the direction of the *PVO* and took two lines: early warning, and short range gun laying. Soviet leaders, like some in Germany, seem not to have grasped the importance of radar to effective air force command and control. As a result, the Red Army and *PVO* probably had no more than fifteen RUS–2 early warning sets, of very limited capability, on June 22, 1941. The German invasion stopped research and production in its tracks until 1942. The first production models probably were not put into use until the end of 1943. Problems associated with manufacture and the training of operators limited Russian use of electronic early warning throughout the war. The lack of radar integrated into a warning and command network was to have serious consequences when the *Luftwaffe* attacked Russian air bases.[39]

Russian antiaircraft defenses for units deployed in the field were the responsibility of the Red Army's artillery branch. The Red Army assigned AA elements to units of division size, and lower if needed. Searchlights, listening posts, and observation stations all came under a single organization in each army region. While this provided some efficiency of operation, the obsolete and varied types of equipment increased supply and maintenance problems, and reduced the ability of the warning network to aid in defense against air base attack. The need to spread AA weapons thinly over the vast Russian land mass left minimal or nonexistent protection in some places. In some ways, however, the Soviets were exceptionally fine performers. In addition to their skill at using heavy small arms and light machine gun fire against low flying enemy aircraft, the Russians had an unsurpassed ability to use camouflage in the open heartland of the country.[40]

## Great Britain and the Commonwealth

British preparations varied from region to region. Their base defense capabilities were least developed in the Far East because of decisions by the home government which essentially discounted the Japanese threat. Few aircraft were assigned in Asia, those present were obsolete, and war plans there were poor. Competing demands for Middle East and home defense put a strain on production capacity, first because of the belief during the 1920s that France was the most serious threat. By the 1930s, a resurgent and militant Germany kept British defense decisions centered on Europe. British scientific advances and a well organized air defense system created a very favorable position in the British Isles, although this would not become clear until after the summer of 1940. British tactical air defense doctrine based upon experience in the Battle of Britain would be used initially in Malta and North Africa.[41]

When Germany announced in 1935 that the *Luftwaffe* was on a par with the Royal Air Force (RAF), the British Chiefs of Staff reevaluated their meager air defense capability. In 1934, AA defense was 17 gun batteries of 8 guns each, and 42 searchlight companies. In 1936, the British increased their planned strength to 76 batteries and 108 searchlight companies, but there was little money to buy the weapons and equipment. Strong antiwar feeling and continued opposition from the Treasury delayed purchase of guns and equipment and training of men. In 1937, Air Chief Marshal Sir Hugh Dowding, Commander-in-Chief, Air Defence of Great Britain, issued a report describing an ideal scheme for the air defense of the United Kingdom. He proposed that 16 heavy guns be deployed around important points such as Navy yards and manufacturing plants and groups of 4 for general defense. That year there were only 146 heavy AA weapons in the entire country. The use of light AA was not yet well understood, as the threat of low level bombing raids from the Continent was just beginning to become apparent. Dowding's report also recommended acquiring 1,200 small guns, but had no specific justification for such a number. The scheme was approved in principle, but it could not be implemented until November 1937 for lack of money. In 1938, when weapon production began in earnest, most guns in use were still the 3-inch from World War I. The Munich Crisis of September 1938, added greater urgency because neither the antiaircraft nor the fighter interceptor force was adequate to the task of defending the RAF's bases in Britain. No more than a handful of the all important Bofors guns, crucial to defense against low-level attacks, was available. Bofors production in Britain and purchases from Sweden slowly increased the number. On September 1, 1939, when Germany attacked Poland, the numbers of both heavy and medium AA guns were far from satisfactory for protection in Britain, much less to send weapons to overseas bases.[42]

A Swedish design of 1930, the 40-mm Bofors gun so far surpassed other midrange weapons that it became the most widely used antiaircraft gun of the war. Licensing agreements allowed its manufacture in eleven countries including Poland, Britain, and the United States; all the countries making it sold the guns on the export market and assigned them to home forces. The Bofors' accuracy and rapid fire (120 rounds per minute) along with its ease of handling and barrel replacement made it a deadly weapon around British and Allied air bases. It had an effective hitting range, allowing for angle of fire, wind, temperature, and barometric pressure, of between 5,000 and 6,500 feet. High altitude air defense requirements were met by a 3.7-inch gun, introduced into service in 1938; followed by a 4.5-inch gun also adopted in 1938. The early model 3.7-inch had an effective range of 23,000 feet, not enough to reach high flying German and Japanese bombers, several of which could exceed 25,000 feet. An improvement was found in the 4.5-inch gun which had an effective ceiling of 26,500 feet shooting 8 rounds per minute. The array of British weapons, then, could theoretically contend with both low and high level attacks. Initial production delays meant, however, that most targets were only marginally defended from the ground, sometimes by only 2 or 3 guns, when the attackers arrived in 1940.[43]

Despite the shortages of AA guns, in many respects the British had the best prepared air defense of any of the World War II combatants in 1940, and it was not by accident that this was so. In 1936, coincident with a reorganization of the RAF that created the Fighter Command, the British began an intense effort to exploit what they called radio direction finding (RDF), or radar. The name RDF was chosen deliberately to mislead German intelligence into believing the development work was related to aerial navigation. Sir Henry Tizard, Chairman of the Committee for the Scientific Survey of Air Defense, and unofficial scientific advisor to the Air Officer Commanding (AOC) Fighter Command, Air Marshal Dowding, believed radar's ability to give bearing, distance, and height of aircraft could be used to guide fighter interceptors to approaching bombers. Tizard thought such a system would eliminate the need for continuous airborne patrols, conserving both men and machines. Experiments at RAF Station Biggin Hill in southeastern England during the summer of 1936 proved him correct. That year the first ground controlled interception guidance techniques were devised. Over the next four years, the techniques were refined and improved, and men were trained to control fighters launched from various airfields. As war with Germany became more probable, the RDF system, named Chain Home, was extended to cover the east coast of the United Kingdom. Tizard's efforts gave Britain an operationally effective detection, warning, and control system, something no other nation had.[44]

This success created a coherent system that gave the British an inestimable advantage over their potential enemy, Nazi Germany. By 1940, the Chain Home (CH) and Chain Home Low (CHL) radar stations, which divided the task of high and low level detection, observed aircraft approaching from the time they took off from airfields behind Calais. In the north of England the protection was not as yet complete, but was being pursued strongly by the Air Ministry. Radar ranges and capabilities were constantly improved as engineering changes were made, but by the summer of 1940 gaps continued to exist. The low level stations, in particular, were beset with problems caused by surface reflections of the signal, causing false returns on the radar screen. To resolve this problem, the British stressed proficiency of radar scope readers and made wide use of ground observers.[45]

Each of the Chain Home sites (*Map 2*) was originally connected to Fighter Command Headquarters. By June 1940, however, they were so numerous that direct reporting was impractical and reports were made to the appropriate fighter group operations room. Chain Home Low stations covered low level approaches to which the high-altitude CH stations were blind and reported to the respective CH location they supported. Information flowed to group and Fighter Command by direct telephone line. Once the information reached an operations room, controllers issued instructions to sectors and airfields by both dedicated telephone lines and the Defence Teleprinter Network. The sector command post then scrambled and controlled the fighter squadrons. The system was not perfect. The CH stations did not always detect each flight of aircraft. In addition, the RAF's 1936 reorganization creating Fighter, Bomber, and Coastal Commands, coupled with the service's slow growth between 1936 and 1938, meant that the new organization was not fully broken in, and not all the RAF's senior officers understood it. Nevertheless, the important advance, the fighter control system, was in place. The question now was how effective it would be.[46]

Supplementing the radar stations was the Observer Corps, originally used during World War I, abandoned, and then reorganized in 1924. This group continued to grow, so that by mid-1940, it contained some 30,000 people serving at more than 1,000 posts. The observers were largely civilian volunteers who put in extra time after work. Observer reports were one of the keys to defense of Fighter Command's inland airfields. Since the radar stations pointed seaward, only the observers could spot enemy aircraft over England's interior. As they became more and more proficient, observers were able to give accurate reports on height and direction of flight of aircraft. Telephones linked the many posts to Fighter Command, and even the most remote location could get a message through in less than 40 seconds. Despite severe problems with report saturation during heavy raids, and difficulty in estimating altitudes by visual observation in poor weather, the observers consistently produced useful information on aircraft formations.[47]

Capping the structure of Britain's air defense system in 1940 was Fighter Command's most important weapon—the squadrons of Hurricane and Spitfire interceptors. Directed by the command and control system, fighter pilots could take off in good time to pounce on enemy formations approaching from the Continent. The growth and development of Fighter Command was not without problems, however. In April 1938, British aircraft production was only 158 machines monthly. Spurred on by the Munich Crisis of September 1938, production increased rapidly. Nevertheless, by

RADAR AND OBSERVER NETWORK GREAT BRITAIN, 1940

LEGEND
● C.H. Stations
○ C.H.L. Stations
▲ Observer centres
—·— Western limit of observed areas
------ Main cover (at 15,000 Ft) Sept 1939
——— Main cover (at 15,000 Ft) Sept 1940

Coltrip
Nether Button
Thrumster
Rosehearty
Hillhead
ABERDEEN
Doonies Hill
School Hill
St Cyrus
DUNDEE
Douglas Wood
DUNFERMLINE
Anstruther
GLASGOW
Cockburnspath
Drone Hill
GALASHIELS
Bamburgh
Cresswell
Ottercaps Moss
CARLISLE
DURHAM
Shotten
Danby Beacon
LANCASTER
YORK
Flamborough Hd
LEEDS
Easington
MANCHESTER
Stenigol
LINCOLN
Ingoldmeis
WREXHAM
DERBY
West Beckham
SHREWSBURY
Happiesburgh
COVENTRY
BURY ST EDMUNDS
NORWICH
Stoke Holy Cross
Strumble Hd.
BEDFORD
Dunwich
CAMBRIDGE
High Street
Haycastle
GLOUCESTER
COLCHESTER
Bawdsey
St. Twynelis
Bromley
Warren
OXFORD
Walton
CARDIFF
WATFORD
Canewdon
BRISTOL
MAIDTONE
Forseness
WINCHESTER
Dunkirk
Truleigh
HORSHAM
Dover
EXETER
YEOVIL
Poling
Rye
Fairlight
Carnanton
Pevensey
Rame Head
Hawks Tor
Worth
Beachy Head
Drytree
W. Prawle
Ventnor

Map 2

**German Würzburg D radar in semipermanent emplacement. The unit was also mounted on a wheeled van.**

mid-1940 Fighter Command had but 756 of its best fighters to form 29 squadrons of Hurricanes and 19 of Spitfires, with the usual 16 to a squadron. Four more squadrons of older, less capable Defiants and Blenheims complemented this force. This was not a large number of aircraft, and the problem was complicated by an accompanying shortage of pilots: 916 at midyear, 946 on September 1, 1940. The relatively small number of pilots and aircraft reflected the inability of the country to respond almost overnight to all of the production and training demands engendered by the military buildup that increased in tempo after Munich. With the organization of Fighter Command, Dowding controlled not only the fighter squadrons, but also radar stations and AA guns; all served one purpose: the defense of the United Kingdom. Dowding and his group commanders focused on that one issue. The years of planning and the leaders' abilities were now to be tested.[48]

By mid-1939, air defense services of the major powers had undergone varying technical and doctrinal changes, most of them coming in the few years before war. Problems associated with high altitude munitions were largely solved, at least in design. Mechanical time fuzes, for example, gave the AA gunners a much improved ability to detonate rounds at specific altitudes. This increased accuracy of AA fire significantly. Production of such fuzes, however, was slow at first, especially in Britain. Complex problems of assembling intricate clockwork mechanisms able to withstand the shock of propulsion out of a gun barrel were slowly solved. In 1939, mass production was not yet under way. Both mechanical and electric computers, used by Japan, Germany, Great Britain, and America, allowed more rapid range calculation and fuze setting, and a variety of excellent machine guns and small cannon of the 20-mm to 40-mm caliber were readily available. No country, however, developed a tracking and gun control system that could follow a fast moving airplane. None would be designed during World War II.

In many ways, World War II was to be an air war. Often, base survival depended on an air force's ability to seize and hold air superiority for a protracted time, and the most effective weapon against air raids became the highly trained pilot flying a fast, well armed fighter-interceptor. How well an air force could function from its flying fields was to be of paramount importance to both sides. The question was most difficult for the German, Japanese, and Russian air forces, as all three were essentially tactical, although they used planes for strategic purposes on occasion. All espoused a doctrine that included attacking enemy airfields as well as logistical and strategic targets.

Lt. Gen. Elwood R. Quesada, wartime commander of the U.S. Army Air Forces' IX Fighter Command, believed that in the years before World War II, none of the the western Allies gave much serious thought to the importance of air base defense.[49] Even by 1939 tactical airfields were still mostly grass with little construction and few paved areas. Many governments were reluctant to spend large amounts of money on air defense during peacetime, and therefore yielded to the belief of many air officers that heavy bombers would defeat an enemy by destroying his homeland and bringing a quick end to the war. Basic planning and consideration for national defense were discussed, and major protagonists had adequate air operation doctrine. In general, however, organization for protection of tactical forces in the field fell by the wayside. One notable exception was in Germany, where the *Luftwaffe* developed an air doctrine calling for the early destruction of an enemy air force in war and an air defense system built on a sophisticated organization that no longer relied on crude adaptations of machine guns shooting at aircraft. The specialization of weaponry for this purpose was not limited to the Germans, although they surpassed all others.

Base defense remained an unfinished and to some extent a still theoretical art at the outbreak of World War II. Virtually every major country had included high altitude artillery and medium and low altitude guns and automatic weapons in its armament, but antiaircraft weapons alone were not the only means needed to defend bases. Faster aircraft and more destructive weapons required efficient warning and control systems for the defenders. In the event, the British combination of radar, well designed fighters under flexible but firm control, and antiaircraft artillery under one command was soon put to the test.

Part 2
World War II

# Chapter III

## *Blitzkrieg* and the Battle of Britain

In the late summer of 1939, the German *Wehrmacht*\* began a series of decisive offensives. On September 1, 1939, the German campaign in Poland precipitated a declaration of war on Germany by France and Britain. Following the success in Poland, German forces rested, reequipped, and devised new plans to carry the fight to Western Europe. In France, the Allied armies watched cautiously, but took no action against Germany in a phase of the war that came to be known as *Sitzkrieg*. Bombing was forbidden, and only reconnaissance aircraft entered German airspace. In April 1940, Hitler seized Denmark and Norway. The next month he turned on France and the Low Countries, smashing the allies in six weeks and forcing Britain to evacuate the Continent. For the Western Allies, this was the bleakest period of the war, culminating in the Battle of Britain in the summer of 1940. By the end of the year, however, the *Luftwaffe* had been dealt a severe blow over England, losing 1,733 aircraft to fighter and antiaircraft defenses, and various other operational casualties connected with the battle. Although few immediately recognized the fact, the *Luftwaffe*'s effectiveness, planning, and doctrine had been called into serious question, and the heavy losses of skilled pilots drained a resource that would be badly needed in the fighting to come. Prepared for a short war, Germany now faced a lengthening conflict of attrition.

During 1939 and 1940, the war was to try severely the military doctrine and planning of all the participants, especially in the new area of tactical warfare. The First World War had been a crude affair for air forces and base

---

\* This term is often used to refer to the German Army. It actually included all of the German armed forces, the Army (*das Heer*), the Navy (*die Kriegsmarine*), and the Air Force (*die Luftwaffe*).

defenders alike. The scale of aerial fighting in World War II dwarfed any-thing experienced in the earlier conflict by even the most seasoned officers. Many of the future air generals and marshals who drew up war plans or doctrine in the 1930s were rudely shocked by the unprecedented events of the new war. Pre-World War II ideas about the effectiveness and relative ratios of antiaircraft weapons to the targets to be defended, the value of air attacks on airfields, and the vulnerability of aircraft conducting them often turned out to be far from reality. From the first, German air strikes against airfields were an integral part of *blitzkrieg*; the German Air Force sought to destroy enemy air strength on the ground by massive surprise attack. Twice the Germans achieved air superiority, only to fail in the most critical test during the Battle of Britain.

## The Attack on Poland

Although not preceded by a declaration of war, the Nazi attack did not catch the Poles unaware, for as early as 1935 Poland began a Six Year Plan to upgrade its armed forces, including the addition of a modern antiaircraft defense with some three hundred 40-mm Bofors guns, Browning machine guns, and other automatics for low-level protection. These weapons would be manufactured in Poland under license from Swedish and American de-signers.[1] Determined to protect its homeland, the Polish government in-tended to spend one third of each year's tax revenue and a two billion franc French loan in the defense scheme. By 1939 some thirty-five to forty-five percent of the original goals had been achieved, despite Poland's sluggish production. In addition to the weapons of foreign origin, the Poles designed and built forty-four 75-mm AA guns, a total of eleven batteries.[2]

Antiaircraft defense played a part in Polish military maneuvers as early as 1927. These units increased in each of the 1937, 1938, and 1939 military exercises. By the summer of 1939, defense plans were well advanced, and Polish leaders were quite aware of Hitler's intentions. Contrary to belief at the time in the West, Poland's air force was not destroyed on the ground on the first day, nor did it lack an ability to protect either itself or the country.[3]

The original German air attack plan centered on a massive surprise blow at Polish bases to destroy support facilities and catch planes on the ground. Germany had clear numerical air superiority in combat aircraft and a tremendous advantage in the quality and capability of equipment. In the East, the *Luftwaffe* deployed two air fleets of some 1,500 planes for the Polish campaign. The *Luftwaffe*'s task was to prevent the Polish air force from taking any effective part in air operations, to support the two army groups, and to destroy military installations and armament factories.[4]

The Poles mustered an air force of about 400 first line operational aircraft; 154 were bombers and 159 fighters in 43 squadrons. These aircraft

54

were divided into 12 army cooperation squadrons for air support of ground forces, 7 reconnaissance, 15 fighter, and 9 bomber squadrons.[5] By 1939 all operational aircraft were of Polish design and manufacture. The main Polish air defense weapon was the PZL 11 fighter (P11), a high wing, open cockpit monoplane first built in 1931. During the 1930s the P11 underwent many modifications and was generally regarded as an excellent airplane, but by 1939, it was completely obsolete and due to be replaced. The P11c then in use was armed with two 7.7-mm machine guns, and modifications adding 2 additional machine guns were under way. The 7.7-mm rounds, equivalent to .30 caliber, were not heavy enough to destroy an opponent without concentrated fire for many seconds. The P11c at 230 miles per hour was much slower than its principal opponent, the German Me109, which could exceed 350 miles per hour. However, because of its excellent maneuverability, the P11c could easily contend with the Ju87 Stuka, whose maximum speed was 242 miles an hour. Although the P11c was slow, it was exceptionally well built and a potentially deadly weapon in the hands of a skilled pilot, even against an Me109.[6]

The Polish Army had 1 regiment and 8 detachments of antiaircraft artillery. It could muster 400 heavy weapons both in fixed emplacements and self-propelled. There were also over 300 light guns and about 170 antiaircraft machine guns. None of the guns had data computing equipment for aiming at moving targets. The Poles did not have radar, and command and control proved weak. German intelligence considered Polish AA effectiveness low due to insufficient numbers of weapons and poor aiming capability.[7]

The Polish air service was part of the Army except for a small naval air section directly under Navy control. In peacetime, the Army's air arm was organized in three large air groups, only two of which were fully operational in August 1939. When mobilizing for war, the Poles planned to break up the big units and allocate squadrons to field army commanders, except for bomber and reconnaissance aircraft which belonged to the Army's High Command. The Polish military command directed conversion to wartime organization five days before the invasion. By August 31, half of the fighters were thus parceled out to various field armies, the other half were organized for defense of major cities, such as Warsaw. (*Map 3*) Except for the bombers and some reconnaissance units, the air arm was now under control of the various ground commanders.[8]

The Polish air arm's ground service units in September 1939 were cumbersome. Although the aircraft were well dispersed, the Germans caught the Poles in the middle of mobilization, and maintenance and service people apparently had not adjusted to wartime operation. The most serious deficiency, however, was communications, especially that used by the air defense forces. There was no Polish communication system dedicated to use by the

**The destruction of the Polish Air Force. Obsolete Polish aircraft abandoned at Deblin, south of Warsaw.**

air and antiaircraft units. The Polish air force depended on Army communicators from local ground units, and there were only ten radio stations to support air operations. Any disruption of the fragile radio and telegraph circuits would quickly affect the commanders' ability to function, the delivery of fuel and spare parts, and the transmission of air raid warning orders.[9]

Despite all of the German planning and effort spent in preparing for war and its preponderance of force, the *Luftwaffe* faced serious problems in trying to destroy the Polish air arm. The weather on September 1 was very poor: fog, rain, and low ceilings with restricted visibility. Only about one-third of the effective force could take off on schedule. Still, the Germans hit nine of the twelve main Polish airfields, but only at Warsaw-Okecie did the they find sizeable numbers of planes. Nineteen secondary airfields were attacked with little effect, and an additional fifteen airfields were reconnoitered but found empty. Poland had successfully dispersed its air capability to a number of secret fields from which it was prepared to operate, although at a reduced effectiveness.[10]

The Germans had excellent air reconnaissance and accurate maps of Poland. The *Luftwaffe* was unable, however, to reconnoiter the whole coun-

**Okechie airfield showing effects of German bombardment in early September 1939. Some Polish squadrons survived on smaller installations and continued to harass the *Luftwaffe* until late in the campaign.**

try. In the flat terrain of East Europe, airfields could be almost anywhere, and the Germans simply could not find many Polish landing places. The Poles capitalized on this by the heavy use of camouflage to protect almost all of their combat aircraft and the first day's damage was to facilities and runways of abandoned bases and to old, noncombat planes. In fact, Poland had employed what the British Air Ministry in 1943 considered of "paramount importance [for defense against air attack] *adequate dispersal of aircraft* and the use of satellite airfields".[11]

Despite the successful air force dispersal, Poland's military weaknesses were evident on the first day of the war. The force of the attack and damage to the communications system confused the Polish air command, which was apparently unable to organize its most effective asset—fighters—in an aggressive, coordinated defense. Similarly, because Polish antiaircraft gunners lacked warning of approaching attacks, their fire was weak and ineffective until September 2nd. Polish reconnaissance planes were aloft then, radioing position and direction of enemy bombers. The highly maneuverable Polish

**POLAND, 1939**

LITHUANIA

EAST PRUSSIA

MODLIN
WARSZAWA

LODZ

DEBLIN

LUBLIN

GERMANY

KRAKOW
KATOWICE

SOVIET
UNION

SLOVAKIA

HUNGARY

## Map 3

fighters attacked the Germans. The ground defenses came into action and the *Luftwaffe*'s 4th Bomber Group faced heavy flak around the three air-fields near Deblin, 55 miles south of Warsaw. Unfortunately, the antiaircraft fire burst 1,000 feet below the planes, the result of poor warning and lack of adequate height and range finding equipment. The *Luftwaffe* easily passed over this potential impediment and carpeted the bases with explosives. Air defense efforts, although remaining unorganized, continued until the Poles exhausted their resources.[12]

The initial defense at Katowice and Cracow air bases were examples of both Polish successes and failures. Attacking suddenly at 900 to 1,500 feet, German aircraft flew too low for the heavy antiaircraft guns, and machine guns had to assume the bulk of the effort. At Cracow, machine guns damaged 3 Do17s, which were forced to land and their crews made captive. By day's end, however, most of the original machine guns had been silenced by the attackers. Army heavy machine guns hastily mounted on truck beds and dangerously exposed to strafing or bomb fragments replaced them. The Poles then used whatever weapons they had at hand throughout the rest of the campaign.[13]

The Polish air force continued to fight, albeit at a diminishing level, until September 16. A lack of spare parts grounded increasing numbers of defenders. German air attacks cut the telegraph system, compounding troubles when orders and information could not be transmitted. Since there was no useful air detection and warning system to begin with, Polish air bases, once found, were in an exposed and dangerously vulnerable position. During the first two weeks of September, however, the *Luftwaffe*'s combat losses numbered 285, or 19 percent of their force. Contrary to some past belief, the Germans had faced significant ground-to-air and air-to-air combat. Several sources give the total number of Polish air-to-air victories as 126 for the 16 days of fighting. In addition to the aircraft lost, another 279 German planes were seriously damaged. Polish bombers made attacks against German infantry up to the final day, but the Poles could not hold out. On the 17th, the remaining planes fled south to Rumania.[14]

Though victorious in Poland, the German military machine did not perform as well as Nazi propaganda of 1939 led the world to believe, both because of Polish resistance and its own internal weaknesses. Inadequately trained German crews missed many of their targets in Poland during the first five days of combat. In 1944, German Air Historical Branch analysts pointed out problems with accuracy of bombing and reliability of aircrew reports during the Polish campaign. Because of the substantial amount of incorrect information, readers were cautioned that, "if the High Command is not to be misled, particular importance must be attached [by the *Luftwaffe*] to the accuracy of such reports." *Luftwaffe* Chief of Staff General Jeschonnek gave vacillating and contradictory operational directives. Early in the campaign, he ordered the sporadic diversion of aircraft from tactical operations to unnecessary strategic targets, such as factories and cities. He also frequently overrode the decisions of senior field commanders, to the point of issuing orders directly to combat units without informing the two air fleet chiefs. The uncertainties and insecurities of many of the air

TABLE 1

# *Luftwaffe* Order of Battle, Losses in the Polish Campaign

Under Direct Command of Goering
Headquarters, Potsdam
8 and 10 Recce *Staffeln*
Signals Unit 100

*Luftflotte* 1 (East)-Kesselring
Hq, Henningsholm/Stettin:

5 Recce *Staffeln*
13 Bomber *Gruppen*
4½ *Stuka Gruppen*
3 Twin engine Fighter *Gruppen*
(Me110)
3 Single engine Fighter
*Gruppen* (Me109)

Total: 824 Serviceable Aircraft

*Luftflotte* 4 (Southeast)-Löhr,
Hq, Reichenbach, Silesia:

3 Recce *Staffeln*
8 Bomber *Gruppen*
4 *Stuka Gruppen*
2 Twin engine Fighter
*Gruppen* (Me110)
2 Single engine Fighter
*Gruppen* (Me109)
1 Ground Attack *Gruppe*

676 Serviceable Aircraft

Total aircraft deployed: 648 bombers, 219 dive bombers, 30 ground attack planes, 210 single and twin engine fighters, 474 reconnaissance planes, plus transports. Figures do not include Army aircraft and home defense fighters.

*Luftwaffe* Losses in the Polish Campaign
Period September 1 through 28, 1939

| | |
|---|---:|
| Reconnaissance | 63 |
| Single engine Fighters | 67 |
| Twin engine Fighters | 12 |
| Bombers | 78 |
| Dive bombers | 31 |
| Transports | 12 |
| Marine and Miscellaneous | 22 |
| Total | 285 |

The Germans counted a further 279 aircraft of all types as temporarily lost to strength, being over ten per cent damaged, but repairable.

**Sources:** Air Ministry, German Translation VII/33, The *Luftwaffe* in Poland
Bekker, *The Luftwaffe War Diaries*

TABLE 2

## Strength and Losses of the Polish Air Force
## September 1939

| Aircraft | Operational Units | Training Schools and Reserves |
|---|---|---|
| Fighters: | | |
| P11c | 129 | 43 |
| P7 | 30 | 75 |
| Light Bombers: | | |
| P23 | 118 | 85 |
| Bombers: | | |
| P37 | 36 | 30 |
| Reconnaissance: | | |
| R XIII | 49 | 95 |
| RWD 14 "Czapla" | 35 | 20 |
| | 397 | 348 |

Losses

Most of the training and reserve aircraft were used as replacements in the first few days of the campaign. Aircraft lost on operations numbered 333, including 82 by the Polish Bomber Brigade. One hundred sixteen serviceable planes were flown over the Carpathians, mainly on September 17th, and were interned in Rumania.

**Sources:** Bekker, *Luftwaffe War Diaries,* quoted from figures issued by the Sikorski Institute in London, and from Adam Kurowski's *Lotnictwo Polskie 1939 Roku*, Warsaw.

commanders remained even as it became evident the Polish air force would be unable to affect the outcome of the fighting.[15]

In spite of the *Luftwaffe*'s earlier limited experience in the Spanish Civil War, some officers found difficulty in dealing with what they viewed as unexpected Polish resistance. Although outnumbered and outclassed, the Poles put up a credible fight. Three Me110s were shot down by P11s in a dogfight on the afternoon of September 2nd. The Polish AA guns were technically some of the best at the time, but they were too few and had no effective aiming mechanisms. A cohesive command organization, the ability to detect and report an approaching aerial enemy in time to intercept him, and improvement of interception tactics and AA control were all hobbled by an overall lack of industrial development in the country. Certainly the skill, spirit, and valor of Polish pilots and crews played a large part in their effectiveness, which was proven when the remnants joined the Royal Air Force in 1940.[16]

## Fighting in the West

When they began the war in Poland, the Germans mobilized their reserves, including flak artillery. The armament industry had not produced all of the weapons desired, but the German antiaircraft artillery was much better than that of any of Germany's potential adversaries. In late 1939 the *Luftwaffe*, which controlled flak units, had 6,700 20-mm and 37-mm guns, and 2,600 88-mm and 105-mm guns; 30,000 20-mm guns, 5,000 37-mm, 8,200 88-mm, and planned 2,000 105-mm guns for the end of 1942. The period of quiet in the West between September 1939 and May 1940 allowed the Germans to continue building AA weapons and gave them the training time to create first line operational units. The French refusal to bomb Germany before May 10 greatly facilitated this training and organizing task, as the young German reservists required a good bit of work to make them proficient.[17]

With the array of weapons they possessed, the *Flakartillerie* protected the German homeland, advanced air bases, and the army on the move. Furthermore, the large numbers and growing size of the antiaircraft establishment clearly showed the importance attached to air defense. The Germans had such strong confidence in defensive guns protecting their heavy industrial areas that overflights of Allied bombers dropping propaganda leaflets in the Rhine-Ruhr district brought no great insistence on fighter protection. Only after May 10, 1940, when the *Luftwaffe* accidentally bombed Freiburg-im-Breisgau, did public pressure bring about the relocation of two fighter groups for south Germany's air defense. Both sides had time to organize and prepare for wartime demands.[18]

In March and April 1939, joint Franco-British staff conversations assessed Allied military needs in facing a German enemy. Discussion included questions of general strategy, the relative capabilities of the various air forces, principles of collaboration between the British and French air forces in attacking German war industries and installations, and the defense of Allied bases. The proposition of Allied air attacks on the *Luftwaffe*'s bases received considerable attention, but was dismissed by the air commanders of both countries, largely because the Allies considered themselves militarily inferior to Germany. The French *Armée de l'Air*'s bomber force, although being expanded and modernized, was neither large enough nor capable of a counterair campaign aimed at German airfields. The French did not wish to provoke German bombing of French territory and so favored general restraint on the question of air attacks on Germany. The Royal Air Force viewed attacks on Germany's airfields as generally infeasible because of the large number of such targets, the high cost of such attacks, and the small potential for successfully destroying or impeding the *Luftwaffe*'s operations. The delegates agreed on tactical areas of operations for their air forces and that enemy air bases could be struck if the situation warranted. They split, however, on the question of methods. The French wanted general attacks on airfields if precise bombing were impossible; the British wished to leave such questions to the local air commander. The upshot of the meetings was general recognition that Allied air forces could not decisively hurt the *Luftwaffe*'s bases.[19]

In the spring of 1940, French officials waited with apprehension. French industrial production, especially defense goods, suffered from political infighting in the French government and poor planning and control during the last half of the 1930s. French air defenses were markedly weaker than Germany's. The prewar French Air Force was oriented toward heavy bombardment and deficient in light and medium ground attack planes. Unlike the *Wehrmacht*, French Army and Air Force staffs failed to develop joint doctrine, especially for the air-armour operations. Neither senior air officers nor Air Ministry planners understood the use of dive bombers and the defense against them. The French antiaircraft commander realized his forces lacked almost everything, but there was little he could do. Aircraft detection relied largely on imperfect sound sensors, supplemented by visual observation. The French also incorporated their balky civil telephone net into their aircraft warning system. They had no tactical radar, and only six British radar sites were located along the Franco-Belgian border from Calais to Le Cateau, the only ones outside Britain. The radar equipment did not work as well over land as over water, it was far from British bomber bases, and there was little networking, especially with the French Air Force, to allow information to flow from radar sites to defending fighters. Only French forward observers reported aircraft sightings along most of the bor-

TABLE 3

# Strength Summary
# French Air Force in Europe,
# May 10, 1940

Fighters

| | |
|---|---|
| Morane-Saulnier 405/406 | 300 |
| Curtiss P–36 | 100 |
| Bloch 152 | 40 |
| Dewoitine 501/510 and Potez 631 (obsolete) | 70 |
| | 510 |

28 Groups: 12 of Morane-Saulnier, 7 of Bloch, 4 of P–36, 5 miscellaneous. On May 10, the Dewoitine 520 was just beginning to be delivered to French Air Force operational units.

Bombers

Thirty-one squadrons were organized. Almost all were equipped with obsolete aircraft. Total strength was 806. Modern bombers were the Loire et Olivier, Martin, and Douglas.

| | |
|---|---|
| Loire et Olivier 45 | 10 |
| Martin Marauder, Douglas DB–7 | 166 |
| Amiot 351, Breguet 693 | 384 |
| Amiot 143, Bloch 210, Farman 221 | 246 |
| | 806 |

Reconnaissance and Observation (all obsolete)

| | |
|---|---|
| Reconnaissance | 152 |
| Observation | 340 |

Note: On May 10, the Dewoitine 520 was just beginning to be delivered to French Air Force operational units.

**Source:** Griffin, "The Battle of France, 1940".

**British 3–inch and 40–mm guns in France just prior to the German assault in May 1940.** Imperial War Museum.

der. This left the area facing the Ardennes Forest and the Maginot Line, almost the entire frontier, without practical aircraft warning capability.[20]

In January 1940, Gen. Joseph Doumenc was appointed special trouble-shooter to raise the parlous state of the *Armée de l'Air.* He found, among other things, a service desperate for 2,100 short and medium range guns for air base defense and almost no production of these weapons. Moreover, the Army wanted 3,000 25-mm guns for protection from air attack, with few to be had from French sources. Immediate foreign purchase of 440 guns, and the use of a few from new domestic production were Doumenc's only solutions. By May of 1940, the British Expeditionary Force deployed to the Continent brought another 550 light guns, but these were used by the British themselves. The French allocated the majority of their antiaircraft artillery to the Army near Belgium or placed it behind the Maginot Line for home defense. Total French production of AA weapons in 1939 was just 1,200, compared to the monthly German output of 1,098. Field artillery pieces were temporarily used as AA guns wherever possible. Unfortunately, they lacked the aiming mechanisms to be very effective. When fighting began in mid-May some airfields in France were without any ground protection.[21]

The French Air Force was visibly weak in modern fighters and the means to control them in combat. Of the 500 fighters in use, few were equal to the Me109. The best was the Dewoitine 520 (D.520), so new to the service that it did not reach the front until May 15. The mainstay was the Moraine-Saulnier 406 (M.S.406), a 300-mile-per-hour craft with a single 20-mm cannon and two 7.5 mm machine guns. Sixteen pursuit groups flew the M.S.406, several of which began conversion to the D.520 in the midst of the fighting. In the fragmented French deployment scheme, some squadrons protected field armies, others were under Air Force control for defense of vital positions. Air raid warning systems were sparse and did not extend beyond field army boundaries; fighters in the Ninth Army area, for example, could not be advised of enemy aircraft approaching from the First and Second Armies on either flank. Lacking radar, ground controllers could not direct fighters to targets. Often the flights dispatched failed to find an enemy formation which had changed course or altitude, or flown into clouds after initial observation.[22]

To the north, Belgian and Dutch air defenses were nowhere near adequate to cope with a German assault. The Netherlands had 355 first rate antiaircraft batteries, but these had to protect the entire country. The AA defenses could put up a stiff local resistance, but could not hope to defeat or even deter an invader. The Germans planned to disable and occupy four primary airfields: a main base at Waalhaven, near Rotterdam, and three others near The Hague: Valkenberg, Ypenburg, and Ockenburg. The Germans wanted Waalhaven intact so they could use it to fly in an infantry division to outflank the Dutch defenders. The Dutch had some warning from their own embassy in Berlin and from the unlikely medium of the Italian Foreign Minister, who warned the Dutch and Belgian ambassadors in Rome. Dutch forces were on alert late on the 9th and began blowing bridges on the German frontier at 0300 on May 10th. At the moment this commenced, Hitler notified the Dutch and Belgian governments of his intent to cross their borders to thwart an expected French and British invasion of the Low Countries.[23]

The *Luftwaffe* attacked Waalhaven at dawn. Trying to approach undetected, German bombers came in from seaward and the direction of England. Dutch defenders saw through the ruse, however, put up a fierce flak barrage, and brought in fighters. While they were busy with the first German group, a low level bomber attack hit Waalhaven. Unsuspecting Dutch soldiers asleep in a hangar were killed and the air defenses paralyzed. Quickly following the bombers, Ju52 transports dropped paratroops of the *Luftwaffe*'s 7th Air Division on the field. The base fell in a short time, despite intense ground fighting. Although Dutch pilots and antiaircraft gunners took a sharp toll, air base defense guns were not numerous enough and intercepts too few to cope with the *Luftwaffe*. The Dutch air force was destroyed, largely in air combat, by noon on May 11. Its twenty-six Fokker G1-As and some old, obsolete fighters were no match for squadrons of Me109s.[24]

From the outset, the *Luftwaffe* had control of the air and followed the Waalhaven attack with assaults on all the main air bases in the Low Countries. (*Map 4*) The few Dutch aircraft that managed to take off were unable to prevent the outcome despite their valorous efforts.

For the Germans, the air victories were essential. The Dutch Army's ground resistance was so effective in places that the threat of disaster hung over the *Wehrmacht*'s air landing operations for two days. The invaders flown to the beaches near The Hague were all but destroyed, and a large number of aircraft were damaged beyond repair. At Ypenburg, the antiaircraft gunners shot down several of the 13 Ju52 troop transports approaching the base. Others wrecked themselves against the obstacles on the ground. Only 2 of the transports of the first wave survived. Late on the morning of May 10 a Dutch bombing raid on Waalhaven destroyed another group of German transports. Dutch defenses accounted for nearly all the 193 German transports lost in Holland in May and the *Luftwaffe* could not mount adequate airlift for some months to come. Dutch antiaircraft may have shot down as many as 315 planes, and German aircraft losses during the 4 day campaign in the Low Countries were very heavy.[25]

Even with these accomplishments, the Dutch defenders were overwhelmed. Their inability to protect the main operational air base at Waalhaven was symptomatic of the problems facing base defenders through-

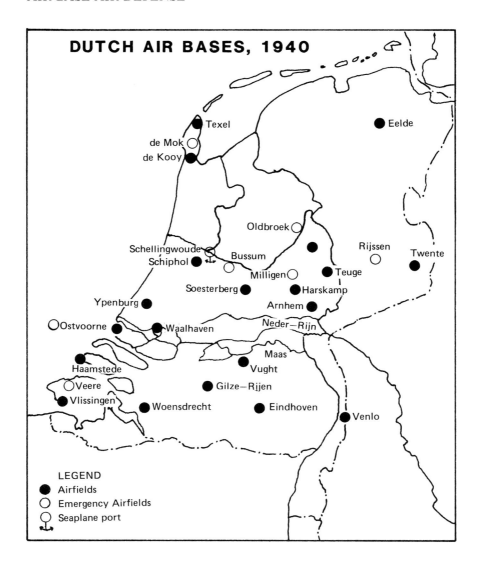

**Map 4**

out Holland. The inadequate size of its air force, confusion in command, and lack of base defense guns concentrated on attacking aircraft gave the Dutch no hope against a much more numerous enemy. Most important, the absence of a coordinated Allied defense plan left the Dutch forces isolated

**In amateur photo taken immediately after the assault, the wrecks of German Ju–52s litter the field at Waalhaven.**

and facing an enemy growing stronger by the day. Most of the Dutch Army surrendered on May 14.

The situation in Belgium was hardly better. During 1939 and early 1940, the Belgians could not count on effective British-French aid in the event of war. Hoping to forestall an eventual German invasion, the country had declared neutrality in 1936 and refused to coordinate defense plans with the major Allies. The Belgians went so far as to refuse both Britain and France any information on airfields in the country. As a result, neither the BEF nor the French could provide help to defend Belgian bases. Early morning attacks on several air bases on the 10th destroyed the Belgian Air Force. Over the next several days, the attacks continued and no effective air defense developed, either on the ground or in the air. By the time the Dutch surrendered, Belgian air operations were also at an end. Some of the force escaped to France, but the planes that made it out were old and of little use to the Allies.[26]

While the Germans attacked all the airfields they could find, the Allies denied themselves an equal chance when their Commander-in-Chief, Gen. Maurice G. Gamelin, stuck to the principles of the year old Allied staff discussions and forbade air attacks across the German border through nearly all of the first day of the German assault. This obligingly enough placed the air war initiative squarely in the enemy's hands. When the reclusive commander finally made German bases eligible for attack, he placed them second in priority to the attacking German armor columns, a prescription that could only divide Allied aviation, since the armor was already in French countryside. The Germans had almost no need to defend their bases from Allied attacks, which were sporadic and of little significance. Gen. Wilhelm Speidel, the 2nd Air Fleet's Chief of Staff during 1940, claimed that there were no French Air Force attacks upon air bases in Germany at any time during the campaign in the West. Ineffective RAF raids struck some German bases, encountering only light flak; the Germans diverted no aircraft or AA guns from their westward attack.[27]

The rapid pace of the German advance created different problems for the *Luftwaffe.* To keep constant pressure on their enemies, German air elements moved forward so quickly that they often outran their own support. At a group of airfields around Guise, the Germans were threatened by several French Army units still wandering about in confusion after the passage of the Panzer divisions. Most of the area was as yet unoccupied. Ju52s supplied the squadrons, but spare parts were in such short supply that fighters and dive bombers could put only half their strength in the air for a time. German flak could not move over the congested roads to the new bases, and the gunners operated without an aircraft warning net. A French night attack on the Guise fields met very little resistance and caused considerable damage to airplanes and uneasiness among crews. Speidel believed the situation so fluid and precarious that the outcome would have been in doubt were not the French in the process of moving air units to the rear in an attempt to regroup.[28]

The British Air Forces in France, commanded by Air Marshal Sir Arthur Barratt, had two main parts. The tactical arm was the BEF's Air Component while the bombers made up the Advanced Air Striking Force (AASF), a bombardment organization independent of the ground force and operationally controlled by Bomber Command in the United Kingdom. The AASF included Battle and Blenheim bombers (*Table 4*) and two squadrons of Hurricanes to to protect airfields, but the force was without its own radar warning system. After struggling with the indecision of the 10th, forced by Gamelin's restriction on bombing, Barratt took matters into his own hands. He ordered the Blenheims of No 142 squadron to attack the German tanks leading the advance through Luxemburg. Next morning, the air attacks continued, and at dawn, aircraft were warming up on the field at Conde

Vraux, the crews ready to climb aboard. To the northeast, bombers from the *Luftwaffe*'s 2nd *Kampfgruppe* were flying from Aschaffenburg at extremely low altitude, just above the housetops. They intended to cross the Maginot Line without warning and bomb Conde Vraux by surprise. There was no radar in the region. No 142 Squadron received no warnings, and neither the base's AA gunners nor the Hurricane pilots saw the approaching formation. Crossing the airfield, twelve Do17s dropped 100-pound bombs all along the line of waiting Blenheims, then circled for a strafing run. One of the last German bombers made a third circuit. The pilot wanted to give his radio operator, Flight Sergeant Werner Borner, a chance to photograph the scene with his movie camera. The Germans flew on toward the Aisne River, still at low altitude. As they departed, a lone Vickers machine gun fired after them. At one stroke, half of the AASF's medium bombers were put out of business. A total lack of warning paralyzed the base force and allowed the destruction of every airplane there.[29]

German air attacks continued without letup through the entire campaign, quite in keeping with the *Luftwaffe*'s initial plan for gaining air superiority. Target planning centered on British and French airfields in France. (*Map 5*) Figures vary, but at least 75 such fields were successfully attacked. Retaliation by Battle light bombers failed. The aircraft were extremely vulnerable and were shot down in great numbers by German gunners and fighter pilots. By May 12, the AASF's original strength of 135 bombers fell to 72. Gallant attacks on German river crossings and columns on the 13th and 14th brought more staggering losses: 40 Battles and 7 Blenheims. At the same time, the *Luftwaffe* closely supported the German army. Mechanized columns drove toward Calais and the French coast, intending to split the Allied force and destroy the French and British piecemeal. Facing annihilation, the BEF with its Air Component and elements of the French Army retreated toward Dunkirk. By the 20th, most BEF aircraft were forced into a narrow strip between the advancing Germans and the sea. On May 23, the Air Component's last planes moved to bases at Hawkinge and Dover across the Channel, from whence they flew to cover the embarkation from Dunkirk's beaches. The airfields in Britain now became targets as the Germans hit the evacuating army. The bases on the English side, however, could not be hammered as hard as those on the Continent. The investment in air defense during the 1930s paid its first dividends as the RAF fended off the *Luftwaffe* and continued operations over the small French seaport. Because it was out of radar and fighter control range, British fighter patrols swept the air over Dunkirk continuously. Hurricanes and Spitfires often forced German bombers and dive bombers away from the beachhead, and air operations clearly showed that the RAF could gain air superiority, especially if it had bases secure from destruction by air and ground forces.[30]

TABLE 4

## Strength Summary, British Air Forces in France
## May – June 1940

Air Component, British Expeditionary Force:

| Squadron | Equipment | Role |
|---|---|---|
| 85 | Hurricane | Fighter |
| 87 | Hurricane | Fighter |
| 607 | Hurricane | Fighter |
| 615 | Hurricane | Fighter |
| 18 | Blenheim IV | Bomber |
| 57 | Blenheim IV | Bomber |
| 53 | Blenheim IV | Bomber |
| 59 | Blenheim IV | Bomber |
| 2,4,13,16,26 | Lysander | Army Cooperation |
| 81 | Dragon Rapide | Liaison |

The Air Component was reinforced by three more Hurricane squadrons, Nos. 3, 79 and 504, after May 10. RAF squadrons usually had 12 aircraft.

Advanced Air Striking Force (AASF):

| Squadron | Equipment | Role |
|---|---|---|
| 1 | Hurricane* | Fighter |
| 73 | Hurricane* | Fighter |
| 12 | Battle | Bomber |
| 88 | Battle | Bomber |
| 103 | Battle | Bomber |
| 105 | Battle | Bomber |
| 142 | Battle | Bomber |
| 150 | Battle | Bomber |
| 218 | Battle | Bomber |
| 226 | Battle | Bomber |
| 114 | Blenheim IV | Bomber |
| 139 | Blenheim IV | Bomber |
| 212 | | Photoreconnaissance |

* The Hurricanes were to defend the area where the AASF was based. Four Hurricane squadrons reinforced the AASF from 11 May. In addition, the following bomber squadrons based in UK operated in support of the AASF during the battle:

No 2 Group: Nos. 107, 110, 21 and 82 (Blenheim IV).

No 4 Group: Nos. 77 and 102 (Whitley)

**Sources:** Ellis, *The War in France and Flanders, 1939–1940*
Richards and Saunders, *Royal Air Force, 1939–1945*

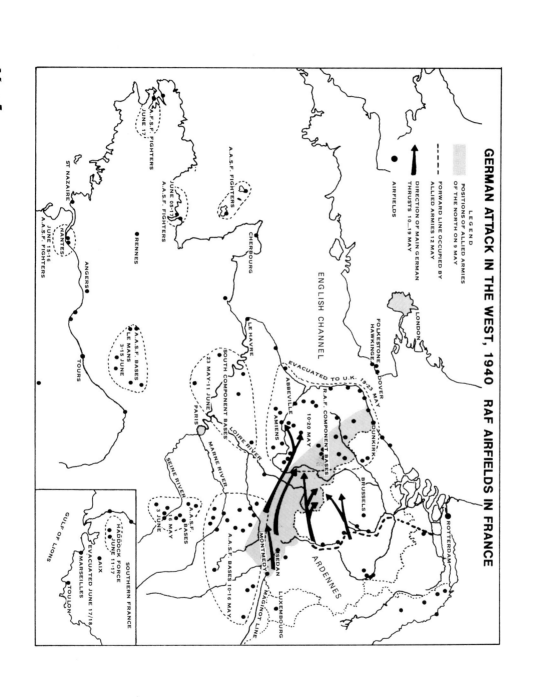

GERMAN ATTACK IN THE WEST, 1940 RAF AIRFIELDS IN FRANCE

LEGEND

POSITIONS OF ALLIED ARMIES
OF THE NORTH ON 9 MAY

FORWARD LINE OCCUPIED BY
ALLIED ARMIES 12 MAY

DIRECTION OF MAIN GERMAN
THRUSTS 10—19 MAY

● AIRFIELDS

TABLE 5

# The *Luftwaffe* in the West, 1940

On May l0, 1940, the first-line strength of the *Luftwaffe* was 5,142 aircraft. Of these, some 3,959 were on the inventories of *Luftflotten* 2 and 3, which had the task of providing air support of the German invasion of France. The order of battle was as follows:

*Luftflotte 2* (Kesselring), in support of Army Group B:

| | |
|---|---|
| IV *Fliegerkorps* (Keller) | |
|     *Lehrgeschwader* 1 | Ju88 |
|     *Kampfgeschwader* 27 | He111 |
|     *Stukageschwader* 3 | Ju87 |
| | |
| VII *Fliegerkorps* (von Richthofen) | |
|     *Stukageschwader* 1 | Ju87 |
|     *Stukageschwader* 2 | Ju87 |
|     *Stukageschwader* 77 | Ju87 |
|     *Jagdgeschwader* 27 | Me109 |
|     *I/Jagdgeschwader* 21 | Me109 |
|     *II/Lehrgeschwader* 2 | He123 |
| | |
| IX *Luftdivision* (Coler) | |
|     *Kampfgeschwader* 4 | He111/Ju88 |
|        (minelaying operations in the North Sea) | |
| | |
| *Jagdfliegerführer* 2 (Doring) | |
|     *Jagdgeschwader* 3 | Me109 |
|     *Jagdgeschwader* 26 | Me109 |
|     *Jagdgeschwader* 51 | Me110 |

II *Flakkorps* (Desloch) -Three antiaircraft regiments

Units temporarily attached to *Luftflotte* 2 for the invasion of Holland and Belgium:

*Luftlandekorps* (Student) comprising 4,500 airborne troops of the 7th *Fliegerdivision,* 12,000 men of the 22nd Infantry Division, 1 regiment of the 46th Infantry Division.

| | |
|---|---|
|     Special Duty *Fliegerkorps* | Ju52 |
|     *Kampfgeschwader* 54 | He111 |

*Luftflotte* 3 (Sperrle) in support of Army Group A and part of Army Group C:

| | |
|---|---|
| I *Fliegerkorps* (Grauert) | |
|     *Kampfgeschwader* 1 | He111 |
|     *Kampfgeschwader* 76 | Do17/Ju88 |
|     *Kampfgeschwader* 77 | Helll/Ju88 |

*Table 5 (Continued):*

II *Fliegerkorps* (Loerzer)

| | |
|---|---|
| *Kampfgeschwader* 2 | Do17 |
| *Kampfgeschwader* 3 | Do17 |
| *Kampfgeschwader* 53 | He111 |
| II/*Stukageschwader* 1 | Ju87 |
| IV/*Stukageschwader* LG 1 | Ju87 |

IV *Fliegerkorps* (von Greim)

| | |
|---|---|
| *Kampfgeschwader* 51 | Ju88 |
| *Kampfgeschwader* 55 | He111 |

*Jagdfliegerführer* 3 (Massow)

| | |
|---|---|
| *Jagdgeschwader* 52 | Me109 |
| *Jagdgeschwader* 53 | Me109 |
| *Zerstorergeschwader* 76 | Me110 |

**Source:** Jackson: *Air War Over France*

On June 3rd, seeking to end resistance in France, the *Luftwaffe* launched Operation Paula, a series of air attacks on 13 air bases and aircraft production facilities in the Paris area. Alerted by various intelligence sources, the French based some 60 fighters around the city, and placed there the heaviest concentration of French antiaircraft artillery in the country. The French flak barrage was the most concerted thus far in the war. German propaganda inflated French losses to an unbelievable 450 airplanes but government figures show 17 fighters lost with 16 more planes destroyed on the ground. Twenty-six German planes were shot down. All of the bases attacked were back in operation within 48 hours. Beginning on June 5th, with the German drive south into France, French air defense stiffened, and the Paris bases were the mainstay of operations for the next week. Speidel noted, "Operation Paula apparently produced no practical results."[31]

The French Air Force could not meet the demands placed upon it with the units then in service, and forces were cobbled together for the defense. Starting on May 11 a number of *Escadrilles Legeres de Defense,* or light air defense flights, were organized from whatever resources were at hand. Test pilots or instructors were rushed to the front in any aircraft available. Very few records survived, but at least one flight, based at Chartres, seems to have acted in an air base air defense capacity and probably damaged three Do17s. These scant victories did nothing to change the outcome of the battle, nor did they give enough protection to air bases. The defense flights were not provided central direction and were no more than a stopgap to vent frustration.[32]

In 1940, Allied tactical air defense was inadequate. The French, British, Belgian, and Dutch armed forces were not united by a common plan aimed at stopping Germany. The ill advised prohibition on bombing enemy airfields aborted any effective counterair campaign that might have been mounted. The dismal air base defense effort in France meant that no base opposing the *Luftwaffe* was secure. Most of the AASF's Blenheims were destroyed on the ground; the Battles were shot from the air by AA and fighter interceptors. The RAF had too few fighters, deficient AA protection, and a woefully inadequate warning system. It was not until the end of the first week of June that air defense effectiveness improved, and then it was far too late. French aircraft production in May and June reached new highs. The modern Dewoitine 520 fighter came off assembly lines at the rate of one an hour and, until the fall of Paris, factories met or exceeded the rate of loss. This rate should have been achieved in the summer of 1939 if any respectable defense was to be prepared for 1940. The Armistice of June 25th simply recognized a fact established weeks before. The only air bases left to face the Germans were now in Britain.[33]

The German success in France brought about a clear realization in Britain and the United States that their tactical air defenses were very inadequate. After the fall of France, both countries produced a large variety of armored, mobile antiaircraft weapons. These vehicles mounted machine guns and light cannon, and were admirably suited to protect both ground troops and air installations. They appeared in great numbers, especially in North Africa, Italy, and Europe after D-Day, where they could readily assist fighter and bomber squadrons as they changed bases with the flow of war.[34]

## The Battle of Britain

The Battle of Britain, one of the most analyzed engagements in military history, began as an apparently unequal contest. Just under 1,000 strong, the pilots of RAF Fighter Command became larger than life heroes in what Peter Townsend described as "one of the most crucial battles in history."[35] Their victory over a well equipped, courageous, skillful, and numerically superior foe relied heavily on the ingenuous use of radar and superior tactics. With electronic warning of an oncoming enemy, RAF ground command centers could plot the direction of the attack and scramble defending fighters to allow them maximum loiter time aloft. With the fall of France in June 1940, the drain of British aircraft to that active warfront ceased, but the flow from factories did not make up the losses easily and could not as yet fill the needs of the existing squadrons. The British had some advantage in that they ran their defense over home territory, where damaged aircraft and

German reconnaissance photo shows British radar masts on the Dover cliffs in 1940. The *Luftwaffe* quickly abandoned its ineffective attempts to destroy these targets.

parachuting pilots could be recovered. On the other hand, the RAF's command structure that had evolved in 1936 into Fighter, Coastal, and Bomber Commands was still untested. Across the channel, the three German air fleets pitted against the RAF had a decided advantage of numbers and at least technical equality in the fighter aircraft deployed. The Me109 fighter was a match for or better than the Spitfire or the Hurricane, and the Me110 outperformed the Hurricanes at altitude. But Air Chief Marshal Hugh C. T. Dowding, commanding Fighter Command and Commander in Chief, Air Defense of Great Britain, also knew from the outset that his force would not have to annihilate the enemy; a standoff would prevent an invasion of the imperiled island. For Dowding, the strategy was to keep his bases and command system fully operational.[36]

The *Luftwaffe*'s attack aircraft, and the targets of the RAF's defending pilots, were the light Ju87 and Ju88, and the medium Do17, He111, and Do215 bombers, all of which required fighter escort. The Me109, the main single-engine fighter, was an excellent airplane, but its limited range gave it only ten to twenty minutes flying time over the United Kingdom, depending on the target and intensity of combat. The Me110 had longer range, but it was vulnerable and could outperform only the Hurricane, and that at high altitude. The real test of battle was how well the RAF destroyed the attacking bombers. Escort fighters could often be ignored by well directed interceptors. Thus, a fighter imbalance in Germany's favor was not necessarily a crucial determinant in the battle.[37]

The first thrust of the German Air Force was at British ports, shipping, aircraft production facilities, and the RAF's operating fields. Although there is considerable dispute about when the battle began and ended, the most intense activity occurred from August 13 to September 15, 1940. Marshal Goering repeatedly attacked the main fighter bases until mid-September when he switched to the cities to terrorize the British population into submission. The key to the battle, though, was how well the British protected their bases.[38]

The air defense control system centered on Fighter Command headquarters at Bentley Priory, Stanmore, which acted as the filter center, receiving all reports from radar stations and the Observer Corps. Each sighting was assigned a raid number which it kept until it was found to be friendly or until it left British skies. Dowding and the brilliant Air Vice Marshal Keith R. Park had designed a command system that integrated all of the warning and control forces available so that the fighters of the various groups could be directed to the best targets. The ability of Dowding's commanders to allocate squadrons to oppose a raid, depending upon how important each was thought to be, allowed Fighter Command to conserve forces. Interceptor squadrons could then be pitted against attacks which controllers at various filter centers judged to be valid and not feints to distract from larger groups out of radar range.[39]

The Fighter Command Filter Center also obtained information from the Admiralty, RAF Coastal and Bomber Commands, and civil, air, and sea agencies so that as much intelligence as possible was available to decision makers. In addition, liaison officers for the antiaircraft, civil defense, and barrage balloon commands were always present at Stanmore. Both the antiaircraft and barrage balloon commands were operationally subordinate to Dowding.[40]

As the air defense system expanded to include Scotland, the Orkney Islands, and the west of England, the growing amount of information and instructions made decentralization of filtering and control increasingly necessary. Decentralization was first introduced in the more remote western areas and then in the eastern and southern areas held by Nos. 11, 12, and 13 Groups, which bore the brunt of the fighting during the summer of 1940. Without decentralization, Fighter Command headquarters would likely have been overwhelmed by the flow of information. The original three fighter groups within Fighter Command were later expanded to five, each having several sectors. The number of sectors depended upon the types of targets in the area, proximity to the Continent, and available fighter forces.

## TABLE 6

# Opposing Forces, Battle of Britain
# August 8, 1940

Operational RAF Fighters

| | 10 Group<br>10 Sqdns | 11 Group<br>23 Sqdns | 12 Group<br>16 Sqdns | 13 Group<br>14 Sqdns | Total<br>62 Sqdns |
|---|---|---|---|---|---|
| Spitfires | 51 | 81 | 100 | 44 | 276 |
| Hurricanes | 69 | 245 | 85 | 150 | 549 |
| Defiants | – | – | 30 | – | 30 |
| Blenheims | 9 | 17 | 21 | 11 | 58 |
| Gladiators | 5 | – | – | – | 5 |
| Totals | 134 | 343 | 236 | 205 | 918 |

There were about 200 additional fighters in squadron reserves. Fighters in storage ready for issue were as follows:

| Defiant | 80 |
|---|---|
| Hurricane | 183 |
| Spitfire | 143 |

*Luftwaffe* Strength
August 13, 1940

| *Luftflotte* (No.) | 2 | 3 | 5 | Total |
|---|---|---|---|---|
| Single engined Fighters (Me109) | 480 | 265 | 35 | 780 |
| Twin engined Fighters (Me110) | 126 | 68 | 20 | 214 |
| Single engine Bombers (Ju87) | 42 | 234 | – | 276 |
| Twin engined Bombers (Ju88, He111, Do17) | 469 | 299 | 100 | 868 |
| Four engined Bombers (FW 200) | – | 7 | – | – |
| Long Range Night Fighters (Ju88) | 14 | – | – | 14 |
| Reconnaissance Aircraft (Ju88, He111, Do17, Me110) | 26 | 26 | 15 | 67 |
| Totals | 1157 | 899 | 170 | 2226 |

**Sources:** Bekker, *Luftwaffe War Diaries*
Price, *The Hardest Day*
Dempster and Wood, *Narrow Margin*

Women auxiliaries surround the plotting table in an RAF filter center during the Battle of Britain. The flow of information to the center kept them busy tracking the location of incoming *Luftwaffe* attacks. (*Below*) Crew reads blips representing German raiders on radar scope in late 1940. (*Right*) Winston Churchill inspects a rocket and cable device at Shoeburyness, Winter 1940. Defenders fired the rocket into the air trailing a cable that entangled an attacking aircraft.

As information on hostile raids developed, each raid was assigned to a group which, in turn, assigned it to a subordinate sector. Sector commanders directly controlled the squadrons, dispatching the units to attack and then informing group headquarters of squadron status. Status notifications were made continuously so that the main plotting boards at each group and at Fighter Command always showed each squadron's position and readiness condition.[41]

One of the most important tools in use was the Identification Friend or Foe (IFF) unit installed in the fighter aircraft. Although not always reliable, this device responded to radar signals from the ground by transmitting a "beep tone" that showed on the radar screen and allowed ground controllers to plot the course of friendly aircraft. Thus, controllers directed the interceptors toward incoming enemy formations, and brought individual aircraft as well as squadrons back to a base after combat.[42] The entire system had some flaws, the most serious being the information load placed on the operations controllers. Once these men, most of them World War I fighter pilots, learned to absorb large amounts of information, they reacted with great efficiency in assigning intercept responsibility.

Both radar operators and the people to whom they passed the information also required special attention and training, done under the guidance of Fighter Command's Operational Research Section.[43] A very important aspect of Dowding's success was his use of scientists as operational researchers to solve technical problems and train operations room personnel. In addition to examining operations matters in general, the scientists wrote procedures for radar sets, devised criteria for selecting men and women best suited to stressful jobs, designed equipment, and often provided on the job training for inexperienced controllers.[44]

A British asset not fully revealed until 1974 was the ability to intercept and decrypt German radio messages. The German *Enigma* encryption machine and its associated code keys had been obtained by a combined British-French-Polish operation in the late 1930s. British intelligence analysts referred to the information derived from this source as ULTRA for the extreme secrecy that surrounded it. It was given only to War Cabinet and select leaders, Dowding and Park among them. Message traffic to and from *Luftwaffe* units attacking Britain usually went by land lines not subject to eavesdropping, thus during the Battle of Britain, ULTRA did not often provide advance information on specific raids. Signals intelligence was nonetheless important. Previous *Enigma* decrypts gave the British a good background on the organization, operation, and order of battle of the German Air Force. Interception of low grade radio transmissions, such as those on air traffic control frequencies, often allowed the RAF to learn of raids forming out of radar range. The information then helped radar observers discriminate between bomber and fighter formations on their screens. On occasion, ULTRA provided key information. The probability of air base raids on August 30 and 31 was known in advance, and appropriate alerts passed to sector commanders. During the same period, Churchill and Dowding knew that the *Luftwaffe*'s aircraft strength had fallen to half of the normal total and that replacements were not arriving quickly enough to cover losses. German production, geared only to a short war, had trouble meeting requirements. Knowledge of German operations and organization gave the British a clear picture on which to base decisions, and daily operational intelligence assisted effective tactical deployment of fighter squadrons.[45]

The RAF's fighter force battled for six weeks and appeared to be nearing at the end of its tether when the Germans shifted emphasis from airfields to attacks on major cities. The Germans thereby admitted they had not defeated the RAF. Subsequently, the Germans dropped their plan to launch a cross channel naval and airborne invasion.

In surviving the British had prevailed. The air defense of Great Britain functioned so well that a report on October 30, 1940, by a board of officers convened by the Chief of the U.S. Army Air Corps recommended adopting much of the system for air defense of the continental United States. The major change projected by the Americans was a more decentralized control, made necessary by the expanse of North America. There is no question that Fighter Command, with its expert leadership, aided by Goering's vacillation, was one of the main reasons for British survival beyond 1940. What is not often seen, however, is the manner in which the air bases were defended from the ground while the Spitfires and Hurricanes were in the air.[46]

In the summer of 1940 Britain's antiaircraft gun defenses were anything but first rate. Attached operationally to Dowding as commander of the Air Defence of Great Britain was the British Army Antiaircraft Command, which controlled all the heavy and medium AA guns throughout the country. The AA Command, formed shortly before the war, was made up largely of a dedicated Territorial Army militia, some of whose members had spent many prewar weekends in training, to the quiet amusement of their countrymen. The antiaircraft units were commanded by a regular officer, General Sir Frederick Pile, who retained his position throughout the war. His command started as one antiaircraft division, which grew in stages to seven by early 1940. During 1939 and early 1940, large numbers of personnel from various, and sometimes dubious, sources were inducted, trained, and organized, all with considerable struggle.[47]

Pile had never enough guns to meet the German onslaught. In January 1940, he had only one-third of the heavy guns (4.5-inch and 3.7-inch) and one-twentieth of the medium guns (40-mm Bofors) needed to protect the entire United Kingdom. Production was not increasing rapidly enough, and there were constant demands from the Army and the Navy to divert weapons to the British Expeditionary Force in France, for the expedition to Norway, and for shipboard use. Many guns were abandoned when the BEF quit the Continent. The lack of medium guns was especially worrisome to the RAF, as the 40-mm was the prime weapon for use against dive bombers and low level attackers, and was needed to protect fighters during the vulnerable times when they were landing or just taking off. To make matters worse, there were only 150 spare barrels for these weapons in mid-1940. The shortage of Bofors guns was made up temporarily by use of Lewis guns, a .30 caliber machine gun from World War I with limited range and rate of fire, hardly suited to the task of shooting down contemporary airplanes. Searchlights were in short supply and the few gun laying radars were very new and so unreliable as to be almost valueless. The AA Command, however, achieved good daytime accuracy using visual observation, which fortuitously coincided with the initial German strategy of daylight raids to achieve optimum accuracy.[48]

As the months of 1940 passed, desperate measures resulted in a slow increase in guns available for air base defense. By July 11, there were 574 Bofors guns of a projected need in excess of 4,000. On August 21, there were a total of 694, and 726 on September 11. If all of these were spread evenly among the 40 stations where fighter squadrons were located, there would have been 18 per location with just 6 left for other places such as ports, aircraft factories, arsenals and the like—a not very impressive score and one kept a closely guarded secret even from the Americans. General Pile even dissembled with the American military attache in June 1940 in claiming that the constant movement of guns made strict accounting impossible. During the battle, Pile settled on 16 Bofors guns and 8 heavy AA guns as the minimum for the defense of each base. Few RAF installations ever acquired so many; the 8 Bofors at Hornchurch and 6 at Biggin Hill were the most at any one location.[49] Pile had to concentrate the Bofors at Fighter Command bases in the south and east that were under the heaviest attack and which formed the linchpin of Dowding's defensive scheme. He supplemented them with Lewis guns and some 20-mm cannon designed for installation in fighters. Airfields to the west and north had few, if any, medium AA guns, and the number of guns in different areas changed as demand shifted among Army, Navy, and other competing agencies.[50]

Camouflage, too, was a victim of the interwar frugality and very little preparation had been accomplished by September 1939. Some practical experiments for aircraft were carried out during the 1935 crisis in Ethiopia, and the following year the RAF established a pattern for coloring planes to reduce visibility from above. For European operations, the upper surfaces were painted in a combination of "dark green" and "dark earth," which reduced detection both while on the ground and in the air. This color pattern, in paint designed to reduce reflection, was in common use by 1939. The increased drag on a dull painted surface slowed the high performance Hurricanes and Spitfires, but, on balance, was an advantage because of the concealment it offered.[51]

Ground targets, especially air bases, were much more difficult to conceal. Most RAF station buildings were of brick construction at the edge of a wide grass field and easily discernible from the air. An attempt at systematic camouflage of vulnerable sites began in 1936 with the formation of a subcommittee devoted to it within the Committee of Imperial Defence. The subcommittee quickly decided that it would be impossible to make targets invisible to reconnaissance cameras and, in any event, most major targets were well known to the Germans or any other potential enemy. With the object of confusing a bombardier, targets were to be made inconspicuous to an airborne observer 4 miles away at 5,000 feet and moving at 180 miles per hour. The distance and altitude criteria matched the average visibility in English skies and the height of English cloud cover. Results were hardly uniform or encouraging.[52]

Biggin Hill was disguised in late 1938. False woods and hedges blending with those of the surrounding Kent countryside were planted and the light color of the concrete aircraft parking apron and the parade ground were subdued with asphalt. Hangars were painted in an orange tone to break up their silhouettes, but a pilot who went up to check from 7,000 feet reported the base clearly discernible. A number of *Lufthansa* commercial airliners passed over, supposedly off course on their approach to the London airport at Croydon. German airline crews observed and photographed the installation in the summer of 1939, much to the distress of the British, who on at least one prewar occasion, fired warning flares at the intruders. Other RAF bases were camouflaged similarly. Their runways were painted a dark color, and buildings were given a diffuse pattern, but all remained visible from the air. A much more effective ruse was the creation of dummy airfields with mock aircraft intended to misdirect bomber pilots. The *Luftwaffe* would have been alert to the possibility of dispersed airfields after their experience in Poland and France and so that tactic lent itself to successful deception. On several occasions these fields were hit instead of the intended targets.[53]

Virtually every RAF station had a ground defense unit of about 150 men armed with rifles and machine guns. Ground defense weapons could also be turned against air attackers, with occasional success. Biggin Hill had 74 men from the Queen's Own Royal West Regiment, supplemented by 70 RAF airmen. In addition, some heavy gun batteries of the 90th Anti-Aircraft Regiment were posted around the base. The Station Commander, Group Capt. Richard Grice, moved them close to the field so that their fire would have a greater effect on dive bombers. At the time of the fall of France, both the ground and air defenses were increased by the addition of half a battalion of the Dorset Regiment and a detachment of the 34th AA

Battalion with Bofors guns. On August 18, Biggin Hill's defense was among the strongest in the country.[54]

The *Luftwaffe*'s main attacks were on the air bases in Kent, Sussex, Surrey, Hampshire, and Essex, closest to the Continent. The fields were easy for the Germans to reach, but RAF fighters operating from them had the greatest combat time after take-off, and German success depended on forcing the British out of their favorable position. In order to defend the bases, the RAF used a variety of passive and active measures in addition to the fighters. To prevent blast damage to parked aircraft, the British spread the planes out behind earth revetments whenever possible. In addition, dispersals were used, and entire squadrons were moved to smaller satellite airfields to increase targeting problems for the *Luftwaffe*. Biggin Hill's aircraft used a small flying club field at Gravesend as an auxiliary airdrome. Kenley, Croydon, and West Malling were also under Biggin Hill's control. Biggin Hill's aircraft operated from them when necessary, supplementing the assigned crews.[55]

From the start of the air battle, the Germans were unsure of the function and importance of the Chain Home stations, although they knew the stations existed and that fighters were directed by radio based upon radar sightings. On August 12, the *Luftwaffe* attacked six stations, but destroyed only the one at Ventnor, on the Isle of Wight. The British kept the remainder in operation and managed to conceal the single loss. Other attacks followed the next day, with stations damaged, but none disabled for more than a few hours. On August 15, Goering dropped radar sites from the target list because, as he said, "not one of those so far attacked has been put out of action." The *Luftwaffe*'s leaders failed to understand fully the importance of radar to Fighter Command's operations. Although they employed radar themselves and knew of the RAF's use of it for at least a year before the battle, they made no apparent study of the British system's vulnerability or of ways to neutralize it. For the RAF, this was a godsend, as three days after Goering's decision, the heaviest blows began to fall on their airfields.[56] (*Map 6*)

Biggin Hill, the fighter control base for the defense sector southeast of London, was one of the most important Fighter Command installations in the area, and closest to the *Luftwaffe*'s French airfields. The Germans hit it repeatedly. The first major raid on August 18, 1940, hit the field and the stations at Kenley, West Malling, and Croydon. About fifty German planes approached Biggin Hill from the direction of Tunbridge Wells. Two of the four RAF squadrons had already taken off to defend Kenley. Only No. 32 Squadron with Hurricanes and No. 610 Squadron with nine Spitfires remained. These the controller held back until he was sure Biggin Hill was the target. Just in time, he ordered them up and everyone one the base not in battle stations went into the trenches. The low level attackers were a mixed

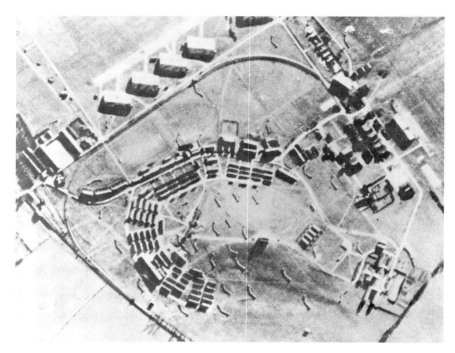

Two German aerial photos show RAF Station Eastchurch, the first before August 15; the second, grainy poststrike view bears German indicators pointing out damage to facilities.

# BRITISH FIGHTER FORCE DEPLOYMENT 1940

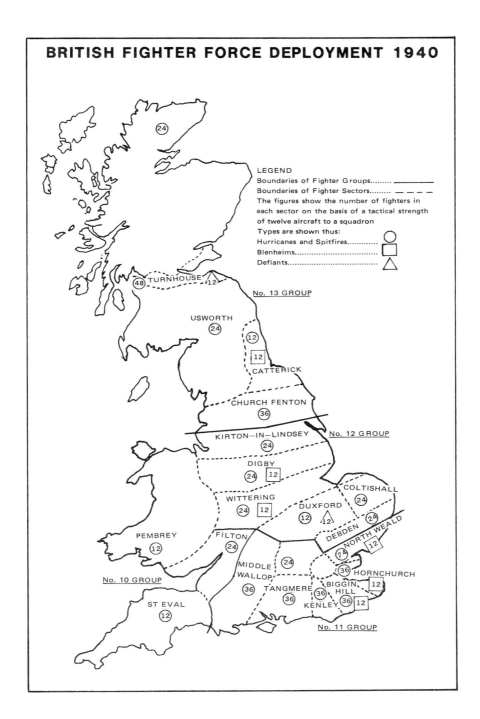

LEGEND
Boundaries of Fighter Groups......... ——————
Boundaries of Fighter Sectors......... — — — —
The figures show the number of fighters in
each sector on the basis of a tactical strength
of twelve aircraft to a squadron
Types are shown thus:
Hurricanes and Spitfires.............. ◯
Blenheims.................................. ▯
Defiants.................................... △

(24)

TURNHOUSE (48) 12
No. 13 GROUP

USWORTH
(24)

(12)

12
CATTERICK

CHURCH FENTON
(36)

KIRTON—IN—LINDSEY          No. 12 GROUP
(24)

DIGBY
(24)  12

COLTISHALL
(24)

WITTERING          DUXFORD          DEBDEN          NORTH WEALD
(24)  12            (12) △12                          12

PEMBREY          FILTON                    (24)
(12)             (24)                                HORNCHURCH
                                          (36)
MIDDLE           (24)                     BIGGIN
WALLOP                                    HILL  12
No. 10 GROUP     TANGMERE        (36)  KENLEY  (36)  12
                 (36)            (36)
ST EVAL                                  No. 11 GROUP
(12)

Map 6

force of Dornier 215s, Junkers 88s, Heinkel 111s and Messerschmitt 110s, accompanied by an escort of Messerschmitt 109s. Bombs began to drop on the far side of the field away from the buildings while the Bofors guns opened up. Near the base a group of civilian Local Defence Volunteers, later redesignated the Home Guard, fired their rifles at a low flying Do215, which caught fire and crashed just beyond the base—much to everyone's surprise. The Bofors guns scored no hits, although one of their positions suffered a near miss from a bomb; one of the crew was killed and several others injured. Above the base a wild ten-minute fight ensued with none of the British planes shot down. At the same time, the two RAF squadrons claimed a total of seventeen *Luftwaffe* planes including one Do17 which Flight Sgt. C. A. Parsons of 610 Squadron, with empty guns, bluffed into landing intact in Romney Marsh. The aggressive attack by Biggin's defenders broke up the German force. The base suffered very little damage, losing only the motor vehicle sheds. No aircraft or other buildings were harmed. Two people were killed.[57]

On August 30th and 31st Biggin Hill received a series of determined *Luftwaffe* raids, preceded by a warning from radio intercepts. At noon on the 30th, two squadrons of Spitfires met the first raid and scattered the Germans, who could not hit the base. Another attack on came at six that evening without warning. A flight of no more than ten German bombers flew up the Thames, turned south and came in at low level. Heavy antiaircraft fire and some ineffective Lewis guns engaged them. Only six Spitfires took off, but failed to stop the Ju88s that cratered the flying field. All electric, water, and gas lines were cut and the airmen's and Women's Auxiliary Air Force dormitories were destroyed. One hangar was hit by a bomb and almost all of the motor vehicles and two parked aircraft were destroyed. The gunners did not account for any aircraft shot down. Even as the Ju88s flew off, the station commander organized a rapid repair crew to free wounded trapped in the rubble, find bodies, and restore the utilities and general operation of the station. Telephone service, crucial to launching fighters, resumed during the night, but other utilities remained out for some days. Flying operations continued on the morning of the 31st with two squadrons, Nos. 32 and 610, going to Acklington for a rest. At noon on the 31st, the Germans returned and this time, despite antiaircraft fire, pitted the runway so badly that the arriving replacement squadron, No. 79, had to land at Croydon, a few miles away, until frantic repairs put the field back into operation by late afternoon.[58]

At six in the evening, the Germans returned and this time put the operations center out of action, destroyed four parked Spitfires and set the armory on fire. Those who could resumed the clean up while the commander and the chaplain prepared a funeral for those killed. During the services, held the following day, the fifth attack took place, but the airfield remained operational. Through four more days of heavy bombing, Group Capt. Grice's command, by dint of aerial combat, ground fire, and almost constant repair, maintained fully operational status on the display board at Fighter Command headquarters. Reading radio intercepts, Air Vice Marshal Park was able to select squadrons for intercept duty and time their return to base for service before the next raid. The RAF's fighters usually avoided destruction on the ground.

During the long series of attacks on Biggin Hill, antiaircraft defenses were heavily relied upon, but scored relatively few hits. The value of the guns lay in disrupting the concentration of attacking pilots. The threat of the Bofors and machine guns sent pilots to higher altitudes, throwing off their bombing accuracy and making their airplanes more vulnerable to interception by the Spitfires and Hurricanes. Antiaircraft guns at Biggin Hill, then, were not a main source of loss for the *Luftwaffe,* but contributed to the defense by creating conditions favoring the defending fighter squadrons and even the repair crews working on runways, communications, and damaged aircraft. The combined efforts kept the base operational, despite heavy and repeated damage.[59]

Hornchurch lay east of London, and, like Biggin Hill, was one of the most heavily attacked bases. With the start of the war in East Europe, camouflage crews worked over the buildings, gunners in the outlying areas practiced their load and fire drills, and the Hurricanes and Spitfires moved to dispersal spots around the field. Within Hornchurch's sector was the field at Manston, right on the coast and a magnet for the *Luftwaffe's* raids.[60]

The strength of Hornchurch's station complement in June 1940, exclusive of fighter squadrons rotated in and out, was 34 officers and 650 airmen and non commissioned officers. Of this number, one officer and 154 enlisted men made up the Station Defence Force, an essentially ground defense unit armed with rifles and machine guns that fired on low flying aircraft. The main air defense was provided by antiaircraft guns. West of Hornchurch lay a detachment of four 4.5-inch heavy AA guns, the newest in use. Low level protection was the responsibility of eight Bofors guns of the 109th Canadian Light AA Battery. Supplementing these weapons were twelve machine guns of the ground defense section. The 40-mm and 4.5-inch weapons were controlled from the station operations room in a small, one story building out in the open where an AA liaison officer was posted with with two signal men. The room's location was so vulnerable that the controllers and communications equipment eventually moved to a Masonic Temple in the town of Romford, finding larger quarters and the advantage of distance as a protection from bombs.[61]

On the 31st, at quarter past one, German aircraft came over Hornchurch at 15,000 feet and dropped bombs diagonally across the station. There was no structural damage, but blast pressure destroyed three Spitfires just as they left the ground. The planes were thrown about like wood chips in a wind. With wings torn off, they hit the earth upside down or without propellers. By a miracle, none of the pilots was killed or even seriously injured. The bombs badly cratered the landing field, but it remained usable. The holes were quickly filled.[62]

Heavy attacks on the base continued for several days. Typical was September 2nd, when all three of the fighter squadrons rose to fend off a large group of Germans who turned back just short of the base and were able to bomb only the perimeter. Four Messerschmitts and a Dornier 215 were shot down. All of this came about after the squadrons had, earlier in the day, fought two battles over France and the Channel. It was not the antiaircraft fire that stopped the raid, but the aggressive defense of the fighters.[63]

In the early part of September, the *Luftwaffe* shifted its attention from air bases to cities due to a deliberate British stratagem. Churchill knew the RAF could not continue to accept punishment indefinitely. Using as a pretext a minor, accidental bombing of London on August 24, he directed retaliatory raids on Berlin. Hitler and Goering were furious and baited into pursuing a policy of terror bombing; they obligingly defaulted on their best chance to defeat Britain. The *Luftwaffe*'s real opportunity was destruction of the RAF's bases in the southeast, which would have forced a withdrawal to northern and western areas of England, exposing the proposed invasion beaches near Dover. Churchill recalled the bitter necessity to accept damage to the civilian population in his account of the Battle of Britain: " . . . we never thought of the struggle in terms of the defence of London or any other place, but only who won in the air."[64] The major urban areas of England, used as a lure, became a weapon in air base defense. The pressure on the RAF's airfields eased, the reserve of fighters grew, and new pilots replaced those lost during the battle.

Despite the continuing arguments over the location of the No. 11 Group bases (west of London as opposed to the east and southeast) or the size of the RAF's attacking force (wings as opposed to squadrons), the system designed, built, and tested over a four year period prevailed. The British were aided in their victory by an enemy air command that chose not to concentrate its forces on the most vital targets—the radar system and Fighter Command's air bases. German target policy shifted first away from radar stations and then from air bases to cities and less important facilities just at a crucial time for the Royal Air Force. Even when airfields were prime targets, the *Luftwaffe* dissipated its offense instead of focusing on Fighter Command. Failure to assess correctly the military situation at the highest German command levels resulted in a loss of the concentration of force needed to win.[65]

Three of the commanding British figures during the Battle of Britain at a commemorative service. *Left*, General Sir Frederick Pile, Air Chief Marshal Sir Hugh Dowding, *center*, and Air Vice Marshal Trafford Leigh-Mallory accept honors.

## Summary

Conventional guns, searchlights, and camouflage did not protect bases in Poland, the Low Countries, or France. In Britain, defenses succeeded, but for reasons not apparent to many even during the Battle of Britain itself. Guns brought down very few airplanes, but forced the bombers higher. Had the RAF relied on them alone to defend bases on British soil, the result would have been much the same as the Allies experience in the battle for France. Camouflage, which some held in high regard, provided only limited protection, and German aircrews found targets by easy reference to known landmarks. By the *Luftwaffe*'s doctrine, most German bombing was from 15,000 feet and above or from 1,000 feet and below. The British prewar decision to conceal or disguise installations from a distance of 5,000 feet thus became moot. The 100 or more dummy airfields with airplane silhouettes were a more effective ruse. Later in the war, the Air Ministry Inspector of Airfield Camouflage, Mr. Norman Wilkinson, decided that much of this effort was waste. He found that quick runway repair and other damage control measures were much more useful during the Battle of Britain.[66] During August and September 1940, the RAF lost 1,379 fighters destroyed or heavily damaged. Less than 70 were caught on the ground by enemy action. The tactics of Dowding and Park and vigorous base defense, rapid airfield repair, the production of new planes, and repair of damaged ones combined to keep Fighter Command operating without letup.[67]

Clear German aerial victories in the first year of World War II came to an end by September 15, 1940. In Poland, the *Luftwaffe*'s attrition of a numerically inferior force followed upon the disruption of its suppy and communications. In France and the Low Countries German air power faced a foe with divided command authority, using tactics and organization more suited to World War I, and, in the case of France, not prepared to fight offensively. The Germans maintained pressure on the Allies and seized air superiority except over the evacuation beaches at Dunkirk. With the bases they gained on the channel coast, Marshal Goering's air fleets could bring pressure on the United Kingdom over short range and with reasonable hope of victory.[68]

The German failure over England had multiple causes. The inadequacy of doctrine, the inability to make correct decisions at senior command levels, and equipment design problems contributed heavily. The inattention of the *Luftwaffe*'s leadership to the importance of the Chain Home stations and their relation to the defense also led to the German failure. Without the ability to direct the squadrons, Dowding's group commanders could not have continued their intense defensive battle. The German failings were almost incomprehensible, but the Battle of Britain was the first in which the *Luftwaffe* fought a major air campaign, and inexperience at strategic direction showed. Vulnerable German bombers, carrying inadequate loads and often left unprotected by the *Luftwaffe*'s short range fighters, could not defeat Fighter Command. In January 1944, a lecturer at the German Air Technical Academy at Berlin-Gatow, said, in referring to the RAF during the Battle of Britain, "the enemy's power of resistance was stronger than the medium of attack."[69]

Clearly, the respite between the fall of France and the large scale attacks on RAF stations was needed by Dowding to reorganize his fighter squadrons after the losses on the Continent. During May and June, of the 432 Hurricanes and Spitfires destroyed in France, 219 belonged to Fighter Command. British factories produced 446 fighters in June, 496 in July, and 476 in August, which barely covered the losses while providing a minimal reserve. Pilots remained in short supply, but 1 Canadian squadron arrived and 4 Polish and Czechoslovak units were formed with veteran pilots who escaped from their now occupied countries.[70] The middle of August 1940, then, found the British in a far better state than might have been supposed, given the debacle across the Channel three months before. The RAF's experience from the Battle of Britain left it ready to employ similar tactics in other theaters as the war progressed. The next tests were to come in the Mediterranean and the Pacific.

# Chapter IV

# Malaya and Malta: 1941–1942

The closing months of 1941 and the first half of 1942 marked the lowest point in Allied fortunes in World War II. Between June and December 1941, the Russians suffered stunning losses; in December they were desperately defending Moscow. The United States had just entered the war as a result of Japan's attack at Pearl Harbor, but could not as yet exert a commanding influence. Early in the following year, Maj. Gen. Erwin Rommel, Commander of the *Afrika Korps,* drove east from Cyrenaica in modern day Libya and, on June 21, 1942, captured the British stronghold at Tobruk. In the Far East, the Japanese forged swift campaigns in the Philippines, Malaya, and the Netherlands East Indies, where they established the defensive outposts of their new Pacific empire and gained the needed raw materials for their armed forces.[1] Landing in Thailand and northern Malaya on December 8, 1941, they pursued and often outran British forces, capturing Singapore on February 15, 1942.

The defenses of Maltese and Malayan airbases present a diverting study in similarities and contrasts. Both were victims of a parsimonious Exchequer in the quiescent interwar years. Faced with a hostile Fascist Italy athwart her Mediterranean lifeline running from Gibraltar to Egypt, Britain organized a hasty defense for Malta, but could not commit large numbers of troops to a garrison. In the event, the successful defense counted on the local leadership's skill and determination and the reluctance of the Axis to accept the costs of overwhelming the exposed island when it had an even chance to do so. Under attack from the time of the Italian entry into the war in June 1940, Malta was in the thick of the fight a year and a half before Malaya met its first onslaught. Yet the Far Eastern bulwark of Empire, adequately warned and more heavily advertised as impregnable, was no match for the Japanese forces thrown at it. The British defense was nowhere concentrated or coordinated on the mainland north of the main fleet anchorage at Singapore. Interservice bickering hobbled prewar planning for Malaya's defense, and faulty, often arrogant intelligence summaries tended to demean Japanese competence and military equipment. The crisis in Europe starved the British command of adequate types and numbers of aircraft for the defense. Malayan bases became easy prey for a greatly underestimated and superior enemy. Lack of British air cover combined with masterful Japanese amphibious strokes employing landing parties of armor and infantry forced continual British retreat, eventual rout, and the loss of a prized Imperial possession in the Far East, another signal of the demise of European colonial dominion in Asia.

## Malaya and Singapore: A Study in Failure

The Malay Peninsula extends south from Thailand toward the East Indies and is connected to Asia at the Kra Isthmus, fifty miles across at its narrowest point, between the Gulf of Thailand and the Indian Ocean. A mountain range runs down the north-south axis to form a rugged backbone for nearly the entire country from the Thai border to Singapore. In 1941, roads generally paralleled the mountains on the coastal lowlands covered with swampland and jungle vegetation interspersed with rubber estates and rice paddies.

A vital part of the British Empire, Malaya was rich in basic goods needed for the war, particularly rubber, tin, and iron. The British Cabinet sought the greatest possible production of raw materials and strongly encouraged foreign sales to help finance the fighting in Europe. Begun in the 1920s, the naval base on Singapore Island was the pivot for the defense of British interests in the Far East. In 1924, when the Curzon Committee* selected the site of the Far East naval base, the Air Ministry proposed using aircraft for the main defense of the island. That agency argued that airplanes could hit a land or sea invader at many times the range of even the largest gun. The aircraft would not have to be stationed permanently in Malaya, but could fly from England in time of need. Neither the Army nor the Navy agreed with the Air Force's argument. The Royal Navy pointed out the obvious advantages of having heavy weapons in place and favored the type that had historically succeeded in deterring warships and seaborne attack. The Army intended to defend the naval base, but not Malaya proper; it believed no enemy force could operate in the rough jungle terrain. The

---

* Lord Curzon was Lord Privy Seal in Stanley Baldwin's 1924 Conservative government and former Foreign Minister. His committee was actually a subcommittee of the Committee of Imperial Defence charged with making a final decision on the location of the naval base on Singapore Island.

interservice rivalries still simmered in Malaya in 1940, when the colony's defense amounted to three Indian Army divisions and a collection of obsolete and wholly inadequate aircraft.[2]

Until 1937, studies of the land defense of Malaya still rejected the possibility of an overland advance down the peninsula. Maj.-Gen. William G. S. Dobbie, General Officer Commanding Malaya, prepared his own assessment at that point, asserting that a seaborne attack and landing on the northeast coast was possible during the monsoon season from October to March. Dobbie made landings to test his belief and found that the monsoons often obscured the forces involved. A land assault from the north, he argued, posed the greatest danger to Singapore; the jungle would not prevent infantry maneuver as had been believed. As a result, an Indian Army battalion scheduled to leave Malaya remained, and the Committee of Imperial Defence allotted £60,000 to build ground defense fortifications on Singapore Island and in Johore State, just to the north.[3]

The improvements to ground defense contributed little. By 1940, the approved defensive plan for the Far East centered heavily on aviation in Malaya. In July of that year, the Chiefs of Staff in London authorized 336 modern fighters and bombers for the purpose, and the RAF sited new airfields throughout the colony to extend reconnaissance and offensive capabilities. At no time, though, did the RAF ask the Army how well the locations could be defended, an ill advised omission, since the Army theoretically provided all ground and antiaircraft protection. Since the Army had not been consulted on the question of base defense, it was not prepared to meet the RAF's expectations. The revised plan in 1941 called for securing all of the air bases on the peninsula so as to give the RAF the range to strike an enemy carrier force before it could strike. While this might have been realistic in 1935, the fall of France in 1940 and Japan's subsequent seizure of French Indo-China in the summer of 1941 gave the potential enemy air and naval bases within easy reach of Malaya. The British garrison of three divisions could not mass enough force in any location to defend either side of the country. In the event of an Asian conflict, the Commander-in-Chief Far East was to hold Malaya until a fleet could arrive, a period assumed to be between 70 and 180 days. The Air Officer Commanding Far East, Air Vice Marshal Conway W. Pulford, realized that his 88 obsolete aircraft in Malaya were not enough, and that air base construction in north Malaya had to be accelerated.[4] A Far East Commonwealth defense conference held in Singapore the October 1940 recommended increasing the combat air strength to 582. The Chiefs of Staff agreed, but could not even send the previously authorized aircraft, let alone the higher number of planes, hard pressed as they were to defend the United Kingdom, Malta, and the Middle East.[5]

The British also reorganized their command structure in Malaya in last minute attempts to meet the coming fury. Late in 1940, the Cabinet created the position of Commander-in-Chief Far East, and appointed Air Chief Marshal Sir Robert Brooke-Popham to the post. On November 14, four days after his arrival in Singapore, General Headquarters Far East began functioning. Subordinate to Brooke-Popham was Pulford as Air Officer Commanding Far East Command. Pulford bore the burden of modernizing and operating the Air Force. Eight months later on July 10, 1941, Group Captain E. B. Rice was appointed Fighter Defence Commander of Singapore and Coordinator of Air Defences of Malaya. Antiaircraft guns remained the responsibility of the British Army.[6]

Other Allied defense meetings in Singapore late in 1940 and early in 1941 involved the British, Dutch, Australians, and New Zealanders, with United States representatives attending as neutral observers. No political commitments resulted, but several recommendations for mutual air and naval reinforcement went to the British and American Chiefs of Staff. Japan was the presumed common enemy. American representatives participated in the meetings through February and March 1941, but Washington publicly raised repeated objections to the conference recommendations, pleading a legally mandated neutrality. The U.S. Chief of Naval Operations refused to be tied to the defense of Singapore. London, meanwhile, did not want to divert United States support for Atlantic operations and so did not press for extensive U.S. involvement in South Asia.[7]

Air base construction in Malaya after July 1940 centered on seven existing installations that needed modernizing and sixteen new sites. Fighter defenses, including the control system, were wholly lacking and had to be started from scratch. Radar had to be acquired and installed, the rudimentary observer operation expanded, and a central fighter control organized along with support, communications, and training of the staff. The work was to have been done by the end of 1941, but this was impossible. Labor and materials, especially asphalt and concrete, were lacking. Construction equipment was old and there were not enough contractors in the country to handle the expansion. The government of New Zealand sent an airfield construction unit in October 1941, which helped but did not solve the problem.[8] The farthest north of the RAF's new bases, Alor Star and Kota Bharu, were small civilian landing fields with tightly grouped buildings close to the runways. Earth revetments there were not sufficient for blast protection. With no thought given to camouflage, hard surfaced runways made excellent targets. Grass fields were easily seen and had their own particular drawbacks: in the monsoon season they became quagmires, difficult to use under any circumstances and especially hard to repair. As a result of the February planning meeting, and in anticipation of a wartime alliance with the United States, four bases, Gong Kedah, Butterworth, Tebrau, and Yong

Peng were to be built or enlarged to accommodate American B–17 bombers. Of the four, only Gong Kedah's runway was complete when Japan invaded. While construction went forward, defenses for the new bases did not keep pace.[9] (*Map 7*).

Defensive batteries and warning nets were incomplete in December 1941. Antiaircraft guns were extremely scarce in Malaya and some locations were totally unprotected. The 3-inch AA guns, about one third of the total heavy weapons, were World War I designs. There was only one regiment of Bofors guns for low level defense.[10] Defense plans called for a total of 20 radar installations for Malaya, but only at Singapore was coverage adequate and there only to seaward. (*Map 8*) Four radar stations on the island provided advance warning of aircraft approaching at 130 miles offshore. Two additional stations, on the southeast and southwest tip of Johore, were operational, but great gaps in surveillance existed and were never closed. Radar was supplemented by an Australian Air Force aerial reconnaissance unit at Kota Bharu, but the normally heavy cloud cover and limited flying time reduced its ability to provide information.[11] Although the Army retained control of AA, the RAF controlled a poorly organized volunteer civilian observer corps on the model of that used in England. The warning net, lacking trained personnel, equipment, and communications, provided little in the way of consistently effective reports of aircraft sightings. The dense, mountainous jungle precluded building observation posts in central Malaya. There were two observer control rooms, at Singapore and Kuala Lumpur, and both were connected to the Dutch East Indies observer system. The general lack of training and observer posts, however, meant that little could be accomplished by the organization. In all, the defense operation held promise of functioning well—but only if it could be put into action with completed warning and communication systems, modern aircraft and trained people.[12]

As it was, the air bases were at risk. In addition to the lack of guns, the outmoded fighters (*See Tables 7–10*), and poor siting of bases, little or no joint planning had been done, and most ground defense units were Indian States Forces, poorly trained and led.[13] North of Singapore, antiaircraft guns were very scarce and height finding and fire control equipment, where it existed, was all manual. Frequent overcast made spotting from the ground difficult, and AA gun crew training was not always possible because of shortages of aircraft to simulate or tow targets. With the shortage of waapons, no installations other than those on Singapore Island mounted the eight heavy antiaircraft and sixteen Bofors guns recommended as the minimum defense by General Pile after the Battle of Britain. Brooke-Popham had to settle for a reduced number for each base: eight heavies and eight Bofors. None of the bases north of Johore Strait reached even this number, and many were totally unprotected. The few searchlights available were all in

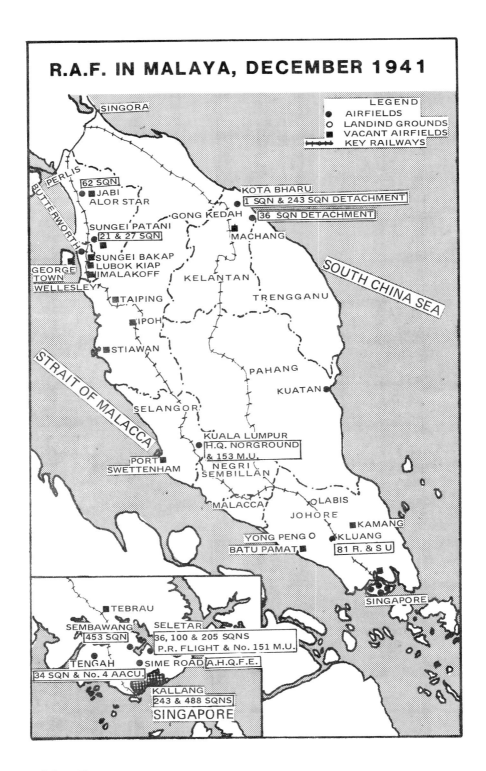

# R.A.F. IN MALAYA, DECEMBER 1941

LEGEND
● AIRFIELDS
○ LANDIND GROUNDS
■ VACANT AIRFIELDS
⊢⊣ KEY RAILWAYS

SINGORA

PERLIS

BUTTERWORTH

62 SQN
■ JABI
ALOR STAR

GONG KEDAH

KOTA BHARU
● 1 SQN & 243 SQN DETACHMENT
36 SQN DETACHMENT

SUNGEI PATANI
21 & 27 SQN

MACHANG

SUNGEI BAKAP
LUBOK KIAP
MALAKOFF

GEORGE TOWN
WELLESLEY

KELANTAN

TRENGGANU

SOUTH CHINA SEA

■ TAIPING

■ IPOH

■ STIAWAN

PAHANG

KUATAN ●

SELANGOR

STRAIT OF MALACCA

KUALA LUMPUR
● H.Q. NORGROUND & 153 M.U.

PORT SWETTENHAM

NEGRI SEMBILLAN

MALACCA

○ LABIS

JOHORE

■ KAMANG

YONG PENG ○ ● KLUANG
BATU PAMAT ■
81 R. & S U

SINGAPORE

■ TEBRAU

SEMBAWANG
453 SQN

SELETAR
36, 100 & 205 SQNS
P.R. FLIGHT & No. 151 M.U.

● SIME ROAD A.H.Q.F.E.

TENGAH
34 SQN & No. 4 AACU.

KALLANG
243 & 488 SQNS

SINGAPORE

**Map 7**

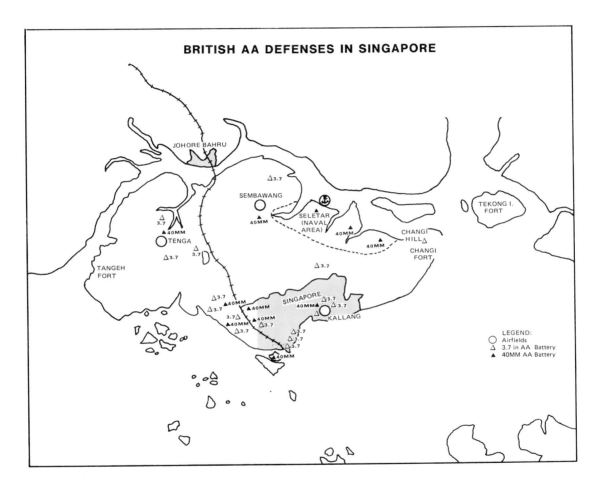

**BRITISH AA DEFENSES IN SINGAPORE**

JOHORE BAHRU

SEMBAWANG

△ 3.7

⚓

TEKONG I.
FORT

SELETAR
(NAVAL
AREA)

▲40MM

CHANGI
HILL△

CHANGI
FORT

△
3.7

▲40MM

○TENGA

△
3.7

△3.7

TANGEH
FORT

△ 3.7

▲40MM

△3.7

▲40MM

▲40MM

△ 3.7

SINGAPORE

△3.7

3.7△
▲40MM

▲40MM

▲40MM

△ 3.7

△
3.7

△3.7

KALLANG

△3.7

△3.7
△3.7

LEGEND:
○ Airfields
△ 3.7 in AA Battery
▲ 40MM AA Battery

▲40MM

**Map 8**

Singapore. Gun crews and air defense controllers were so deficient that on the night of December 8, 1941, when Japanese bombers first raided the city, fighters were forbidden to take off. Nobody knew how to coordinate gunfire with airplanes, and there was fear that the wrong aircraft would be hit.[14]

To prepare for combat with the British, the Japanese had Lt. Gen. Tomoyuki Yamashita's veteran 25th Army, the subordinate 3rd Air Corps, and the attached 22nd Naval Air Flotilla. Since his forces lacked adequate maps for the Malayan operation, the Chief of the 25th Army's Operations Planning Staff, Lt. Col. Masanobu Tsuji, reconnoitered north Malaya in an unarmed plane. Fine weather on November 22 allowed him to see Singora and Patani in Thailand, and the east coast airdrome of Kota Bharu. Crossing the mountains and entering rain clouds, Tsuji and his pilot dropped to 6,000 feet and overflew the air bases at Alor Star, Sungei Patani, and Taiping. The size and extensive development of the British installations surprised Tsuji. Knowing the RAF could destroy the few planes his forces could initially operate from Singora and Patani airfields, he decided to recommend quickly capturing the major British air installations of Alor Star and Kota Bharu. Tsuji's reasoning was clear; possessing the bases would drive the RAF from Northern Malaya and allow the Japanese greater operating freedom. On Tsuji's return to Saigon, the Japanese altered their plans and reinforced the Army Air Forces' units intended for the Malay campaign. General Saburo Endo's 3rd Air Group, with 3 regiments of medium bombers and one of fighters, was added to the 3rd Air Corps on December 2.[15]

Both the 3rd Air Corps and the 22nd Naval Air Flotilla possessed fighter and bomber squadrons. The majority of the naval flotilla's squadrons were land based, operating from Indo-China. Although missions of the 3rd and 22nd differed, both had to collaborate in preventing British attacks on newly established Japanese airdromes. In addition to fighter protection, the 3rd Air Corps prepared mobile antiaircraft organizations to protect their new bases. The Corps' four airfield construction units could repair captured enemy airfields and rapidly build new establishments.[16]

In mid-1941, the British plan to thwart a Japanese invasion was Operation MATADOR. MATADOR postulated a British advance to a line across the Kra Isthmus just north of the Thai ports of Singora and Patani and their airfields to deny them to the Japanese. The War Cabinet complicated this simple plan with an insistence that Britain violate no part of Thai territory until Japan did so, or unless America agreed to provide support to the British in the Far East.[17]

On December 5, amid reports of Japanese movements, Brooke-Popham was authorized to begin MATADOR if he faced a Japanese landing on the Kra Isthmus. He agonized while trying to get full reconnaissance surveys from the Gulf of Siam. Even as the British minister in Thailand was insisting on continued respect of Thai neutrality, General Yamashita seized Singora and Patani on December 8, 1941. The two airfields, inadequate at first, were rapidly improved.[18] On the same morning, the Japanese launched air attacks from Singora, Bangkok, and Indo-China designed to neutralize the northern Malay air bases. Japan's air commanders wanted to preserve the fields for their own use, so they avoided cratering the landing areas. With no warning system, the British installations were vulnerable to surprise raids, and scarcity of British and Indian AA guns made retaliation feeble. Group Captain Rice's fighter control center in Singapore was just becoming operational and could provide little help.[19]

Nothing seemed to avail the defense. The RAF attacked troops landing at Patani, but Japanese interceptors were waiting in the air and British losses were heavy. The RAF was too weak to follow up, and the Japanese retaliated quickly. Twenty minutes after No. 62 Squadron's Blenheims returned to Alor Star, Japanese bombers came over at 13,000 feet dropping antipersonnel and high explosive fragmentation bombs. The only warning came from an airman waving a white handkerchief on the base's far perimeter. There were no fighters aloft, and the four old 3-inch guns could neither hit nor disperse the attackers. Four Blenheims were destroyed, five were damaged. No Japanese planes were shot down and the bombing formation was not disrupted. Brooke-Popham thought the antiaircraft guns unable to reach the bombers, but their range was 20,500 feet. Inexperienced crews, the outmoded design, and the poor aiming capability of the all too few antiaircraft guns led to the complete failure of the defense. The Japanese hit airfields at Sungei Patani, Gong Kedah, Machang, and Butterworth repeatedly on the same day. None had any passive defense except for dispersal parking at Gong Kedah.[20]

Kota Bharu, on the northeast coast, was also in difficulty. The Japanese wanted the base to support the 25th Army's advance. Air attacks began early in the morning, avoiding the landing field when possible. The Japanese assault force landed on the beach and began to move inland toward the base under heavy British fire. By late afternoon of December 8, the ground offensive pressed so close to the perimeter that the RAF evacuated the base—prematurely as it turned out. While the British moved their 3-inch AA guns to the south, the Japanese seized their first functioning airfields in Malaya. No other British air base or satellite field on the east coast had any antiaircraft defense. Bypassing the nearby but overly vulnerable Gong Kedah, the retreating British aircraft landed at Kuantan, several hundred miles down the coast.[21]

On December 9, Pulford tried again to strike at Singora airfield with six Blenheims from Tengah and Butterworth. The attackers bombed the Japanese aircraft, but found fighters of the 12th Air Group in abundance. With their sound detectors and searchlights, Japanese antiaircraft units contributed effective AA fire. Three of the six British planes did not return. The

TABLE 7

## Royal Air Force Strength and Disposition in Malaya, December 7, 1941

| Airfield | Squadron No. | Type | Strength |
|---|---|---|---|
| Alor Star | 62 | Blenheim I | 11 |
| Sungei Patani | 21 (RAAF) | Buffalo | 12 |
| Sungei Patani | 27 | Blenheim I | 12 |
| Kota Bharu | 1 (RAAF) | Hudson II | 12 |
| Kota Bharu | 36 | Vildebeeste | 6 |
| Gong Kedah | 100 | Vildebeeste | 6 |
| Kuantan | 60 | Blenheim I | 8 |
| Kuantan | 8 (RAAF) | Hudson II | 8 |
| Kuantan | 36 | Vildebeeste | 6 |
| Tengah | 34 | Blenheim IV | 16 |
| Kallang | 243 (RNZAF) | Buffalo | 16 |
| Kallang | 488 (RNZAF) | Buffalo | 16 |
| Sembawang | 8 (RAAF) | Hudson II | 4 |
| Sembawang | 453 (RAAF) | Buffalo | 16 |
| Seletar | 100 | Vildebeeste | 6 |
| Seletar | 205 | Catalina | 3 |
| | | Total | 158 |

No. 60 Squadron had arrived from Burma for bombing practice, and was retained in Malaya on the start of the war with Japan. About the middle of December the personnel returned to Burma by sea, the aircraft remaining in Malaya to replace combat losses in other squadrons.

Hurricane fighters did not arrive until January 1942, because of demands at home and in the Middle East.

There were two maintenance units, No. 151 at Seletar and No. 153 at Kuala Lumpur.

| Reserve Aircraft in Malaya | |
|---|---|
| Blenheim I and IV | 15 |
| Buffalo | 52 |
| Hudson | 7 |
| Catalina | 2 |
| Total | 88 |

**Source:** Kirby, *The War Against Japan,* Vol I.

TABLE 8

**Antiaircraft Artillery Forces**

| Singapore | Malay Peninsula |
|---|---|
| 1st HAA Regt (Less 1 Btry) | Butterworth – 1 Lt. AA Btry |
| 2nd HAA Regt (Less 1 Btry) | Alor Star – 1 Lt. AA Btry |
| 3rd HAA Regiment | Sungei – 1 H.A.A. Btry |
| 3rd Lt. A.A. Regt (Less 1 Btry) | Gong Kedah – 1. H.A.A. Btry |
| 1st AA Regt (Indian Army) | Kota Bharu – 1 H.A.A. Btry |
| 5th Searchlight Regt | |

Heavy AA regiments normally had guns in 3 batteries of 12 guns each but this varied by type of gun in use and location of the unit. Both 3-inch and 3.7-inch weapons were in Malaya.

The light AA regiment was assigned 3 batteries of 18 Bofors guns.

**Sources:** Kirby, *The War Against Japan*, Vol I

Percival: Second Supplement to *The London Gazette,* No. 38215, 26 February 1948

Japanese Monograph No. 68: Report on Installations and Captured Weapons, Java and Singapore.

# TABLE 9

## Major Malayan Air Installation Defenses
## December 8, 1941

| Base | AA Guns | Dispersal Capability | Runway Surface |
|---|---|---|---|
| Alor Star | 4 × 3″ guns | Complete | Hard |
| Butterworth* | None | Not complete | Hard, being extended |
| Jabi | None | None | Graded, not surfaced |
| Lubok Kiap | None | None | Partly surfaced, partly graded |
| Penang | None | None | Grass |
| Sungei Patani | 7 × 3.7″ guns | Almost complete | Grass |
| Gong Kedah | 2 × 3″ guns | Almost complete | Hard |
| Kota Bharu | 4 × 3″ guns | Almost complete | Grass |
| Machang | None | None | Hard |
| Kuantan | None | Complete | Grass |
| Ipoh | None | None | Grass and hard |
| Kuala Lumpur | None | None | Grass |
| Kluang* | None | Complete | Grass, hard surface under construction |
| Kahang | None | Complete | Grass |

### Singapore Island

| | | | |
|---|---|---|---|
| Kallang | ** | Complete | Grass |
| Seletar | ** | | |
| | 8 × 40-mm Bofors | Complete | Grass |
| Sembawang | ** | Complete | Grass |
| Tengah | ** | Partly complete | Grass and concrete |

* Eight Bofors guns arrived at Butterworth on the morning of December 10; a battery of guns arrived at Kluang on or about December 28.

** AA protection was provided by Singapore and Naval air base air defense guns.

**Sources:** Maltby, Third Supplement to *The London Gazette*, No. 32816, 26 February 1948
RAF Narrative (Draft), *The Campaigns in the Far East*, Vol I

TABLE 10

## Japanese 3rd Army Air Corps

### (Lt. Gen. Michiyo Sugawara)

| Unit | Aircraft Type* | Numbers |
|---|---|---|
| | 3rd Air Group (Brigade) | |
| 59th Air Flt (Regt) | Model 1 (Oscar) and | |
| | Model 97 (Nate) Ftrs | 24 |
| 27th Air Flt | Model 99 Bombers (Lily) | 28 |
| 75th Air Flt | Model 99 Bombers | 25 |
| 90th Air Fleet | Model 99 Bombers | 23 |
| | 7th Air Group | |
| 64th Air Fleet | Model 1 and Model 97 Ftrs | 41 |
| 12th Air Fleet | Model 97B Bombers (Sally) | 27 |
| 60th Air Fleet | Model 97B Bombers | 60 |
| 98th Air Fleet | Model 99B Bombers | 42 |

\* Allied code names for Japanese aircraft appear in parentheses.

| | | |
|---|---|---|
| | 12th Air Group | |
| 1st Air Fleet | Model 97 Fighters | 42 |
| 11th Air Fleet | Model 97 Fighters | 39 |
| | 15th Independent Air Fleet | |
| 50th Recon. Sq. | Model 97 and 100 Bombers (Helen) | 5 |
| 51st Recon. Sq. | Model 97 and 100 Bombers | 5 |
| | Other Assigned Units | |
| 81st Air Fleet (Recon) | Model 97 and 100 Bombers | 26 |
| 15th and 7th Air Transport Units | Model 97 Transports | 55 |
| 83rd Indep. Air Unit (Recon) | | 3 Recon Squadrons |
| | Antiaircraft Artillery Forces | |
| 20th AA Regt | | |
| 32nd AA Fld Battalion | [4 companies each, armed | |
| 36th AA Fld Battalion | with 20 and 25-mm automatic cannon and 75-mm heavy guns.] | |

**Sources:** Japanese Monograph No. 55, Record of Southeast Asia Air Operations

TABLE 11

## Japanese Navy 22nd Air Flotilla
Rear Adm. Sadaichi Matsunaga

| Malaya Operation Strength | |
|---|---|
| Type O Fighters (Zeke or Zero) | 36 |
| Light Attack Bombers Land Based | 96 |
| Reconnaissance Aircraft, Land Based | 9 |
| 21st Air Flotilla Units (Attached for the Operation) | |
| Light Attack Bombers, Land Based | 42 |

According to Lt. Gen. Saburo Endo, Commander of the 3rd Air Group, the total Army and Navy air strength on December 8, including reserve aircraft, was about 800.

**Sources:** Japanese Monographs, No. 55, Record of Southeast Asia Air Operations, and No. 107, Malaya Invasion Naval Operations
Kirby, *The War Against Japan,* Vol I
Endo Interrogation, Interrogation No. 278, *USSBS, Pacific*

ease with which the Japanese brought AA battalions to their bases indicated their capacity to move equipment and supplies quickly.[22]

Continued southward pressure by the Japanese on both sides of the mountains made the RAF's position extremely tenuous. On the ninth, at noon, the first Japanese bombing raid hit Kuantan air base. After the high and low level attacks, the Japanese naval pilots reported fierce antiaircraft fire. Since Kuantan had no protection, the source of the fire is uncertain, but it may have come from the rifles and machine guns of the 5th Sikhs, providing the ground defense. Perhaps it was imagination, stimulated by the sense of danger felt by the pilots. Another Japanese attack on Butterworth at five that afternoon disrupted the imminent departure of another flight of Blenheims for Singora. The eight Bofors guns sent by the 11th Indian Division were just being set up, and could not influence the fight. At about the same time, British Air Headquarters decided that an evacuation of all the northern bases was necessary. Most of the squadrons there no longer existed; the RAF north of Singapore was largely a reconnaissance agency.[23]

Japan's Nate and Zero fighters were a complete surprise to British pilots. The high performance aircraft quickly destroyed the Buffaloes, leaving the Blenheim bombers unescorted and vulnerable. Although most British pilots were unaware of the existence of the Japanese fighters on December 8, a great deal of information about a Zero shot down in China in May 1941 reached Air Headquarters Far East in Singapore months before the Japanese attack. By the end of September, the British knew the aircraft's range, speed, and armament and oxygen arrangement, yet none of this was given to the aircrews because there were no intelligence officers in the flying squadrons. The small intelligence staff at air headquarters was simply unable to make up for the inadequacies caused by poor prewar staff organization and manning.[24]

Until December 10, the Japanese were wary of the British Far East Fleet, the battleship *Prince of Wales* and battle cruiser *Repulse* and their supporting destroyers, which could disrupt Japanese naval support and ground operations in Southeast Asia. That day, the Japanese Naval Air Force, flying from Indo-China, found the British fleet units off the Malay coast near Kuantan, and sank both capital ships in two hours. This was a stunning blow to the British; for Japan it opened new combat options and allowed them a free hand in advancing on Singapore.[25] At the end of the first week's fighting, the RAF was forced to fall back to Kuala Lumpur airfield. Here the retreating Indians, British, and Australians assembled their fighters and supporting antiaircraft weapons. Gunners manning six 3.7-inch, four 3-inch, and eight Bofors guns along with the pilots of the Royal Australian Air Force's No. 453 Squadron, flying Brewster Buffaloes, fought Japanese fighters and bombers attacking the airfield. By nightfall of the 22nd, only three of the original fifteen fighters were able to fly, and the field was abandoned the following day to a much superior Japanese air force operating from nearby captured British fields. The remnants of the RAF were now centered on the reputedly impregnable Singapore Island.[26]

Air defense of the four bases at Singapore itself benefited at first from their distance from the fighting, radar warning, modern airfields, and the antiaircraft guns protecting the city and the naval base. Of the 172 heavy and light AA guns in the colony, more than half were in the Singapore area on

December 8.* The forces retreating to the city brought back many of the weapons that had been deployed up-country, but the most serious problem continued to be a shortage of fighters. Japanese ability to repair and use abandoned British air bases added to the difficulties facing Singapore's defenders. While the retreating RAF was able to remove spare parts and equipment, large stocks of gasoline and bombs were left behind.[27]

Throughout the remainder of December, combat losses reduced the Commonwealth squadrons to a total of twenty-five bombers and thirty Buffalo fighters, all based at Singapore. Acting in support of the prewar mutual assistance plan, the Dutch East Indies Air Corps sent fifteen Martin B-10 bombers and a squadron of Buffaloes. The Air Ministry in London ordered reinforcements from the Middle East: fifty-two Hudson III bombers, and fifty-one Hurricane fighters. The convoy carrying the crated Hurricanes arrived on January 13, and they were ready for use by the 20th of the month.[28]

While awaiting the reinforcements, British night air strikes at Japanese occupied bases continued at every opportunity. Because of the heavy losses of Blenheims, attacks were small and sporadic. Most were made before dawn, timed to take advantage of darkness and to arrive when the Japanese planes were on the ground. Some raids were effective. One attack on Sungei Patani during the night of December 27–28 destroyed seven Japanese fighters and damaged ten fighters and bombers, but the RAF flew only eighty sorties between December 20 and January 15. The Japanese did not take the RAF lightly. General Saburo Endo, commander of the Japanese 3rd Air Group at Sungei Patani, was very concerned lest his unit's strength be badly depleted. The RAF pilots, flying over familiar territory, found their targets fairly easily. Detection and warning, not a strong feature of the Japanese Army Air Force in 1941, was inadequate or nonexistent at their newly captured bases. Japanese operational records did not completely reflect their losses on the ground, yet they easily replaced aircraft from depots in Indochina and Taiwan. The British had no replacement aircraft easily available to them and had to depend on those that arrived in midmonth.[29]

Early in January the Japanese began concerted attacks against airdromes in the Singapore area. By this time, the retreat down the peninsula put most of the ground observers out of business. The incomplete radar net could not provide more than thirty minutes warning of bombers at 24,000 feet; it took longer than thirty minutes for the Buffaloes to reach that height. The heavy guns could engage immediately, yet the 3-inch pieces on hand could not reach this altitude.[30]

---

* A Japanese survey in May 1942 reported the capture of 152 antiaircraft guns in Singapore. Seventy-six were Bofors guns, the rest assorted heavy weapons.

On January 20th, the new Hurricane squadrons began flying intercept missions from Seletar, Kallang, and bases in Johore State. Heavy Japanese attacks on Singapore's air bases did not allow full, effective use of the new units, however. Bomb damage was severe, and native labor for repair disappeared; British airmen, soldiers, and civilians had to be diverted to the work. Aircraft shelters were both inadequate in number and protection. To complicate matters, bomb damage at Kallang, built on reclaimed swamp land, could not be easily fixed. Water and mud seeped up from bomb craters, and elaborately reinforced gravel fill was needed to stabilize the repaired surfaces. All was not yet lost, however. The new Hurricanes improved the RAF's defenses. Many of the pilots who arrived to fly them were veterans of the Battle of Britain. The skilled fliers and first rate fighters began to take a sharply higher toll of Japanese aircraft.[31]

Relentless pressure by the Japanese Army forced the British south once again. Between January 23 and 25, the airfields at Kahang, Kluang, and Batu Pahat, all equipped to handle Hurricanes, were abandoned. Kluang and Kahang possessed protected dispersal parking; Seletar, to which the Hurricanes were now restricted, was not as good. Work had begun late in December to build six dispersed emergency landing strips on Singapore Island, but air attacks were so severe that none was completed. Because of the poorly designed and protected parking at Singapore's four main bases, Japanese raids destroyed many airplanes on the ground. Singapore's air bases were protected by the heavy AA guns defending the naval base and city. Only Seletar had its own Bofors guns. Yet the Army's heavy antiaircraft weapons were remarkably ineffective. Japanese airplanes crossing the island rarely broke formation under fire. One battery of the 5th Battalion, 16th Heavy Anti-Aircraft Regiment, with four new 3.7-inch guns, had no usable height finding equipment. The height finder pedestals had been sent by mistake to the Middle East, and there were no replacements.[32]

During the latter part of January, sixteen to twenty Hurricanes operated each day. Normally, the Japanese aircraft outnumbered the defenders during a raid by anywhere from six to one to fifteen to one. Congested aircraft parking made for easy targeting and increased the danger of damage from secondary explosions and fragmentation during a raid. The scheduled arrival of carrier borne Hurricanes promised more serious crowding. Air Marshal Pulford had no choice but to remove some of the flying units to Sumatra.[33]

The first squadrons to leave Malaya were the Dutch bombers. Then on January 27, three RAF squadrons moved to Palembang airfield on the Dutch East Indian island of Sumatra. The RAAF's reconnaissance units remained in Malaya, as did a few Hurricanes to serve as an advance fighter force. The Singapore airfields would now be used primarily as service and ground alert locations. The withdrawal of the Army to Singapore Island on

January 30 put three of the four main fields there in range of Japanese artillery in Johore. Although the RAF continued some flying from Kallang until February 10, for all practical purposes air defense of the remaining bases was no longer possible.[34]

Just before the surrender of Singapore, Group Captain Rice, the air defense commander, estimated that the British destroyed about 180 Japanese aircraft in counterair strikes on Japanese bases. A further 130 were destroyed in aerial combat, most by the Hurricanes. The effort was not enough. A modern fighter force did not arrive until the campaign was nearly over, and it did not have secure bases from which to operate. An adequate, coordinated air defense was never in place, and the bases became littered with damaged and unflyable aircraft. Once the Japanese seized the initiative and ousted the RAF from its northern bases, they did not lose air superiority.[35]

The improperly sited British air bases could not be protected against Japanese ground or air attack. Without sound interservice planning in the thirties, the RAF built such bases as Kota Bharu near invasion points on the Malay Peninsula instead of inland where terrain and vegetation could favor ground defense and help disguise the installations from air observation. When Japanese air superiority forced the RAF out of the northern bases, the Army further spent itself in vain attempts to deny them to the enemy.

The many long standing problems affecting defense in Malaya and the tyranny of logistics in a global war acted to British disadvantage. Japanese planning and execution in the Malay expedition demonstrated a unity of purpose unmatched in their opponents. Battles over England and Malta and in North Africa absorbed most of the first-rate Hurricane and Spitfire fighters. When new airplanes could be spared for Malaya, the Japanese firmly held air superiority. Antiaircraft artillery reinforcement units arriving in January 1942, were hardly organized for combat before they were swept into prisoner-of-war cages.[36] The British found themselves at the end of a very long supply line with obsolete aircraft; they were outnumbered by a much more modern and determined air force, one which they did not understand. The Japanese were able to fly from airfields and depots adjacent to the theater of operations. As the Japanese Army advanced south, the British could not continue flying from fields threatened by air and ground attack. Japanese squadrons, on the other hand, took over airdromes abandoned by the RAF and protected their new bases. The most costly prewar British mistake was the disparagement of Japanese ability and equipment. Air Vice Marshal Paul Maltby, who took command of the RAF in southeast Asia when Pulford died while evacuating his headquarters to Java, realized too late the ability of his enemy. Maltby noted that "the speed and aggression of his follow-up [to each successive thrust south] came as a surprise." Even so, had the British applied the air defense lessons taught them during the campaign in France and the Battle of Britain, they could have given a much better account of themselves.[37]

As in France, the RAF's bases in Malaya were grossly underprotected. Antiaircraft weapons were not sufficient in either quality or quantity, radar surveillance was largely nonexistent, and Group Captain Rice's air defense control center in Singapore, once it began a rudimentary operation, lacked the information and communications needed to launch and control even the small fighter force at its disposal. Moreover, it is doubtful the center had firm command of all the air defense assets. The longstanding interservice bickering probably insured that it did not. This situation existed more than a year after the Battle of Britain had demonstrated conclusively that such an arrangement was essential.

The complicating factor least apparent on the surface was the failure of the three services to cooperate fully in preparing the defense of Malaya. Air Marshal Brooke-Popham found that welding the three forces into a cohesive entity was one of his most pressing jobs in late 1940. Months passed before he was able to see results in the attempt to unify his organization. Jealousy and a decided tendency to work within their own spheres of operation characterized not only the relations between the military services, but also between the military and civil authorities as well. The result was the fragmented effort at defense clearly visible in the precarious position of the air bases.[38]

Inadequate early warning, uncoordinated antiaircraft gunfire with questionable accuracy and rate of fire, poor facilities for protecting ground assets from blast and bomb fragment damage, and a lack of modern fighters and AA guns were all symptoms of difficulties which could not be corrected in the few weeks available before the fall of Singapore. The failure to come to grips with problems seen emerging years before, when the need of a Commander-in-Chief Far East was first debated, created a situation fraught with disaster fully realized in the course of events.

## The Siege of Malta, 1940–1942

Even as the drama of Singapore played itself out, Malta was entering a new phase of its own siege. At five o'clock in the morning of June 11, 1940, Italian bombers attacked Hal Far airfield and Grand Harbor and continued a sporadic and intermittent air campaign against the island for six months.[39] In January 1941, Hitler, determined to prop up his Italian ally reeling from British attacks in North Africa, committed German troops to the desert to drive the British finally from the Mediterranean and secure Axis predominance there. The *Luftwaffe* would protect the shipping lanes carrying Rommel's supply to North Africa. In May, having momentarily subdued the island's defenders, the Germans moved to the conquest of the Balkans, and

Malta quickly resumed its role as a center of the British sea interdiction of Axis supply.[40] Unable to ignore this thorn in their logistical side, the Germans turned their attention to the island again in December 1941.

Malta resembled Singapore in few respects other than size. Lying some sixty miles across the Malta Channel from Sicily, its strategic importance was in its position as the only Allied operational base and refuel point between the Atlantic and the Middle East during 1941 and most of 1942. (*Maps 9, 10*) It was open to attacks by the *Luftwaffe* and the *Regia Aeronautica* based in Sicily, a half hour from their targets and closer than the Japanese in Indo-China were to Malaya or Singapore.

The island's air defenses were almost nonexistent in 1939. Air force protection consisted of four old Sea Gladiator biplanes found crated in a warehouse, assembled, and manned by pilots hastily assigned. One regiment of Royal Artillery heavy antiaircraft provided gun defenses. A prewar plan called for 4 fighter squadrons and 112 heavy and 60 light guns. Demands of the British Expeditionary Force in France and home defense, however, made deployment of the projected force impossible. In July 1940, the Chiefs of Staff believed they could provide the necessary antiaircraft guns by April 1941, and hoped to send the 4 fighter units as soon as possible. By December 1940, only 1 squadron of Hurricanes was in place along with a squadron of 12 Martin Maryland reconnaissance bombers. Seventy-two heavy and 34 light AA guns made up the remainder of the air defenses.[41] British naval and air forces nevertheless invited attack by their effectiveness in sinking 31 enemy ships totaling 101,636 tons through the first five months of 1941.

When the *Luftwaffe* supplanted the Italians in dealing with Malta, *Fliegerkorps X* was based on Sicilian fields with a strength that reached 443 fighters and bombers by the end of March 1941. The fury of their unremitting attack in the first half of the year is clear from the use rates of antiaircraft munitions on Malta. From January through March, British gunners expended four-and-a-half times the heavy AA ammunition used in the last six months of 1940. Light AA artillery fire increased thirty-three times, to 18,660 rounds, for the same period.[42] A few Hurricanes fitted with fuel tanks flew from Egypt to Malta, but they could not manage the 1,100 miles from Gibraltar to the island. RAF bomber and Royal Navy flying boat units temporarily moved to Egypt in March. Fighter activity continued, but combat losses and operational wear reduced the size of the force. Replacement fighters sent via the Western Mediterranean had to be shipped most of the way to Malta on aircraft carriers, which normally launched the planes about 400 miles west of their destination. During April, May, and June 1941, 109 arrived by this route. An attempt in late April to send crated aircraft by ship failed when the merchantman carrying them hit a mine and sank off Cape Bon, Algeria. With British offensive capability on Malta eroded and needing aircraft in May 1941 for action on Crete and the projected invasion of

Russia, the Germans returned responsibility for the island to the *Regia Aeronautica.* The *Luftwaffe*'s first campaign against Malta cost it 60 aircraft; the Italians lost 16. Royal Air Force losses were 42 fighters and 36 bomber, reconnaissance, and other aircraft. The British continued to use Malta as a stopping point for flights to the Middle East, and as soon as German pressure abated, the British bombers returned to the island.[43]

Given Malta's ninety-five square mile area and the relatively short range of the fighters, defense in depth was not possible. Early warning radar was available, but in early 1941 did not give complete coverage of the air space surrounding the island, nor could it give accurate heights of targets. British ground-to-air radio was so poor that fighters could not be directed to locations far from land. The Hurricane's moderate rate of climb made it necessary to fly south to gain altitude, after which the flight leaders were responsible for sighting an enemy and controlling the attack. These maneuvers worked well enough for early 1941, but improvements both in the ground organization and in air tactics were needed to blunt heavier enemy attacks.[44]

The Germans made good use of Malta's reduced circumstances. During February and March 1941, fifteen of their convoys reached Tripoli carrying the 5th Light Division with large numbers of vehicles and supplies. During May the 15th Panzer Division was brought over to complete the *Afrika Korps.*[45]

In the summer of 1941, Air Vice Marshal Sir Hugh P. Lloyd became Air Officer Commanding Malta and opened a new phase of defense operations. Lloyd began heavy improvements to the three active fields at Hal Far, Luqa, and Takali. A landing strip lay between Hal Far and Luqa at the village of Safi. At all of the bases there was dispersed parking for about five squadrons, but it was generally close to the runways. More parking was needed for transient aircraft passing to and from the Middle East required protection, as would any additional aircraft assigned to the island. The terrain and villages near the existing bases made expansion a difficult undertaking. Begun in June 1941, the first major enlargement was a series of taxiways linking Luqa and Hal Far via the Safi strip. Construction equipment on Malta was in even shorter supply than in Malaya. All of the excavation was done by civilian labor using hand tools and pony carts. The taxiway and dispersal parking work continued for a year, through the most intense air bombardment the island experienced. Materials to seal the runway and taxiway surfaces were almost nonexistent. Rolling equipment was old, too light for the work required, and in short supply. Nevertheless, the goal was to build 240 protected parking spots at the three bases by January 1942. All were to be far enough away from any airdrome so that airplanes were near a runway only when landing or taking off. In addition, at least two of the bases, Luqa and Hal Far, required longer runways to accommodate bombers

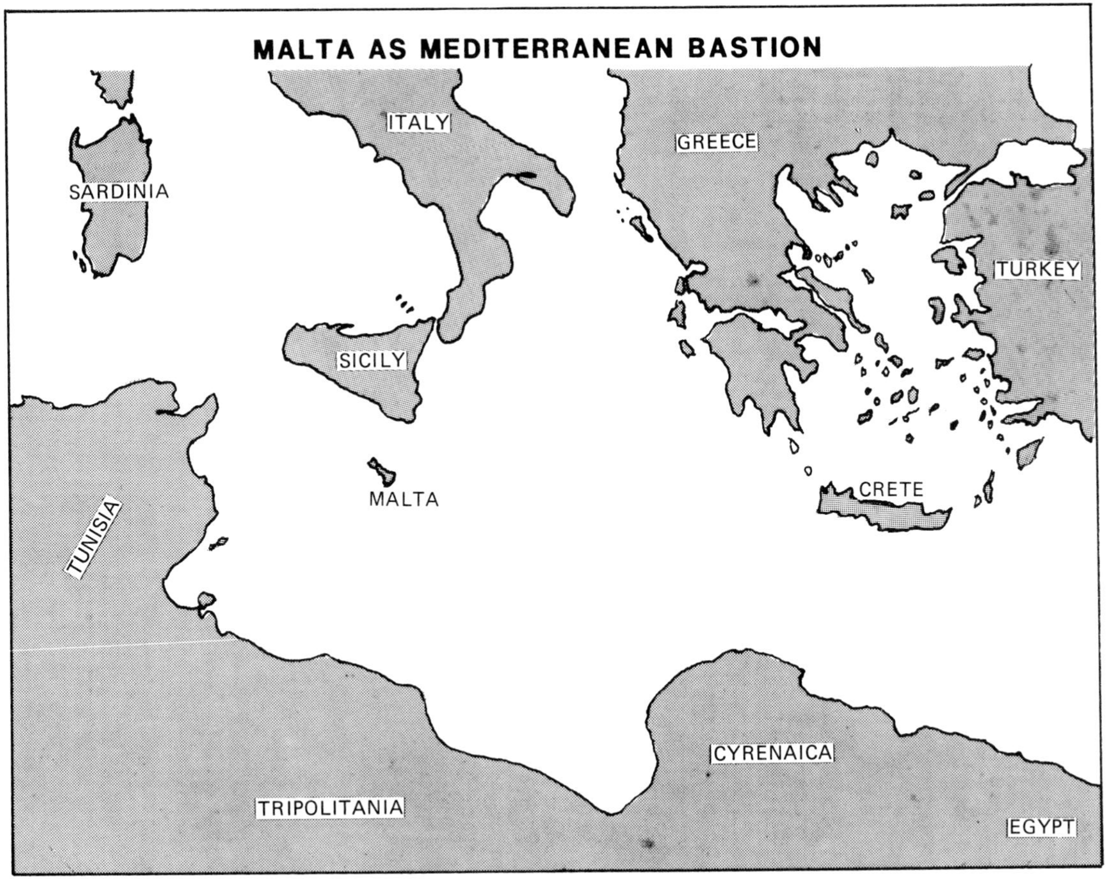

# MALTA AS MEDITERRANEAN BASTION

SARDINIA

ITALY

SICILY

GREECE

TURKEY

CRETE

MALTA

TUNISIA

TRIPOLITANIA

CYRENAICA

EGYPT

**Map 9**

**Grand Harbor, Malta. Damage to dockside structure at left is evident; bomb throws up spray beyond the harbor breakwater.** Imperial War Museum

so that those arriving during a raid would have a choice of landing sites that might be relatively free of enemy activity.[46]

Battalions of infantry and those with time free from other duties swarmed to the repair work. By May 1942, 43 miles of taxiway were in service connecting 600 revetted or tunneled parking spots. The runways and taxiways were not the only projects to be undertaken. Takali airfield lay on the central plateau of the island and was bounded to the south by a limestone bluff. The face of the bluff was ideal for building underground shops where extensive repair work could be carried out in safety. To exploit this advantage, the British began to dig a number of caves and connected them to the airfield by both road and taxiway. A cave cut into the wall of a ravine at the end of Luqa's runway accommodated a large engine and instrument repair shop. One of the most important projects was the preparation of several underground radar operations rooms and space for an air defense control center. The latter was in a cavern dug out of the hill overlooking Valetta Harbor. Here all work was done by hand. Workers cleared debris from narrow air shafts by loading rock in buckets that were hauled by hand to the surface. In addition to underground shops, the RAF dug into the cliff face to create protected parking spaces. The rock, however, would not sup-

**AIRFIELDS ON MALTA**

GOZO

COMINO

AERODROMES

ST PAULS BAY

SLIEMA

VALETTA

IMTARFA

NOTABILE

TAKALI

RABAT

LUQA

KRENDI

SAFI STRIP

HAL FAR

MARSA XLOKH BAY

**Map 10**

port the large undercut areas needed, and the excavations were not used for operational aircraft. The work was not entirely in vain as derelict aircraft were parked there and often fooled the attacking Germans.[47]

Blast shields were also necessary around each parking space and to protect precious construction equipment. Work had to be done by hand, with laborers piling rock, earth or, more often, filling 5-gallon gasoline cans with rubble, then stacking and wiring them into place. A single revetment for a Wellington bomber required 60,000 such cans and took 200 men working 9 hours a day 3 weeks to complete. All of the service equipment and two steam rollers essential to bomb damage repair needed similar protective revetments. Steady work was not possible as the airfield commander diverted men to repair bomb damage and craters on airfields. In late 1941, weeks went by with no progress in dispersal construction. Lloyd fretted and fumed, but there was nothing he could do; day and night bombing attacks required constant repair work. The civilian labor force quickly fell behind in the task and men from the infantry brigades on the island were pressed into service. Workers, military and civilian alike, were additionally hampered by an inadequate diet, the result of the Axis blockade of Malta. From October into the new year the three airfields remained open except for a few short periods.[48]

The control of the defense improved amid the continuing expansion of installations. Late in 1941, the Air Defense Operations Centre moved into expanded underground quarters that held the fighter operations controller, antiaircraft artillery control room, and radar filter center. It was not until February 1942, however, that the fighter operations room was completely organized and staffed with experienced controllers. After that, the joint facility greatly increased efficiency. Drawing on experience from the Battle of Britain, there was now direct liaison between all of the functions and their administrative and communications support. RAF squadrons, Fleet Air Arm units, and the antiaircraft artillery all came under Lloyd's control. Defense of the air bases required an ability to intercept an approaching enemy with fighters directed by radar. Ground weapons engaged the enemy that got past the fighters. Damage repair was directed where needed immediately after an attack. All of the functions required constant coordination by a central authority well versed in the needs of air operation and ground-air cooperation.[49]

While air base construction continued, the island's bomber and torpedo aircraft and submarines from the naval base kept up steady attacks on Axis shipping bound for Africa. The British estimated that between July and December 1941, they sent down another 581,000 tons of shipping with Rommel's supplies. German leaders began seriously to contemplate invasion in late 1941, but concluded that the Italians were not equal to the task of subduing the island's defense.[50]

**Scenes from the Siege** (*Clockwise from above*) **Repairs to taxiways on Malta used extensive hand labor. (2) Revetments of cut stone, sandbags (3), and later, rubble filled jerry cans (4) were common. A Hawker Hurricane is fueled by gravity feed tank in protected emplacement. (5) Bristol Beaufighter in revetted stand at Takali airfield.** Imperial War Museum

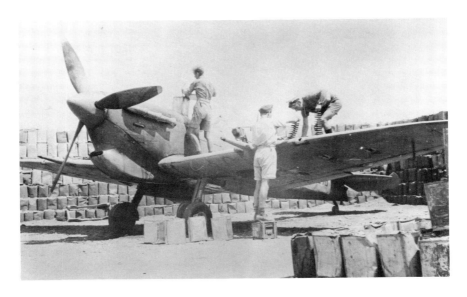

TABLE 12

# Royal Air Force, Malta
## Order of Battle
## 1941–1942

### January 1941

| | |
|---|---|
| No. 261 Sq. | Hurricanes–12 |
| No. 228 Sq. | Sunderland Reconnaissance Flying Boats–5 |
| No.  69 Sq. | Maryland Reconnaissance Bombers–4 |
| No. 148 Sq. | Wellington Bombers–12 |
| No. 830 Sq. | Swordfish Torpedo Bombers–10 (Fleet Air Arm) |

### January 1942

| | |
|---|---|
| No. 126, 185, 249 Sqs. | Hurricanes – 16 planes each |
| No. 1435 Flight | Hurricanes – 4 planes |
| No. 69 Sq. | Maryland and Beauforts Reconnaissance Bombers–8 |
| No. 21 and 107 Sqs. | Blenheim Bombers – 12 |
| No. 37 and 40 Sqs. | Wellington Bombers – 18 |
| No. 828, 830 Sqs. | Albacore and Swordfish Torpedo Bombers – 20 (Fleet Air Arm) |

**Sources:** Richards and Saunders, *Royal Air Force 1939–1945*, Vol II.
Playfair, *The Mediterranean and Middle East*, Vol II.
Report, RAF Operations in the Western Desert and Eastern Mediterranean.

Table 13

**Order of Battle
Malta Antiaircraft Defenses
November 1941**

10th Heavy Antiaircraft Brigade

2nd Heavy AA Regt. ⎫
11th Heavy AA Regt. ⎭     Royal Malta Artillery

4th Heavy AA Regt. ⎫
7th Heavy AA Regt. ⎬     Royal Artillery
10th Heavy AA Regt. ⎭

Each regiment was assigned 24 guns, either 3.7-inch or 4.5-inch. Regiments were divided into three batteries, each battery consisted of two troops of four guns per troop.

7th Light Antiaircraft Brigade

3rd Light Antiaircraft Regt., Royal Malta Artillery
Four batteries with 72 Bofors guns assigned

32nd Light AA Regt. ⎫
65th Light AA Regt. ⎬     Royal Artillery
74th Light AA Regt. ⎭

Each Royal Artillery Regiment was assigned three batteries of three troops each, with six Bofors guns per troop.

225th Light AA Battery, Royal Artillery

14th Heavy AA Battery (Relief), Royal Malta Artillery

**Sources:** Playfair, *The Mediterranean and Middle East*, Vols II and III.
Attard, *The Battle of Malta*

TABLE 14

## *Luftwaffe* **Order of Battle**
## **Sicily**
## (*Fliegerkorps II*)
## **March 1942**

| Type of Unit | Type of Aircraft | No. of Aircraft |
|---|---|---|
| Long Range Recon. *Staffel* | Ju88 | 17 |
| Single Engine Fighter *Geschwader*, Organized in four *Gruppen* | Mel09f | 146 |
| Twin Engine Fighter *Gruppe* | Mel10 | 19 |
| Night Fighter *Gruppe* | Ju88 | 14 |
| Bomber *Geschwader* Organized in five *Gruppen* | Ju88 | 131 |
| Dive Bomber *Gruppe* | Ju87D | 25 |
| | | Total 352 |

**Source:** Felmy: "The German Air Force in the Mediterranean Theater of War"

On November 28, Field Marshal Albert Kesselring of the *Luftwaffe* arrived from Russia to become Commander-in-Chief South (*Oberbefehlshaber Süd*) with authority over all operations in the Mediterranean area. He also commanded *Fliegerkorps II*, transferred from Russia. *Fliegerkorps X* continued to operate in the eastern Mediterranean. On May 6, 1941, The Germans rescinded a directive from the *Luftwaffe*'s Chief of Staff making German air units on Sicily subordinate to Italian Air Force headquarters. Destruction of the RAF's air and ground operation on Malta became first priority for the Germans.[51] Kesselring planned a three-phase air operation to destroy the British defenses and open the island to invasion. First, he planned to neutralize the antiaircraft guns. By forcing the gunners to intensify their fire for a period of several days, Kesselring believed, they would exhaust their ammunition, and the Axis blockade would prevent the arrival of replenishments. This was sound in theory, but the Germans were unaware of the large stocks of AA shells on Malta, enough for three months of defensive operations and 1,000 rounds per gun in an invasion reserve. Then he intended to eliminate the fighters and the bombers by severe and continued air base bombardment. Finally, a series of attacks would reduce the naval facilities and ports of the island.[52]

From December 1941 through the following spring, bombardment of the RAF's bases increased in both tempo and quantity of explosives dropped, the result of the better organized and larger force directing itself against what Kesselring referred to as "that hornet's nest."[53] Axis fliers gave special consideration to the destruction of the underground areas at Takali. Ju88s launched rocket propelled armorpiercing bombs, either from a shallow dive or on low altitude runs toward the cliff face. German tests led them to believe the bombs could penetrate from thirty-six to forty-nine feet of rock before detonation and then collapse the caves. In addition, they dropped oil filled bombs in front of the entrances to the caves. The oil was ignited by a fuze and was supposed to flow into the caves, burning the contents. Neither weapon worked. The limestone was too hard for the armorpiercing bombs, and the oil was absorbed by the crushed rock of the the tunnels and burned without entering the excavated area. March 20, 1942, marked beginning of the most violent air attacks on the fortress. For six weeks, until April 28, the bombing was far heavier than anything directed against the bases in England during the Battle of Britain. In February, 993 tons of bombs fell on Malta; March's figures increased to 2,174 tons, and April's to 6,728. In April, 1,200 tons of ordnance fell on the three airfields within few days.[54]

To oppose the Axis onslaught, Air Vice Marshal Lloyd had an assortment of aircraft. The Hurricanes were Malta's first line defense. They could turn inside a German Me109f at moderate altitudes, but could not fly as fast or handle as well at greater heights. But all the Hurricane's speed was needed to catch the Ju88 bombers, and the fighter's .303 caliber machine guns could not penetrate the Junkers' armor. Only the RAF's few fighters with 20-mm cannon were superior in this regard. Constant combat rapidly wore down the Hurricanes, the Wellingtons, and the Blenheims. To repair the fighters, Lloyd ordered a halt to all major maintenance on the bombers and impressed new aircraft transiting the island *en route* to the Middle East. Old aircraft in need of major repair, inspection, and service were sent out, the new ones kept.[55]

**One of many Bofors gun crews on Malta stands ready near Valetta. Their determined defense claimed 1,000 Axis aircraft in two years.**

Imperial War Museum

In the midst of all this punishment, the British defenders managed to strike back. During the winter of 1941–1942, heavy rain made Luqa and Hal Far (*Map 11*) unusable for several weeks. All working aircraft were scattered about Takali airfield (*Map 12*), immobile targets for the *Luftwaffe.* Hugh Lloyd surmised that the Germans might have similar problems with mud and water at their bases on Sicily. British photoreconnaissance reported the enemy had shifted many of his planes to Catania, Castel Vetrano, and two other airdromes. Since the RAF had been concentrating attacks on North Africa-bound shipping and had neglected attacking their enemy's air bases, Lloyd also detected in his opponents a false sense of security. On January 4, 1942, flying at no more than one hundred feet, ten Blenheims found the Germans parked wingtip to wingtip at Castel Vetrano and destroyed thirty planes while damaging many others. A following attack by Wellingtons set fire to another fourteen planes and a gasoline storage area. In the confusion of that night, the RAF set a trap for German bombers returning to Catania. As German aircraft circled awaiting their turn to land, Hurricanes and two Fleet Air Arm Fulmar fighters shot down three. As an added benefit to the British, the German gunners directed antiaircraft fire into the melee, damaging some of their own planes.[56]

124

Such success was rare, and the steady offensive by Field Marshal Kesselring continued to reduce Malta's air defense force. On February 15, only eleven Hurricanes were serviceable, and the main German effort was more than a month in the future. German raids were so frequent that the RAF's pilots often did not have enough time between attacks to land, refuel, and rearm. By default, the Germans had no air opposition on those occasions; only the antiaircraft guns could carry on the fight. Until more British aircraft reached the island, the overriding problems were fending off German attacks with ground fire, maintaining airfield operations, and avoiding starvation. Kesselring's campaign had reduced a typical day's rations to four or five slices of bread with a thin smear of jam, bully beef at all principal meals, a still adequate supply of sugar, but dwindling stocks of oil and margarine. Axis shipping losses declined markedly after mid-February until only seven percent of German supply vessels bound for Africa were sunk in April and May.

Antiaircraft weapons on the ground were crucial to the defense of Malta. The British positioned most of the guns to protect the four main military areas. No more than ten miles separated major targets. Operating in an area about one-seventh the size of London, the defenders had to exercise strict gun control. If flak appeared too early, the Germans chose an alternate target. If it began too late, there was not enough time for British guns to disrupt the formations. Axis fliers had an advantage because their bombing effort aimed at a relatively small area; but within the area almost all the guns waited for the approaching airplanes. Since the antiaircraft defense was concentrated on less than half the island, at least two and one-half guns were available for each square mile. By grouping the four-gun batteries to take advantage of their effective ranges, as many as eighty heavy guns fired into the air above the most important points. Furthermore, the small size of the target areas shortened the distance that repair crews had to move material, thus allowing the work to be completed quickly. The continuing addition of dispersal points greatly complicated the targeting tasks of Kesselring's staff.[58]

Before the arrival of gun laying radar, gunners often fired so called box barrages, where every available gun fired as fast as it could at its own predetermined point within a defined cube in the sky. The heavy flak the attackers had to fly through was daunting to any pilot, yet the Germans and Italians did so repeatedly. Box barrages appeared ferocious, but in reality were very inefficient. Most of the fire at fixed, predetermined points in the sky came nowhere near a moving target. Diving aircraft emerging from the high level barrage met much more effective fire from Bofors guns. Bombing remained quite accurate, with most of the explosives falling on or near the targets.[59]

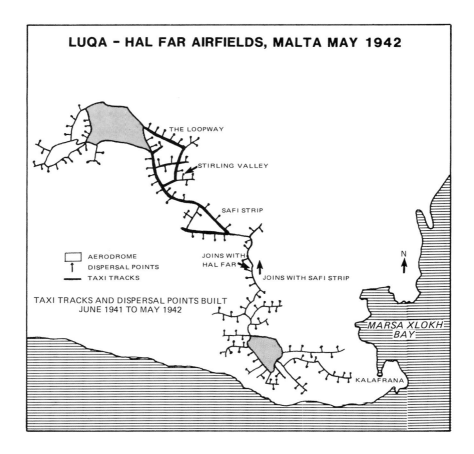

LUQA - HAL FAR AIRFIELDS, MALTA MAY 1942

## Map 11

By the beginning of 1942, two MkII gun laying radar sets were on Malta. This equipment provided the distance, bearing, speed of approach, and elevation, of a formation, and allowed much more accurate concentrations of fire than the box barrage. Air defense controllers had the guns fire into designated layered zones in the air. Air Marshal Lloyd reserved other zones for fighters and bombers to give free passage to friendly aircraft, especially those involved in night raids.[60]

Malta's stock of AA ammunition was so great that conservation measures were not needed until March and April 1942, when fear of an invasion prompted the desire to keep some on hand for that eventuality. The blockade reduced new ordnance supplies to that which could be carried by submarines

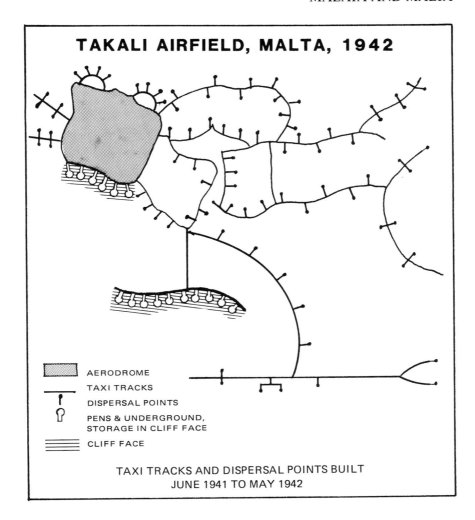

**TAKALI AIRFIELD, MALTA, 1942**

AERODROME

TAXI TRACKS

DISPERSAL POINTS

PENS & UNDERGROUND, STORAGE IN CLIFF FACE

CLIFF FACE

TAXI TRACKS AND DISPERSAL POINTS BUILT JUNE 1941 TO MAY 1942

**Map 12**

and the fast mine layer HMS *Welshman*. The firing restrictions presented no serious defense problems. Increased accuracy made possible by the gun laying radar and firing only by guns in range of the targets compensated for the reduced volume. During April, antiaircraft gunners claimed 102 victims. As a result of their mounting losses to AA, the Germans concentrated on flak suppression. Having calculated that at least 47 guns could reach any given spot over each sector, the Germans realized they had to reduce the effectiveness of British gunners. As a result, one-third of all their aircraft in

**British serviceman at Malta airfield contemplates spare rations. The garrison endured a semistarvation diet during the second year of the siege.**

Imperial War Museum

the siege of 1942 went for the AA positions. The attackers tried dive bombing to destroy the batteries or prevent accurate aiming. Often, time delay bombs were dropped amid the batteries. The crews then either evacuated the area, defused the weapons, or, on some occasions, disregarded them. Losses were sometimes heavy, and whole AA crews were occasionally killed. The Royal Malta Artillery organized a gun relief battery to replace losses and provide rest for crews.[61]

Well conceived deception schemes forced the enemy to choose among alternate targets and sometimes bluffed attacking formations into retreat. An unfinished airdrome at Krendi became a night target and absorbed frequent attacks. Special teams kept Krendi's runway lighting working, and a crew in a protected bunker switched it on as radar reported approaching formations. The size of the island again became an advantage as the German pilots, unable to differentiate quickly, dropped their bombs on what they mistakenly believed was their target. During the day, Safi strip served as the decoy when crews shifted irreparably damaged aircraft around the area.

**German bomb leaves smoke column over Maltese airfield, 1942.**

Imperial War Museum

These derelicts attracted dive bombers and confused enemy intelligence. An Italian Air Staff summary stated that the RAF kept the number of fighters constant at about forty between March 20 and April 10. In fact, many of the airplanes included in this count were the decoys parked at Safi. Radio deception played out fictitious fighter unit designations, and radio conversations between ground stations simulated directions to airborne Hurricanes. On several occasions, Axis bomber crews listening to RAF frequencies jettisoned their bombs and retreated rather than face the imaginary interceptors.[62]

Among the Axis fliers, the reputation of Malta's defense forces continued to grow with each raid. During the spring siege a commonly believed story held that the British found a dead Italian pilot with a disciplinary charge sheet referring to some indiscretion for which he had been sentenced to participate in air raids on Malta.[63]

Five radar stations detected raiders approaching Malta from Italy or North Africa. Reports of sightings were relayed to the filter room in the Air Defense Operations Centre at Valetta. The radar net was invaluable in scrambling Hurricanes and, later, Spitfires, to intercept Axis formations, but it often broke down. Technicians trickled in to handle the problems and continue installing new equipment. In May 1942, the British added night interception to their defense, using heavily armed Beaufighters that were

129

guided to within three miles of their targets by ground control intercept radar and then took over for final approach with their own airborne radar.[64]

During more than two years of conflict, the Axis air forces attacked none of the radar stations. Occasionally a telephone cable connecting the stations to Valetta and the bases was cut, but this was sheer happenstance and service was quickly restored. It is difficult to understand why the Germans left the radar alone. The *Luftwaffe* had radar in Sicily, used it in their own base defense, and regularly tracked RAF flights around Malta. On one occasion in April, they detected a flight of 47 Spitfires ferrying in from the American carrier USS *Wasp* and sent Ju87s and Ju88s that destroyed two RAF planes and damaged six shortly after the fighters landed. Jamming attempts from Sicily were common and caused some problems for the RAF's operators. In November 1942, the Germans used radar and flak to protect their airfields in the Bizerte -Tunis area, so their tactical air forces were by no means ignorant of its value. Apparently, Kesselring still had not realized either the full importance of radar to tactical warning and aircraft control, or the fragility of the equipment as demonstrated during the Battle of Britain, in which he was one of the *Luftwaffe*'s senior tactical commanders.* On Malta, some radar rooms were under many feet of rock, but the antennae were on the surface and could not be protected. Without them, radar could not function, aircraft could not be controlled effectively, and gun crews would have to remain on alert almost constantly, an extreme strain that could quickly reduce the undernourished men to uselessness. The Germans may have believed that jamming alone was a sufficient countermeasure, but if so, it was a serious error, as they did not know what countermeasures the British might use. The most likely explanation was the German air leaders' inability to absorb technical information and apply it to

---

* By 1942 the British had discovered widespread use of radar in Germany but were, as yet, unable to neutralize it. Not having faced bombing efforts against the home radar, the Germans may not have disseminated either warnings to protect the units or staff opinions on how best to destroy an enemy radar. See F.H. Hinsley, *et al., British Intelligence in World War II*, 3 volumes (New York: Cambridge University Press, 1979-1984), Vol. I, pp 238-257. Postwar German discussions of the Malta campaign did not mention radar as a target. See Helmuth Felmy, *GAF in the Mediterranean Theater of War*, USAF Historical Study 161 (Maxwell AFB, 1955), and Albert Kesselring, *Kesselring: A Soldier's Record* (New York: William Morrow and Company, 1954), Ch 13 and 14. The Italian versions of the plan for capturing the island did not mention radar as a target. Kesselring's plan directed jamming of radar, but did not discuss British antijamming measures or prelanding attacks on radar. Generals Paul Deichman and E. A. Marquard, in their reconstruction of German target selection methods, did not list a specific target category for radar stations. Other categories, such as communications stations, apparently included radar. Deichman and Marquard listed the type of weapon preferable for attacking radar stations, but did not tell when it was added to the weapons list. See USAF Historical Studies 186 and 187. Writing after the war, Kesselring spoke of disabling radar by seizing the stations with paratroops. See *A Soldier's Record*, pp 68-70.

tactical situations. The same failing that plagued their efforts during the Battle of Britain haunted them at Malta.[65]

Throughout 1941 and 1942, British intelligence helped keep Malta fighting, especially by predicting movements of enemy convoys to North Africa. Lloyd withheld attacks on Italian shipping until an independent source was found to duplicate the information, thus protecting ULTRA and other eavesdropping activities. In addition to the *Enigma* decrypts, the British regularly read the Italian medium and low grade naval codes, and the RAF's Y-Service teams analyzed radio messages throughout the Mediterranean area. Radio intercept, however, yielded little information of direct help to Malta's defenders. Most of the message traffic to and among the German air bases on Sicily went by cable and could not be intercepted. The attacks on Malta were so frequent and intense that even if specific times and routes of raiding formations were known, it could have added little to the effort. Radar warnings were a more significant factor because they gave immediate information of course and altitude exploited by the Spitfire's high speed, rate of climb, and its heavier armament.[66]

Because of the intense pressure on the air bases, fighter wastage was great. The number of serviceable fighters fluctuated, often declining to as few as five. The British pilots contended with almost 500 German and Italian aircraft. Many times when British fighters were too few or the pilots exhausted, the antiaircraft guns bore the defense burden. During April there were 248 air raid alerts on the island, during which the Axis hurled 5,715 sorties at the island. Malta's heavy guns fired 72,053 rounds, the Bofors guns 88,176.[67] The intensity of the fire and the accuracy of the Bofors gunners made the enemy release bombs at altitudes of 5,000 to 6,000 feet, not the optimum for dive bombing accuracy and one of the reasons why flak suppression was not as effective as it should have been. Heavy defensive fire notwithstanding, by early May the Axis had curtailed Malta's offensive power and much of her air defense. Rommel's drive toward Egypt had isolated the island yet more, but the air bases did not stop operating except for short periods of restoration after each attack. Some days flying halted to allow the mechanics an opportunity to ready more planes and create a more potent force. Use of the island as an air staging area did not cease. Almost half the aircraft replacements sent to Egypt and the Middle East in 1941 and 1942 used Malta's bases.[68]

On May 9, 1942, Malta's air operation was again reinforced, this time with 64 Spitfires flown from the carriers USS *Wasp* and HMS *Eagle*. Reception preparations were much improved and the arriving Spitfires orbited at very low altitude under protection of Bofors guns while waiting to land. This time the Germans attacked Hal Far, not Takali where the new Spitfires were. The airplanes were serviced and flew 74 interception sorties the same

**Maltese terrain, with numerous depressions and stone walls, presented a forbidding aspect to a prospective German glider invasion.** Imperial War Museum

day. On May 10, the *Welshman* arrived at Valetta with a 340-ton cargo of airplane parts, some AA ammunition and a small amount of food.[69]

On May 10, Kesselring believed the island's defenses neutralized. Hunger and stress achieved what the air raids could not. Much of *Fliegerkorps* II was transferred to Libya and the *Luftwaffe* once again shared responsibility for the island with the Italian Air Force. Rommel's advance opened the port of Benghazi, and when the Germans captured Tobruk on June 21, Axis supply convoys could sail farther east and avoid attacks from the island's bomber force. Unfortunately for the Axis powers, their plan for the seizure of Malta was not carried out. German leaders remembered the high costs of taking Crete in May 1941, when two German airborne divisions suffered almost 4,000 casualties and lost a large number of Ju52 transports and gliders. Goering especially had little desire to lose more of his prized paratroops. Believing that shipping supplies to Tobruk and Benghazi was more efficient than seizing Malta, he would not authorize the operation. The British continued to threaten Rommel's supply line and ultimately the shortage of material helped force him out of North Africa. That Malta could have successfully resisted an invasion in May or June 1942 is difficult to imagine. The demonstrated excellence of leadership and determination of the garrison would have exacted a higher price than Kesselring believed, but the defenders were in such serious straits that had he attempted the invasion, he would probably have succeeded.[70]

Because the Axis hesitated, the British could again reinforce their base defenses. On May 18, seventeen Spitfires arrived, increasing the number of fighters on the island to more than a hundred. The bomber squadrons were restored to full strength and returned to the offensive against Africa bound shipping. Transfer of the *Luftwaffe*'s forces away from Sicily and the renewed strength of the Royal Air Force returned local air superiority to the British. The Axis opportunity to seize the island lapsed. Though they hotly contested the relief of the island by convoys in June and July, the Axis could no longer support the simultaneous campaigns in North Africa and Russia and continue the aerial destruction of Malta; the island's worst trial was over.[71]

## Comparison of the Campaigns

A study of air base air defense during the Malayan and Maltese campaigns shows that neither of these British bases was ready for war when hostilities began. Malta had the nine months from Germany's invasion of Poland to Italy's declaration of war to prepare. Singapore had less than a day after Japan's attack on Pearl Harbor, but British leaders should have fathomed Japan's intentions long before the bombs began falling. In both instances, war priorities directed resources to other theaters, primarily home defense. While planning was done before fighting began, in neither case was it adequate. In Malaya, defense preparations underway on December 8 were far from complete. Lack of dispersals, revetments, modern fighters and antiaircraft weapons, and poor intelligence and command and control planning were the most deficient areas.

At Malta, the planning for AA and fighters to be based on the island also proved deficient. Large increases in force size and constant resupply were necessary. Few passive defensive measures, such as underground facilities, were complete. Almost no blast shields and little dispersal parking were ready in June 1940. Construction began in earnest only after large scale bombing by the Germans in 1941. The need to repair while constructing new defenses put a very heavy strain on the engineers.

The garrisons of both islands had several airfields to defend, Singapore four and Malta three. Both commands placed heavy reliance on antiaircraft guns for air defense and heavy gun density was roughly equal. Singapore had three guns per square mile, Malta two and one-half for the critical eastern part of the island. Half of Singapore's heavy guns were the old 3-inch type; all of Malta's were modern 3.7-and 4.5-inch. Gun laying radar was used to assist AA in both locations.[72] The number of Bofors 40-mm guns available in Malta and Singapore differed significantly. There were 234 protecting the Maltese targets; no more than 76 were in use by the Singapore garrison. With great accuracy and a high rate of fire, these weapons instilled fear in German and Italian fliers. Between June 1, 1941, and mid-July 1942, the defenders shot down 693 aircraft during attacks on Malta. By October 13, 1942, 1,000 were claimed by fighter and gun defenses during 28 months of war. The antiaircraft score was heaviest in April 1942, when gunners believed they had accounted for 102 raiders.[73]

The most striking dissimilarity between these two cases is in the varying determination among the military forces and civil governments to keep the air bases functioning. The British never viewed the prewar threat to Singapore as seriously as that to the United Kingdom itself and misjudged Japan's intent and strength. They allocated fewer resources to the Far East. The Japanese as a consequence drove the thinly spread British defenders in Malaya 400 miles down a peninsula thought to be impassable. The defenders of Singapore were exhausted and much of their equipment had been left behind as they scrambled south. The Japanese used British bombs and gasoline abandoned at several northern bases in their final bombardment of the airfields, ports, and Army positions on Singapore Island. Stunned by the brilliance of the Japanese concept and the enormity of their losses, the leadership lacked the will to defend Singapore and in any event had lost much of the means to do so. The senior British leaders failed to organize a coherent defense of the island and the adjacent part of Johore so vital to its protection.[74]

The leadership on Malta was totally different, buoyed by a number of factors, not the least of which was a psychological one. The island was a vital link to Egypt, the Middle East, and India, and the British were determined to hold it. Not having seen their forces retreat in disorder while trying to protect a land mass like Malaya, Malta's commanders did not adopt an attitude of inevitable failure. Even under the most intense bombing, Royal Air Force pilots and mechanics and Army artillery gunners resisted fiercely. Airplanes frequently arrived from England and Egypt, and the island's garrison never lost communication with other British forces. In Malaya, a growing feeling of isolation and abandonment eroded morale as the battle progressed. Even while training to fight an invading force, thousands of soldiers joined the civilians and airmen in patching Malta's taxiways and runways. Malta's weapon batteries fought for two years, and there were few glaring failures such as the lack of critical parts for height finding equipment that prevailed at Singapore. The consistent willingness of Malta's population to repeat the repair jobs and the proximity of other British and Allied forces were the keys to success.[75]

The disparity in tonnages of bombs dropped was striking. Between March 12 and May 10, 1942, almost 10,000 tons of bombs fell on Maltese bases, an average of over 160 tons a day. On some peak days, the three airfields absorbed 600 tons of explosives.[76] Air base attacks by the Japanese were never as severe. During the fifteen days of the final attack on Singapore, the Japanese 7th Air Group dropped 773 tons of bombs on all targets, including those at sea. The amounts expended by the 3rd Air Group and the 22nd Naval Flotilla were probably similar.[77]

German and Japanese bombs used in these two campaigns were quite adequate for air base attacks, except for the destruction of underground facilities at Malta. The *Luftwaffe* used mostly 550-pound fragmentation and high explosive bombs and incendiaries. The Japanese employed generally lighter weapons and bombs captured from the British. Throughout the Malta campaign, bombing was consistent; responsibilities for targets were assigned to specific units, intelligence was good, and the targets were struck repeatedly in an attempt to prevent recovery of the RAF. Damage caused to flying fields and parking areas on Malta was quickly repaired. At Singapore, however, the available work force was too small, and materials were not readily at hand to accomplish the same results.[78]

Whereas Malta had a more modern fighter force than did Singapore, until late April 1942 there were so few planes available, and the odds they faced were so formidable, that air interception was as difficult there as in Malaya. Isolation of both Singapore and Malta made reinforcement extremely difficult, although aircraft carriers could bring replacement fighters to within flying distance of both battles. Those sent to Singapore, via convoy or carrier, were far too few and arrived too late to be a significant factor. The fighter replacements to Malta served only to sustain an operational force of ten or fewer planes through March and most of April 1942. While never without resources, on some days Air Vice Marshal Lloyd chose not to commit his handful of fighters and entrusted the defense of the island base to the guns. Even when a small number of fighters did fly, the British still depended heavily on ground guns. The artillery gunners and the people who repaired the airfields, then, were the factors that sustained a minimal base operation through the most intense fighting.

Malta differed most obviously from Malaya in the courage and determination of Air Vice Marshal Lloyd, Maj. Gen. C. T. Beckett, the antiaircraft artillery commander, and their crews who refused to concede the closing of the air bases. Britain could replace Malta's aircraft losses only in small increments, but those few planes at a time, a bristling collection of antiaircraft guns, and a defensive system proven during the Battle of Britain were enough to keep at bay an enemy whose Cretan venture left him unwilling to rush into a similar attempt in 1942.

# Chapter V

# Campaigns in Africa

For the Western Allies, the two year war in North Africa was the proving ground for new tactical air warfare ideas and for newly raised units fresh to combat. By 1942, under the influence of Air Marshal Arthur Tedder, British air commander in the Middle East, the RAF's tactical air operation was closely aligned with that of the Eighth Army. Both air and ground defenses drew on each service's inherent mobility, intelligence gathering and processing ability and the firepower of fighters and light and medium AA guns. The desert conflict also made clear the need for dedicated base defense units, organizations that could repel raiders in the air or on the ground. In addition to fighter squadrons, the Royal Air Force looked back to the experience of World War I to organize armored car companies for mobile defense. Later, in Northwest Africa, squadrons of the Royal Air Force Regiment protected landing fields. In 1942 and 1943, the Americans, new to the war, adopted some of the proven techniques to defend their air bases during the Allied drive from the West across French North Africa.

The Axis powers countered with forces that were so skillfully used that at times they were nearly overwhelming. Both sides competed fiercely for air supremacy; losses were heavy, and landing grounds were frequent targets for air attack. Two problems haunted the German-Italian armies, however. The continued existence of a British base on Malta whose commanders used the advantage of ULTRA to attack resupply from Italy and an air support system that was not meshed closely enough with its ground forces in the Western Desert. As a result, many excellent opportunities to damage the enemy slipped by unrealized.

## War of Movement in the Western Desert

When Mussolini declared war on Great Britain in June 1940, large Italian armies in Eritrea and Libya threatened the British positions on the Suez Canal, in Palestine, and in Egypt. The fall of France left the greatly outnumbered British without an ally. In August, Italian forces under Marshal Rodolpho Graziani advanced cautiously from Libya as far as Sidi Barrani, sixty miles into Egypt, where they paused to build a forward supply base. For the next three months, the armies watched each other from fixed emplacements. The British were unsure how the Italian Army, then still well regarded, would fight, but General Sir Archibald Wavell, Commander-in-Chief Middle East, moved first. He sent his Western Desert Force, consisting of an infantry and an armored division and the Royal Air Force, Egypt, on a five day raid into enemy territory.[1] Results were immediate.

On December 9, 1940, the British attacked under the command of one of the most highly respected officers in the Middle East, Lt.-Gen. Sir Richard N. O'Connor. O'Connor revised Wavell's plan and sought to outflank the Italians by maneuvering in the vast open area between the Nile and Tunisia which the British called the Western Desert. In rapid succession O'Connor took the fortress at Tobruk, drove west over the Cyrenaican desert, and trapped the Italian army near Benghazi. With a numerically inferior air force, the British won air superiority by staging a series of heavy attacks on the *Regia Aeronautica*'s bases. In less than a month, the British captured 200,000 prisoners and nearly all the enemy's war supplies in Libya. The Italian collapse left the Axis with only a small foothold along the Tripolitanian coast, centered on the port of Tripoli.[2] (*Map 13*) Before he could finish the job, O'Connor received orders from Winston Churchill on February 7, 1941, to hold in place and extend all possible aid to Greece, which Italian forces had invaded from Albania the previous October. Most of the British force facing the Italians in Libya returned to Egypt for refitting or was sent to assist the Greeks. Then, on February 12, 1941, Rommel arrived in Tripoli to command Axis ground forces. His immediate goal was to rally the Italians and organize two arriving German divisions into a force that could stop the British and expand the Axis-controlled land area sufficiently to allow the German Air Force, already in Libya, room to operate.[3]

In the Balkans, the Greek advance into Albania and the presence of a British expeditionary force on the Hellenic peninsula rapidly brought German intervention; Hitler felt compelled to prevent a second Italian military disaster at least as great as the recent defeat in Libya. The German columns pushed south, and by the end of April British forces had retreated to the island of Crete. On March 31, while attention was riveted upon events in Greece, Rommel, contrary to orders, seized the opportunity to outflank the British in the Western Desert. With a small force of tanks and mechanized

**Map 13**

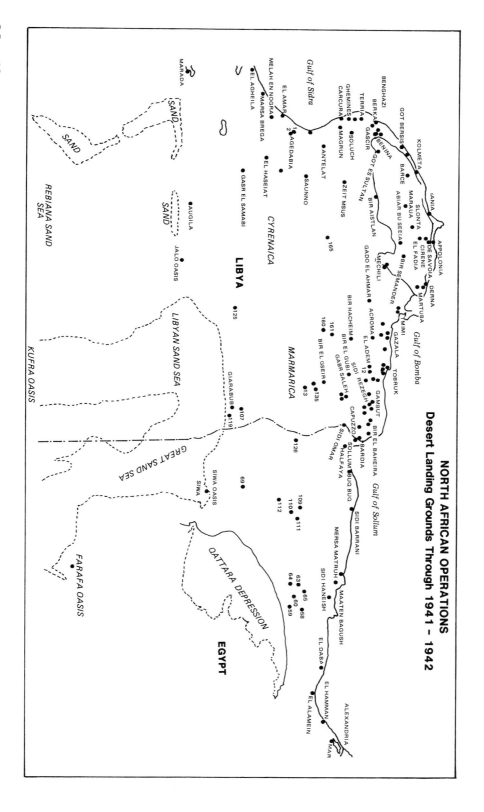

NORTH AFRICAN OPERATIONS
Desert Landing Grounds Through 1941 – 1942

infantry, his fledgling *Afrika Korps*, supported by the *Luftwaffe*'s X *Fliegerkorps*, raced across Cyrenaica, invested Tobruk, and in mid-April came to a halt at the Egyptian border. By a stroke of good fortune, German troops captured O'Connor, who was attempting to restore order in the disorganized Eighth Army. The German Air Force now joined with the artillery, trying to force Tobruk's perimeter. Attempting desperately to salvage something from the disaster, the British decided to hold the Germans where they were in North Africa and defend Crete, thereby keeping a foothold at the entrance to the Aegean Sea. Defense of the island centered on 3 airfields and consisted of some 30,000 men, but less than a squadron of British fighters at Heraklion and Maleme airdromes. German opposition came from a string of bases in southern Greece and the Italian Dodecanese islands. The issue of air defense of the troops on Crete was never in doubt. Combat losses quickly ended the RAF's air operations on the island, which lay beyond the range of any British fighters based in Egypt. The meager bombing effort by Wellingtons flying from Egypt could barely dent the German forces.[4]

Although fiercely opposed on the ground, the *Luftwaffe*'s parachute and glider borne troops, supported by tactical air bombardment, landed at Maleme. In ten days they overcame all ground opposition on Crete, but with heavy losses. One of the mildest German assessments said that although successful, the seizure of Crete "was not easy and involved a great deal of bloodshed." Tedder, in summing up the British loss, attributed the RAF's inability to operate in Greece and Crete to "a lack of secure airbases," which, in turn, gave the *Luftwaffe* the initiative. By May 31, the British abandoned Crete with the Royal Navy evacuating about half the defending force. Bleak as the British situation appeared, the Germans lacked the naval force needed to cross from Crete to Alexandria. Furthermore, they were powerless to advance farther into Egypt from Libya. The *Afrika Korps* was tired, its armor reduced by combat losses and its supply lines stretched to the limit. Tobruk's perimeter could not be penetrated without heavy German reinforcements, and none was available.[5]

With both sides temporarily exhausted, the situation stabilized. The German aviation and artillery, however, continued to press the attack on Tobruk, a small but developed seaport that served as the main logistic and troop marshaling area in eastern Libya. The British had turned it into a strongpoint protecting Egypt and lying astride the only road the Axis could use. Ground and antiaircraft defenses were tenacious and withstood German attempts to seize the position throughout the summer. Antiaircraft guns were in short supply and several additional batteries were brought in by the Navy. Radar warning came only from two gun laying sets which could not search the sky adequately, but did help with aiming and fire control. The RAF's airfield at Tobruk was too exposed to bomber and artillery attack and quickly became unusable. Cut off from the Eighth Army and supplied only by ships under intense attack, Tobruk's fighter force dwindled rapidly. The remaining aircraft of the two original squadrons withdrew on April 24. Air Marshal Sir Arthur Longmore, Air Officer Commanding in Chief Middle East, and his deputy, Tedder, had 54 Hurricanes left in Egypt to face an enemy air force capable of deploying some 400 aircraft from bases in Libya and the eastern Mediterranean area.[6]

The RAF now faced several serious problems. Pilot morale after the loss of Greece and Crete and the retreat in the Western Desert was low. The German aircraft outnumbered and outperformed the Hurricanes. The distance from sources of new aircraft (England or America) was great; delivery times were lengthy. As a result, the RAF seemed unable to match its opponents in combat and operational support. Tedder began by establishing a more coherent organization for the job. He got Longmore to decentralize control of aerial operations and created a tactical force in the Western Desert responsible to himself. Bombers and the air defense forces of the Nile Delta remained under command of Headquarters Middle East Air Force in Cairo. Upon Longmore's recall to London on May 1, Tedder took command of the RAF in the Middle East and immediately placed Air Vice Marshal G. G. Dawson in charge of all repair and maintenance in the theater over the Air Ministry's demurrers. Tedder knew Dawson's unit to be utterly essential, and it became the key to sustaining the Air Force in isolated areas.[7]

Of equal importance was the division of each fighter and fighter bomber squadron into two parts. The ground echelon of each half squadron was equipped with vehicles, enabling the divided components of the tactical air forces to leapfrog forward or backward to match the movements of the armies. The British established desert landing grounds quickly, often within a few miles of the maneuvering ground units. The landing grounds were dirt strips with minimum supplies of gasoline, essential parts, and ammunition which allowed the RAF's mechanics to service aircraft quickly. Tedder added mobile radar stations to forward bases so the aircraft would not be surprised by a German or Italian attack. In moving his forces about the country, one of Tedder's first rules was to locate fighter fields close to bomber airdromes, to allow fighters to intercept enemy aircraft and escort British bombers.[8]

The restructuring did not leave the Desert Air Force problem free. By September 1941, Tedder still judged air base defense to be the RAF's "weakest spot." Moreover, he encountered opposition to his changes from both the Army and the Navy. The Eighth Army commander feared the outcome of any battle in which each of his division commanders did not have bombers and fighters at his disposal. The Navy voiced the same concerns, having lost half its Mediterranean fleet to Axis air attacks while supporting the withdrawal from Greece and Crete and supplying Tobruk. Bitter arguments ensued in staff meetings. Neither the Army nor the Navy wanted Tedder to control tactical air. Tedder, refusing to yield, cited Prime Minister

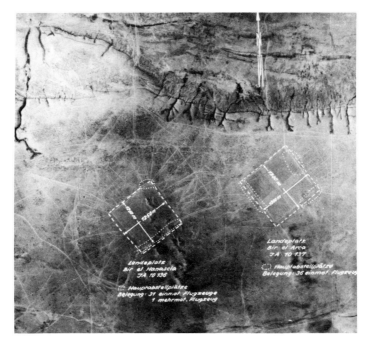

**German aerial reconnaisance photo plots the location of British desert landing grounds between Tobruk and Bardia.**

Churchill's support for his position and finally brought the sister services around by convincing General Sir Claude Auchinleck, now Commander-in-Chief Middle East, of the necessity of concentrating the attacking power of the Desert Air Force at the most effective spot.[9]

Tedder further insisted, in the face of great resistance from the Army, that the forward tactical air headquarters (Western Desert Air Force, commanded by Air Vice Marshal Sir Arthur Coningham) be adjacent to that of the army commander. Moreover, he created a command organization that was highly mobile and could communicate directly with the commander of subordinate groups, with supply and repair points, radar stations, the AA gun operations room, or rear headquarters. Within Western Desert Air Force, No. 211 Group was responsible for fighter defense. The Western Desert became a fighter sector, another sector was formed to cover rear areas. Both resembled sectors in England during the Battle of Britain.[10]

The division of air defense guns and equipment supported the new organization. Eighth Army assigned 12th AA Brigade to work with No. 211 Group, and the brigade's operations room quickly came to share quarters with the fighter controllers. Assigned to the 12th were thirty-two 3.7-inch

142

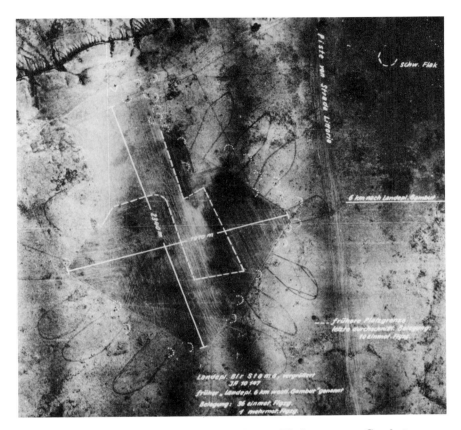

**German intelligence outlines the British field at Bir Stama, near Gambut.**

and seventy-two 40-mm Bofors guns. Four radar sets, observer units, and some of the RAF's Radio Field Interception Units (of the Y-Service intelligence organization) also reported to the fighter controllers. Radar filter rooms were not used; time response was so critical that no delays could be tolerated. The fighter control that developed was not a true ground controlled intercept system such as used over Britain; the controllers did not work directly with radar scopes. Rather, they used a variety of data passed to them to maneuver their airborne fighters. Moreover, a GCI system would not have worked because most of the RAF's aircraft had high frequency radios with a range of fifty miles. It was not until 1942 that the RAF began to change to VHF radios in Africa, giving them an extended range of one hundred miles or greater. Additional defense against low level attack was available from the machine gunners of the station defense forces, predecessors of the Royal Air Force Regiment. During 1941 and 1942, station defense

143

force units in the Middle East served largely as airdrome guards or on general base details. They were poorly trained and did little AA work. In 1942, however, the Regiment assumed control of 8,000 of the RAF's antiaircraft gunners in the Middle East theater, where, after September, they were made into AA flights with up to 360 men. A much greater role for the Regiment came with the Northwest African invasion late in 1942. There, the Regiment deployed both ground and air defense units.[11]

Tedder defined air superiority as an ability to destroy an enemy air force or limit its operations against friendly forces. In his view, air superiority was gained by operating from secure air bases, bases protected by a combination of early warning, fighter interceptors, and enough AA guns to deflect an attacker during his final bombing or strafing run. He clearly realized that superiority could not be held permanently; relative strength could and did change from day to day. Risks must be taken, especially at the start of a campaign when there might be no assurance of secure bases. Furthermore, numerical superiority alone was never a determinant; effective strength, concentration of force, and adroit leadership were more important. Before the November 1942, Anglo-American landings in Northwest Africa, the RAF held clear numerical superiority rarely—and then only if one did not count total Axis strength in the Mediterranean that could be used as reinforcements.[12]

Late in 1941, the most important British air base in the Western Desert was extremely vulnerable. Located at Sidi Barrani, just east of the front line, it was within easy reach of the *Luftwaffe* and *Regia Aeronautica*. The British quickly moved gun defenses from Mersa Matruh airfield and installed numerous machine guns for use against low level attack. Parachute and cable rockets, first used in the Battle of Britain, were set out, and radar and Hurricane fighters were placed on alert. Even so, Italian air attacks during September destroyed many aircraft on the ground, and defending fighters shot down no intruders. Better protection was needed, for Tedder feared an attack by pilots of greater skill could destroy his operation.[13]

Churchill, the ever present force in British military planning, added more urgency by demanding an offensive into Libya. On November 18, 1941, Operation CRUSADER began. As the operation opened up, rains and mud immobilized the enemy's air force; there was little Axis air reaction and no direct threat to the British air bases. The RAF's fighter sweeps neutralized enemy airfields. Advancing British forces found 172 damaged or destroyed airplanes on aerodromes near Derna. Ground threats to RAF bases from Rommel's maneuvering divisions were a far greater menace, and two advanced landing grounds had to be evacuated under the guns of *Afrika Korps* tanks. Throughout CRUSADER, however, the air threat to Tedder's bases was negligible. By Christmas 1941, the British once again controlled Benghazi. They then paused to re-equip their forces. During the rapid ad-

TABLE 15

## Axis Air Forces in Africa
## December 1941

### German Air Force

| | |
|---|---|
| Reconnaissance | |
| Africa Flight, 1st *Staffel*/121 *Gruppe* (Ju88) | 4 |
| | |
| Dive bomber | |
| 3d Bomber *Geschwader* (Ju87, Me110) | 72 |
| | |
| Twin Engine Fighter | |
| 3rd *Gruppe*/26 Fighter *Geschwader* (Me110) | 18 |
| | |
| Single Engine Fighter | |
| 27th Fighter *Geschwader* (Me109) | 64 |
| | |
| Night Fighters | |
| 1st *Staffel*/3 NF *Gruppe* (Me110) | 10–12 |

A *Staffel* in the Mediterranean area usually consisted of nine aircraft, though special purpose units varied in strength. Support and reinforcements were also available from *Luftflotte* II in Rome. Normally, half the assigned aircraft were operationally ready at any time. Total German aircraft in the Mediterranean area was 523.

### Italian Air Force

| | |
|---|---|
| Fighters | 100 |
| Fighter bombers | 90 |

Italian Air Force operational rates were about fifty percent.

Sources: Felmy, "The GAF in the Mediterranean Theater of War"
Air Ministry, German translation VII/2

Table 16

# Royal Air Force in Africa
## November 1941

Air Headquarters, Western Desert

| | | |
|---|---|---|
| 30 Sq | Sidi Haneish, L.G.* 102 | Hurricanes |
| 33 Sq | Gerawla, L.G. 10 | Hurricanes |
| 60 Sq (So. African) | Fuka, L.G. 16 | Marylands |
| 80 Sq | Fuka, L.G. 103 | Hurricanes |
| 113 Sq | Maaten Bagush, L.G. 115 | Blenheim Fighters |
| 223 Sq | Fuka North, L.G. 17 | Marylands |
| 272 Sq | Gerawla, L.G. 10 | Beaufighters |
| 805 Sq (Fleet Air Arm) | Fayid | Martlets |
| 815 Sq (Fleet Air Arm) | Dexheila | Swordfish/Albacores |
| 826 Sq (Fleet Air Arm) | Maaten Bagush | Albacores |

261 Wing

| | | |
|---|---|---|
| 11 Sq | Maaten Bagush, L.G. 116 | Blenheims |
| 12 Sq (So. African) | Dara, L.G. 24 | Marylands |
| 21 Sq (So. African) | Qotafiya, L.G. 21 | Marylands |
| 24 Sq (So. African) | Fuka Main | Bostons |

270 Wing

| | | |
|---|---|---|
| 8 Sq | Fuka Main | Blenheims |
| 14 Sq | L.G. 15 | Blenheims |
| 45 Sq | Fuka, L.G. 16 | Blenheims |
| 55 Sq | Fuka North, L.G. 17 | Blenheims |
| 84 Sq | SW Maaten Bagush L.G.116 | Blenheims |
| Lorraine Sq (French) | Abu Sueir, L.G. X | Blenheims |

253 Wing

| | | |
|---|---|---|
| 208 Sq | Sidi Barrani, L.G. 75 | Hurricanes |
| 237 Sq (Rhodesian) | Gerawla, L.G. 11 | Hurricanes |
| 451 Sq(RAAF) | Sidi Barrani, L.G. 75 | Hurricanes |

258 Wing

| | | |
|---|---|---|
| 2 Sq (So. African) | Sidi Haneish, L.G. 101 | Tomahawks |
| 3 Sq(So. African) | Sidi Haneish, L.G. 102 | Tomahawks |
| 4 Sq(So. African) | Sidi Haneish, L.G. 101 | Tomahawks |
| 112 Sq | Sidi Haneish, L.G. 102 | Tomahawks |
| 250 Sq | Sidi Haneish, L.G. 13 | Tomahawks |
| Royal Navy Sq. | Sidi Haneish, L.G. 13 | Tomahawks |

*TABLE 16 (Continued):*

262 Wing

| | | |
|---|---|---|
| 1 Sq(So. African) | Kenayis | Hurricanes |
| 94 Sq(So. African) | Maaten Bagush, L.G. 103 | Hurricanes |
| 229 Sq | Jesaka, L.G. 10 | Hurricanes |
| 238 Sq | Sidi Haneish, L.G. 12 | Hurricanes |
| 260 Sq | Maaten Bagush, L.G. 115 | Hurricanes |
| 274 Sq | Fuka, L.G. 103 | Hurricanes |

\* Landing Ground

In addition, No 205 Group with 6 squadrons of Wellingtons, No. 201 Group (Naval Cooperation) with 5 squadrons of Dorniers [prewar acquisitions by various Balkan and Mediterranean powers, captured or otherwise pressed into service by British forces at this point], Blenheims, Ansons, and Sunderlands, and two squadrons of Hurricanes assigned to Air Hq Egypt were available as reinforcements.

British squadrons normally had twelve to eighteen aircraft, however, this varied by area and operating conditions.

**Source:** Rpt., "RAF Operations in the Western Desert and Eastern Mediterranean," 512.421B

vance both Army and Air Force accommodated themselves to the new methods of close cooperation.[14]

In December, as the British advanced into Cyrenaica, Eighth Army's engineers rapidly built or repaired landing grounds. Using whatever transport was available, the RAF delivered gasoline and began flying operations. At Gazala, engineers spent two days under Axis shellfire clearing three airfields ahead of British lines. Protection was provided by the RAF fighters flying to and from targets in the near vicinity, but such cover could not be continuous and the engineers were at great risk. Nevertheless, the construction efforts paid off handsomely by placing planes on fields close enough to Eighth Army to support it directly. At Msus, a landing ground with some dispersed parking and fifty thousand gallons of gasoline was ready two days after the British Army took the area. Eleven fighter squadrons, a close air support squadron, and Blenheim bombers soon occupied it and an adjacent airstrip.[15]

Because of the vast area of responsibility, the distance from England, and the varied locations of landing grounds, the total number of weapons protecting desert airfields remained inadequate until well into 1942. The fluid nature of the desert war left some bases with great numbers of guns, others with few or none. The desert dust was notorious for fouling weapons, and rough terrain wore the gun mounts, resulting in extra work for the

**American B–25 weathers Egyptian sandstorm, 1942. Maintenance and flying operations under these conditions were arduous.**

gunners who had to clean and repair the pieces. Gun positions could not be prepared readily in the hard, rocky soil, and gun crews began blasting instead of digging emplacements. Much of what was learned would prove invaluable in the summer of 1942, especially when the British faced Rommel's renewed offensive, which was designed to force the British to withdraw far into Egypt.[16]

Backing away before CRUSADER, Rommel safely withdrew through Agedabia to Mersa el Brega, where he reorganized and re-equipped. On January 21, he lashed out again, quickly recaptured Agedabia, and turned once more toward Egypt. Recoiling from the renewed Axis threat, the RAF retreated in stages across Cyrenaica to airfields at Gazala and Tobruk. Resupplied, Rommel renewed his drive in May, broke Tobruk's defense, captured the port, and chased Auchinleck into Egypt, behind the El Alamein line. During the retreat, Axis fliers made 211 attacks of varying size on the RAF's landing fields, forcing No. 262 Wing to abandon the fighter base at El Adem. The Axis attacks were, however, almost entirely limited to landing grounds near the front. The RAF believed this was due largely to their enemies' inability to move attack squadrons rapidly from airfield to airfield. Cooperation grew between the gunners of the 12th AA Brigade and 211 Group. Because both the RAF's operations center and the 12th AA Brigade's gun operations room were highly mobile, they quickly abandoned any location threatened by Rommel's advancing army, and rapidly restored operations at a new airfield. The swiftness with which Royal Air Force squadrons could move from base to base prevented losses during the retreat. On several occasions the departing aircraft were screened from the enemy only by a few of the RAF's armored cars.[17]

Several negative aspects of this fluid process emerged, too. The continuous exchange of information between gun and fighter defenses quickly overloaded the 12th Brigade's telephone and radio circuits, and communications often broke down. Tanks and trucks cut the wires while moving into position and only the most ingenious solutions and hard work kept a satisfactory operation going. Fortunately, the communication difficulties were not a major impediment because of Tedder's insistence on close and continuing liaison between Desert Air Force and the AA Brigade. Tedder himself often remained near Eighth Army's headquarters where he and the ground commanders could quickly solve problems. Joint staff meetings were held daily, and a close understanding arose between the air and ground leaders facilitated by the design of the air force's operations center.[18]

American observers were not impressed at first. In June of 1942, after Maj. Gen. Lewis H. Brereton and his staff arrived in Egypt to organize the United States' Ninth Air Force, they formed an impression that British air defenses had been improvised and were somewhat ramshackle. Maj. David H. Likes reported to Brereton that "the mobile desert units [used only] rudimentary plotting methods and often only a vehicle for an operations room." Although the system appeared crude to the Americans, they quickly came to appreciate that it was a well thought out, battle tested scheme. In the operations room the information was sorted, assessed, and given to the controllers who dispatched fighters to contend with large groups of intruding Axis aircraft. Small flights of two or three enemy planes were ordinarily ignored by fighters and left solely to ground gunners regardless of what their target might be. In using its fighters, the RAF tried to intercept Axis raiders before they reached the front lines, thus preventing them from penetrating to the relatively unprotected rear areas, where radar detection and control was lacking. Once directed toward an enemy, fighter pilots were under tight direction until they were near combat. Only while fighting were they on their own; immediately after they broke off, the fighter controllers sent them to another target or back to their bases. The result was a very efficient allocation of weapons; the British avoided any ineffective prowling of the skies by pilots who had no knowledge of an enemy's location. During daylight, the RAF used AA guns to drive off or deter enemy pilots who avoided the interceptors. At night, guns were only allowed to fire if the enemy found a landing ground. Otherwise, they would lie low, depending on camouflage or blackouts to fool the pilots.[19]

During the last year of fighting in Africa, British forces probably received more information about the enemy's tactical air operations, especially logistics, than at any other time in the Second World War. How well ULTRA was used will probably never be known since no commander ever published revelations on how he appreciated or applied the secret intelligence. This was partly for security reasons, but also because commanders at the time were not always aware of the relative importance of the information, nor was ULTRA the only source of good intelligence. Many were also reluctant to put on paper accounts of their decisions and deeds that proved in hindsight to be mistakes. The effects of this special intelligence on every aspect of Allied military operations in North Africa, including air base air defense, were nevertheless pronounced. Auchinleck, the Commander-in-Chief Middle East (after August 15, 1942, General Sir Harold Alexander), received daily ULTRA reports from London summarizing high level German messages. Although the nature of ULTRA information often precluded its immediate tactical exploitation, or even open discussion of the material, experts at Bletchley Park provided the commanders in Egypt information against which RAF Y-units could compare their own intercepts. In addition, the RAF's radio operators at various radar stations picked up radio conversations between enemy pilots and ground stations and various enemy ground units. Frequently, radio intercepts confirmed compass bearings of radar sightings (most of the radar sets in the Western Desert were accurate only for height and distance). The confirmation allowed immediate actions by fighter controllers at No. 211 Group headquarters who had been alerted earlier by Tedder. The *Luftwaffe*'s logistics problems and force dispositions were almost as well known to Tedder and Coningham as to Lt. Gen. Stefan Froelich and his successors who commanded the *Luftwaffe*'s forces in Africa.[20]

By the summer of 1942, Rommel had advanced to El Alamein, some fifty miles from Alexandria, Egypt. The British Middle East Command, hard-pressed to halt the enemy and, at the same time, provide aircraft to bolster the Far East against the advancing Japanese, requested American air units to reinforce the RAF. On June 2 a detachment of B–24s arrived, followed shortly by Brereton's task force from India. Shortly thereafter, the Army Air Forces organized the Ninth Air Force with Brereton commanding. The Americans only provided flying units; they relied on established British air base defenses throughout their stay in the Western Desert campaign. In fact, Brereton enthusiastically embraced many of Tedder's ideas, including placing the 57th Fighter Group operationally under No. 211 Group, dividing it into two sections to support rapid movements, and sending American officers to the fighter controller school at Heliopolis, near Cairo.[21] In the days before the second battle of El Alamein began in late October, combined RAF-USAAF air strikes repeatedly hit the Axis' airfields as well as other advanced positions. Allied fighter cover was heavy and Axis reconnaissance planes could not cover the front. On October 27, the 57th's P–40s took off in the darkness from Landing Ground 174 using truck headlights to mark the dirt runway. Flying low to avoid German radar, they surprised an airdrome

**Blenheims of 82 Squadron strike German field at Tamet, Libya, on June 17, 1942. Two aircraft are wreathed in smoke and dust, while a Ju–88 waits helplessly. Other equipment and structures lay open to the attack.**

near Fuka at dawn and heavily damaged parked Italian and German aircraft.[22]

With the Axis retreating toward El Agheila, Tedder and Coningham once again tried audacity to disrupt further Axis transport and air bases. Landing Ground 125, 120 miles west of the Libyan-Egyptian border, and deep within the Cyrenaican desert, lay abandoned, and served only as a rendezvous for air transports supporting patrols of the British Long Range Desert Group and the commando teams of the Special Air Service. Tedder and Coningham, however, saw the area as the perfect place from which to operate fighters in the Axis rear. They counted on rapid redeployment and the remoteness of the desert strip for both air and ground defense. Nevertheless, British Middle East Headquarters objected that the risk to the air transports supplying the fighters at the field would be too great. Coningham, convinced the plan would work, promised to protect the supply aircraft with his fighters; he received a reluctant approval. In early November, the RAF's No. 2 Armoured Car Company drove west unobserved over the forbidding terrain. They would give light AA protection for the fighter headquarters at the field and a ground detection screen 50 miles out to the north. On November 12, the RAF flew supplies and ground personnel to the landing ground. On the 13th, two Hurricane squadrons landed, refueled, and took off to attack Axis lines of retreat. For three days the British fighters shot up the crowded roads along the coast. In addition, they made surprise raids on at least two airfields—Agedabia on November 14 and

151

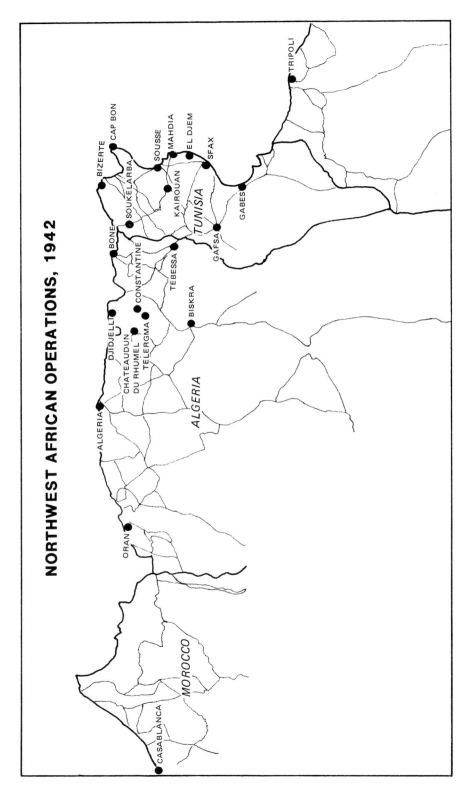

# NORTHWEST AFRICAN OPERATIONS, 1942

TRIPOLI

CAP BON
BIZERTE
SOUSSE
MAHDIA
EL DJEM
SFAX
SOUKELARBA
KAIROUAN
*TUNISIA*
GABES
BONE
GAFSA
CONSTANTINE
TEBESSA
DJIDJELLI
BISKRA
CHATEAUDUN
DU RHUMEL
TELERGMA
ALGERIA
*ALGERIA*
ORAN
*MOROCCO*
CASABLANCA

**Map 14**

Giala on the 15th. Pilots reported heavy damage to both the road traffic and the air bases.[23] By the 15th, the thoroughly aroused enemy sent ground and air units to find and destroy the British base, which beat off an approaching Italian artillery unit, inflicting heavy losses. Coningham abandoned LG 125 by noon on November 16. Two fighter squadrons were not enough to be decisive, but they disrupted the Axis retreat and hammered the morale of the defeated army. The 21st *Panzer* Division's report for the period noted heavy air attacks on nearby units to the south; many of these attacks were probably made by Hurricanes from the mid-desert landing ground. The British decision to use the field took agility and daring, for it was almost entirely lacking conventional warning and air defense equipment. The RAF moved in stealthily, operated with great success for four days, and deftly withdrew.[24]

Throughout the time they pressed the retreating Axis forces, the Allied commanders capitalized on ULTRA and their own air superiority. They knew the extent to which interdiction from Malta sapped the fuel and supply of their opponents. The result was an effective campaign that denied air support to Rommel's army. During the period October 24–November 2, the *Luftwaffe*'s daily sorties exceeded 200 only once, on October 31. On the 24th, just 107 sorties were flown. The low numbers indicated not only gasoline shortages, but also pilot fatigue and the heavy punishment meted out by the RAF and the Americans. General Sir Bernard L. Montgomery, the Eighth Army's new commander, drove west in collaboration with the RAF. He forced Rommel, now extremely short of fuel, into a long retreat to Tunis.[25] (*Map 14*)

## The Desert *Luftwaffe*

On the German side in North Africa, the relationship between air and ground commanders diluted German efforts. Rommel described the problem in organizational terms: "One thing that worked very seriously against us was the fact that the *Luftwaffe* in Africa was not subordinate to the *Afrika Korps*."[26] The root cause was the continuing friction between Rommel and senior German air officers and complicated equipment and organizational deficiencies that prevented the formation of a responsive, mutually supporting headquarters so apparent under Tedder's leadership. Unlike the British and later the Allies in North Africa, the Germans were unable to unify the control of air power within their African forces. Rommel's chain of command ran through the Italian High Command in Africa to the *Commando Supremo* in Rome. The *Luftwaffe*'s command lines, however, went from North Africa directly to Kesselring in Rome. Within the German air elements in Africa, the ground organization, including flak, was separate from the fliers and responsible not to Germany's African air commander, but to *Luftflotte* II in Rome. The Axis alliance did not establish a clear theater command responsibility for African operations until the final battle in Tunisia.* Regardless of Kesselring's superior position as *Oberbefehlshaber Süd* and their usually genial personal relationship, Rommel did not always take him too seriously. Rommel also distrusted the Italian field commanders. Believing that they leaked his plans to the British, he often acted without consulting his Italian superiors or subordinates. The Desert Fox also had a tendency to communicate directly with Berlin, bypassing all intervening commands. The upshot of the situation in Africa was an early estrangement between Rommel and his air support—to the detriment of both.[27]

In contrast with the British practice, the Axis' ground and air forces did not have adjacent operations centers. During most of the fighting in 1941, Froelich kept his headquarters at the major airfield then in use. His successor, Brig. Gen. Otto Hoffman von Waldau, never improved on this. Thus, while Rommel was operating at Tobruk or in Egypt, the *Fliegerführer Afrika* (Air Commander, Africa) was usually at Derna, more than one hundred miles west of Tobruk. With no air liaison officer on Rommel's staff, the air commander could not keep up to date on the movement of friendly forces or easily track enemy units that could threaten his operation.[28]

German military doctrine called for close coordination between Army and Air Force, but practical considerations overrode the printed manual, this time with serious consequences. *Luftwaffe* Directive 16, published in 1940, called emphatically for the Air Force to achieve air superiority at the start of a campaign. However, Hitler emphasized instead that air units primarily provide close air support for maneuvering ground forces, and when Froelich went to Africa, he was told that his main mission was "maximum support of the army units," not seizure of air superiority. While trying to resolve coordination problems, the Air Commander, Africa, continued to receive instructions from Kesselring which placed both convoy protection and close air support ahead of air superiority in mission priority.[29]

Prior to the war, the *Luftwaffe* had not prepared a ground based fighter control system. The service tried three different systems between 1939 and 1942; none worked very well. One of the most serious unresolved problems was the development of an IFF capability that could interface with and mark friendly aircraft on a radar operator's screen. In 1941, the Germans used a radar directed system in France. Shortly thereafter, they started using radar controlled fighters to defend Germany. To a lesser extent this was also seen on the Eastern Front in Russia, but tactical intercept control systems,

---

* The *Luftwaffe*'s combat structure, organized in terms of fronts, was unlike that of the Allies, based on theaters. When several commanding generals worked on a front, their operational responsibilities were divided according to area or duty.

such as those employed by the RAF in the Western Desert, were absent from the German theater organization. Day fighters were scrambled when German radar picked up approaching intruders, but after receiving directions on approximate distance and bearing, the pilots were on their own.[30]

Not only was radar's use retarded, but the Germans also had a deficient aircraft reporting service in North Africa. Air and ground patrols went out, but, von Waldau noted, "British aircraft approaching over a wide area cannot be located." Improvements were made over the next year, however, they remained inadequate by September 1942. At least two radar stations were in use near El Alamein in 1942, but they seem to have been intended only to warn the advance forces of aircraft approaching from British bases. Once the planes passed on a flight to the west, the stations did not track their courses. In May 1941, a squadron of radar equipped Me110 night fighters came to Benghazi to protect the port and airfield. The Me110s were used, however, for reconnaissance and close air support, and never succeeded in their intended mission.[31]

To correct the problem, and to improve operations and defense in general, the *Luftwaffe*'s fighters in Africa were grouped under the control of a *Jagdfliegerführer* (*Jafü*, literally, a fighter leader or commander), who provided a specialized staff to plan for and support combat flying. The *Jafü*'s office coordinated fire of flak batteries near air bases and with its communications net, sent aircraft to attack RAF bases or intercept flights of enemy aircraft. Analogous to Tedder's mobile operations center, the fighter commander control system worked rather well within its limited framework. It might have compared favorably with that of the RAF, had it not been for the lack of liaison between the services and a shortage of almost all varieties of supplies, parts, fuel, and aircraft because of interdiction of convoys from the British flanking position on Malta and the demands of the Russian front.[32]

Throughout the campaign in Africa the *Luftwaffe* could not match the RAF's ability to move quickly. The smallest German fighter unit capable of shifting operations from base to base was the *Gruppe*, usually composed of two or three squadrons totaling some forty aircraft. Station changes were preceded by an advance party which arrived at the new location a day or two before the move. After the aircraft flew to the new airfield, the remainder of the command and support people followed by truck. Only rarely did a single squadron move, and then under unusual circumstances. The German system was more cumbersome than the British and could not match it for speed and efficiency. During February 1942, while Rommel advanced toward Egypt, the lack of squadron mobility caused the Axis to forfeit air superiority over Cyrenaica. Lacking motor transport for their service echelons, the air forces could not keep up with the rapidly maneuvering ground forces. When *Luftwaffe* and Italian squadrons arrived at Benghazi, Derna, and then Martuba, they were left exposed. Fortunately for the Germans, the RAF was sending aircraft to the Far East and India to meet the specter of Japanese seizure of Singapore. The rapid British withdrawal in fact gave the *Luftwaffe* an opportunity to destroy Air Vice Marshal Coningham's tactical air force on the ground at this juncture, but German air elements could not pull themselves together and strike the vulberable bases.[33]

Relying heavily on its own ground based weapons for base defense, the *Luftwaffe* brought flak units to Libya early. Shortly after Rommel's arrival and before most German army units were in place, there were five and a half motorized battalions of AA guns (subsequently organized as the 19th Flak Division) and a mobile flak gun repair shop in Africa. The German AA quickly gained a reputation among RAF pilots for accuracy. No less impressed were the Eighth Army's tank men who experienced the fire of the 88-mm batteries used against them. The German Army frequently commandeered 88-mm and 37-mm flak guns, as their range, muzzle velocity, and flat trajectory made them ideal for tank killing. When the German Army did not take AA weapon units for its own use, Axis airfields were well defended by flak, radar, and searchlights, but their abrupt removal from air defense left gaps not readily filled. To avoid effective German fire, British pilots sought to attack the guns either at very low altitude or between the 3,500 foot maximum range of the 37-mm guns and the lowest altitude at which the 88-mm could be used, about 9,000 feet.* In the latter case, bombers joined the attacks to keep the gunners pinned down. Finding the defending gun batteries was not easy, for they were spread out and away from the flying fields.[34]

Although Axis air base defenders usually had enough guns, they failed to use camouflage to their advantage. This too, may have been due to interdiction of shipping by the RAF's Malta air force, for nets, paint, and equipment were all in short supply. German motor vehicles and aircraft were often not repainted from the dark gray-green used in northern Europe. The dark color gave protection during the short wet season, but with the summer months light earth tones would have been far more effective. Little attempt was made to conceal dispersed aircraft and AA guns were not always hidden. Fuel storage, however, was better concealed; it was kept in small caches scattered over wide areas. The few such sites located by British aerial reconnaissance were well covered by brush and earth. Fuel containers, rather small in size, were more easily concealed in the terrain; the larger gun pits and airplanes were not.[35]

The German guns protecting airfields outnumbered those of the British in the Western Desert, but antiaircraft artillery was necessarily a reactive

---

* Minimum effective range was governed by the elevation of the gun barrel, fuze design, speed of the target, and of ability of the gun crews to traverse the guns.

TABLE 17

## Axis Air Forces in Africa
## May 1942

### German Air Force

| | Strength |
|---|---|
| Reconnaissance | |
| 4th Short Range *Staffel* (Me109, Me110) | 21 |
| 1st Long Range *Staffel*/121st *Gruppe* (Ju88, Me109) | 13 |
| | |
| Dive Bomber | |
| 3rd Bomber *Geschwader* Hq. (Me110, He111) | 2 |
| 1st *Gruppe*/3rd *Geschwader* (Ju87) | 44 |
| | |
| Twin Engine Fighter | |
| 7th Sq./26th *Geschwader* (Me110) | 12 |
| 9th Sq./26th *Geschwader* (Me110) | 11 |
| | |
| Single Engine Fighter | |
| 1st *Gruppe*/27th *Geschwader* (Me109) | 34 |
| 2nd *Gruppe*/27th *Geschwader* (Me109) | 31 |
| 3rd *Gruppe*/27th *Geschwader* (Me109) | 30 |
| Fighter-bomber *Gruppe*/27th *Geschwader* (Me109) | 10 |
| | |
| Night Fighter | |
| 2nd Sq./2 NF *Gruppe* (Ju88) | 9 |
| | |
| Bombers | |
| 12th Sq./1st *Luftwaffe* Area Command (Ju88) | 17 |
| | 234 |

### Italian Air Force

| | |
|---|---|
| 1 Ground Attack Wing | 90 |
| 1 Fighter Wing | 75 |
| Reconnaissance, misc. | 20 |
| | 185 |

Support and reinforcements were available from elsewhere in the Mediterranean area. Normally half the assigned aircraft were operational at any one time.

**Source:** Felmy, "The GAF in the Mediterranean Theater of War"

TABLE 18

# Royal Air Force in Africa
# May 1942

## Air HQ Western Desert

No. 211 Group (Fighters)—Gambut

| | | |
|---|---|---|
| 233 Wing | | |
| 2 Sq (So. African) | Maaten Bagush, L.G.* 115 | Tomahawks |
| 4 Sq (So. African) | Maaten Bagush, L.G. 115 | Tomahawks |
| 260 Sq | Maaten Bagush, L.G. 115 | Kittyhawks |
| 239 Wing | | |
| 3 Sq (RAAF) | Sidi Haneish, L.G. 12 | Kittyhawks |
| 112 Sq | Sidi Haneish, L.G. 12 | Kittyhawks |
| 450 Sq (RAAF) | Sidi Haneish, L.G. 12 | Kittyhawks |
| 243 Wing | | |
| 33 Sq | Sidi Haneish, L.G. 13 | Kittyhawks |
| 73 Sq | Sidi Haneish, L.G. 13 | Hurricanes |
| 80 Sq | Sidi Haneish, L.G. 13 | Hurricanes |
| 274 Sq | Gambut | Hurricanes |
| 805 Sq (Fleet Air) | Maaten Bagush, L.G. 14 | Martlets |
| 889 Sq (Fleet Air) | Fuka Satellite | Fulmars |
| 3 Wing (So. African) | | |
| 12 Sq (So. African) | Qotafiya | Bostons |
| 24 Sq (So. African) | Qotafiya | Bostons |
| Detached Squadrons | | |
| 1 Air Ambulance | Western Desert | |
| 2 Flight (Photo Rec) | Western Desert | Various |
| 15 Sq (So. African) | Amriya, L.G. 98 | Blenheim Fighters |
| 21 Sq (So. African) | Amriya, L.G. 99 | Baltimores |
| 40 Sq (So. African) | Sidi Azeiz | Hurricanes |
| 60 Sq (So. African) | Ahbassia | Marylands |
| 208 Sq | Sidi Azeiz | Hurricanes |
| 250 Sq | Sidi Haneish, L.G. 12 | Hurricanes |

No. 205 Group (Bombers)—Ismailia

| | | |
|---|---|---|
| 231 Wing | | |
| 37 Sq | El Daba | Wellingtons |
| 70 Sq | El Daba | Wellingtons |
| 236 Wing | | |
| 104 Sq | El Daba, L.G. 106 | Wellingtons |
| 147 Sq | L.G. 224 | Wellingtons |
| 148 Sq | El Daba, L.G. 106 | Wellingtons |

TABLE 18 (Continued):

| 238 Wing | | |
|---|---|---|
| 38 Sq | Shallufa | Wellingtons |
| 40 Sq | Shallufa | Wellingtons |
| 242 Wing | | |
| 108 Sq | Fayid | Wellingtons |

\* Landing Ground

No 201 Group with 11 squadrons of Beauforts, Blenheims, Dorniers, Ansons and Beaufighters in Alexandria, and 15 assorted squadrons of Spitfires, Hurricanes, Beauforts, and Tomahawks assigned to Air Hq Egypt. All were available for reinforcement.

Most squadrons had 12 or 18 aircraft assigned, but this varied greatly depending on intensity of combat and repair or service facilities available.

Source: Rept., "RAF Operations in the Western Desert and Mediterranean," Hq RAF Middle East

force, subject to the flow of highly mobile fighting. After October 1942, as the weight of British forces sent the Axis retreating a thousand miles toward Tunis, the German air base defenders were rendered temporarily impotent. During the course of the retreat the *Luftwaffe*'s 19th Flak Division and its 88-mm guns came under control of the Army as an antitank force and was no longer able to protect bases and ports. With the Allied landings in Morocco and Algeria in November 1942, the German and Italian Air Forces began the final battle for North Africa.[36]

## TORCH and the Drive to Tunis

Late in 1942, a redirection of Anglo-American strategy took the western allied war effort to North Africa. Early in the year, the American Chiefs of Staff planned for a contingency invasion of Europe should the Russians appear on the verge of collapse. The British saw little possibility of success for such a venture. Prime Minister Churchill sought to win the fight in Egypt and deny the Vichy French regime its North African possessions. He proposed instead the seizure of those territories to President Roosevelt. This thrust would place a force in Rommel's rear and inject Allied influence into the western end of the Mediterranean.[37]

The Germans controlled Northwest Africa through an Armistice Commission set up in 1940 to enforce the neutrality of Morocco, Algeria, and Tunisia. The French actually administered the region with the limited military forces allowed them by the imposed 1940 agreement. No Axis forces were in French North Africa, but it was obvious that Germany and Italy could occupy both it and Vichy France at Hitler's whim. Covert diplomacy aimed at gaining French acquiescence to the landings on the Moroccan Atlantic coast and at Oran and Algiers were only partially successful. Though negotiators presented the enterprise as a primarily American one, the French were still bitter at the memory of their apparent abandonment by the British in 1940 and Royal Navy's later attack on the French fleet at Oran. Amid these uncertainties, Operation TORCH began.[38]

The landings took place on the morning of November 8, 1942. A lack of shipping reduced the size of the forces originally planned for TORCH, but the troops got ashore at all three invasion points against enough resistance to rescue French honor. An American naval task force, with the carrier *Ranger* and three escort carriers, provided air cover for the landings in Morocco and seizure of airfields at Port Lyautey and Casablanca. The escort carrier *Chenango* carried P–40s of the 33rd Fighter Group, a contingent of Brig. Gen. James H. Doolittle's Twelfth Air Force. The 33rd was to fly from the carrier to fields near Casablanca. The Royal Air Force provided the newly formed Eastern Air Command, under Air Vice Marshal Sir William A. M. Welsh. The two Allied air forces were organized as complete units, capable of performing several missions. Each was to carry out strategic bombing, counterair, coastal patrol, and similar duties in its geographical area.[39]

At the landing sites, French ground and coastal defenses were potentially strong. Air defenses were active at first, but easily overcome. The Germans had permitted only a few obsolete AA weapons among the French defenses. Radar was not to be found. American aircraft losses in Morocco were due largely to inexperienced pilots' landings on fields damaged by naval shells. The French agreed to an armistice with the Allies, and on November 11, their units joined the drive against the Axis. The Allies turned their attention east hoping to capture Tunis by the end of December.[40]

In support of the offensive, eastern Algeria became the center of air action. Paved runways there were rare, hard surfaced parking rarer; everywhere a sticky mud quickly trapped any airplane taxiing into it. The resulting congestion presented exceptional targets for enemy bombers. On November 18, Maison Blanche airfield, near Algiers, received one of the first air attacks. Eighteen airplanes of the 14th Fighter Group were badly damaged. Overcrowding prevented some fighters from taking off to engage the *Luftwaffe*. British and American engineers began to lay out new airdromes and bring in equipment, but a severe shortage of road and rail transportation and the Allies' ignorance of terrain and soil conditions impeded construction.[41]

The burden of defending against air attack devolved early on the RAF and the AA units of the British First Army; theirs was the only radar

**Wreckage of American B–17s at Maison Blanche, Algeria, on November 21, 1942. The absence of any protection left these aircraft vulnerable to a German strike.**

available until early 1943. Most American radar sets sent to the three Signal Aircraft Warning battalions were slow in arriving, sometimes several months late. Moreover, they were too delicate to unload over beaches and too heavy to be easily transported overland, save over good roads. Unlike the U.S. Marine Corps, which had brought similar equipment to Guadalcanal a few months previously, the U.S. Army was not yet accomplished at amphibious operations. When American radar arrived it was used mostly along the coast west of Algiers. Mountains and terrain variations caused echoes or gaps in coverage, and some sets were moved a dozen times until they were satisfactorily placed. For an interim solution to the many air defense warning problems, the Allies turned to British ULTRA and Y-Service intelligence to report impending German air attacks on bases in Algeria. Intelligence officers could not predict every raid, and every precaution was taken to avoid tipping off the Germans that their messages were being read. Nevertheless, the results were satisfactory and knowledge of the *Luftwaffe*'s order of battle was extensive. The signals intelligence staff at Allied Force Headquarters was quickly increased in size and function.[42]

Radar siting difficulties were overcome as the Allies gained experience, but the early problems with operating the systems were more serious. No entirely satisfactory solutions were found during the North African campaign. The Eastern Air Command staff had no officer responsible for coordinating radar, fighter operations, and communications. On November 21, Group Capt. D.E.W. Atcherly reported to Welsh that, among other problems, the situation created "an air of uncertainty, no one being entirely certain of his own individual responsibility in setting up of the [defensive]

**Algerian laborers help stack pierced steel planking for use in airfield construction on the advance to Tunisia.**

fighter coverage." More than three weeks were needed to establish radar detection around Algiers, the stations then being connected to Maison Blanche airfield "somewhat nebulously" by unreliable field telephone. Station operators were not sure they could reach the air base when necessary.[43]

As a result of earlier wartime experiences, the British established interservice rules for operational control of air defense in overseas areas. When an air defense system was created in major operating areas, the air officer commanding controlled all defense resources including guns, fighters, radar, and searchlights. At isolated bases the service with the predominant interest would appoint a defense commander. Apparently this was not clearly understood in Northwest Africa, for the Chiefs of Staff in London found it necessary to reiterate the policy in a message to their forces. The less experienced Americans had an even vaguer understanding of tactical air defense. The Signal Corps' air warning service contingent assigned to XII Fighter Command headquarters arrived in Casablanca on November 19. From its arrival until April 11, 1943, the organization moved from station to station without apparent purpose, performing routine drill and details, finally taking over duties of the 412th Signal Company, which were not related to air warning.[44]

In addition to a questionable warning system, active air defenses for the Allied bases in Eastern Algeria and Tunisia were poor or nonexistent. Thelepte airfield had no warning net, only four 40-mm Bofors, and four .50 caliber machine guns to ward off attackers, and had to depend on expensive daylight fighter patrols for protection. By late December 1942, Biskra airfield had just twelve .50 caliber machine guns and an air warning system for the British and American bases had yet to be organized. Except for a few RAF Regiment AA flights, Air Marshal Welsh did not command AA defenses at his airfields; operational control of the heavy and medium guns was retained by the armies.[45]

Lacking the battle experience of the Western Desert, the Allies in Northwest Africa did not work as closely as necessary. During the first two years of desert fighting, the British learned that concerted air attacks on air bases made below 4,000 feet could be deflected only by heavy defenses. At least a dozen 40-mm guns, and another twenty to twenty-six positions armed with 20-mm cannon and machine guns were needed. Double or quadruple mounted light guns were best. Many extra firing positions had to be prepared in advance as the guns had to be moved often; once seen by pilots or reconnaissance cameras they could be successfully attacked. Above all, training in the proper use of weapons was essential. Although the Air Ministry prepared studies incorporating battle experiences and gun and radar operating standards, neither Allied army in North Africa drew upon the knowledge until forced to do so by the weight of German and Italian attacks. Inability to perform well on offense or to protect friendly forces made the Allies review doctrine on use of tactical aviation.[46]

In mid-February 1943, the Allies unified their military organization in North Africa. The air component, under Tedder, was named Mediterranean Air Command; the ground echelon became the 18th Army Group. Gen. Dwight D. Eisenhower's reorganization was intended to consolidate the Allied position in preparation for an invasion of Italy and drew heavily on British experience and leadership.[47]

The Mediterranean Air Command was not a strong, coherent air force, however. Its primary purpose was to supervise planning and overall air operations, but its leaders now set about changing the Allied view of the use of air power. Most of the senior officers of both armies and air forces in Northwest Africa were relatively inexperienced in combat. Many army commanders believed firmly in almost constant air cover, available on call, to fend off enemy airplanes. Doolittle and Welsh were unable to influence those views, and it took the new command structure to bring about a significant change. Tedder and Air Marshal Sir Charles Portal argued the air arm's first job was to destroy an enemy air force and then concentrate to destroy the enemy army's ability to reinforce and continue the battle. Success in the air would protect both ground forces and air bases from air attack. The contrary practice of using air power to try to defend army positions simply dissipated scarce resources. The air marshals' achievements in the Western Desert loomed large in the continuing debate. In mid-February General Montgomery and Air Vice Marshal Coningham spoke to many of the senior

**Allied military leaders at Casablanca Conference, January 1943.** *Front row, left to right*, **General Dwight D. Eisenhower, Air Chief Marshal Arthur W. Tedder, General Air Harold Alexander, Admiral Sir Andrew Cunningham.** *Rear*, **Harold MacMillan, Maj. Gen. Walter B. Smith and two British officers.**

officers at a meeting in Tripoli, convincing them, too, of the need to change the employment of aviation. Coningham characterized close air-ground cooperation in the Western Desert by citing examples of rapid deployments to remote landing grounds, sometimes with supporting armor elements.[48]

Subordinate to the Mediterranean Air Command were Middle East Air Command, RAF Malta Air Command, and the American Northwest African Air Forces (NAAF). Within NAAF, led by Maj. Gen. Carl Spaatz, were several subcommands, two of which were responsible for air defense: Northwest African Coastal Air Force in all areas up to a line fifty miles from the front, and Northwest African Tactical Air Force forward of that line. Within Allied Force Headquarters an Antiaircraft and Coast Defense (AA and CD) Section was created and charged with coordinating defensive fire zones and allocating and controlling AA weapons within the theater. Even with the reorganization, however, the problems caused by inexperience and the formerly fragmented command structure could not be rectified at once.[49]

Not only had the Allies neglected warning and defense systems, but training of radar operators was deficient. The U.S. Army usually assigned less well educated men to operate and repair the Signal Corps' radar sets than did the British. The Royal Air Force required radar operators to be college graduates with appropriate civilian experience. On the other hand, few of the U.S. Army Air Force's operators were high school graduates and repairmen were of similar caliber. Captain August W. Mysing, a fighter controller with the American 3rd Air Defense Wing, remarked, "Our radar units weren't worth a dime, and if it hadn't been for some English units with us, we would not have been operational. I believe the [U.S.] personnel were green and didn't know how to maintain the apparatus or read the scope." Brig. Gen. Lyman L. Lemnitzer, commander of the 34th Coast Artillery Brigade, described the Signal Corps' radar maintenance as "non-existent . . . one of the blackest situations of [the] campaign." The experience gained by the British in North African fighting gave them the basis of a plan to correct the problems, although it took months—in fact until after the conclusion of the campaign—to resolve them all. The command also transferred many skilled people from Egypt to form a core of repair and operations specialists on the NAAF staff.[50]

The rapid Allied advance to the east after the November landings left behind the airfield defense and warning units set up at the Allies' first Northwest African bases. On March 31, Northwest African Strategic Air Forces found its bases near Constantine, Algeria, without a warning service. The commander appealed to General Spaatz to provide one to avoid a "successful attack by the enemy upon our airdromes [which] would decimate . . . our heaviest air striking forces." In fact, those bases were already under frequent attack. Spaatz's staff referred the warning problem to Northwest African Coastal Air Force, which was able to offer little immediate aid other than to change the reporting circuits to increase warning time for attacks approaching from directly east, that is, from Bizerte and Tunis. The radar coverage for the Strategic Air Forces' bases continued to have holes, however, since aircraft attacking from fields in southern Tunisia could not be detected.[51]

Eventually, British mobile radar units were linked by radio or telephone to the Coastal Air Force's 3rd Air Defense Wing or 242 Group, which launched fighter interceptors. Two British AA brigades sent some guns for base protection and assigned the American 34th Coast Artillery Brigade, with its 192 40-mm guns, to the task.[52]

Before the war and through 1940, the Royal Air Force depended on the British Army for both AA and ground airdrome defense. During the summer of 1940, some bases in England augmented their defense with machine guns manned by RAF airmen. It became more and more apparent, however, that the Army had neither the men nor the organization to continue in the

**D–7 bulldozer fills crater torn into a North African airfield. Rapid repairs ensured near continuous operations.**

base defense role. Realizing that an army commander in combat would almost always be forced to support his own units before those of another service, the RAF began to take a more active interest in protecting its bases from both air and ground attack. Inability to defend air fields in Greece followed by the loss of Crete in May 1941, gave added impetus to the movement. The dangers of depending on an *ad hoc* ground defense, especially when facing an airborne or highly mobile enemy, had been clearly illustrated on Crete when the Germans seized Maleme airfield and used it to reinforce their assault units. In February 1942, after extensive study of how best to solve the problem, the Royal Air Force formed the Royal Air Force Regiment. It was intended to be a highly mobile organization capable of protecting airfields from both ground and air attack. The Air Ministry handled recruiting, equipping, and deploying the new unit, although the Army provided its first commander and much of its original training. The Regiment was first used in England, but the clear need for similar units overseas was readily apparent.[53] Several of the RAF Regiment's well trained defense squadrons accompanied the Allied force to Algeria. In addition, it sent five separate light AA flights armed with air transportable 20-mm

166

cannon. One of the flights was quickly deployed with No. 322 Fighter Wing to Bone airdrome, where it immediately engaged the attacking *Luftwaffe*. In a short time its commander and four gunners were killed. Other AA flights were assigned to airdromes near Canrobert and Souk el Arba.[54]

The light AA flights were attached to the RAF Regiment's ground defense squadrons. Early in 1943 the squadrons and AA flights became responsible for seizing forward landing grounds as the armies advanced. After clearing mines and mopping up stray enemy forces in the immediate area, the units set up base defenses. Because the air defense flights were not heavily armed, usually having only nine 20-mm cannon and three .303-caliber Browning machine guns, they supplemented rather than replaced fully the army AA. Often, however, the Regiment's AA flights were the only defenders at a newly acquired and operating airfield for some time. They quickly gained a reputation for effective work.[55]

In January 1943, the British moved two mobile radar stations through their front lines and then by land to Cap Serrat to control air attacks on the German airlift of men and supplies into Tunis. One ground defense squadron and an AA flight went along to protect the equipment. Since the stations were in an area where the *Luftwaffe* held air superiority, they were often attacked *en route*. The AA flight's gunners shot down at least one attacking FW 190 fighter. Once at Cap Serrat the unit camouflaged its radar sets and supporting equipment, the AA guns kept silent, and the ground defenders moved out as a protective screen blocking frequent Axis patrols. The radar stations functioned unseen until March 3, when a German offensive forced them to evacuate to the west.[56]

So successful were the AA flights that by the end of 1942 the British formed twenty-four more in North Africa. In a reorganization of May 1943, the twenty-nine flights became eleven light antiaircraft squadrons, three fully mobile, each with twenty-four 20-mm cannon. The eight remaining squadrons temporarily used twenty-nine .303-caliber machine guns apiece and enough vehicles to move one flight at a time. The intent was to use the partially mobile units at rear bases or areas not susceptible to heavy attack, whereas the squadrons with cannon helped defend the more heavily used airfields and would accompany the first Allied forces to Sicily.[57]

In addition to the RAF Regiment, other base defense improvements appeared as the Allied Force reorganization took root. Early in February 1943, Allied Force Headquarters (AFHQ) and Eastern Air Command, responding to Portal's reminder about air defense control, established specified air defense areas. By spring 1943, the areas were fully developed, guided by the new Antiaircraft and Coast Defense Committee, chaired by Maj. Gen. R. B. Pargiter, Eisenhower's new antiaircraft chief. Inner Artillery Zones (IAZ) were designated at certain locations that could best be defended only by antiaircraft guns. Any aircraft entering such a zone was to be

**British Bofors gun crew on guard on a beach near Tripoli. A downed Italian Macchi fighter rests where its pilot left it in the sand.**

U.S. Army Air Defense Museum.

engaged by gunfire unless the local British or American fighter controller directed otherwise. By the use of code words and improved communications, the Allies closely coordinated AA fire and fighter operations. Gun Defended Areas (GDA) were less important locations where heavy antiaircraft weapons were in place and where an inner artillery zone was not normally in use. When necessary, friendly aircraft could enter a GDA after identifying themselves. Allied Force Headquarters further specified that an IAZ could exist within a Gun Defended Area, and specific rules of engagement, varying according to the situation, governed defensive fire in such an area. Special Areas were the designated third category, established to protect the most important, vulnerable, or unusual sites. Flying discipline was stressed and became more detailed over the next few months to accommodate AA gunners, who had to determine that a plane was hostile before they fired. Pilots were enjoined from flying low over troop locations without previous coordination, from diving toward bases out of the sun (a favored mode of attack), and from test firing weapons except in specific places. In addition, aviators were to approach GDAs through specified corridors.[58]

Air defense sectors for Northwest Africa were established under the control of Coastal Air Force. The British and Americans assigned fighter squadrons to each sector and supporting command structures improved. Sector commanders were air officers with operational control of AA in their areas. The USAAF redesignated its Composite Wings in Morocco and Algeria as the 1st, 2nd, and 3rd Air Defense Wings; aircraft warning services were integrated in their structure. NATAF also operated fighter control sectors, protecting its bases with AA and aircraft within its fifty mile area along the front. Most important, the Allied pilots carried the offensive to the German and Italian airdromes, destroying the enemy air force by high and low level bombing of its airfields, and in air to air combat. Each week the attacks increased in intensity. Airfields within the shrinking German perimeter became pitted with craters and covered by rubble and wrecked equipment. Axis air strikes at Allied airfields ceased in April, and remaining enemy air forces were thrown into desperate support of the army. American fighter groups, accustomed to operating independently, at first chafed at flying within the rules. This was overcome in time, and by the capture of Tunis on May 13, the Allied air defense, combined with air superiority, provided safe operational bases.[59]

## The Axis Defense Of Tunisia

In September 1942, in a major change, Kesselring became commander of all German forces in the Mediterranean, except for Rommel's army, still under nominal Italian control. Maritime transportation to North Africa continued under the direction of the *Commando Supremo.* German success depended upon a rapid buildup of reinforcements for Rommel and keeping the new aggregate supplied with food, fuel, equipment, and ammunition. On November 9, 1942, the *Luftwaffe* began moving to airfields in northern Tunisia; army units followed shortly in strength unexpected by the Allies. Brig. Gen. Martin Harlinghausen, *Fliegerführer Tunis,* led 3 fighter *Gruppen,* 1 dive bomber *Gruppe,* and a reconnaissance *Staffel* to Tunis with a single flak regiment giving AA protection. By December, Axis air strength in Tunisia grew to 850 planes with strong ground-attack capability. The entire *Kampfgeschwader* 76, with 90 airplanes, flew from the Caucasus to Bizerte. German Army units were brought to Tunisia faster and in much larger numbers than the Allies anticipated. By the time they were ready to move on Tunis, the Allies had lost the race. Now they had to fight to take the country; gone was the chance to scoop Rommel and his men quickly into the bag.[60]

Twenty-two airfields of varying size and construction were available to the *Luftwaffe* and *Regia Aeronautica* throughout Tunisia. The most important, at Tunis, Bizerte, Gabes, Sfax, and Sousse, were heavily defended. Moreover, major airfields in Sicily and the lower Italian peninsula, no more than 170 miles away supported and reinforced the bases in Tunisia. The single AA regiment at Tunis soon grew into the 20th Flak Division, while the 19th Flak Division continued its largely antiarmor role in the south with Rommel. In addition to the 19th and 20th Divisions, Italian fighters and AA defended their bases, though the Germans did not consider their comrades in arms effective. If nothing else, the Italian weapons increased the total number of guns available. The relatively small area which the Axis attempted to hold provided several advantages. Fighters could be more effectively deployed and radar could survey virtually all approaches used by enemy attackers.[61]

German radar units, now much more efficiently used than in the Western Desert, established a warning net connected by an excellent communications system. The Germans moved several *Freya* sets to Tunisia, siting ten of these installations in such a way that they had a range of up to 160 miles. The radar did not have GCI ability, but the Germans were able to detect impending air strikes—some as much as two hours in advance, while the Allied groups were still assembling after take off.[62]

German reinforcement could not stave off defeat indefinitely. By December 1942, Hitler had still failed to conquer Malta. RAF and USAAF squadrons, based ever closer to their targets in the Mediterranean, attacked air bases in Sicily, Tunis, and Bizerte, disrupting fighter operations and the airlift of men and equipment. Of nearly 500 airplanes on overcrowded bases in Sicily, 62 were reported destroyed between April 4 and 6, 1943, alone.[63]

German military studies on the southern theater returned constantly to the difficulty of shipping supplies across the Mediterranean. From June 1941 on, Italian shipping could not meet demands in the face of Malta's air strikes, and supply starved German forces in Africa rarely operated at full effectiveness. The Allies were aware of their enemy's plight and attacked ships and ports relentlessly. Intercepted *Enigma* messages gave virtually complete information on shipping losses, and by March 1943, Allied air attacks on the sea supply routes became decisive.[64]

Axis attempts to hold a constricted base in Africa were further eroded by Allied heavy bombers. Flying near 30,000 feet, they were above the effective range of most of the German 88-mm guns, only the newer models of which could reach that height. As their perimeter contracted in Tunisia, the Germans used half of the 138 guns available as antiarmor weapons, severely restricting the base defenders. The constant need to fly fighters to cover for close air support missions, protect airlift aircraft, or intercept high flying bombers strained German pilots and planes and rapidly used up fuel and spare parts.[65]

TABLE 19

## Axis Mediterranean Air Strength
## Tunisian Air Corps
## April 1943

|  | Strength |
|---|---|
| 53rd Single Engine Fighter *Geschwader* (Me109) | 90 |
| 77th Single Engine Fighter *Geschwader* (Me109) | 90 |
| 3rd *Gruppe*/1st Close Support *Geschwader* (Me109) | 25 |
| 3rd *Gruppe*/4th Close Support *Geschwader* (FW190) | 25 |
| 2nd and 4th *Staffeln*/14th Recce. *Gruppe* (Me109) | 16 |
| Desert Rescue *Staffel* (Fiesler Storch) | 21 |
| Mine Detector *Staffel* (Ju52) | 3 |
|  | 270 |

The *Luftwaffe* could also draw from forces elsewhere in the Mediterranean totaling 767 aircraft capable of immediate deployment.

German Flak Strength in Tunisia (19th and 20th Divisions):

| | |
|---|---|
| 105-mm guns | 4 |
| 88-mm guns | 138 |
| 37-mm guns | 12 |
| 20-mm guns (single barrel) | 208 |
| 20-mm guns (four barrel) | 59 |

The 19th Flak Division was engaged mostly in antitank and army force protection. About half the available 88-mm guns were in that role.

**Sources:** Felmy, "The GAF in the Mediterranean Theater of War"
Air Ministry, German translation VII/25

The German-Italian air force faced heavy odds. In mid-February, *Luftwaffe* intelligence estimated that 2,769 aircraft were closing in from Libya and Algeria. This was short of the mark as the Americans had 1,855 aircraft added to an RAF total of about the same. On the other hand, many German and Italian airplanes used to counter the Allies, such as the Stuka, were obsolete. The demands of the Russian front and home air defense

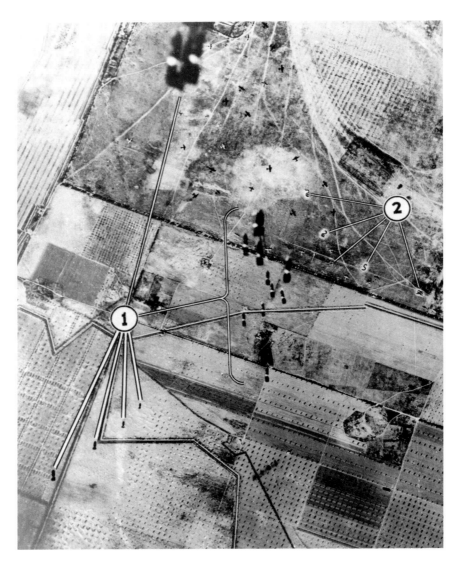

**Allied bombs fall on Axis airfield at Tripoli. Indicators point out bombs falling (1) and aircraft revetments below (2).**

groups severely limited available German reinforcements. During the fighting for Tunisia, Allied air and naval attacks on Mediterranean supply routes kept a choke hold on available fuel and parts.[66]

After mid-March 1943, the *Luftwaffe* in Tunisia was unable to go on the offensive. Air operations continued and some replacement aircraft arrived from Italy, but parts and fuel shortages restricted flying. Only the most important missions could be flown as more and more derelicts collected on the hard pressed bases. The situation worsened in mid-April when the Allies gained complete air superiority and began Operation FLAX. FLAX was Tedder's plan to cut the Axis aerial supply effort. It was based partly on *Enigma* information, but more on the RAF's Y-intercepts. Carefully scrutinizing message traffic, intelligence specialists gave the Allied air force leaders times, routes of flight, and types of aircraft heading for Tunis. Three squadrons of South African Air Force P–40s repeatedly attacked the Ju52s and Me323s, the latter being six engine transports able to lift 40,000 pounds, while other Allied fighters took on Axis escorts. German and Italian air transport losses approached or exceeded those at Stalingrad a few months earlier. In April alone, the Germans lost 125 Ju52s and 23 Me323s; 65 more aircraft were badly damaged.[67]

Fuel and parts now became almost impossible to obtain. As the Allied armies approached Tunis, the Germans increasingly diverted their flak units from AA to ground combat. By April 29, the *Luftwaffe* could no longer find the daily 35 gallons of fuel needed for each of its radar sets and power-generator units. The capability of the German air force declined at an accelerating rate until, on May 8, 1943, surviving air units were withdrawn to Sicily, leaving behind 600 unflyable aircraft. The army held out a few days longer, until May 13. By then, control of the air had long since passed to the Allies who were preparing to invade southern Europe.[68]

## Summary

The keys to successful Royal Air Force operations in the Western Desert were the liaison with Eighth Army and the mobility of the fighter and gun defenses. The British ability to create a profusion of landing grounds in barren, rocky desert greatly compounded German efforts to destroy the RAF. The Germans, on the other hand, lacked both the air organization and warning services that could have given them an opportunity to challenge Allied air superiority. After the fighting west of El Alamein in mid-1942, during which the Eighth Army was badly mauled and pushed back, Rommel wrote, "[On the night of June 30, while pursuing the Eighth Army] . . . we soon heard the guns of British low flyers, which had apparently settled in on their new airfields."[69] The ability to move quickly and the large repair and maintenance facility in Egypt provided the Allies with an air force that could vacate threatened areas, replace battle losses, and quickly repair airplanes. In short, it was an air force that could survive a long battle of attrition.

From November 1942 to May 1943, 2,047 Commonwealth aircraft were destroyed or damaged in the Western Desert. The intense fighting placed a premium on quick replacement. The RAF was forced to ship new airplanes from England or America via the Cape of Good Hope, ferry them through Gibraltar and Malta, or land them from ships at Takoradi, in present day Ghana, and fly them to Cairo. During the same period, the RAF assessed Axis losses at 2,587 destroyed and damaged, but new German and Italian aircraft could fly a short, direct route from Europe or be repaired at Bengazi and Tripoli.[70]

When Air Marshal Coningham spoke to senior Allied officers in February 1943, he characterized the cooperation that enabled the British to seize, prepare, and defend airfields:

> The advanced forces of the spearhead of the 7th Armored Division took with them a landing ground party and one or two specialist personnel. They reached the landing area [at Sedala, 120 miles east of Tripoli] at dusk, and on breaking camp next morning threw off the aerodrome party, 18 to 20 prized Bofors, M. T. and the Ambulance Holding Unit. By nine o'clock word was received that a landing strip was ready. Two squadrons of fighters escorting a transport plane with the necessary RDF and immediate requirements, landed. They flew on their auxiliary tanks which were immediately dropped and they were then at readiness.

By noon the airfield was in full use. By nightfall the AA guns departed, moving another thirty miles to yet other airfields.[71]

The smooth operation evident in the Western Desert was not apparent during the TORCH landings and only rarely during the subsequent campaign in Tunisia. The Allied armies that sailed from England and America were inexperienced, their leaders had yet to try maneuvering a sizable force against a determined enemy. None of the TORCH planners visited Egypt to observe air operations or air defense there, nor did they absorb much information from reports sent home by the RAF. Only two staff officers doing TORCH planning in London thought about use of radar. An equally small section at the USAAF's Fighter Command school in Florida planned deployment of American radar to Northwest Africa. Both British and Americans planning and commanding TORCH operations failed to use the RAF experiences of the previous two years to insure air base security. The failure to prepare was clearly seen in the most significant problem the Allies faced in protecting their bases: poor organization of the air forces and air defense until late in the campaign. The result was the halting employment of air warning and air defense forces in Algeria and western Tunisia. Even after the reorganization there was continued confusion and needless duplication of resources. As late as the end of 1943, Maj. Gen. H. R. Oldfield, AA liaison officer to General Arnold, noted deficiencies in the AA protection of air bases because of cumbersome organization and poor training.[72]

Not all of the Allied efforts were so beset with difficulty. *Enigma* and Y-Service decrypts provided revelations about most of Rommel's secrets. Tedder used ULTRA information and tactical radio interception to formulate FLAX, which delivered the final blow to Axis supply. After the destruction of most of the German-Italian airlift by mid-April 1943, Axis planes flew to Africa only at night, and in greatly reduced numbers. Ironically, Rommel learned from British officer prisoners, a source he regarded as reliable, that Montgomery knew of his plan to attack Alamein on August 25, 1942. He always suspected some disloyal senior Italian officer was passing information to the allies and never dreamed the Allies were reading German message traffic.[73]

Rommel himself shares a heavy burden of blame for the *Luftwaffe*'s setbacks in Africa. He and all of the successive German air commanders in Africa failed to reach an understanding on the use of air power and on the command and control of base defense units until the final reorganization in Tunis in early 1943. Tedder and the British Army commanders, though they had problems initially understanding one another's views on air support before CRUSADER, created a far more efficient and cooperative way of operating. The Commonwealth force reaped rewards in the Western Desert fighting. This was not so for the TORCH forces, whose inexperience and organizational problems caused American air combat losses between November 1942 and April 1943 to mount to unacceptable levels, reaching 666 machines by the end of the campaign. Antiaircraft defenses accounted for only 14 percent of the total, Axis fighters for 80 percent. During the same period the Axis lost 1,183 aircraft to American attack, of which 188, or 16 percent, were hit while on the ground. On the day the Germans surrendered in Tunis, Brig. Gen. Laurence S. Kuter, Deputy Commander of North African Tactical Air Force, sent General Arnold a blistering indictment of the U. S. Army's doctrine on air employment as it existed in Africa before the reorganization and continued to exist both in official doctrine and other theaters.[74]

Kuter saw as the most serious deficiencies the subordination of air forces to ground commanders, inadequate organization of flying commands, and shortages of equipment which prevented, among other things, establishing an air warning system until March 1943. The overall effect, in Kuter's opinion, was an air force "unsound in battle," that exercised a " . . . vague . . . concept of Air Support."[75] The British did not escape his wrath either when he suggested that "the organizational lessons learned by the R.A.F. in the Battle of Brittain [sic] have been applied too broadly and are not appropriate in a mobile situation." In referring to the RAF, though, Kuter was painting with a broad brush, as he was familiar only with the RAF's operations in North Africa under Air Vice Marshal Welsh, not the campaign in the Western Desert. The subsequent changes under Coningham, brought on by the Allied reorganization, had not yet developed fully into the type of organization that succeeded in the Western Desert.[76]

The ability of the Allies to bring enormous resources to bear in ousting the Axis from Africa, to adapt their air and ground organization to the needs of the conflict and to exploit the advantage of cryptanalysis led them to eventual victory. That it took longer than anticipated and cost more than expected was a testament to the importance of organizing the air-ground command relationship. In the summer of 1943, the U.S. Army issued new air-operations guidelines incorporating the experience gained during the first year of war. This new directive adopted in large measure the lessons learned in North Africa, and became the bedrock of air doctrine for the next half century.[77]

# Chapter VI

# The Eastern Front: 1941–1944

Outnumbered more than two to one in aircraft strength in the east, the *Luftwaffe* depended on a heavy, surprise aerial blow to destroy as much as possible of the Red Air Force on the ground in June 1941. Russian aircraft losses when Hitler invaded seemed at first incomprehensible—even to the Germans, who had direct evidence in the form of burned out and wrecked aircraft. The Russians had not taken seriously the possibility of such a devastating assault, but the Red Air Force survived. Over the course of the war, its decimated regiments were re-equipped with new and better aircraft. Soviet fliers absorbed heavy losses and gave proportionally heavier in return in a bloody war of attrition. Bereft of many experienced leaders by Stalin's purges, the Soviet Army Air Force or *Voyenno-Vozdushnyye Sily* recovered only slowly at first from the surprise of June 22, 1941. When the recovery took hold the invaders, especially the German Air Force, found an enemy more formidable than expected. The *Luftwaffe* became progressively less able to control its opponent. German bases grew more vulnerable as Russian commanders gained ability and experience. German losses rose to the point where they could not be sustained. In May 1945, the *VVS* was triumphant in the sky over Berlin. It had destroyed a foe which a few years before seemed the certain victor.

## Operation BARBAROSSA

Before dawn on June 22, 1941, the *Wehrmacht* launched Operation BARBAROSSA against the Soviet Union, achieving nearly complete surprise along most of the 2,500-kilometer eastern front. (*Map 15*) Soviet historians themselves record the destruction of at least 1,200 aircraft, 800 of those on the ground, in the first German attack. German claims of 1,489 planes

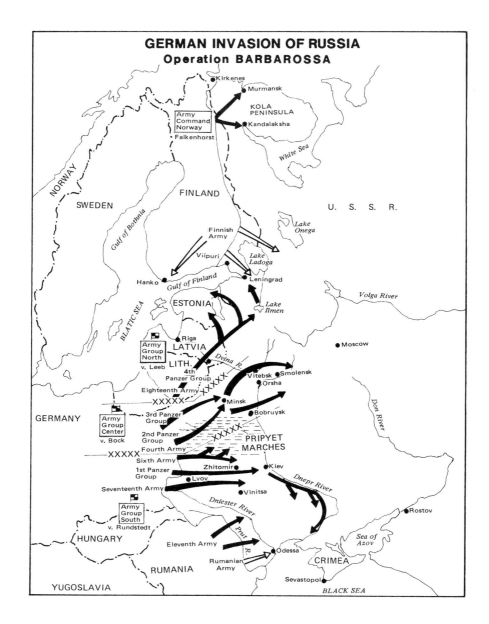

**GERMAN INVASION OF RUSSIA**
**Operation BARBAROSSA**

Map 15

**Russian I–16 biplanes sit disabled and abandoned as German forces overran their fields in June 1941. Soviet forces lost 1,200 aircraft to German air strikes in first days of the attack.**

destroyed on the ground and 322 shot down were so astonishing that Goering initially refused to believe them.* He ordered a recount, only to find the total even higher. The published Soviet statistics are still sketchy, and the true figures will probably never be known, but it was clear that within a week the Red Air Force was almost completely deprived of first-line operational combat aircraft. For more than three months, the *VVS* remained incapable of performing any significant combat missions; indeed, except for the defense of Moscow during November and December of 1941, it was not a significant factor in the war again until late in 1942.[1]

This stunning failure had its roots in Joseph Stalin's purges of the Communist Party during the late 1930s, which destroyed much of the military leadership and retarded technical advances. Stalin himself contributed greatly to the military paralysis by refusing, even on the eve of the attack, to consider seriously the danger presented by Germany. Stalin seems to have held a firm belief in Hitler's intent to uphold the terms of the Nazi-Soviet Non-aggression Pact of 1939. He apparently roused himself to confront reality on the afternoon of June 21, and by then it was too late to take any

* Conflicting claims relative to aircraft losses in Eastern Europe are very difficult to resolve. Many German records did not survive the war and we cannot determine with accuracy how many aircraft were in the three air fleets they deployed against Russia. In addition, Soviet histories cannot always be taken at face value.

effective action. It was evident that the country was unprepared for the assault. Stalin's despotism may have put him in a position where he had little other choice. Perhaps he believed that he could arrange as much as two more years of quiet, during which he could restore the confidence and capability of the military.[2] The wish was in vain.

Faced with the German invasion, new *VVS* air commanders were often unable or unwilling to exercise initiative in meeting the threat. By and large, they did not protect their bases or launch effective counterattacks. German radio intercept services often heard units under attack ask for instructions from their headquarters. The quandry continued, and as late as July Red Air Force headquarters still had to instruct commanders to put no more than nine aircraft on a base. After the debacle of the 22nd, Stalin had General Pavel Rychagov, the *VVS*'s Chief of Staff, and the air commander in the Kiev Military District shot. The Western Military District's commander was either shot or committed suicide when he lost 600 aircraft. During the last days of June, many other Soviet Air Force officers died by their own hand or Stalin's order.[3]

German photoreconnaissance and radio intercept services had been excellent. Flying from several bases in East Prussia, Poland, and Rumania, the *Luftwaffe* pinpointed virtually every major target in the weeks before the invasion, including some 2,000 airfields. From intercepted radio messages German intelligence identified most of the major units near the border.[4]

The Red Air Force had committed several errors which, coupled with the lack of effective leadership, created the desperate situation. Combat units were concentrated on relatively few exposed bases near the border. On June 22, the *Luftwaffe*'s first wave of bombers, operating in small flights, struck thirty-one of the most important and found aircraft parked close together with little or no blast protection. A reporter for the *Frankfurter Zeitung* accompanied one of the first flights of bombers to attack an airfield in Russian occupied Poland. He saw Soviet fighters "lined up as on parade," so that German bombs exploding at one point sent fire and detonation to plane after plane. He reported only desultory flak and some ineffectual Russian fighter sorties. Gen. Franz Halder, Chief of the German Army General Staff, noted in his war journal that some units had not even uncovered their aircraft in preparation for the day's flying. The same situation prevailed everywhere along the front save for the far south, where the area commander, Maj. Gen. M. V. Zakharov, dispersed some of his planes and mounted air patrols. Only there were the losses nearly equal on each side.[5] Many Soviet air units reequipping with new aircraft like the LaGG–5, MiG–3, and Yak–3 remained at forward operational bases. Camouflage was rarely evident, Russian fighters were unaggressive, and there was no organized air defense.[6] From the Baltic to the Black Sea the Germans succeeded at every major attempt, both in the air and on the ground.

German bombing attacks concentrated on Russian airfields with small, 4-pound fragmentation bombs were generally used to disable airplanes. Three Do17 or Ju88 bombers hit each base at low level with these munitions after crossing the frontier at high altitude to avoid detection. Lack of Russian radar insured the surprise. Stukas made follow-up attacks to finish destroying planes, fuel, ammunition dumps, and support equipment. The second and succeeding waves of German attackers on June 22 were met by the alerted fighters and flak, but each took only a small toll.[7]

From the opening day of BARBAROSSA to the year's end, the *VVS*'s attacks employed predictable tactics. Soviet bombers raided German bases in Poland with great determination and courage, but little effect. Capt. Herbert Pabst of the *Luftwaffe* reported seeing twenty-one Russians shot down at his base. The Soviet aircraft flew straight on, with no effort at evading either the defending fighters or intense AA gunfire. None escaped, and no serious damage was inflicted on the Germans.[8] Throughout 1941 the Soviet Air Force sporadically attacked German airfields. German and Russian estimates of the effectiveness of these raids differed, but there was no question that the Red Air Force threw itself against the German bases whenever it massed enough aircraft to support a substantial blow.

The general pattern of the *VVS*'s attacks allowed the Russians to return to their lines as quickly as possible after a strike, but remained otherwise costly to Soviet fliers. They would circle a base in exactly the same way each time, then make a single pass, dropping light bombs. German flak was prepared, fighters aloft, and Soviet losses were high. On occasion, all of the attacking Russian planes were shot down. When the *VVS* did try something inventive, it stood a much better chance of success. One such raid at Smolensk-North airfield in September 1941 saw the Russians come in at low altitude over a wooded area, avoiding both detection and flak positions. This time the attackers did not flee immediately, but made repeated passes, firing at defending gunners and successfully blowing up an ammunition dump. A number of veteran German aviators, including Hans-Ulrich Rudel, Pabst, and Heinz Joachim Jaehne, commented on these tactics after the war, invariably praising the Russians for bravery, but condemning the inexperience and inflexibility of the Red Air Force.[9]

The poor initial showing of the *VVS* should not, however, be attributed solely to the inexperience of Russian commanders. Russian military doctrine and the beliefs of Joseph Stalin precluded defensive preparation and did not at first accept retreat. Stalin insisted upon repeated attacks, even in the face of insurmountable opposition. For example, on the night of June 22, 1941, Marshal S. K. Timoshenko, at Stalin's instruction, issued Directive No. 3 ordering the Red Army to begin a full scale counterattack. Consider-

**Camouflaged German Air Force radio vans park near tree line.**

ing the disorder along the front and the overwhelming effect of the German attack, compliance with Timoshenko's instruction was impossible. Nevertheless, on the 23rd Stalin stuck by it and refused to allow his field commanders to withdraw and regroup. Roy A. Medvedev, a Soviet writer who has analyzed Stalin's career, attributed the dictator's failure to his poor understanding of tactical military problems, his harsh, mean temperament, his intense suspicion of others, and his cruelty.[10] Leadership in the field was brutish and unimaginative. The secret police often peremptorily shot commanders who did not display a willingness to attack. There were reports that members of Russian units surrounded by the enemy, even briefly, were killed upon return to their own lines. Certainly they were often arrested and sent to unknown fates. Stalin's own daughter reported a statute providing for punishment of families of captured men. Her father, she said, "considered everyone taken prisoner, even if wounded, to have surrendered voluntarily to the enemy."[11]

The *Wehrmacht* advanced rapidly on all fronts and on June 30 captured Lvov. By July 13 the Russian railway system supplying the front was largely destroyed by air bombardment. On August 13, Red Army units began to withdraw east of the Dnieper River. During September Marshal Semeon

**Field Marshal Albert Kesselring boards FW-189 aircraft.**

Budenny's five armies were surrounded in the Kiev pocket. With their surrender late in the month, the Russians suffered almost 1,000,000 men killed or captured. Large amounts of equipment, particularly tanks, fell into German hands. As the German army groups advanced, the *Luftwaffe* shifted its focus from counterair operations to attacking ground targets. Air defense of Army units and air bases became a secondary, although still important mission.[12] The heavy flak units also changed their emphasis from AA defense to ground support, destroying Red Army tanks and bunkers with armor piercing 88-mm ammunition.[13]

Despite the overwhelming victories of the *Luftwaffe*, there were disturbing signs seen by German commanders. The *VVS* seemed to have an almost inexhaustible supply of aircraft. Some German fighter groups amassed credits for destroying aircraft exceeding 1,000, but Russian planes continued to appear. Red pilots were plentiful also. The attacks of June 22 destroyed hundreds of planes on the ground, but did not kill or disable the crews. These men were assigned to reorganized units, and given new, often modern aircraft. Graduates, both men and women, of the many civilian flying and gliding clubs (*Osoaviakhim*) formed in the 1930s provided a valuable resource since they all had a basic knowledge of flying and could prepare for combat in less time than raw recruits.* The ready availability of new planes and crews were factors not incorporated in German intelligence estimates. Additionally, the Germans were misled by the magnitude of their tactical victories. They failed to follow up by destroying Soviet war industries.[14]

The Soviet Union relied heavily for recovery on its own industry. Western estimates indicate that as early as the Czech crisis of 1938, Russian aircraft and engine factories in threatened western areas of the country were moved east into and beyond the Ural mountains. The German attack accelerated the move, and from these plants soon emerged a steady flow of fighters, fighter bombers, and ground attack airplanes. The Germans had seriously underestimated Russian industrial capacity. Domestic production was able to meet the immediate needs of the *VVS* and was supplemented, beginning in the autumn of 1941, by aid from Britain and the United States, thus allowing the Russians eventually to achieve a numerical superiority in aircraft on the eastern front.[†15]

One of the most famous products of Russian aviation industry was the Ilyushin IL-2 *Sturmovik,* an armored ground attack airplane that was exceedingly difficult to bring down. Light and medium AA fire at ranges of 900 to 1,200 meters had little effect on it unless the gunners scored a hit on some vulnerable point, such as the tail. This aircraft was to be the principle weapon used to attack German air bases in Russia.[16] Other aircraft also appeared, especially fighters such as the Yakovlev Yak-1 and -3, the Lavochkin LaGG-3 and La-5, and the Mikoyan MiG-1 and -3. All the fighters were high performance craft, well armed, and able to be serviced and maintained on the profusion of Russian airfields.

## The Russians Regroup

Six months of harsh treatment by the *Wehrmacht* taught the Russians much in the way of protecting their bases from the German *blitzkrieg.* Their attempts at reinforcement went hand in glove with revised organization and operating procedures, all of which slowly brought their air forces to a level of operating efficiency. Even as the German drive was blunted in early December 1942, new measures began taking effect.

---

* At least three combat air regiments within the *VVS* were composed of women. Their organization began in 1941, and by 1943 they were involved regularly in major air battles.

† Soviet factories produced some 140,000 aircraft between 1941 and 1945. United States Lend Lease provided 14,589. The British added another 4,280, mostly fighters. In contrast, the Germans built 92,666 between 1941 and 1944, and about 2,500 more early in 1945. Between 1941 and 1945, Britain built 108,560 (1941-1945), Japan 67,065 (1941-1945), and the United States 295,486.

Reorganization for the defense changed the structure of Soviet air units. A *Stavka* (Red Army General Staff) order of June 29 created the post of *VVS* Commander with an Air Staff subordinate to him. The Staff and its headquarters received central responsibility for planning, training, logistic support, and aircraft design. In the field, the air units assigned to military districts now came under the command of Red Army *fronts*. The army *front*, which had its closest equivalent in the army group of the western allied armies, controlled its own aviation. Within the *front*, air operations were unified under *VVS* sector commanders. The resulting smaller units were far less vulnerable than the former air divisions and regiments that started the war and were much easier to maneuver, disperse, and camouflage.[17]

By mid-October, the Soviet leaders thought the situation so bleak that the Politburo left Moscow. In November 1941, however, the extreme distances over which the Germans had to operate, mud caused by autumnal rains, and fresh divisions brought from Siberia to stiffen the defense had slowed the German advance. On December 5, the *Wehrmacht* made its closest approach to the Russian capital. A Russian counteroffensive sent the Germans, reduced by combat losses and the severe early winter, into near rout. The resistance of Gen. Walter Model's Ninth Army, after Hitler's "no retreat" order, finally stabilized the front in January 1942.[18]

The dispersal of units among one large and several smaller satellite bases in an area became standard practice. Soviet doctrine did not require sophisticated fields, and their number proliferated on the Soviet side with time. Intermediate size airfields had only rough buildings and sometimes some fuel and spare parts. Runways were usually of rolled dirt, but also occasionally constructed of octagonal concrete slabs fitted together. Frost could shift them, and enemy bombs scattered them, but the surfaces were easily repaired. Airfield engineer battalions of up to 500 men, supplemented by locally conscripted labor, prepared airfields in as little as three days with only the most rudimentary tools. Slit trenches and dugouts served as living space and shelter during attack. Roads were few, and barrels of gasoline were hand rolled into place, usually by forced civilian labor, sometimes over distances of ninety miles. Parts, ammunition, bombs, and food were hand-carried in by gangs of civilians. The very simplicity of the bases thus created added to the mobility of the Red Air Force and gave the Germans little to destroy in their air attacks. The very crude nature of the landing fields, the hundreds of sites from which to fly, and the emphasis on mobility created an air base system with built in defenses. Russian forces brought about 1,000 aircraft from Asia and the Caucusus for the defense of Moscow and sustained them on these primitive bases even as the *Luftwaffe,* without subzero lubricants or warm clothing for crews, froze in place.[19]

TABLE 20

## *Luftwaffe* Antiaircraft Strength
## Eastern Front
## June 1941

Fourth Air Fleet (Army Group South)
  II Flak Corps (3 Regiments)
    13 mixed (light and heavy) AA Battalions
    4 light AA Battalions

Second Air Fleet (Army Group Center)
  I Flak Corps (3 Regiments)
    16 mixed AA Battalions
    7 light AA Battalions

First Air Fleet (Army Group North)
  3 AA Regiments without corps organization
    8 mixed AA Battalions
    3 light AA Battalions

Mixed battalions contained 3 to 6 batteries of guns. Each battery normally had 4 to 8 heavy guns (88-mm) and 12 to 15 light or medium guns (37-mm, 20-mm) plus 4 sixty centimeter searchlights.

Light battalions had 3 batteries of 20-mm guns, often a battery of nine 37-mm guns, and a searchlight battery.

**Sources:** Plocher, "The German Air Force vs. Russia, 1941"
        War Department, "Air Staff Post Hostility Intelligence Requirements on German Air Force"
        War Department, MI Service, Special Series publication No. 10

Soviet Air Force commanders made increasingly widespread use of camouflage and decoys. Parked aircraft were hidden by trees, brush, or snow. Taxi lanes covered by nets and branches ran far into the woods, sometimes half a mile. Roads and tracks leading to the dispersal fields were forbidden. Trucks and equipment were not parked in view and repair was

TABLE 21

## Soviet Antiaircraft
## June 1941

Tactical antiaircraft organizations were part of the Red Army and were formed in divisions assigned to a Front Area.* Fronts were similar to German Army Groups. A normal division had the following:

3 to 8 regiments with sixteen 76-mm, 85-mm, or 105-mm guns
1 Light regiment with varying numbers of 37-mm guns
1 to 3 regiments of 12.7-mm AA machine guns
2 to 4 searchlight regiments
1 to 3 barrage balloon regiments
1 to 3 independent AA batteries

Russia had almost no radar in use when the fighting began.

* The strength and number of regiments and divisions varied from area to area.

**Sources:** Liddell Hart, editor, *The Red Army*
Mackintosh, *Juggernaut*
Schwabedissen, "The Russian Air Force in the Eyes of German Commanders"
Hq. USAF Air Intelligence Report No. 100-45-34

done at night or in bad flying weather. On the open steppe, aircraft were hidden in false houses or covered with hay, dirt, or snow piled to simulate snow drifts. At various places, dummy airfields were constructed, often in large numbers. Landings and take offs were simulated by passing aircraft, vehicles were used to indicate activity, and containers of gasoline were placed in dummy aircraft to ignite when strafed or bombed. German air commanders described the Russian camouflage and deception accomplishments as masterful.[20]

Early in the war, AA guns for defense of Russian bases were hard to obtain. Satellite fields might sometimes be protected by a battery or two of light guns supplemented by machine guns taken from damaged aircraft. Main bases might be defended by medium or heavy guns. In general, the accuracy of the heavy gunners was not rated highly by the Germans or

British observers, largely because tracking and aiming mechanisms were crude. Having learned their lesson in June 1941, Russian air commanders kept frequent fighter patrols in the air above bases. Protection by fighters was one of the most significant active defense measures of the early war years. Another type of defense frequently reported by German pilots was intense small arms fire at low altitudes. Russian soldiers and airmen were well trained in this so called "everyone shoot" technique. Aircraft attacking bases often flew into a hail of bullets.[21]

Soviet operating doctrine and equipment did not require sophisticated airfields. Onc tactical air base could function as a main installation supporting numerous smaller and less well developed flying fields. The number of fields, some of which were no more than dirt runways, proliferated with the passage of time. Intermediate size airfields sometimes had a few rough buildings and, occasionally, small amounts of fuel and spare parts. Runways on the intermediate fields were often constructed of octagonal concrete blocks fitted edge to edge on level ground. The blocks shifted with mud and frost and retained a relatively even surface.[22]

Little effort was expended in airfield preparation. Mobility and rapid deployment were extremely important, and most fields were completed in two or three days. Serviced at the support bases, aircraft would deploy in small numbers to the satellite stations. Airfield engineer battalions of 400 to 500 men, freely supplemented by conscript labor drafts made up of local peasants and townspeople, prepared a system of fields simultaneously. Widespread conscription was carried out under an order of June 22 from the Supreme Soviet, and large numbers of people were put to work building bases and other military facilities. Only the most primitive equipment was used. Sometimes no more than clearing an area of brush, trees, and then rolling the ground was done. The construction procedure and simple needs of the *VVS* allowed hundreds of fields to be built in as little as a month.[23]

The targeting problems which the *VVS*'s system of base operation presented to the *Luftwaffe* were significant. The dispersal basing theme was adopted for more than defense reasons, however. The *VVS*, as part of the army, helped carry out the Soviet doctrine of attacking every enemy element in an area simultaneously. As such, the *VVS* was as much an extension of artillery as anything else. It conducted little long range bombing, nor did it ordinarily pursue complex interdiction missions. Early in the war, Russian ground commanders employed the *VVS* as they thought best and in conjunction with ground maneuver units. This requirement, as much as defense, was responsible for airfield proliferation.[24]

## German Air Base Defense

The *Luftwaffe*'s position within the *Wehrmacht* was markedly different from that of the Red Air Force within the Soviet military establishment. While the *VVS* was a tactical air branch of the Red Army, the German Air Force was an independent service which worked closely with the German Army, but had its own responsibilities. Within the *Luftwaffe* were antiaircraft units charged with home air defense, air defense of army units and depots, and air base air defense. In the field, the *Luftwaffe*'s senior commander on a base or in a unit higher in the chain of command, such as an air division or air corps, was responsible for air defense of his organization. The *Luftwaffe* lacked a clear strategic bombardment doctrine or capability. In the Russian campaign it acted as a tactical force which carried out little strategic bombing until 1943 and was reduced, over several years' time, to a position similar to that of the *VVS*: subordinate to Army needs. As the Army field forces lacked sufficient artillery and antitank weapons, the *Luftwaffe*'s aircraft and flak units became more and more a substitute for these and less an organization capable of independent action. As the guns and crews drained away to stop Soviet counteroffensives, German air base defense declined.[25]

The *Luftwaffe* believed that defending a battlefield, including air bases, from air attack was a cooperative responsibility of fighters and antiaircraft artillery. The goal was to achieve air superiority, the essential first step toward battlefield defense. Attacking enemy airfields was part and parcel of defense. The Germans discouraged direct conflict with a defending enemy fighter force except for self protection; they much preferred to strike an enemy when they held the advantages of surprise and maneuver. Such actions conserved their forces and were in keeping with their preference for offensive operations. Examples of the German preference for attacking enemy bases were the air actions of July 1942, near Voronezh, about 350 miles northwest of Stalingrad. Supporting the German Second and Sixth Armies, two *Kampfgruppen* and a *Jagdgruppe* attacked a number of Russian airfields. By German claims, at least 92 Russian planes were shot down and 35 destroyed on the ground. In the same month, the same tactics were repeated further south with similar success and reportedly light German losses. The constant pressure kept the Red Air Force off balance and reduced its ability to reply in kind.[26]

German bases in forward battle zones in the USSR did not support the same flying units indefinitely. Squadrons were often reassigned on short notice to keep up with the advancing armor and mechanized infantry. During rapid movement, air defense was very fluid, varying according to the numbers and types of weapons available and the degree of *Luftwaffe* air superiority. As a result, bases would not always have AA defense units until

TABLE 22

## *Luftwaffe* Air Strength
## Eastern Front
## June 1941

|  | Strength (approx.) |  |
|---|---|---|
| *Luftflotte* 4 (Löhr) |  |  |
| 12 Bomber *Gruppen* (He111) | 360 |  |
| 7 Fighter *Gruppen* (Ju88, Me109e and f) | 210 |  |
| 3 Reconnaissance *Staffeln* (Ju88) | 30 | Poland and |
| 2 Air Transport *Gruppen* (Ju52) | 60 | Rumania |
| 3 Liaison *Staffeln* (Ju88) | 30 |  |
|  | 690 |  |
| *Luftflotte* 2 (Kesselring) |  |  |
| 8 Bomber *Gruppen* (Do17, He111) | 240 |  |
| 8⅓ Dive Bomber *Gruppen* (Ju87) | 250 |  |
| 9 Fighter *Gruppen* (single engine-Me109f) | 270 |  |
| 2 Fighter *Gruppen* (twin engine-Me110) | 60 |  |
| 2 Ground Attack *Gruppen* (Ju87) | 60 | Poland |
| 2 Reconnaissance *Staffeln* (Ju88) | 30 |  |
| 2 Air Transport *Gruppen* (Ju52) | 60 |  |
|  | 970 |  |
| *Luftflotte* 1 (Keller) |  |  |
| 9 Bomber *Gruppen* (Ju88) | 270 |  |
| 3⅔ Fighter *Gruppen* (Me109f) | 110 |  |
| 5 Reconnaissance *Staffeln* (Ju88) | 50 |  |
| 1 Air Transport *Gruppe* (Ju52) | 30 | East Prussia |
| 2 Liaison *Staffeln* (Do215) | 20 |  |
|  | 480 |  |
| Total | 2140 |  |

*Luftflotte* 5 in Norway was not a significant force. In addition to the above, the Rumanian Air Force added 504 first-line planes. The Hungarian Air Force of 368 entered the war on Germany's side on June 27. The Finnish Air Force, which supported Germany, had about 550 aircraft, not all modern.

**Sources:** Wagner, editor, *The Soviet Air Force in World War II*
Bekker, *The Luftwaffe War Diaries*
Plocher, "The German Air Force vs. Russia, 1941"
Air Ministry, German translation VII/34

TABLE 23

## Soviet Air Force Strength
## June 1941

| Location | Bombers | Fighters | Total |
|---|---|---|---|
| Leningrad Military District, Leningrad | 570 | 585 | 1,155 |
| Baltic Military District, Riga | 315 | 315 | 630 |
| Western Military District, Minsk | 660 | 770 | 1,430 |
| Kiev Military District, Kiev | 460 | 625 | 1,085 |
| Other Districts: Odessa, Kharkov, Caucasus | 395 | 445 | 840 |
| Moscow, Orel | 320 | 240 | 560 |
| Total* | 2,720 | 2,980 | 5,700 |

\* Precise information not available; forces were being reorganized during period.

To the above, add 1800 transport and liaison aircraft and 3000 aircraft probably in Asia.

These tabulations were made by the *Luftwaffe* from photoreconnaissance. The Germans assumed 50 percent would be serviceable at any given time. The estimates were too low. Reserves and new types coming into service were not correctly anticipated. In reality, there were some 12,000 to 15,000 military aircraft in the USSR.

The *VVS*'s units were organized into air regiments of 60 to 64 aircraft. There were 4 or 5 squadrons in each regiment. Air divisions were made up of 4 or 5 regiments and could operate independently.

**Sources:** Wagner, editor, *The Soviet Air Force in World War II*

Greenwood, "The Red Air Force in the Great Patriotic War, 1941–1945"

**Luftwaffe 88-mm gun crew sets up in finished, timber lined emplacement at captured Dugino airfield in Russia.**

territorial gains were consolidated. Through 1942 this did not present a serious problem, as the Russians did not attack frequently. Many German AA units thus became free to help destroy enemy armor and fortifications.[27]

As the war on the eastern front became more settled, German air bases tended to be increasingly well established, with buildings and support services. Defense became more evident, and was the responsibility of the station commander. Each base was assigned an Aerodrome Command, responsible for administration, supply support of flying units, and station defense. The organization was more complex and sophisticated than that used by the Russians and reflected the different composition and mission of the *Luftwaffe*. Major air installations were normally provided with an attached flak unit of eight to twelve heavy AA guns (one to one-and-a-half 88-mm batteries) and twelve to thirty 20-mm cannon. Less important bases received fewer weapons, and bases where only an Aerodrome Command was present, with no flying units, had only a small number of 20-mm guns. Base personnel supplemented the antiaircraft artillery with rifle and machine gun fire. Attached construction platoons handled bomb damage repair and construction of dispersal areas and defense fortifications. Labor Service companies (German civilians who were not part of the *Luftwaffe*) were often assigned to assist with the work. Local civilians, often forced to serve, also worked on construction projects.[28]

After the Russian Winter Offensive of December 1941–January 1942, the *Luftwaffe* formed field infantry divisions. Battalions and regiments of these divisions varied in size and deployment according to the terrain, location of the station, and nature of the enemy threat. Assigned detachments were under the operational control of the station commander. When at an airfield, these ground defense units also fired on low flying attackers with small arms. Late in 1943, all of the divisions were absorbed by the Army.[29]

As with the Russians, camouflage played an important part in German air base defense. Aircraft were painted with a color pattern designed to increase the difficulty of observation from the air, and whenever possible, they were parked under nets or in the protection of forests. Guns were similarly hidden, and command posts disguised to resemble natural features or native houses. Where blast protection was not available, the Germans quickly dispersed their aircraft and sent damaged or worn planes to rear stations in order to reduce congestion. Because German industry could not produce the numbers of aircraft to match Russian factory output and British and American aid, the *Luftwaffe*'s tactical commanders were more sensitive to the need to protect and repair their assets than were their opponents.[30]

## The Struggle on the Steppe: 1942–1943

The exact geographic placement of airfields in the vast expanse of European Russia was not crucial in the first years of the Soviet-German war. Possession of a particular base or group of bases was rarely a prerequisite for continued military operations. During the battle of Stalingrad, however, the need for a more focussed defense became acute. Between November 19, 1942, when the Soviet pincers began to encircle the German Sixth Army, and January 30, 1943, when the Sixth Army surrendered, the main contact with and resupply of the trapped Germans was by air,[31] and airfield defense assumed a greater importance for the German command. Within the Stalingrad pocket were five airfields: Pitomnik, Bassargino, Gumrak, Gorodische, and Stalingradsky. Because it was in the best condition, Pitomnik took most of the load. Gorodische was almost useless due to its rough, pock-marked surface, and the other three were only marginally better. If the trapped army was to be sustained, a steady flow of some 750 to 900 tons of food, fuel, and ammunition had to be provided every day. Security of the bases within the pocket and at the transports' originating locations was absolutely necessary.[32]

**German airfield construction in Russia, 1941. Reich Labor Service battalions pour footings and emplace primitive but durable wood stump taxiways.**

**German aerial shows typical Russian air strip at Kirovsk. The overprinted figures delineate the field parking areas, open and covered revetments, flak pits, barracks, several Russian built aircraft and six Hurricane or Tomahawk fighters supplied by Western Allies.**

The *Luftwaffe*'s 9th Flak Division, attached to von Paulus's Sixth Army, was the Germans' main air defense force at Stalingrad. The 9th had 11 heavy and 19 light artillery batteries (37 88-mm, 162 20-mm, 49 37-mm, and 3 50-mm guns). It had been well supplied with ammunition and was able to maintain fire throughout the period. When it ceased fighting at the end of January 1943, the 9th still had thousands of rounds of 88-mm ammunition and an unknown amount of ammunition for its lighter weapons. Also within the pocket were various air units, including a squadron of about twenty Me109 fighters. The fighters were active for only a short time. Attrition, caused largely by the poor airfield conditions and lack of service facilities, rapidly reduced this force. The 9th was commanded by Brig. Gen. Wolfgang Pickert, a highly experienced and capable AA specialist and the *Luftwaffe*'s most senior officer in the Stalingrad area. He was placed in charge of all air operations in the pocket, including fighters and airlift services, in addition to his artillery command. Pickert was not a flier but was highly regarded by both Field Marshal von Paulus and his Air Force contemporaries.[33]

Despite the exposed position of the German bases, both inside and outside the pocket, the Russian Air Force does not seem to have made an

**German light flak crew fires on Russians overhead during the approach on Stalingrad, 1942.**

effort to destroy them completely. At first, severe logistics problems, shortages of fuel, parts, and spare engines retarded Soviet air operations. In August, the *VVS*'s commander, Lt. Gen. (later Marshal of the Soviet Air Force) Alexander A. Novikov, took personal charge at Stalingrad and ordered changes to improve both the logistic and command systems. The *VVS*'s performance improved, and during December, 28 percent of its sorties were directed at airdromes (apparently on both ends of the supply line). In January, the figure dropped to 7.8 percent. The *VVS*'s pilots concentrated on attacking German transports, a more vulnerable and profitable target. Postwar German studies of the battle insisted that the Russians were unable to attain air superiority for any lengthy period. This is open to argument, given the enormous losses of transports by Germany (German records admit the loss of 488 aircraft from enemy action, accident, wear and tear, and weather; the Russians claimed double that from combat losses). Whatever the true losses, they were heavy. Even so, the *Luftwaffe* was able to continue operations into airfields until the end of January, finally resorting to air drops on the last few days because the bases had been overrun on the ground. Despite the true method of its employment or the extent of its air superiority, the action at Stalingrad was a singular achievement for the Red Air Force. Late in 1942, it was not yet equal to the Germans in quality of aircraft, crews, or command. Novikov's decision to attack heavily took a great deal of faith, and months of effort. His forces applied intense pressure on the *Luftwaffe*'s transport traffic around Stalingrad.[34]

Advantages continued to favor the Russians as the battle dragged on. Russian fighters flew from fields less than 20 miles from Stalingrad, their fighter-bombers from bases 60 to 90 miles away. The *VVS* increased the

**German field at Demyansk. The sod field could sustain heavy traffic and withstand attack. At lower right is a boneyard of wrecked German aircraft.**

number of its sorties until the Germans had to operate over much greater distances from fewer airfields. The Germans, on the other hand, traversed up to 180 miles of enemy air space with their slow and unmaneuverable Ju52, Ju86, and He111 transports. Most of the craft were lost or badly damaged during flight, the victims of Russian fighters or antiaircraft gunfire. To support their increased fighting, the Russians created an extensive radio-equipped observer and fighter-control net to detect and attack flights of transports. They never had a fighter direction system at Stalingrad, but may have used a rudimentary radar system, which probably did little more than detect aircraft approaching over the Red Army's units west of Stalingrad. Between November 19, 1942, and February 2, 1943, the *VVS*'s pilots logged 35,920 sorties.[35]

The improvised German airfields in use at both ends of the operation could not have offered a sustained defense against a systematic Russian air assault. Long range German fighters were not available and an adequate number of fighters could not be kept within the pocket. Antiaircraft artillery positions were rudimentary, although the gunfire was heavy and accurate. Shelters for people and equipment were often no more than huts or snow houses. Few could be constructed by the weakened men in the bitter cold. On January 18, 1943, the *VVS* attacked the Ju52 staging base at Zverevo.

The base was, in reality, a cornfield, with no facilities save for essential services. Rumanian and German AA forces protected the field, but the Rumanians apparently did not fight. Only the platoon of German 20-mm gunners gave resistance, shooting down a *Sturmovik*. The Russians destroyed ten Ju52s and badly damaged twenty others. Other German airfields supplying Stalingrad were also attacked. Sal'sk twice suffered heavy losses, and was threatened on the ground by the middle of January.[36]

In addition to interception by Russian aircraft, the *Luftwaffe*'s transports were under constant Russian AA fire on their flights into and out of Stalingrad. Although the German pilots could vary their altitude and direction, some routes were unsuitable because of lengthy flight time and heavy fuel requirements. As the most used flight paths became known, the Russians positioned AA to cover them. The Germans flew above the accurate low level gunfire and risked the sporadic 85-mm fire. As dire for Sixth Army as the Soviets were the bitter winter weather and the airlift utterly unable to meet the needs of the trapped men. The highest daily total of deliveries was 289 tons on December 19. Deliveries from December 1 to 11 averaged 97.3 tons, and from December 13 to 21, 137 tons, several hundred below the daily requirement. On many days, drifting snow, clouds, ice, and wind combined virtually to close air transport operations. Indeed, the only bright spots of the effort were the courage of the crews and the evacuation of about 30,000 wounded by return flights. The last German units in the pocket surrendered on February 2, 1943.[37] It is reasonable to suppose that using an effective aircraft warning service (even without radar) and coordinating the use of aircraft at their disposal, the Russians could have stopped the entire airlift. By a combination of fighter interception and constant airfield bombardment the *VVS* could have isolated the Sixth Army more quickly. In the fighting for Stalingrad and during the German withdrawal from the trans-Caucausus, the Red Air Force, it is generally conceded, became a fully offensive organization, capable of carrying out attacks on targets of its choosing and executing them with increasing finesse, although not without some problems. German air defense units were a major part of that fighting withdrawal. On February 7, 1943, the 9th Flak Division was reorganized around the remnants of the division's staff that had not been at Stalingrad. The division was subordinate to the First Flak Corps, in turn a part of the Fourth Air Fleet. Its commander was again General Pickert, who had been away from the pocket at the time of surrender, organizing air defenses in the Kuban-Crimean area. The 9th was initially assigned three regiments totalling fourteen heavy and fifteen light flak batteries with some searchlight units. Because of the need to protect air and naval bases, the air force added an additional forty-seven heavy and thirty-one light flak batteries in early March.[38] The 129th Air Signal Battalion of the 9th Flak Division built a communications net that enabled Pickert to control his antiaircraft forces throughout this wide area. Warnings of Russian aircraft relayed by radio and telephone to the local AA commanders allowed intense fire both day and night.[39]

Heavy air and ground fighting continued through the spring and summer, with consequent heavy aircraft losses on both sides. By early October, the Germans evacuated the Kuban area, bringing most of their units across the strait to the Crimean Peninsula. Operating from their air bases on the peninsula, the German Air Force claimed 1,045 tanks destroyed. Antiaircraft battalions and fighters reportedly shot down or destroyed on the ground 2,280 Soviet aircraft.[40] The claims were high and probably excessive, although the Germans used a variety of defense measures and aggressive air attack policies. The Kuban struggle proved above all that the Red Air Force had overcome its organizational and logistical problems. Now it began the task of grinding down the *Luftwaffe* in the east.

## The Battle for Kursk

The attrition of German forces in the East continued during the year with another clash that irrevocably wrested the initiative on that entire front from the hands of the *Wehrmacht*. Soviet operations through late winter 1943 resulted in a large salient separating Army Groups South and Center in the German lines just west of the city of Kursk. (*Map 16*) Perceiving that Stalin could counter any German move from this position or launch his own offensive to the west, Hitler ordered a late spring attack on the salient under the code name Operation CITADEL. Heavy fighting in the Mediterranean and the German withdrawal from the Crimea in the spring continually drew off German air strength, and Hitler postponed the operation repeatedly. Both sides poured resources into the preparations for the battle: 4,000 Soviet tanks were poised on the Russian side and Hitler arrayed 2,700 tanks and several hundred of the Ferdinand self propelled guns against the bulge in hopes of pinching it off around its base.[41] Facing some 3,000 Russian planes, the Germans amassed 1,850 aircraft in support of the effort at bases around Orel, Bryansk, and Kharkov. The *Luftwaffe* also emplaced the I Flak Corps under Maj. Gen. Richard Reiman to protect Kharkov; subordinate to the Sixth Air Fleet, the 12th Flak Division under Maj. Gen. Ernst Buffa moved in at Orel and Brig. Gen. Paul Pavel's 10th Flak Brigade guarded the bases and other potential targets around Bryansk. The 18th Flak Division was charged with air base air defense around Smolensk for the operation. Russian attacks on the German bases around Orel and on rail depots and supply points were particularly heavy. As early as April 30, the Russians received a British warning of the buildup based on *Enigma* intercepts that confirmed their own information of German intentions garnered from their efficient

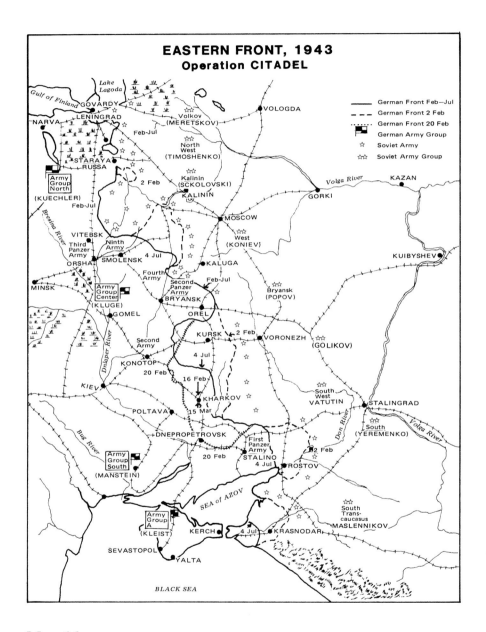

**EASTERN FRONT, 1943**
**Operation CITADEL**

German Front Feb–Jul
German Front 2 Feb
German Front 20 Feb
German Army Group
☆ Soviet Army
☆☆ Soviet Army Group

Lake Lagoda
Gulf of Finland
GOVARDY
LENINGRAD
NARVA
Volkov (MERETSKOV)
VOLOGDA
Feb-Jul
North West (TIMOSHENKO)
STARAYA RUSSA
Army Group North (KUECHLER)
2 Feb
Kalinin (SCKOLOVSKI)
KALININ
Volga River
KAZAN
GORKI
Feb-Jul
Bresina River
VITEBSK
Third Panzer Army
Ninth Army
SMOLENSK
4 Jul
MOSCOW
West (KONIEV)
ORSHA
Fourth Army
KALUGA
KUIBYSHEV
MINSK
Army Group Center (KLUGE)
Second Panzer Army
BRYANSK
Feb-Jul
Bryansk (POPOV)
GOMEL
Dnieper River
OREL
Second Army
KURSK
2 Feb
VORONEZH
(GOLIKOV)
KONOTOP
4 Jul
20 Feb
16 Feb
KIEV
KHARKOV
South West VATUTIN
STALINGRAD
POLTAVA
15 Mar
Volga River
Bug River
DNEPROPETROVSK
First Panzer Army
20 Feb
STALINO
4 Jul
2 Feb
Don River
South (YEREMENKO)
Army Group South (MANSTEIN)
ROSTOV
SEA of AZOV
South Trans-caucasus MASLENNIKOV
Army Group A (KLEIST)
KERCH
4 Jul
KRASNODAR
SEVASTOPOL
YALTA

*BLACK SEA*

**Map 16**

espionage network in Berlin. They redoubled the construction of defensive belts that featured some of the densest minefields ever seen.[42]

Both sides installed new airfields for the battle. Near Orel the Germans constructed 12, but the Russians were even busier. For 325 miles in either direction north and south of Kursk, they built or reconditioned a total of 154 strips. They stocked each main base with 10 to 15 days of supply and camouflaged everything carefully. Numbers of dummy airfields went in around the operating bases. A small force at each dummy field simulated operations by moving planes around and displaying lights at night. If a field were attacked twice, it was abandoned in favor of another in a continuing game that deceived German reconnaissance seeking out the real bases. The quality of Soviet early warning nets at Kursk varied and we are uncertain how they used radar. The few Russian radar sets that were probably present had a range of 70 to 90 miles.* The *VVS* compensated with many ground observers who quickly reported any aircraft they saw. In addition, the *VVS* kept fighters aloft over its fields, but the multiplicity of targets the Soviets created was the chief reason for the survival of so many usable installations.[43]

Russian aerial tactics had improved vastly by 1943, but were still unimaginative by German standards. Large numbers of attacking planes were lost in head on attacks. Russian official histories offer a highly sanguine but dubious view of the performance of the *VVS*, claiming a total of 506 German craft destroyed in a single surprise attack on German fields on May 6, 1943, and another 145 German planes destroyed during an attack on Russian rail facilities behind Kursk in June. The Russian claims were clearly unrealistic as the *Luftwaffe*'s strength rarely exceeded 2,500 operational aircraft on the Eastern Front in 1943.[44] Russian aircraft were only sparsely equipped with radios, and many of those in use could only receive messages; only flight leaders had transceivers and maps. German gunners and pilots learned to concentrate on the lead plane in an attack. Destroying it would usually scatter the rest of the flight. Once over their targets, however, the Russians were tenacious in the attack regardless of their losses. German military opinion held that while the Russian attacks could be dangerous, they were so inconsistent as to reduce their overall effectiveness.[45] The Soviet fliers, however, had become more adept at flak suppression, and used the Il-2 *Sturmovik* to good effect. Flying at the rear of an attacking serial, these robust planes strafed and bombed gun positions at or near German airfields that revealed themselves by firing at the lead aircraft in the attack.[46] Night attacks on German positions were common. To counter them, the *Luftwaffe*

---

* In August 1941, Britain sent the USSR a GL-II gun laying radar that was pressed into service during the defense of Moscow. The American Lend Lease program provided the Russians 135 early warning and gun laying radars, but these arrived after the Kursk operations.

fixed a mobile radar on a rail car, itself protected by flak, and brought in five night fighter squadrons from the West. Their excellent communications allowed the Germans to correlate radar and ground observer reports and alert interceptors.[47]

Hitler finally ordered CITADEL to commence on July 5. For the first few days German qualitative superiority was evident. German bombers of *Fliegerkorps* VIII near Kharkov assembled for take-off when Russian planes on a night mission nearly upset their timetable. Radar and ground observers spotted the large flight of Russians headed for the corps' five fields, and fighters scrambled to meet the assault. A swirling melee developed in the clear morning sky. General Hans Jeschonnek, the *Luftwaffe*'s Chief of Staff, was at the corps headquarters watching in astonishment as the Russians bored straight in and lost most of their planes. Few bombs fell where intended.[48] In the 1st German Air Division area near Kharkov later in the day another large air battle drew on with the Germans demonstrating clear dominance of the air. But the German aircraft could not continue to fly mission after mission, and German pilots were hard pressed to contain the *VSS*. As the ground battle wore on, the Germans stripped their air defenses to utilize the 88-mm guns in an antitank role for the Army. On July 13, Hitler declared CITADEL at an end. The Allied invasion of Sicily on July 10 forced him to divert forces to the aid of the collapsing Italian Army. Between May and early July, the German Air Force's airfield defenses centered on warning, fighters, and heavy concentrations of antiaircraft fire. The *Luftwaffe* seems to have held its own and continued flying from its bases. The overall German effort, however, fell to bristling Russian defenses, miles deep and laid by Stalin and his generals in the full knowledge of the *Wehrmacht*'s plans. The battle of Kursk marked the final German attempt to destroy the Red Army. For the remainder of the war, the Luftwaffe operated on the defensive in the East.[49]

The year 1943 marked the end of German aerial domination on the Russian front. The Kuban-Crimean and Kursk air battles were among the most savage and prolonged of the war. The Soviet Air Force prevailed because in the long struggle of attrition, Russian industry and training schools produced more airplanes and pilots than did Germany. German weapons and aircraft were more sophisticated, and their pilots generally better. Often they used radar, while the Russians rarely did. The *Luftwaffe*, operating in the Soviet Union at the end of a long logistics line, could not replenish flying squadrons and send sufficient spare parts to service its fleet. The *VVS*'s ability to counter German attacks by widespread dispersal, excellent use of camouflage, antiaircraft artillery, and, most of all, replacement of worn or damaged equipment provided the long term success denied Germany. Only fragmentary statistics on Russian air losses are available. One reliable Russian report puts the *VVS*'s losses at Kursk between July 5 and 8, 1943, at

**German antiaircraft crew mans a predictor to determine height and range of approaching Russian aircraft at Dugino, 1943.**

566. Clearly, had the *VVS* not been able to disperse forces over a wide area and quickly replace lost or damaged aircraft, they would have risked destruction by the *Luftwaffe*. The turnaround in Russian proficiency in the air war begun in the Kuban was now complete.[50]

The continuing German losses at Kursk and elsewhere on the Eastern Front could not be replaced because the *Luftwaffe* was fighting an air war on three fronts: in Russia, Italy, and over Germany itself. While the Germans increased aircraft output, they could not produce enough fuel, guns, and other equipment, and the population was too small to replenish the lost army divisions. Nor could the *Luftwaffe*'s instructors turn out sufficient numbers of pilots. For the Germans, air base defense in the East became a succession of actions designed to safeguard their forces on the retreat to Germany. The German Air Force was able to strike hard, and occasionally it did so. One such attempt provided a clear picture of Russian base defense.[51]

## The Attack on Poltava Air Base, June 21, 1944

On November 28, 1943, at the Tehran Conference, W. Averell Harriman, American ambassador to the Soviet Union, again approached Stalin about the use of Russian air bases by the U. S. Army Air Forces to bomb targets in the eastern part of German held territory. The targets were out of round trip range of B–17 and B–24 bombers stationed in England and Italy and the Soviet Long Range Bomber Force was too small and ill-equipped to undertake such a task.[52] In Harriman's scheme for shuttle bombing, American bombers would fly from England or Italy, attack targets, land in Russia to refuel and rearm, and hit new objectives on the return. Though approving in principle, Stalin only gave permission on February 2, 1944, and on the 5th the first substantive meeting to discuss the project was held in Foreign Minister Vyacheslav M. Molotov's office. The Red Air Force was represented by its commander, Novikov, and Col. Gen. A. V. Nikitin, in charge of the *VVS's* air operations. Ambassador Harriman, Maj. Gen. John R. Deane, Chief of the United States Military Mission to the Soviet Union, and their aides presented the American ideas.[53]

Deane described the purposes of shuttle bombing, the Russian support desired, and the need for reconnaissance facilities. After some discussion, Marshal Novikov proposed use of bases in the south, at Poltava and Kiev, where weather was better and the sites more readily prepared than in the north. German destruction in the north precluded using fields there, Novikov continued. During a discussion of general support requirements, the Marshal told the Americans that defense of the bases was a Soviet responsibility and that they would provide it. Both sides agreed that American personnel would be kept to a minimum consistent with the needs of flying operations. Gasoline and bombs would be provided by the Russians, who would notify air defense units of arriving aircraft. Unable to agree on bases, the group left a decision on the specific airfields to be used for later.[54]

In March 1944, Nikitin and Deane discussed the question of a suitable base in a meeting at the *VVS's* General Staff headquarters in Moscow. Poltava, Mirgorod, and Piryatin, in the Ukraine, had been tentatively selected after several survey trips by the planners. Nikitin pointed out the vulnerability of Poltava. It was well known to the Germans, who occupied it for more than a year, was within range of German bombers and could not be camouflaged easily. He suggested another location farther east. The Americans, however, were concerned about distance to and from England and Italy; they wanted Poltava. In addition, the constant delays encountered in getting a decision from the highly centralized Russian bureaucracy prompted them to accept the fields in the Ukraine and go ahead with the project, code named FRANTIC.[55]

**American aviation engineers lay out pierced steel plank runways at Poltava in the spring of 1944.**

Soviet preparations seemed overshadowed with the traditional and pronounced Russian xenophobia. Distrust was more evident at the higher government levels than within the *VVS*, whose members were most willing to assist and cooperate with the Americans. The selection of bases in the Ukraine served to heighten official Russian apprehension as that region was commonly viewed as being less than completely loyal to Moscow. The Soviets harbored a long memory of Allied intervention in North Russia and Siberia from 1918 to 1920 when the United States had fought the infant Red Army and generally supported the White faction in the civil war. The experience left the Soviets, and especially Stalin, with a distrust of foreign intentions.[56]

While the Russians were deciding the question of American troops in the Ukraine, construction of the airfields was not affected. At Poltava, a mile long steel mat runway and taxiway were rapidly laid. Mirgorod, too, would handle bombers, but its concrete block runway did not need as much work. Piryatin was to be a fighter installation, and runway and taxiway preparation was also not as extensive as at Poltava. Final visa approval and other problems related to admitting Americans to Russia were resolved in late May 1944 in time for the first mission, Frantic Joe. It was conducted from Italy by Fifteenth Air Force units led by their commander, Lt. Gen. Ira C. Eaker. They arrived at Poltava at one in the afternoon, June 2, 1944.[57]

Americans at the base had questions from the beginning about air defense. The primary Russian weapons were 85-mm and 37-mm guns, although precise types and numbers were never made known to the Americans. The *VVS* also had varying numbers of fighters, mostly Yak–9s, at Poltava. Passive defenses consisted of slit trenches to shelter personnel during attacks and German built revetments around the bomb storage. Located on the open steppe adjacent to the town of Poltava, the base had no natural features to afford protection or concealment of aircraft, people, or equipment. No known decoy bases operated in the vicinity of the three locations and the only concession to camouflage was the tarpaulins covering the bombs. There were no aircraft blast shields, so ground dispersal offered the only measure of protection.[58] Maj. Gen. Alexei R. Perminov, the *VVS*'s commander at Poltava, originally had control of the heavy air defense batteries and the fighter forces at the station. Perminov and Brig. Gen. Alfred A. Kessler, Commander of Eastern Command, United States Strategic Air Forces, conferred often and agreed to greater dispersal of fuel and bomb storage. On April 22, a German reconnaissance plane overflew Poltava, after which Perminov directed a relocation of the AA guns. The artillery commander assured him that no other enemy plane would repeat such a visit. Perminov was extremely cordial to the Americans, and he and the other Russian fliers gave every indication of providing a viable and effective defense. No air raid drills were held, however. When American officers sought information on details of the Soviet defense system, the Russians became extremely sensitive and upset, insisting they "were well capable of handling the situation." It required great tact on the part of Maj. Albert Lepawsky, the AAF's Executive Officer at Piryatin, to smooth the ruffled feelings that day.[59]

On May 25 General Deane queried General Nikitin about base defense. Apparently, control of fighters and antiaircraft artillery had been shifted to Moscow. If this were so, Deane wanted to know how defense would be affected. The Soviets never clarified the issue, but the American fears were allayed when Russian fighter crews and planes began ground alert and heavy guns appeared in greater abundance. At Piryatin, American P–51s, which escorted the FRANTIC JOE bombers, joined the ground alert force. During early June, German reconnaissance aircraft were reported near the bases at least three times, although they were not pursued. After bombing a number of targets in east Europe, providing a small diversion after the Allied landing in Normandy on June 6, 1944, the Fifteenth Air Force contingent returned to Italy on June 11.[60]

The second FRANTIC mission arrived at Poltava from Eighth Air Force bases in England at half past three in the afternoon of June 21, 1944. It was commanded by Col. Archie J. Old, Jr., and had bombed targets near Berlin *en route*. East of Warsaw, Old noticed a German fighter following his formation at a distance, retreating only when challenged by American escorts. A photoreconnaissance plane also showed up to follow the B–17s to their new base. Old's flight landed at Poltava and Mirgorod, the P–51s at Pi-

**Luftwaffe Sergeant Hans Mueller shot this aerial of American B-17s lined up in the open at Poltava. A few hours later, using this photo as a guide, German bombers devastated the field.**

ryatin. The bombers taxied to dispersal points and began refueling, a long process given the lack of fuel trucks and the extensive hand labor involved. American generals and newsmen met the incoming crews, and the senior elements of the command sat down to a late supper at the base. The German reconnaissance pilot, Sgt. Hans Mueller of *Kampfgeschwader* 55 at Minsk, crossed the field at Poltava and recorded the scene below. His chief, Col. Wilhelm Antrup, had received orders to send his wing and the three others into the attack. Shortly after Mueller brought his photographs back to Minsk, German bombers took off into the night to destroy American air power in the Soviet Union.[61]

Air raid alarms sent all the diners and the station crews at Poltava into the slit trenches or behind other protection. Just after midnight on June 22, AA opened up fifteen minutes before the German pathfinder dropped flares over the middle of Poltava. For two hours, Antrup's bombers plastered the parked American planes with what Old reported as heavy demolition and incendiary bombs along with thousands of small antipersonnel devices. An investigating board decided that 110 tons of explosives had hit the base, most of one or two kilogram size. Ninety-eight percent of the load fell directly on or near the Eighth Air Force's planes.[62]

Fire fighting and rescue began immediately. The Americans assisted in the living and administration areas, the Russians claimed the right to try and save the bombers. Only Soviet personnel were allowed to approach the aircraft. In fact, Colonel Old described the Russian attempts to protect his people as "rather embarrassing," because it was so solicitous. Soviet soldiers did all of the live ordnance disposal work. The American surgeon, Lt. Col. William M. Jackson, later cited Mechanic Sgt. Tubisin and Mechanic Georgy Lucknor for heroism. These two men, directed by a Soviet lieutenant, walked ahead of a jeep picking up the small antipersonnel devices known as butterfly bombs, laying them aside to let the rescue workers reach wounded men at the north end of the field. Bomb disposal continued for months in much the same fashion; at least thirty Russians were killed in the process, and many more wounded.[63]

Every American B–17 was hit, and 50 were written off. Twenty-nine were still usable, but required extensive repair. By June 24, only 9 were flyable and recovery work was hampered by the thousands of unexploded butterfly bombs, which littered the ground and would often detonate if moved, or even in the event of ground tremors and heavy rain. The *VVS*'s aircraft losses on the other side of the base were 1 C–47 and 25 assorted fighters and trainers. In addition, the German attack destroyed 200,000 gallons of gasoline and a great deal of machine gun ammunition. In addition to the 30 Russians killed and 45 wounded, two American officers were killed at Poltava, and six other Americans were injured. Confidence in the Russians, built up over several months, was severely shaken.[64]

The Germans failed to carry through their attacks on the bombers at Mirgorod on the 21st, probably because of a navigational error. At daybreak on the 22nd, American aircraft dispersed to bases in the east. That night the *Luftwaffe* attacked, but did little damage. No aircraft were lost, though ground facilities at Mirgorod suffered. The attacking force missed Piryatin altogether, dropping their bombs three miles east of the installation.[65]

The overwhelming German success in the Poltava raid has led to suspicions of Russian duplicity and even of cooperation with the Germans to discourage the western Allies from continuing to use Russian bases. Some theories are rather far fetched. There is enough room for other explanations

This scene on the ground is the only known photograph taken by the allies during the German attack on Poltava airfield, June 21, 1944. Tracers etch the sky as German flares illuminate the unprotected bombers. (*Below*) The morning after. Burned hulks of Eighth Air Force B–17s cover the Poltava field on June 22. Nearly fifty bombers were completely destroyed.

Soviet Yak–9s were part of the base defense at Poltava. (*Below*) Soviet General Alexander R. Perminov listens to citation read at an awards ceremony. As the Russian commander at the Poltava field, his relations with Americans were cordial, which may have contributed to his disappearance after the war.

by taking into account Russian capabilities in air defense.[66] The *VVS* lacked doctrine, command structure, and the equipment to defend the base. The Russians did not have many heavy bombers, and the *VVS* probably was not familiar with defense needs for such a force. Soviet unease with the project seems to to have surfaced momentarily early in the planning when General Nikitin pointed out the exposed position of Poltava. The Russians had very little gun control radar, and their airborne intercept radar did not appear until late in the war. In addition, they lacked a ground controlled intercept system capable of contending with a large scale German attack. Lacking adequate gun laying radar, the antiaircraft artillery could not be accurately aimed at night. Every American present who subsequently made a report commented on the ineffective AA fire. Soviet gunfire shot down no aircraft, and none was deterred from bombing or strafing, though medium calibre guns continued shooting long after the raiders left. General Deane reported that Russian antiaircraft gunners fired 28,000 rounds into the air. Such a figure would confirm Old's opinion that there was a preponderance of 37-mm fire as these guns could fire faster than heavy artillery, but not as high. Accuracy was terrible. Old said that only one searchlight located a plane, and ground fire could not bring it down. In fact, only one Ju88 failed to get away, and it crashed in Russian territory on the return flight. The AA units were not prepared for night combat, and Colonel Antrup's raiding force flew high enough to avoid most of the rounds. The premature firing, fifteen minutes before the Germans were in range, served only to aid the bombers by pinpointing the target.[67]

Very few Russian fighters, if any, of the thirty at Poltava took off, and no German aircraft was intercepted. This would have been the natural result of an underdeveloped air defense fighter-control system in an air force oriented toward ground attack rather than air superiority. It is significant that after the raid, the *VVS* offered other bases, near Kharkov and Dniepro-petrovsk, for dispersal. Spreading their forces thinly had served the Russians well, and the suggestion was a logical reaction on their part. General Kessler had asked the Russians to provide more space at Poltava some weeks before the attack, but no local resolution to the problem was achieved. Both air forces needed to use the limited space at that location. Blast shields and revetments were not common on the *VVS*'s airstrips and were not built at Poltava. Had they been, the damage could have been reduced considerably.[68]

The Americans were not without blame either. Little thought seems to have been given to any German initiative. The American bombers were not painted in subdued, nonreflective colors, and their silver finishes readily reflected light from the flares, making them starkly visible to German pilots. Inadequate camouflage preparations meant that no airplanes were hidden from view.[69]

The Soviet military opinion of defense also mitigated against defensive measures. Except when incidental to consolidating gains made by an aggressive assault, or while preparing for an offensive, defense was not appropriate as a mode of combat operation. What the Soviet histories refer to as an "active defense," was, in reality, an attack or series of attacks. The following quotation from the official Soviet history of the war illustrates:

> In the course of such defensive operations the Soviet troops exhausted the enemy, inflicted heavy losses on him and created the conditions for a counteroffensive. A characteristic feature of the organization of a strategic defense was the availability of large numbers of mobile troops and the use of artillery corps and divisions for break through purposes.

This strategic defense would "develop . . . into a strategic offensive to be pursued until the complete defeat of the enemy's assault groupings."[70] Within this line of thought a place for the defensive military post was singularly lacking. The Red Army and the *VVS* were tools of attack. The Red Air Force, as a branch of the Army, received direction from ground commanders. It had little opportunity to develop comprehensive doctrine counter to that of the prominent army marshals who, in turn, reflected the thinking of Joseph Stalin. Stalin considered defense tantamount to "loafing."[71]

## Summary

The tremendous production potential of Russia, so seriously underrated before the war, allowed the *VVS* to triumph by attrition. Its planes were well suited to the task of offensive ground attack and air escort of fighter-bombers. Soviet acceptance of material and human loss did not vary throughout the war. The Russians could replace lost materiel far more easily than their enemies could. It was better to attack from a multiplicity of bases, abandoning those badly damaged, than to flail away from behind a protective wall.[72] When Maj. Gen. Robert L. Walsh, commander of Eastern Command, United States Strategic Air Forces in Europe, asked Perminov where the Russian fighters were during the Poltava raid, the Russian base commander told him they had been attacking German air bases. True or not, the reply refelcted Russian practices.[73]

Aversion to defense was based partly on skepticism of its efficacy. Only in a few instances between 1941 and 1945 did the Soviet leaders adopt defense as a matter of policy—Kursk, Moscow, Leningrad, and Stalingrad were the most prominent examples—and each was tenaciously defended for special reasons. Moscow, Leningrad, and Stalingrad were very important symbolically, less so militarily. In planning for Kursk, the Russians knew, from the British and through their espionage net in Berlin, of the impending

**German Ju–52 transports ablaze on a field in Soviet Russia during the German retreat in 1944.**

German offensive; they busied themselves building an immense trap. In general, however, defense being a suspect tactic, largely foreign to the thinking of the Red Army and the *VVS*, one could not expect an in depth system of protection for air bases.[74]

To an extent, the *VVS* was denied an opportunity to learn the techniques of integrated tactical air defense commonly used in the West because of the separate strategic defense force, the *PVO Strany*. The *PVO Strany*'s position and operational control were not clearly understood by Western observers during and after World War II. The *PVO Strany* seemed, however, to have controlled most of the Soviets' AA guns and large numbers of fighter regiments. Late in 1941, the air defense force engaged in its most prominent wartime battle, the defense of Moscow. There it joined the *VVS* and bomber force in a common, desperate effort to save the city. Even at Moscow, the *PVO Strany*'s fighters often attacked German ground targets, including airfields. But the emphasis on ground attack by the *PVO Strany* also reflected Stalin's thinking. German strategic bombing was not an important factor in the aerial fighting on the Eastern Front, especially after 1942, thus continued development of the *PVO Strany*'s doctrine, tactics, and command and control systems was not as extensive as that found in western Europe and the Pacific. The experience gained by the *PVO Strany* did not become part of the *VVS*'s doctrine or thinking on a scale large enough to influence tactical air defense command and control. The *PVO* could have provided a defense screen not only for the American bases, but also a much more extensive one for the *VVS* which lacked enough radar fighter control systems, including enough airborne intercept radar, to contend with heavy night raids such as that mounted by Colonel Antrup. Consequently, Poltava had less than adequate active protection.[75]

Air base defense employed by the *VVS* in World War II was quite unlike the same art in the West. Despite huge losses on the ground to German attacks, the Russians maintained air base operations even during the darkest periods of the war. At times it seemed as if will power and determination carried the Red Air Force through. Disregarding the active base defense systems in use by the Western powers, the Soviets built a profusion of airfields, some 8,545 by war's end, and used them with increasing skill. Defensive schemes incorporating early warning, coordinated gunfire, and fighter interception under the command of a single authority were not the mark of the *VVS*. A constant proclivity to attack carried the fight to the opponent. The Russians could, in turn, absorb heavy losses to German counterair strikes because of an enormous industrial and training capacity. Although the Soviet Union may have lost between 70,000 and 80,000 aircraft during the war, many of them on the ground to the *Luftwaffe*'s best pilots, the Germans were unable to subdue their stubborn and increasingly more skillful foe.[76]

In addition to quick replacement of machines and crews, the *VVS* depended on using many small, well concealed landing strips. These airfields were often prepared in advance of a battle so carefully that they were unobserved by German reconnaissance. The Red Air Force kept airplanes at bases fifty to a hundred miles behind the front lines until the day before an offensive. They would then disperse the force to forward camouflaged areas and strike from these, often without being detected and attacked.[77]

The devastating German attack on the Eighth Air Force's units at Poltava came about more because the Americans assumed too much about Russian base defense than because of communist treachery. The Soviet leaders probably wanted to be rid of the American bases as quickly as possible, but their own doctrine, organization, and practices did much to hinder an effective defense.

The German Air Force relied to a far greater extent on an organized, active defense. It created well equipped and well trained flak divisions, assigning one or more to each air corps. The guns were coordinated by a commander who also served on the air corps or air fleet staff. Radar detection was often used and fighters were launched to fend off attacking formations. The air defense of the *Luftwaffe*'s bases in early July 1943 near the Kursk salient was much more understandable to Western military thinking than the Red Air Force's practice of dispersal, replacement, and expenditure of lives and equipment. At Kursk, as elsewhere, the German efforts were effective, but German defense suffered in the long run from an inability to replace lost and damaged guns, planes, and most of all, pilots in a manner that even approached that of the *VVS*.

# Chapter VII

# The Solomons and New Guinea: 1942–1944

Japanese forces advanced from one success to another after the fall of Singapore. In a war fought over islands and wide expanses of ocean, aviation became a central element in military operations, and base defense accordingly took its place in the military concerns of both sides. While the Japanese Army was driving through Malaya and the Indies, Imperial Japanese Navy forces from the Caroline Islands took the port of Rabaul on New Britain island in the Territory of New Guinea. After capturing nearby New Ireland and constructing an air base at Kavieng, the Japanese turned their attention to New Guinea. In March 1942, they landed at Lae and Salamaua on the northeast coast and were poised to seize Port Moresby, the major Australian position in Papua. Capture of this small trading center would give the Japanese control of all New Guinea, and leave them ready for a land assault on Australia. To protect this drive to the south, air bases in the Bismarck and Solomon Islands were crucial as staging areas and guarded against an Allied flank attack from the sea.[1]

During the first months of 1942, the American, British, Dutch, and Australian Allies (ABDA) faced a pincer movement aimed at isolating Australia and New Zealand from North American supply and reinforcement. Fortunately, the Japanese moved cautiously while exploiting advances in the Indian Ocean, and did not arrive in the Solomon Islands until March. They then waited until May 3 to take the administrative center of Tulagi. Reacting to an attempt to take Port Moresby, the U S. Navy clashed with the Japanese in the Coral Sea between May 5 and 8,[2] blunting Japan's drive south and forcing its Port Moresby invasion group to return to Rabaul.[3] (*Map 17*)

In the Solomons, the Japanese at first evinced little interest in Tulagi's neighboring island of Guadalcanal until July 6, when they landed to begin building an airstrip. The new military dispositions were quickly reported to

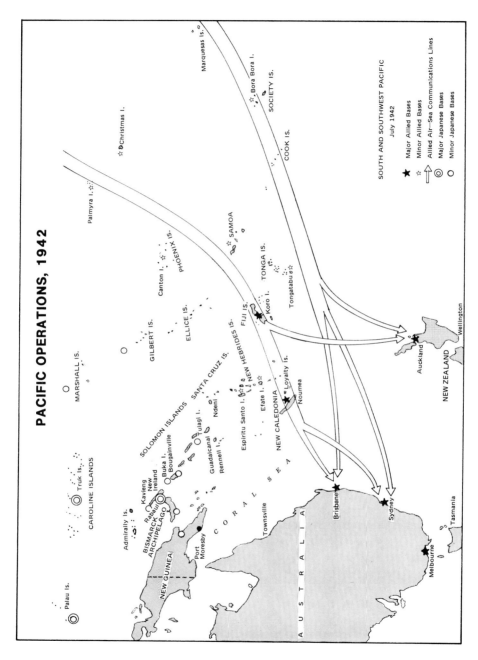

# PACIFIC OPERATIONS, 1942

SOUTH AND SOUTHWEST PACIFIC
July 1942

★ Major Allied Bases
☆ Minor Allied Bases
⇧ Allied Air—Sea Communications Lines
◎ Major Japanese Bases
○ Minor Japanese Bases

**Map 17**

the Australian Navy by coastwatchers* in the Solomons and thence to the Joint Chiefs of Staff in Washington.[4] The Americans had planned since early June to move north from the Fiji and New Hebrides Islands to block any further Japanese advance. Discussions among General Douglas MacArthur, Commander-in-Chief, Southwest Pacific Area, General George C. Marshall, Chief of Staff of the U. S. Army, and Admiral Ernest J. King, Commander-in-Chief, United States Fleet, resulted in a directive of July 2 to drive the Japanese from the New Britain-New Ireland-New Guinea area and preserve the Australian lifeline. The first objective was to seize or secure the Santa Cruz Islands, Tulagi, and islands adjacent to Tulagi—Guadalcanal lay just twenty miles across Sealark Channel.[5]

## Guadalcanal and Munda

The main Allied landing force at Guadalcanal on August 7, 1942, was the 1st Marine Division, commanded by Maj. Gen. Alexander A. Vandegrift. Vandegrift intended capturing Tulagi and securing a foothold on Guadalcanal in the Lunga Point area, taking at the same time the nearby uncompleted airstrip. As soon as the airfield was made ready for flying operations it would be occupied by an assortment of fighter and fighter-bomber squadrons that would be Vandegrift's only consistent air support.[6] Immediate Japanese opposition at Lunga Point came from some 2,230 troops and laborers of the Special Naval Landing Force supported by the Japanese Navy's Twenty-fifth Air Fleet and strong naval surface units. Vandegrift's Marines found little initial opposition on Guadalcanal, but encountered much stronger resistance on Tulagi and the adjacent small island of Gavutu.[7]

To protect the landing, B–17 bombers of Maj. Gen. George C. Kenney's Allied Air Forces, Southwest Pacific Area (SWPA), attacked airfields near Rabaul. These raids of August 7 and 8 found Japanese fighters and bombers, many of which were unprotected on the runways, at Vunakunau, near Rabaul. Kenney, newly established in his position, estimated that his fliers destroyed some seventy-five aircraft and believed the losses limited the Japanese ability to oppose the Marine landing. Intercepted radio messages confirmed the disruption of Japanese operations and their inability to offer immediate help to their forces on Guadalcanal. Kenney's attack surprised and pleased MacArthur, frustrated by the previously disorganized state of

---

* In the mid-1930s certain members of the Royal Australian Navy saw Japan as a potential adversary in a Pacific war. Australian naval intelligence officers began looking about for possible future sources of information and hit upon the idea of using people familiar with the territory to observe and report. Both Australia and New Zealand had coastwatching stations during World War II.

his hard pressed air forces. This modest success buoyed American spirits, but losses among American bombers were heavy and could not be sustained. The B-17s could not face Japanese interceptors alone, and no Allied fighters had the range to escort them on long flights. Protection was essential during the next eighteen months, but at the outset of the island campaigns only Japanese bombers had aerial protection.[8]

The Allies needed desperately to hold Henderson Field, but faced a strong Japanese reaction. Without air operations on Guadalcanal, the Solomon Islands position would collapse. The Japanese, on the other hand, had to destroy the Marine air base to protect their ships landing reinforcements on the island. A months long battle of attrition determined the outcome. On August 9, the Japanese Navy sank four Allied cruisers and a destroyer in the first battle of nearby Savo Island, a direct threat to the first Allied lodgement in the Pacific. Worse yet, the Japanese attack forced the withdrawal of the Marines' supply ships, leaving them short of much equipment, including that needed for anitaircraft defense of the island. Fortunately when it came ashore, the 1st Marine Division captured a variety of Japanese trucks, earth movers, and rollers. With these unfamiliar vehicles Marine engineers and Navy Seabees managed to complete and lengthen the runway at Henderson Field, named after Maj. Lofton Henderson, a Marine squadron commander killed at the battle of Midway. Nineteen fighters comprising Marine Fighting Squadron 223 (VMF-223) arrived on August 20. They were quickly joined by twelve dive bombers of Marine Scout Bomber Squadron 232 (VMSB-232). On August 22, fourteen P-39s of the United States Army Air Forces' 67th Fighter Squadron landed.[9] The Japanese operated from several air bases at Rabaul, Kavieng, Buka, and Buin, supplied from their home islands and the East Indies.[10]

In the first assault wave General Vandegrift split the Marine 3rd Defense Battalion between Guadalcanal and Tulagi. This unit, the first of several of the same type to serve in the Solomons, had the dual function of beach defense and antiaircraft protection. The 3rd and its sister units were created late in 1939 as a result of a long recognized need to protect forward naval bases, but it was not fully proficient on arrival in the Pacific.[11] Unable to cope adequately with high speed and nighttime targets, the unit had a great deal to learn in a short time, for Japanese pressure mounted rapidly.[12]

The battalion was equipped with 90-mm antiaircraft guns, capable of firing to a height of 33,800 feet, and 5-inch guns for shore defense. The antiaircraft group also had 20-mm and 40-mm cannon and .50-caliber machine guns for defense against low altitude attack. Fire control was the responsibility of the various battery commanders in conjunction with the 1st Marine Air Wing's air operations officer. The liaison between the two sections was not always effective, however, and gunners sometimes inadvertently fired into the paths of defending fighters, forcing the aircraft away from Japanese attackers and endangering friendly pilots.[13]

The 3rd Battalion had two SCR-268 gun control radars and an SCR-270B search radar as well as optical tracking devices. The gun control radars proved unable to locate an airborne target precisely. The SCR-268 was originally designed for searchlight control, which required aiming only to within 200 meters of a target but the bursting radius of the 90-mm shells was less than fifty meters. The SCR-270 was not much better. It was a crude instrument that could provide speed and bearing of a target, but not altitude. Moreover, local terrain features produced clutter and bad readings.[14]

The battalion lacked heavy weapons. Although the 90-mm was an excellent gun, the unit had only twelve assigned. The first battery of four guns fired on August 11, but the demands of fighting to secure Tulagi and the work necessary to complete the airfield runway delayed the arrival of the remainder until September 19. The battalion commander soon found out that he had not been given enough small weapons, such as .30-and .50-caliber machine guns to protect the 90-mm crews from low-level attacks.[15] Battery E, on Guadalcanal, defended Henderson Field. (*Map 18*) Since there were so few guns, they fired from near the midpoint of the runway to concentrate their aim over the airfield. They were dug in so that the crews were not exposed to blast and shrapnel during Japanese attacks.[16]

The main American defense weapon was the Grumman F4F-4 Wildcat fighter. This well armored aircraft carried six .50-caliber machine guns and had a top speed of 330 miles per hour at 19,000 feet. It was not as fast or as agile as its main adversary, the Japanese Mitsubishi A6M Reisen fighter (known as the Zero and later as the Zeke). The Zeros, however, had no armor or self sealing fuel tanks. Additionally, the Japanese used a two engine medium bomber, the Mitsubishi G4M, later designated the Betty by the Allies. The G4M also lacked armor, and its nonsealing fuel tanks, located between the engines and the fuselage, made them so infamous for exploding when hit that their crews referred to them as flying cigarette lighters. The Grumman fighters were joined by the 67th Fighter Squadron flying Bell P-39 and P-400 Airacobras (an export version of the P-39 intended originally for the RAF). The Airacobras could not operate at the 23,000 to 25,000 feet where the Japanese normally flew and, after August, served largely for surface attack.[17]

Marine and Navy engineer battalions were to repair damage to Henderson Field. Once the builders had completed the runway, they piled sand and gravel nearby. After an air raid or naval shelling, the material was quickly moved, the holes shaped, filled, and tamped, and the field restored to operation. Aircraft often began landing shortly after an air raid, which required rapid repairs. Japanese cruisers, destroyers, and sometimes battleships shelled Henderson Field at night, as did enemy artillery on the island.

**Marine 3d Defense Battlion 90–mm guns sited at the midpoint of Henderson Field's runway.**

These bombardments, frequently very heavy, could cause more damage than aircraft attacks.[18]

Early in the campaign, the most essential part of the air-warning system was the network of coastwatchers established in the northern Solomon Islands. On Bougainville and adjacent Buka Island, a group of men worked for senior coastwatchers Jack Read and Paul Mason. From their posts, these men reported by radio movements of the Japanese air and naval forces to Navy headquarters in Australia and to Henderson Field. The route of Japanese bombers from Rabaul and Kavieng past Bougainville, Choiseul, and New Georgia kept them in view of the coastwatchers for much of this flight. On Segi Island, 160 miles northwest of Henderson Field, District Officer D. G. Kennedy confirmed the reports of other coastwatchers. His position allowed calculation of speed and an approximate arrival time of the Japanese attackers even before they were within radar detection range.[19] Coastwatcher reports arriving up to one hour and forty minutes before an attack often gave sufficient time for the Wildcats to take off and climb to an altitude above that commonly used by Japanese bombers. The American fighters normally made only one diving pass from either side through the Japanese formation, avoiding the Zeros. The dive allowed a clear shot at the Bettys while staying clear of their dangerous 20-mm tail cannon.[20]

**F4F Wildcats in open maintenance revetment at Henderson Field, Guadalcanal, February 1943.**

The information radioed by the coastwatchers was collected at Henderson Field by a small team headed by Hugh Mackenzie, an Australian Naval Intelligence officer, who passed it to fighter operations which then directed the air interception effort. After a raid, as the returning Japanese passed Jack Read's coastwatching station on New Georgia, he reported their numbers and confirmed Japanese losses. As they became aware of the coastwatchers, the Japanese often flew farther out to sea or through clouds. The Marine radar sets then had to provide the missing information, but the 650 miles between the Japanese bases and the targets still limited the ways the Japanese could avoid the direct route.[21]

Because the U.S. Navy was forced out of Sealark Channel around Savo Island on August 9, the Americans could not land their search radar for some days. On the day of the invasion, the 1st Marine Division had captured several Japanese radar sets that they tried to use to no avail before shipping them home to the Naval Research Laboratory. Japanese communications equipment, however, including a variety of radio and telephone components, was quickly incorporated into the alerting system. Finally, the Defense Battalion's SCR–270B radar was installed just before Henderson Field's fighters arrived. Another SCR–270B went into service about September 15. It was assigned to the Marine Air Wing's Fighter Direction Center

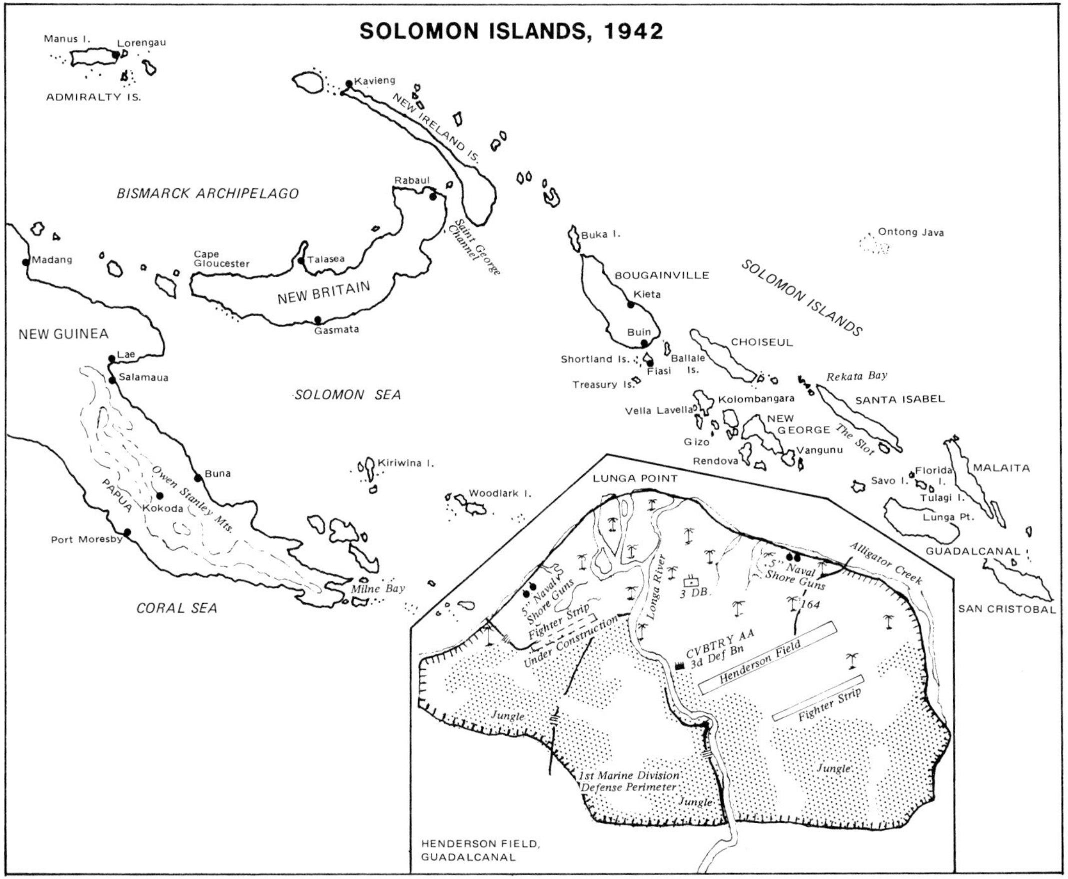
SOLOMON ISLANDS, 1942
Manus I.
Lorengau
ADMIRALTY IS.
Kavieng
NEW IRELAND IS.
BISMARCK ARCHIPELAGO
Rabaul
Saint George Channel
Madang
Cape Gloucester
Talasea
NEW BRITAIN
Gasmata
NEW GUINEA
Lae
Salamaua
SOLOMON SEA
Owen Stanley Mts.
Buna
PAPUA
Kokoda
Port Moresby
Milne Bay
CORAL SEA
Kiriwina I.
Woodlark I.
Buka I.
BOUGAINVILLE
Kieta
Buin
Shortland Is.
Fiasi
Ballale Is.
Treasury Is.
SOLOMON ISLANDS
Ontong Java
CHOISEUL
Rekata Bay
SANTA ISABEL
Kolombangara
Vella Lavella
NEW GEORGE
The Slot
Gizo
Vangunu
Rendova
Savo I.
Florida I.
Tulagi I.
Lunga Pt.
MALAITA
GUADALCANAL
SAN CRISTOBAL
LUNGA POINT
5" Naval Shore Guns
Fighter Strip Under Construction
Longa River
3 DB
5" Naval Shore Guns
164
Alligator Creek
CVBTRY AA 3d Def Bn
Henderson Field
Fighter Strip
Jungle
1st Marine Division Defense Perimeter
Jungle
Jungle
HENDERSON FIELD, GUADALCANAL

**Map 18**

**Crew poses with 20–mm antiaircraft guns at the Henderson strip.**

under control of Master Tech. Sgt. Dermott H. MacDonnell,* who became in his own right one of the keys to the air defense system on the island.[22]

At first the fighter control system was crude. As soon as the radar operators sighted a target, they sent the bearing and distance to Henderson's air operations officer, Maj. Joseph N. Renner. Lacking nearly every kind of reliable radio and signaling equipment and with almost no staff, the major launched planes as he received radar or coastwatcher reports. Later he supplemented his equipment with a salvaged aircraft radio installed in his truck. Renner also acted as an observer, identifying aircraft as friendly or enemy when they were in sight, then sounding the air raid alarm if necessary. The strain on the one man carrying this burden was heavy.[23]

---

* MacDonnell was born on August 16, 1921. He received the Silver Star for gallantry under fire at Henderson. He left Guadalcanal on March 8, 1943, and returned to the United States where he was commissioned, rising eventually to lieutenant colonel in the Marine Corps Reserve. He died in April 1976.

TABLE 24

## United States Air Defense Units
## Guadalcanal

| | |
|---|---|
| Marine Fighting Squadron 223 (F4F–4)* | August 20–October 11, 1942 |
| Marine Fighting Squadron 224 (F4F–4) | August 30–October 16, 1942 |
| AAF 67th Fighter Squadron (P–39, P–40) | August 22–February 8, 1943 |
| Navy Fighting Squadron 5 (F4F–4) | September 11–October 16 |
| Marine Fighting Squadron 121 (F4F–4) | October 9–December 30 |
| Marine Fighting Squadron 212 (F4F–4) | October 16 into 1943 |
| Marine Fighting Squadron 112 (F4F–4) | November 2, 1942 into 1943 |
| Marine Fighting Squadron 122 (F4F–4) | November 12, 1942, into 1943 |

| | | |
|---|---|---|
| Third Defense Battalion | 12 | 90-mm guns |
| | | .50 caliber machine guns |
| | | 20-mm cannon |
| | 8 | 40-mm cannon |

Third Barrage Balloon Squadron, USMC
> Arrived with balloons and .30 and .50 caliber AA machine guns. The balloons were not used on Guadalcanal. Anchorages were difficult to find, and there was fear the balloons would draw attacking aircraft and interfere with the operation of Henderson Field. Squadron personnel were used to augment various AA positions on Guadalcanal and Tulagi.

First Marine Aviation Engineer Battalion

Navy Construction Battalion 6 (Seabees)

* The strength of flying squadrons varied almost daily. Replacements arrived frequently and without regularity. Any attempt to list numbers of aircraft assigned is almost impossible.

**Sources:** Miller, *The Cactus Air Force*
        USMC Historical Files

TABLE 25

## Japanese Navy Air Units
## Solomon Islands

25th Air Flotilla
(Rear Adm. Sadayoshi Yamada)
August 1942

| | | |
|---|---|---|
| Tainan Air Group | Model 0 Fighters (Zeke) | 24 |
| 2nd Air Group | Model 0 Fighters, square Wing (Hamp) | 15 |
| | Model 99 Dive Bombers (Val) | 16 |
| Yokohama Air Group | Model 97 Flying Boat | 9 |
| | Model 0 Fighters (float type) (Rufe) | 11 |
| 4th Air Group | Model 1 Medium Bombers (Betty) | 32 |
| | | 107 |

11th Air Fleet
(Vice Adm. Nishizo Tsukahara)
30 September 1942

Rabaul

| | | |
|---|---|---|
| 25th Air Flotilla (Rear Admiral Yamada) | | |
| Tainan Air Group | Model 0 Fighters (Zeke) | 8 |
| 2nd Air Group | Model 0 Fighters (Hamp) | 16 |
| 6th Air Group | Model 0 Fighters (Zeke) | 12 |
| | Model 0 Fighters (Hamp) | 13 |
| 3rd Air Group | Model 0 Fighters (Zeke) | 20 |
| Kanoya Air Group | Model 0 Fighters (Zeke) | 8 |
| | | 77 |

Kavieng

| | | |
|---|---|---|
| 26 Air Flotilla (Vice Adm. Jinichi Kusaka) | | |
| Kisarazu Air Group | Model 1 Medium Bombers | 15 |
| Misawa Air Group | Model 1 Medium Bombers | 12 |
| Takao Air Group | Model 1 Medium Bombers | 19 |
| Kanoya Air Group | Model 1 Medium Bombers | 16 |
| | | 62 |

**Sources:** IIS 43–4, Jan 7, 1943
Miller, *The Cactus Air Force*
USMC Historical Files

**Control panel of captured Japanese radar installation, Guadalcanal, October 1942. The unit was sent to the Naval Research Laboratory for evaluation.**

On October 8, Lt. Lewis C. Mattison and Ens. W. A. Noll, both naval officers sent from the Navy's fighter director school at Pearl Harbor, arrived on Guadalcanal. There they found two rudimentary radar air search operations. One was used by the 1st Marine Air Wing's fighter controllers, the other by the 3rd Defense Battalion. The two search efforts at first were not integrated and not always mutually supporting, although there was contact between them. Moreover, the early radar sets were not very reliable and reported false returns from the surrounding mountains and hills. Sergeant MacDonnell was often the only man who could interpret the zigzag lines on the oscilloscopes and tell how many airplanes were in an attacking formation. Lieutenant Mattison gave much of the credit for the radar's success to MacDonnell, who could tell from the radar set's A-scope not only how many aircraft were in a formation, but could also frequently identify medium bombers, dive bombers, fighters, or long range seaplanes.

MacDonnell was a harried commander's dream who specialized in getting around shortcomings in his equipment. For example, radar operators could get speed and bearings of approaching raids on the SCR–270 but had

228

The SCR-270 radar had ten degrees of tilt designed into its frame. Master Tech. Sgt. Dermott H. McDonnell used this feature to advantage in the defense of Guadalcanal.

to wait for the enemy to come within 25 miles before the SCR-268 gave them the accurate altitude reading. The sergeant knew that the 270's frame was tiltable 10 degrees backward, so that the antenna could be adjusted for terrain contour when installed. MacDonnell used this feature to take two readings on a target, one with the antenna perpendicular, another with the antenna slightly reclined. He could then calculate an approximate altitude. Fighters vectored to the heading waited above that level. More exact determination could be made when the Japanese came within the SCR-268's range, and the American interceptors closed in.[24]

Defending fighters rarely tried to attack the Japanese before they reached the target area. Poor ground to air radios limited the intercept zone to an area ten to fifteen miles from Henderson Field.[25] In the sky above the field, the Wildcat pilots' dive and run tactic was very effective and compensated for the limited interception zone. The resilient airplane in the hands of capable pilots shot down or damaged a disproportionate number of enemy

Maj. Gen. Roy S. Geiger surveys the situation on Tulagi in January 1943. Geiger's grit alone was a major factor in the American air defense of Guadalcanal.

aircraft. As the Americans did well under the able leadership of Brig. Gen. Roy S. Geiger, the Marine air commander at Guadalcanal, they became more confident, but difficulties persisted.[26]

Command and control of the air defense operation was shaky from the start of the battle. Both Lieutenant Mattison, the chief fighter director, and Col. Robert H. Pepper, the 3rd Defense Battalion's commander, recommended improving liaison between radar sets and fighter operations. Colonel Pepper also cited an insufficient information exchange between battery commanders and fighter squadrons as the cause of frequent conflict and confusion. On some occasions, the gunners fired on friendly planes. At others, confusion between the two units was so serious it prevented accurate tracking and interception of enemy aircraft. Neither Pepper nor his gunners were apparently aware of what was expected of them. In his after action report, Pepper begged to have the defense battalion commander sit in on the planning of operations in which his defense battalion was to be involved. Such a request from the man responsible for antiaircraft and shore defense operations seems inconceivable, yet neither the Marine commander nor his staff sought Pepper's consistent participation. The situation illustrated clearly the problems which faced the willing, yet inexperienced, American amphibious group.[27]

Other problems also dogged the Americans. At first, dispersal was poor, revetments and blast shields could not be built, and the aircraft had to be scattered widely about the open field. Fortunately, the 90-mm guns of the defense battalion kept the Japanese bombers high, making their bombardiers' aim uncertain. By early October, the engineers had finished a fighter strip about one mile from the original field. This dirt runway was rolled when necessary, but was excessively muddy after a rain. Nevertheless, use of two fields allowed separation of dive bomber and fighter squadrons and provided further dispersal. Construction continued throughout the campaign, and by the end of the year three adjacent strips were in use with revetments and blast shields to shelter most of the planes and equipment.[28]

Japanese naval air units bombed the fields heavily. Most of the raids came during the day, but night bombers harassed the defenders, keeping pilots awake or making them run for shelter in foxholes or trenches. Exhaustion resulted in accidents and unnecessary combat losses. General Geiger could do little about the night attacks as he had no radar equipped night fighters. Inadequate radar aiming meant the AA gunners could help little. The stress was so great that pilots returning from combat at times climbed out of their aircraft and collapsed in tears. On occasion, Geiger was hard pressed to get the men to fly again the same day.[29]

The attackers were not without their own difficulties. The distance from Rabaul and Kavieng forced the Japanese to leave early in the day, usually arriving over Henderson Field between eleven and twelve o'clock in the morning. The escorting fighters had to use external fuel tanks that could not be jettisonned, thus reducing their maneuverability. After October 20, Japanese fighters flew from Buin, but that was still 300 miles from their targets. Moreover, the flights invariably arrived from the northwest, often after forewarning from coastwatcher stations and radar. The long distances, American awareness of impending attacks, and inadequately armored Japanese planes gave the defenders an important advantage, which they used repeatedly to ambush the Japanese. After slashing through the flights of bombers, the Wildcats dove to safety at Henderson. Moreover, American airmen shot down could be rescued. Downed Japanese pilots were normally lost at sea or captured.[30]

The American ability to recover both pilots and damaged aircraft was important to the course of battle. Fighter strength, not great to begin with, often fell to no more than a handful of operational aircraft during August and September. Lack of spare parts, battle damage, and accidents caused constant loss. Only replacements flown from carriers and islands to the

**White smoke marks direct Japanese hit on American hangar on Henderson Field, September 1942.**

south enabled the squadrons to offer resistance. Working each night, the mechanics kept the force at a barely effective level.[31]

By mid-October American fighter strength had improved somewhat, just as air defense of Henderson Field reached a critical stage. Repeated bombings, coupled with Japanese naval and land-based artillery fire exerted severe pressure on the Marines. Japanese attempts at reinforcing their garrison were constant and could be defeated only by air attacks on the transport ships, campsites, and supply areas.[32] Fierce combat continued into November. Lieutenant Mattison and his fighter directors improved the radar warning system by linking all the radar sets on the island to their operation and tightening the liaison with fighter operations. Sergeant MacDonnell's adept use of the sets gave more reliable and useful information.[33] The 3rd Defense Battalion recorded eighty-two air attacks on the Marine air base before heavy Japanese losses caused the number of air raids to decline significantly after November 15. By November 22 it became apparent that the American position could be held, though heavy ground fighting on the island continued.[34]

Japan's failure to retake Guadalcanal was due largely to air operations from Henderson Field. Continued destruction of Japanese supply and reinforcement shipping, culminating in the defeat of a large Japanese naval relief attempt on the night of November 14–15, left the enemy starving. The Marines, now reinforced by the Army's 164th Infantry Regiment, beat back several frontal attacks. During December and January the Japanese, weakened by disease and hunger, were forced into a small area on the north end of the island. The Japanese Navy withdrew the few survivors in early February 1943.[35]

American air defense of Guadalcanal and Henderson Field succeeded almost in spite of itself. The Marines were inexperienced and ill prepared for sustained combat after the Navy support ships departed precipitously on August 9th with much of their equipment. Even if the ships had stayed, however, the Marines were far from home, at the end of a long supply line, and in an unfamiliar area. Fortunately for the Americans, the Japanese, operating at the extreme range of their aircraft, were funneled toward a small target area. The defenders, fighting desperately and commanded by strong men like Geiger and others, used their advance warnings to great advantage. Many people on the isolated Guadalcanal battlefield were driven by a combination of desperation and a sense of duty. Others found the challenges well suited to their talents. Sergeant MacDonnell's innovative use of radar was not the only example of initiative and skill, but his remarkable accomplishments were more significant than many. Men like him provided Lieutenant Mattison's fighter direction center as well Geiger's aviators with the resources they needed to repel the Japanese air assaults. In addition, the Americans benefitted from British success in 1940. Naval officers who learned the art of fighter direction from the RAF in England taught men like Mattison and Noll. They in turn used the knowledge to fend off the Axis Pacific partner.[36]

The small number of American fighters wrought disproportionately heavy losses, although an exact comparison cannot be made because of a lack of adequate records. American pilots may have destroyed as many as 535 Japanese planes by December 28 with a corresponding loss of 78. In addition, the 3rd Defense Battalion gunners added 49 with another 13 probably shot down.[37] A postwar Japanese study estimated that they lost only 136 aircraft during the Guadalcanal campaign (53 bombers and 83 fighters), but this is almost certainly too low. In all probability, the Japanese lost some 300 fighters and an equal number of bombers and torpedo planes in action in the Solomons and adjacent waters. Considering American aircraft losses at the battles of the Coral Sea and Santa Cruz Islands, there was a rough casualty ratio of four to one in favor of the Americans.[38]

Interception of Japanese radio transmissions played only a small part in the Allies' victory. A U.S. Navy Strategic Direction Finder station was established on Guadalcanal in November 1942. This station was part of the Pacific intercept and direction finding (D/F) net responsible for locating Japanese radio transmissions and reading enemy radio traffic. The Guadalcanal station did both D/F and intercept work, but little is known of its operation before June 1944. It is unlikely this station provided significant information of approaching air attacks until after the main battle, if at all. The operation's late start and problems caused by loss of some equipment in

233

an aircraft crash probably limited the station's intelligence output until after November 22. Intercept work may not have begun on Guadalcanal until early 1943. At that time, the information gained normally went to the net control unit at Pearl Harbor, unless it was immediately recognized as pertaining to the island. During the heaviest fighting, occasional warnings came from the Commander-in-Chief Pacific (CINCPAC) at Pearl Harbor, but were not always accurate. In any event, the coastwatchers and radar provided a much faster and more reliable warning.[39]

Although its hold was tenuous at times, the defense at Henderson Field stopped the Japanese advance and kept open the lines of communication to Australia. Guadalcanal marked the limit of Japanese expansion in the South Pacific area. The Americans, at the same time, learned a great deal about the relationship between air superiority and air base defense. Except for the debacles at Hickam and Clark Fields in December 1941, Henderson Field was the first major American attempt at defending an airfield in a combat theater during World War II. Many of the problems faced in August 1942 were due to inexperience, but were overcome by the end of the year. As the Americans seized other airfields, they applied the knowledge gained in radar operation, fighter control, and AA gun cooperation with increasing success.

Having secured themselves on Guadalcanal, the Allies began to take the offensive. Several Japanese bases in the South Pacific posed a danger to their position. Throughout October, reports from coastwatchers and search aircraft indicated considerable Japanese use of airfields at Buka and Kahili. Allied aircraft attacked Buka during October and November with limited success. Airplanes and facilities were damaged, but even after a strong attack on November 18 there were thirty fighters operating. Then, in early December, a coastwatcher reported a new base being built at Munda, New Georgia, within 250 miles of Henderson Field.[40]

The construction being done by the Japanese at Munda was almost entirely under camouflage. Tree tops were held in place over the new runways by nets and wires while the trunks were removed and construction went on beneath. On December 5th, pilots of two USAAF P–39s flying over Munda sighted two airstrips with five trucks, two rollers, and many carts. Before leaving with this information, the Americans made a strafing pass at fifty feet, the first of many attacks.[41]

Through the rest of December the Americans hit Munda frequently, two and three raids a day being not uncommon. On December 12, B–17s from Australia began a series of raids on the airfield. The Japanese doggedly continued work, bringing fighters to protect the field late in the month. The heaviest strikes came on Christmas Eve of 1942, when three separate raids found more than twenty Japanese planes on the ground. Ten were shot down as they took off, another ten or twelve were destroyed on the field. The attacks continued into the new year and the Japanese faced an increasingly difficult situation.[42]

The Japanese never used radar at Munda. They relied on reports from Japanese soldiers, some on Guadalcanal, who radioed reports of American air activity, much as did the coastwatchers. Ground observation by the Japanese had limited utility because of the vast area, the frequent cloudy weather, and the deteriorating Japanese situation in the southern Solomons. As a result, the American raids from Guadalcanal and New Guinea frequently surprised the defenders and inflicted heavy losses.[43]

The heavy fire of numerous Japanese antiaircraft guns failed to prevent constant cratering of the runways. During the first 6 months of 1943, attacks by American aircraft killed some 200 Japanese gunners, and the AA crews' discipline suffered. In early March 1943, Admiral William F. Halsey, commander of all U.S. forces in the South Pacific, had his staff analyze the loss rates for fighter escorted missions to Munda. The results clearly showed the difference between Japanese defense against bomber attacks made with and without fighter participation. During the period from December 1942 to February 1943, the Americans lost 12 aircraft on 2,183 sorties where only AA fire was seen. During the same period, there were 607 sorties against combined AA and fighters, with 56 aircraft lost.[44]

Generally, throughout the Solomon campaign, land based Japanese antiaircraft guns were not particularly effective. Japanese gunners could not make range corrections quickly enough to bring attacking aircraft under fire. It was common for American crews to observe AA bursts behind and below their formations. In contrast, Japanese naval AA gunners were more accurate, given their central shipboard fire control, excellent range finders, and the much higher quality of their training. Most of the gunfire faced by Americans attacking Munda's airfield was not from ships, however.[45]

In aerial combat during this time the results favored the Allies by a ratio of 3.34 to 1. The heaviest Allied losses were sustained by American torpedo bombers flying on missions against enemy shipping. Loss rates for missions directed against the air base at Munda heavily favored the Americans. The reasons for such aerial success were, as at Guadalcanal, better armed and armored aircraft, increasing pilot experience, and the Allied ability to bring firepower to bear on a target. At the same time, veteran Japanese pilots could not be replaced quickly and the AA defense lacked the warning, the gun density, and the accuracy needed to deter attacks.[46]

Despite the defense's lack of success, the Japanese were able to repair most bomb damage in forty-eight hours. Runway repairs were accomplished largely by sheer determination on the part of base construction crews, and it was necessary for the Allies to bomb the field daily to keep it closed. Heavy cratering prevented Munda's use as a fighter base, and there was little the Japanese could do to stop the almost daily raids. When B-26s entered the fray, the pressure on Munda continued, forcing the Japanese to remove their air operations. After the end of December 1942, the field was used only to service aircraft. Repeated heavy bombing, however, continued up to the American seizure of New Georgia in July 1943. Any significant respite would have allowed the Japanese forces to restore the field fully.[47]

Beginning on June 30, 1943, the Allied landings on New Georgia Island developed into 37 days of fighting against intense Japanese resistance. The air campaign included neutralizing the nearby Japanese air bases. Not only Munda was attacked, but also airfields at Kahili, Ballale, Vila, Rakata Bay, Buka, and Rabaul. Five hundred thirty-three Allied aircraft began the effort against New Georgia's enemy positions. Japanese reaction included air raids by as many as 120 aircraft directed mostly against supply and equipment storage areas. Major targets of the Allies included AA sites, storage areas, runways, and aircraft parking spots on which were dropped 1,900,000 pounds of explosives in 5 weeks. Other bases on neighboring islands were attacked as heavily as necessary to keep them out of operation. The Japanese lost 348 aircraft, the Allies 121. Most of the American losses were the result of aerial fighting and attacks on Japanese shipping.[48]

Although Japanese air power in the Solomons was largely destroyed by mid-July, the bitter campaign for New Georgia went on until August 4, far longer than anticipated. The American planners had underestimated Japanese determination to fight to the end, their skill at deploying forces in fortified positions, and their tenacious leadership. A major factor in the final American victory was the Allied counterair campaign. Denying the Japanese the use of their bases eased the job considerably and allowed the land and naval forces to extract the defenders from their fortifications.[49]

## Fifth Air Force: Port Moresby to Hollandia

The American victory on Guadalcanal drove the Japanese north in the Solomons, but to the west, the collapse of the ABDA command in February 1942, after the fall of Singapore and the destruction of major Allied forces in Southeast Asia had left a dangerous threat to Australia from the East Indies. Blocked temporarily at the battle of the Coral Sea, the Japanese did not give up their designs on Port Moresby. (*Map 19*) The small town soon became the key to the defense of Papua and the center of Allied air and land forces in the area. The Japanese threatened Port Moresby not only by invasion from the sea, but also by an overland attack from northeast New Guinea via the Kokoda Trail over the precipitous Owen Stanley Mountains.[50]

In early 1942, Port Moresby's airfields were small and virtually undefended. (*Map 20*) Japanese air attacks were such a threat to Allied aircraft on the ground that few were based there. Bombers used Port Moresby's Seven Mile airdrome as a staging base on flights from Australia, landing in

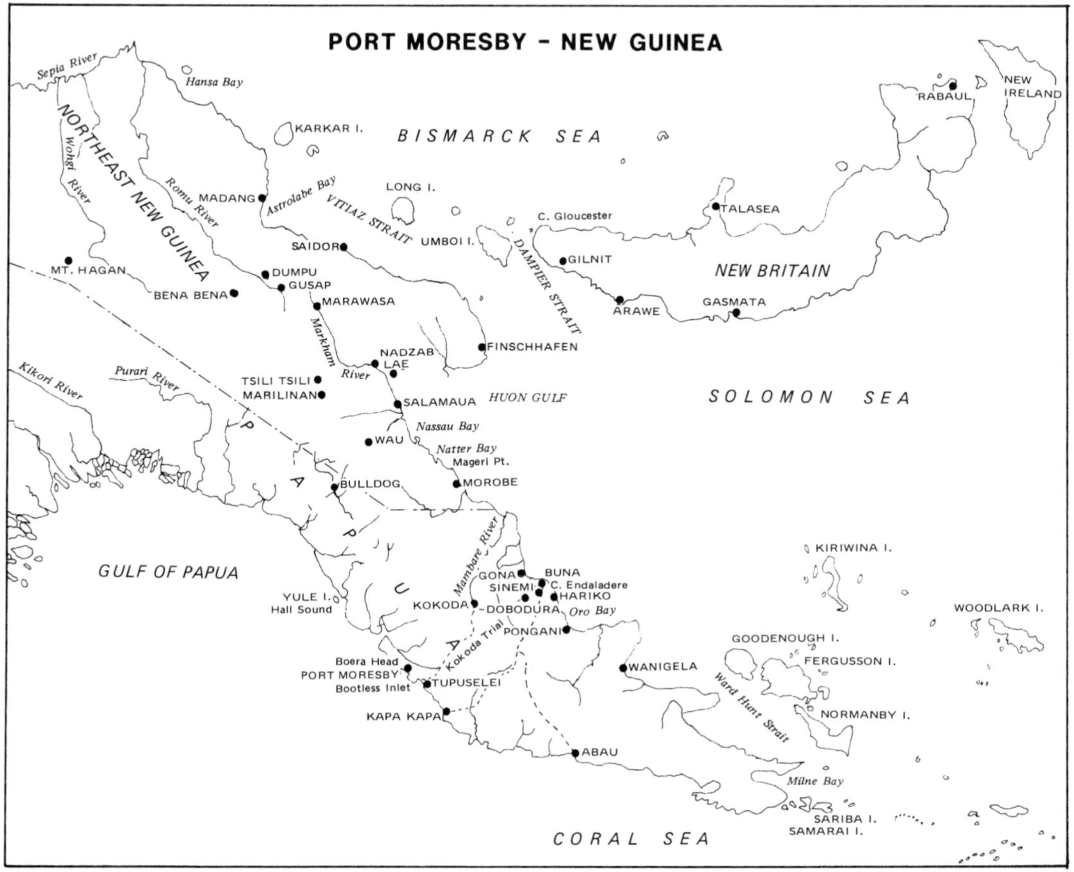

Map 19

PORT MORESBY – NEW GUINEA

BISMARCK SEA

NORTHEAST NEW GUINEA

GULF OF PAPUA

Sepik River

Hansa Bay

Wohat River

Ramu River

MT. HAGAN

BENA BENA

Karoa River

Purari River

TSILI TSILI

MARILINAN

DUMPU

GUSAP

MADANG

SAIDOR

MARAWASA

Markham River

Astrolabe Bay

VITIAZ STRAIT

KARKAR I.

LONG I.

UMBOI I.

DAMPIER STRAIT

C. Gloucester

GILNIT

ARAWE

GASMATA

NEW BRITAIN

TALASEA

RABAUL

NEW IRELAND

NADZAB

LAE

SALAMAUA

FINSCHHAFEN

HUON GULF

BULLDOG

WAU

Nassau Bay

Mageri Pt.

MOROBE

SOLOMON SEA

YULE I.

Hall Sound

PORT MORESBY

Bootless Inlet

Boera Head

KAPA KAPA

TUPUSELEI

KOKODA

Kokoda Trail

Mambare River

GONA

SINEMI

DOBODURA

PONGANI

BUNA

C. Endaiadere

HARIKO

(Oro Bay)

ABAU

WANIGELA

CORAL SEA

GOODENOUGH I.

FERGUSSON I.

NORMANBY I.

Milne Bay

SARIBA I.

SAMARAI I.

Ward Hunt Strait

KIRIWINA I.

WOODLARK I.

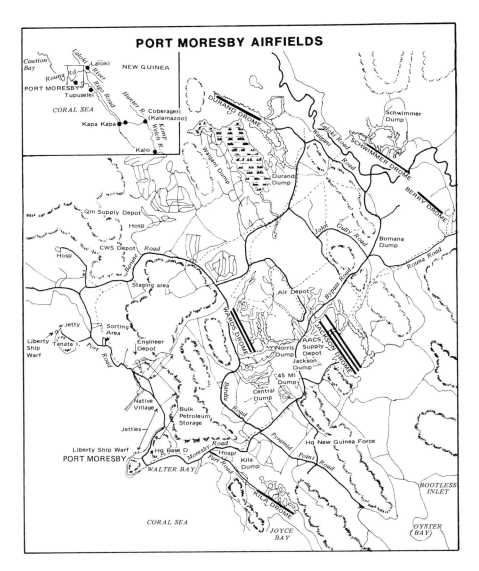

# PORT MORESBY AIRFIELDS

**Map 20**

the evening, after dark, and departing the following dawn.[51] On June 22, 1942, General MacArthur directed construction of an airfield at Milne Bay, at the eastern end of New Guinea. The base was occupied by a squadron of Royal Australian Air Force P-40s late in July. In all, the Allies built three landing strips at Milne Bay while rushing seven to completion at Port Moresby. Because of an almost complete lack of road and rail transportation in New Guinea, these air bases, with their associated seaports, and others to be built during the course of the campaign, became the key to sustaining the ground force and the ultimate Allied success in defeating the Japanese in New Guinea.[52]

A Japanese landing in the Buna–Gona area late on the night of July 21, 1942, blocked an Allied plan to occupy the region. By mid-August, Maj. Gen. Tomitaro Horii's Army and Special Naval Landing Force units held the trail junction and small airfield at Kokoda, northeast of the Owen Stanleys. They then stood poised to cross the mountains and push the Australians out of New Guinea. To do so, however, Horii's troops had to cross the roughest terrain found in any theater of World War II. The jungle covered Owen Stanley mountains were exceptionally steep. Rainfall averaged 200 to 300 inches per year and there were no roads. Where the muddy, slippery Kokoda trail passed through a mountain gap it was wide enough for only one person at a time. Much of the passage had to be cleared with machetes or bolo knives, and supplies could be hauled by either side only with great difficulty. The tired and undernourished men with inadequate inoculation easily contracted a variety of tropical diseases.[53]

The Allies, not initially expecting an overland Japanese thrust, quickly reinforced Papua's defenses. Two brigades of the 7th Australian Infantry Division landed at Port Moresby, a third at Milne Bay.[54] In bitter fighting between August 25 and September 6 an Allied force cleared a Japanese landing force from Milne Bay. Defense of the Kokoda trail was, however, more difficult. Outnumbered by the Japanese, the Australian Army and militia units fell back repeatedly until, reinforced by an additional brigade, they stopped the enemy about twenty miles from Port Moresby in mid-September. To prepare for a flank attack on Japanese positions north of the mountains, General Kenney organized a successful airlift of the United States 128th Infantry Regiment from Australia to Port Moresby. This was the first American attempt at moving a unit of this size by air, and some at SWPA headquarters doubted it could succeed. Delivering on what many considered a rash promise, Kenney saw his standing with MacArthur rise again. At the same time, his Southwest Pacific Air Forces launched an air campaign against the Japanese logistics system, attacking supply bases, trails, bridges, and the airfield at Buna.[55]

During the fighting in 1942, Kenney's main base was at Port Moresby's several landing strips. Designed to handle fighter planes and transports, the

Strip at Durand Airdrome outside Port Moresby offers no protection to parked Fifth Air Force planes. A P–47 (*below*) in earth reventment at Ward Airdrome.

**U.S. Army troops of the 128th Infantry arrive at Port Moresby from Australia.**

initial strips were rapidly enlarged. At first, there were almost no air warning or antiaircraft artillery units available, and early warning of attacks came either from ground observers or fighter patrols. As a result, the early air defense of the Port Moresby–Milne Bay area rested largely on fighters and wide dispersal of aircraft and supplies on the ground. The Port Moresby base area became a sprawling affair, characterized by numerous taxiways and revetted parking areas similar to those on Malta. American P–38s, P–39s, and USAAF and Australian Air Force P–40s stood ground alert, to be launched at the approach of a Japanese force.[56] Fortunately for the Allies, Japanese air strength in New Guinea was slight during the summer of 1942. Kenney estimated on August 2 that there were only 35 enemy airplanes on the island. Most of the air threat came from Rabaul, and that base would be preoccupied with the Guadalcanal operation for some time. Even so, the Japanese mustered frequent, if not always heavy, attacks on Kenney's air bases.[57]

The inexperienced Americans found difficulty organizing air base defenses. In 1942 the United States Army lacked trained manpower enough to fight both a European and an Asian war. The mobilization begun in 1940 had yet to meet military requirements, and warning, antiaircraft, and fighter units arrived in the theater in small numbers. Some units arrived without all of their equipment, others had outdated guns or aircraft that were to be replaced when industrial production caught up to the Army's needs.[58]

The first of the United States' air warning units to reach New Guinea, a plotting platoon of the 694th Air Warning Company, came on August 8, 1942. The first American radar set arrived a month later to supplement an Australian fighter sector radar recently installed near Port Moresby. The Allies organized their fighter sectors after those developed by the RAF in Britain, and they became the standard Allied air defense unit in the SWPA. As more air warning companies arrived in the theater they joined the 565th Signal Air Warning Battalion and operated within specific fighter sectors, giving information to the sector commander and the antiaircraft gunners. Establishing a warning service was, however, a time consuming process with little progress visible for months. It was not until December 29, 1942, that the Allies developed a comprehensive radar coverage plan for New Guinea. Shortly thereafter, another Air Warning Battalion, the 583rd, began operating. The battalions provided detection of enemy aircraft by both ground spotters and radar. Each had one or more plotting and control centers, depending upon the size and needs of the fighter sectors.[59]

In theory, all air defense functions (warning, AA, and fighters) were under the operational control of Maj. Gen. Ennis C. Whitehead, Commander of the Advance Echelon, Fifth Air Force, and an exceptionally able planner and leader. Whitehead exercised control through the V Fighter Command and subordinate fighter sectors. It was to the sector commanders that the warning battalions provided their information. There was, however, another source of similar reports. Each of the USAAF fighter groups that arrived in New Guinea had an assigned fighter control squadron charged with the responsibility of dispatching fighters to intercept an approaching enemy force. Each fighter control squadron had as its center a plotting and control section analogous to the plotting platoons of the air warning companies and battalions. Although the control squadrons lacked radar, they were designed to work independently of warning battalions. Information about approaching enemy formations came from airborne patrols, ground observers, and the aircraft warning units in the area.[60] When the warning battalions and fighter control squadrons were in place, Whitehead found they duplicated each others' functions to a great extent. Neither type of organization intended to relinquish its duties to the other and each possessed elements the other lacked.[61] The inexperience, poor planning, and divided responsibilities that plagued cooperation between American ground and air forces during the summer of 1940 still plagued operations in New Guinea.

The problems of managing a system in which rival units did similar jobs grew throughout 1942 and 1943. Because the warning battalions possessed radar stations and plotting and control ability, they gradually became the primary sources of attack alerts. The fighter control squadrons were relegated to operating the various fighter control centers. Hampered by the confusion, Allied effectiveness did not improve quickly. Serious problems in coordination between fighter sectors existed as late as March 1943. Communications were poor, radar plotters were not familiar with procedures, and IFF responses appearing on one sector's radar screens were not seen on others'. Emphasis on training and procedural standards helped, and by late April major Japanese air raids were repulsed by fighters scrambled with adequate warning. At the same time, the difficult experiences of its units overseas were not lost on the AAF's headquarters, which improved the training of fighter control units still forming in the United States.[62]

The majority of the AA units sent to the Southwest Pacific by the Americans were former National Guard cavalry hastily redesignated and brought into federal service in 1940 and 1941. Many were originally issued .50-caliber machine guns for initial training at Camp Davis, North Carolina. As heavier weapons became available, the units were converted to automatic weapons battalions (37-mm or 40-mm), or gun battalions (90-mm). The majority of those organizations sent to the SWPA went first to Australia, but two automatic weapons battalions (the 101st and 211th) with thirty-two guns each went directly to Port Moresby. Another, the 104th, the Americans divided between Merauke, Dutch New Guinea, and Milne Bay. One 90-mm gun battalion (the 745th), with sixteen guns, defended Port Moresby. General Kenney had the 709th AAA Machine Gun Battery (Air Transportable), airlifted to Milne Bay on August 24, 1942.[63] A few days later, the eight machine guns of this unit, used for ground defense, played a major part in turning back the Japanese attempt to capture the Milne Bay air strip. Few other such organizations arrived before mid-1943, however. The weapons in place had to suffice for the interim.[64]

The most obvious aspect of Allied air base defense was Kenney's policy of aggressive attack of Japanese bases carried out by the V Bomber and V Fighter Commands, both organized late in 1942. These two commands took control of the American squadrons which had been operating in Australia and New Guinea since March of that year on a more or less independent basis under the control of Allied Air Forces Southwest Pacific Area. It was the fighter and bomber squadrons, used in a consistent application of air power, that gave Kenney secure bases.[65]

General Kenney was an ardent air power advocate and a man who believed in aggressive low altitude attack. He was a gregarious extrovert who

**Men of Battery D, 101st Coast Artillery, watch a C–47 take off at Ward Airdrome near Port Moresby, February 1943.**

always wanted what he referred to as "operators" in charge. By that term he meant pilots who could "shoot up" any target, preferably with machine guns, and who embodied to some extent the qualities of scrounger and pirate. In short, Kenney wanted his subordinate leaders to be self sufficient men who did not have to be pushed to do a job and did not always adhere to regulations while doing so. From the day he assumed command of the Southwest Pacific Air Forces, Kenney was convinced that the best way to protect his air force was to destroy that of the enemy, either in the air or on the ground at home bases. He thus began a series of modifications to his A-20 and B–25 aircraft that gave them great forward firepower from as many as eight or ten .50-caliber machine guns. He also acquired from the United States several thousand small fragmentation bombs fitted with parachutes (para-frag bombs) that could be dropped on airfields from low altitude, and he abandoned use of the A-24 attack aircraft (the AAF's version of the Navy's SBD dive bomber), which he said was worthless because of its low firepower and high loss rate. Actually, dive bombing did not fit Kenney's concept of jungle warfare, and he had little use for the plane in New Guinea.[66]

244

Kenney combined his fondness of attack with a belief that he could supply by air the Allied ground forces north of the Owen Stanleys. To do this, he had to seize or build bases wherever those forces moved. The first major bases the Allies set up north of the Owen Stanleys were taken by air. They were actually nothing more than open fields at Wanigela and Dobodura (*Map 21*), which Kenney's men quickly converted to landing strips that supported Australian and American infantry assaulting strong Japanese positions in the Buna-Oro Bay area late in 1942. After the capture of Buna on December 31, the Allies quickly established bases at Nadzab and the upper Markham Valley. Each base put Kenney's forces closer to the main Japanese air installations at Wewak and Hollandia. Kenney's advance bases were rapidly constructed by RAAF engineers or U.S. Army aviation engineer battalions assigned to the SWPA Engineer, Maj. Gen. Hugh J. Casey. For special operations, such as those in the Markham Valley, the Army temporarily attached aviation engineer units to the Fifth Air Force, which airlifted them to the new work site. In February 1943, Kenney tried to take control of the aviation engineers, but Casey argued persuasively to MacArthur that central control would allow more effective use of their small numbers and limited types and amounts of equipment.[67]

Despite the fact that there were so few antiaircraft weapons available, Kenney argued for his forward base concept at every opportunity. It is doubtful that the lack of Allied AA guns ever impeded Kenney's efforts to establish forward bases. His wartime diaries contain no second thoughts on the matter; throughout the New Guinea campaign he remained assured of the efficacy of attack aviation. Kenney's view of an air campaign was to hit enemy targets, especially air bases, with a preponderance of machine gun fire to suppress defenses followed by heavy bombing. He continued attacks against the same target until it was destroyed, thus eliminating potential threats to his airfields.[68] Because of his successes at reorganizing the SWPA air forces, airlifting the American infantry to Port Moresby, the defenders to Milne Bay, and bombing Rabaul on the morning the Marines landed on Guadalcanal, Kenney found that General MacArthur readily accepted most of his ideas. More important, MacArthur fully supported Kenney in his drive to obtain more fighter and bomber units from Army Air Forces headquarters in Washington.[69]

Kenney was not a man to get tied up with organizational wrangling, and he left the problems of sorting out the confused warning and fighter control situation almost entirely to General Whitehead. It was not until early 1943, while the Allies were pushing into the Markham Valley, that Whitehead began resolving the air defense problem. Some time passed before he saw success, and all the while the Japanese strengthened their air forces in New Guinea. A radio net linking the Allied bases at Buna, Goodenough Island, and Normanby Island was not completed until February, although an Aus-

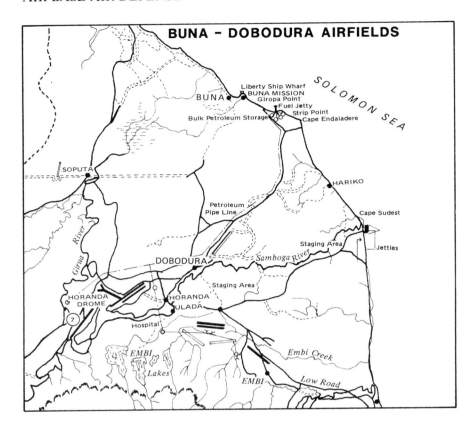

**BUNA - DOBODURA AIRFIELDS**

**Map 21**

tralian radar unit operated at Oro Bay from the first of the year and was joined by American air warning equipment in February. Except for a battery of air transportable .50-caliber AA machine guns, Dobodura airdrome did not receive AA protection until mid-April because the guns could not be hauled the few miles from Oro Bay, the road being not yet complete. Kenney and Whitehead had outrun the ability of the ground defenses to keep up. At the end of May, the frustrated Whitehead described the antiaircraft protection at Dobodura as "a helluva mess." That was an understatement. He could not find out what guns were available for the job, nor could he make his ground force contemporaries understand that air defense of air bases and adjoining areas handled by separate commands was impractical. Less than ten miles separated Dobodura and Oro Bay, but a corps boundary ran between the two. Each area's AA had a different line of command and their fire could not be centrally controlled.[70]

The problems Whitehead found in New Guinea resulted in part from the generally inexperienced American military, but were largely caused by the attempt of General Headquarters, Southwest Pacific Area, in Brisbane, Australia, to do all of the detailed antiaircraft planning though far removed from the scene. Whitehead firmly believed that "the fighter sector which handles the fighter defense of the locality must also control the antiaircraft [weapons]." Fortunately, Whitehead and the senior American AA officer in the Southwest Pacific, Maj. Gen. William F. Marquat, were on good terms personally, and could devise a solution. With General Kenney's assistance, and the approval of General MacArthur, Marquat, late in October, asked Washington's permission to organize the 14th Antiaircraft Command.[71]

Marquat's request detailed the seriousness of the problem and approval was promptly granted. The 14th AA Command was activated November 15, 1943, taking over the functions of several other intermediate organizations that were simultaneously abolished. The 14th's operations centered on New Guinea, but also included Australia. It would coordinate, administer, and control all of the AA units in the area. More important, the AA command's operations were subordinate to the air commander. By this stroke of cooperation, the underbrush of confusion was cleared away. From then on, tactical air defense began to improve.[72]

Placing AA units into one command eliminated many problems and allowed a much more effective response to air defense needs. It did not, however, resolve the difficulty of confused and overlapping duties of the AAF's fighter control squadrons and the Signal Corps' air warning battalions. The most serious problems continued into 1944 and resulted in clashes between fighter controllers and air warning commanders with a steep decline in morale in many locations. A conference called in April 1944 to resolve the issue found that fighter control squadrons had little or no practical function because they had not been given any guidelines as to what they were to do. Consequently, the units tended to operate aimlessly. The conferees recommended a system to end the overlapping efforts, and Whitehead quickly agreed.[73]

The 583rd Signal Aircraft Warning Battalion was assigned to the newly arrived 85th Air Defense Wing headquarters. The 85th was shortly joined by another air defense wing headquarters and the two began controlling all air warning and fighter defense in northern New Guinea. The air warning units operated radar stations and ground observer sites, sending information to their plotters at filter centers supporting the Aitape, Hollandia, and Wakde Island fighter sectors. At the centers the fighter control squadrons took the information, plotted it on an area grid, and used it to guide their aircraft elements. Daylight ground controlled intercepts became common, although

**Lt. Gen. George C. Kenney and Brig. Gen. Paul Wurtsmith share a moment with newly decorated pilots in New Guinea.**

night GCI actions were rare as there were no fighters able to carry heavy radar equipment to an altitude where Japanese airplanes could be attacked. Finally, after two years, the problems of coordination and control were being solved. Ironically, it came about just as the Allies forced the Japanese out of New Guinea.[74]

## The Japanese Respond

The Japanese, in their attempt to seize New Guinea, created a string of air bases on that island's northern coast and on adjacent islands. By mid-1943, airfields at Wakde, Hollandia, Wewak, Madang, Alexishafen, Rabaul, and Kavieng were the main threat to the Allies. (*Map 22*) The aggressive Japanese often launched major strikes at Port Moresby or other bases from these sites. On March 11, 1943, they swept over Buna destroying thirty-eight

C-47s land at strip at Nadzab, New Guinea, while engineers are still laying out the facility. Mobility and surprise were the hallmarks of Kenney's operations.

Allied aircraft on the ground. On April 14, twenty-eight more met the same fate at Port Moresby when Japanese aircraft crossed the Owen Stanleys and raided the base, catching the Allied defenses without warning. The Japanese bases, like the Allied, depended heavily on guns and revetments for defense. For the Japanese, antiaircraft gunfire became increasingly important as Allied air power grew. Because the Japanese lacked radar equal to that of the Allies, their warning system was less effective than that of their opponents. Also, the Japanese lacked heavy construction equipment and their aircraft dispersal parking was nowhere as elaborate as at Allied bases. Attacks often caught the Japanese with planes on the ground, and losses were sometimes heavy, but they brought replacements rapidly from the Pacific islands, the Philippines, or the East Indies.[75]

Early in the New Guinea fighting, Japanese land based AA fire was inaccurate and ineffectual. Japanese AA troops did not have an active aerial enemy before 1942 and they, like the Americans, had little experience in counterair fire. As the Japanese did not, at first, establish major air bases in New Guinea, having concentrated on Burma and the Bismarck Archipelago, there was little air base air defense development. Finally, the Japanese gun aiming mechanisms were obsolete and could not adjust quickly to a target's changes of altitude, speed, or direction. Japanese AA gunners eventually

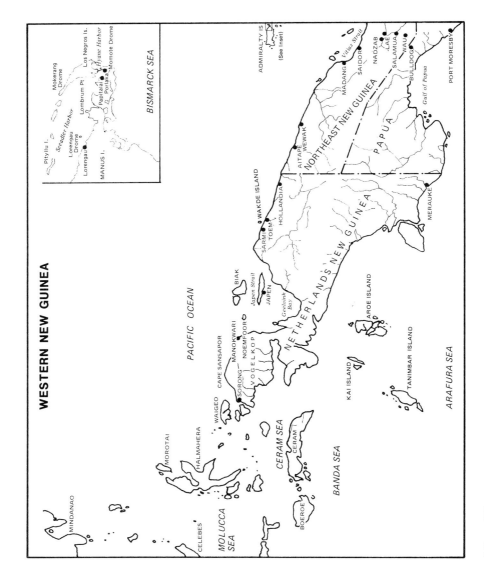

WESTERN NEW GUINEA

Map 22

**Vegetable gardens give away the locations of nearby Japanese gun emplacements at Wewak, New Guinea, February 1944.**

became more proficient and their weapons much more numerous, but few modern guns or fire control systems became available to them.[76] Early in the war, Japanese weapons remained close to the defended area, often concentrated within a mile of the runways. While this increased the volume of fire over the area, it reduced the length of time the guns could shoot at a low level target. Aircraft attacking at low altitude were in range only a short time and the gunners rarely reacted fast enough to maintain effective fire. After November 1943 this changed, and the Japanese dispersed their guns to increase the time an enemy was under fire. During World War II the Japanese usually did not camouflage their antiaircraft guns. New Guinea was an exception to this practice and there camouflage was excellent. Camouflage and the new dispersal scheme made gun positions more difficult to find and attack. Japanese gun crews, however, seemed intent on undoing all the good. They often planted vegetable gardens near their gun sites, allowing Allied photointerpreters to identify some locations that otherwise would have have gone unnoticed.[77]

At the same time that the Japanese began dispersing weapons, they made other changes in their AA positions. Attacking aircrews noticed the use of more light and medium guns (20-mm, 25-mm, and 40-mm). This was both a response and a distinct threat to Kenney's low level tactics. The Japanese abandoned the practice of dual siting in which they used the same guns for both AA and ground defense fire. Antiaircraft guns concentrated on their primary mission and a new type of weapon site with higher, concentric revetments gave the gunners greater protection.[78]

The changes in Japanese antiaircraft weapon deployment and gun revetment construction seem to have stemmed from growing Allied success in attacking air bases. The Allies crowned their achievements with an especially successful assault on Wewak during August 1943. American radio intercept intelligence, by then excellent, found indications of a large Japanese increase in air strength.[79] Reconnaissance confirmed the information and General Whitehead launched his forces on successive days between August 17 and 21. The Japanese lost more than 200 aircraft in 4 days, almost all of them on the ground. On the 17th the attackers noticed no AA fire and little fighter interference. Defenses were not much better on the following days. The combination of surprise and a low altitude approach put the aircraft over the target and then out of the area so quickly the gunners had little chance to react.[80]

Japanese radar was not as plentiful, nor was it as well developed as that of the Allies. Few Japanese airfields in New Guinea had radar for search and warning and gun control radar was almost unknown on the island. Compensation for their lack of radar came from natural sources—the weather and terrain. In order to avoid heavy and frequent thunderstorms, the Allies often attacked Japanese bases between ten o'clock and noon. For Kenney and Whitehead this was not desirable, but bad weather was always a severe handicap to them, and during the campaign in northern New Guinea they had little choice. Like the Americans on Guadalcanal, the Japanese could prepare for the daily raid and, where their bases lay near mountains, they could predict not only the time, but the probable direction of approach.[81]

As American attacks on their bases became heavier and more frequent, Japanese airfield battalions and antiaircraft regiments increased in number. Whereas they had only a single battery of the 47th Field AAA Battalion defending their base at Buna late in 1942, by early 1944 Japan had heavy AA concentrations at a number of bases around Wewak, actually a collection of airfields within a thirty mile area encompassing Boram, Wewak, But, and Dagua.[82] Wewak and Boram were the most heavily defended by far, having thirty-six 75-mm, twenty-five 37-mm, and forty-eight 20-mm guns along with warning radar and fighters. American crews found their fire accurate and intense.[83]

By late 1943, the continuous Allied air attacks forced the Japanese to repair runways and taxiways constantly. They could not be abandoned as the heavy jungle and mountainous terrain allowed few alternate sites. Damage repair, especially to the airfield's surfaces, was the responsibility of the airfield battalions. Labor was drawn from any available source of enlisted men on the base and natives in the surrounding area. Morale suffered heav-

TABLE 26

## Allied Air Units Used Against Wewak

Bombardment*

| | |
|---|---|
| 90th Bomb Group (B-24) | 4 Squadrons |
| 43rd Bomb Group (B-24) | 3 Squadrons |
| 22nd Bomb Group (B-24) | 2 Squadrons |
| 38th Bomb Group (B-25) | 4 Squadrons |
| 345th Bomb Group (B-25) | 4 Squadrons |
| 3rd Light (Attack) Bomb Group (A-20) | 4 Squadrons |
| 312th Light Bomb Group (A-20) | 4 Squadrons |

Fighter Protection—Normally 15 aircraft per squadron

| | |
|---|---|
| 7th and 8th Sqdns. | P-40 |
| 9th, 39th, 40th, 340th, and 342nd Sqdns. | P-47 |
| 431st, 432nd, and 433rd Sqdns. | P-38 |

* Numers of bombardment aircraft used each day varied. Usually the A-20 squadrons provided twelve while the medium and heavy bomb groups sent six to twelve aircraft daily.

**Sources:** Air Evaluation Board, Southwest Pacific Area "Neutralization of Wewak," Letter, A-2, Fifth Air Force Advance Echelon, 29 March 1944

ily, but it was imperative that existing airfield operations continue as Allied pressure made new construction virtually impossible.[84]

The Allies made their most severe air base attacks on the four Wewak fields between March 11 and 27, 1944. These attacks destroyed hundreds of airplanes and forced Japanese airpower into the confines of Hollandia. The result was to drive the Japanese from the air over northern New Guinea but in carrying out these attacks, General Kenney's forces encountered the most dangerous Japanese air defenses thus far in the Southwest Pacific Area.[85]

The Wewak and Boram airfields were separated by about three miles of coconut plantation, within which the Japanese located great quantities of supplies as well as living and work areas. Antiaircraft artillery was posi-

# TABLE 27

## General Kenney's Estimate of Japanese Air Strength
## February 1944

Fourth Air Army—Wewak, Hollandia
| | |
|---|---:|
| Fighters | 108 |
| Light Bombers | 27 |
| Reconnaissance | 45 |
| Miscellaneous (mostly cargo) | 100 |
| | 270 |

Reinforcements to Wewak and Hollandia from Sumatra:
(mid- to late-February arrival)

Eighth Air Brigade (Army)
| | |
|---|---:|
| Fighters | 54 |
| Light Bombers | 54 |
| Medium Bombers | 27 |
| | 135 |

Additional Air Forces in the East Indies:

Seventh Air Brigade (Army)
| | |
|---|---:|
| Fighters | 54 |
| Medium Bombers | 27 |
| Reconnaissance | 18 |
| | 99 |

Naval Air Forces:
| | |
|---|---:|
| Various Aircraft | 100 |

Note: Japanese accounts report the 8th Air Brigade with the 33rd, 45th, 60th, 75th, and 77th Air Regiments were sent to the Wewak-Hollandia area. Kenney's information came from intercepted radio transmissions and was exceptionally accurate.

**Sources:** Letter, Kenney to Whitehead, February 12, 1944
Japanese Monograph No. 39, Eighteenth Army Operations, Vol III.
Rinsuka Kaneko, Interview No. 440. *USSBS, Pacific*

tioned at each airfield, on the plantation, and on coastal capes and promontories, allowing crossfire by mutually supporting positions. Fighters could be launched on radar warnings, and Japanese pilots could hide in the clouds before diving on the Allied attackers.[86]

Fifth Air Force reconnaissance and intelligence organizations constructed a very accurate picture of the base area. Kenney and Whitehead knew that as long as the fields were fully operational, the Japanese would send reinforcements from other islands. Destruction of the bases was essential to protecting General MacArthur's advance to the Philippine Islands. Neutralizing the Japanese bases near Wewak would also protect the Allied airfields of Gusap, Finschhafen, and Nadzab, and curb any Japanese reaction to the planned Allied seizure of Kavieng, Manus Island, and Hansa Bay in April.[87]

The first attack on Wewak began at half past ten, March 11. These assaults were carefully planned to destroy progressively the defenses and then the Japanese ability to operate in the area. American fighters made the first thrust. At their approach, the Japanese launched some thirty fighters from Wewak, beginning an hour and a half of combat with the P-47s. When they landed to refuel, B-24 bombers appeared. The heavy bombers dropped eighty 1,000-pound demolition bombs with instantaneous fuzes on the antiaircraft artillery positions. Similar suppressive strikes hit Boram and the two other fields. Heavy clouds obscured some of the targets, and the effects were not as great as expected. The third attack, by B-25s and A-20s at low level, was made shortly after one o'clock and was intended to destroy ground facilities and impede use of the airfields.[88] Japanese gunners fired some of the most intense AA yet observed by Fifth Air Force crews. The crossfire from the well placed Japanese guns lacked effectiveness due in part to the suppression bombing, and in part to the outdated Japanese aiming devices. The Allies lost only one B-24 and one P-47. Thirteen other aircraft were damaged, but all returned home.[89]

At 10:30 the next morning the Americans went back. The AA positions near Boram and the surrounding area were the prime targets. Forty 2,000-pound bombs, half of them fuzed for aerial burst, and thirty-two 1,000-pound bombs with instantaneous and .025-second delay fuzes fell on the gun positions. The purpose of the fusing was to stun the gun crews by concussion, allowing free rein to the following low level attackers intending to hit other targets.[90] Japanese fighters again intercepted; all other Japanese planes took off from Wewak and Boram. Two fighters departed as the Allies approached the base. They remained low and headed out to sea, trying to lure some unwary Americans to follow. About 30 more Japanese fighters remained in the clouds waiting to pounce on any that pursued the decoys. There was no pursuit and no attacking aircraft was shot down. Because of the heavy fighting under way, the Japanese were forced to land at But and

Dagua to refuel. When they did, a well timed strike hit these bases with intense strafing and hundreds of para-frag bombs released from tree top height. Defensive ground fire was unable to deter the approaching formations.[91]

During the second day's raids many bombs burst close to the AA positions, yet ground fire remained heavy from guns which had not been hit. Japanese defenders damaged eighteen aircraft and 2 A-20s were reported missing. Postattack interrogations of crews indicated that many AA batteries began to show reduced effectiveness as a result of the bombing. Daily attacks continued.[92]

On March 16, the Japanese fighters withdrew to Hollandia to protect approaching convoys. Wewak's air defense was now without an important component. The raids continued in the same general pattern except for a pause on March 20 for maintenance and on March 24 when bad weather precluded an attack. By March 21, the AA fire was so reduced in volume and accuracy that attacks on these gun positions were made only twice more, and then half-heartedly, on the 22nd and 26th. After March 27 it was evident that the damage to the Wewak bases was irreparable. Aircraft no longer operated from the four airdromes.[93]

Allied aircraft losses for the 16-day assault totaled 34. Only 6 were directly attributed to enemy action, 8 failed to return for unknown reasons, and the remainder fell victim to various operational problems. The Allies estimated that they shot down 28 Japanese fighters; 170 more aircraft were destroyed on the ground. Continued reconnaissance and bombing insured that the bases could not be used again. General Kenney's air forces imposed an air blockade of ocean areas between the Wewak fields and Hollandia, isolating the Japanese 18th Army headquarters and its subordinate divisions and halting further transit of vital Japanese airplane parts. Since overland travel by more than small groups and stragglers was virtually impossible, a large number of combat troops and aircraft maintenance specialists were trapped. The Allies now faced the last major enemy air base in New Guinea—Hollandia.[94]

The air assault upon Hollandia was almost anticlimactic. Beginning on March 29, 1944, air attacks on the airfields near Sentani Lake used essentially the same tactics as at Wewak, except that heavy ordnance was not dropped on the runways, as the Allies wanted to use the field without extensive repairs. Hollandia's air defense was without radar, but the Japanese maintained communication with their forces elsewhere on the New Guinea coast. Warning of the Allied strike came from Wewak, where either the radar continued to operate or the Fifth Air Force formations passed so close on their way to Hollandia as to inform the defenders of their intent.[95] Antiaircraft fire was heavy but inaccurate. Some forty Japanese fighters sent out were not aggressive, and several defenders were shot down. Many Japanese aircraft, some grounded for lack of parts, were destroyed. AA positions and aircraft on the ground took severe damage. The Japanese relieved their air commander at Hollandia, Lt. Gen. Giichi Itabana, of his command. Lt. Gen. Kunachi Teramoto, of the Fourth Air Army, moved the remnants of his command to Manado in the Celebes. Japanese air forces were no longer a threat in New Guinea, and between April 22 and 29 Hollandia was seized by U. S. Army ground forces, ending any further Japanese use of the bases.[96]

## Summary

Two years of unremittingly aggressive fighting by both sides ended in Japanese expulsion from New Guinea. In 1942, when the campaign began, neither side had extensive air bases on the huge island, and neither was prepared to defend the bases it had. The Americans were not fully mobilized, their Australian and Dutch allies weak, and the Japanese occupied elsewhere. The fighting in New Guinea lasted far longer than that at Guadalcanal, but some of the reasons for Allied victory were the same. Japanese aircraft could not withstand battle damage as well as Allied models and Japan lacked an armor protected bomber. As American military planners directed the flow of new airplanes to the South and Southwest Pacific, it became evident that the performance of American aircraft exceeded that of the Japanese. Allied attacks on Japanese shipping put an increasing strain on their supply system; many aircraft could not fly because they could not be repaired. Long before the devastating two-week campaign against Wewak, the Allies seized and held air superiority. General MacArthur, in fact, claimed control of the air from late 1942. General Kenney agreed, and the Japanese conceded the point privately in a document captured by the Allies early in 1944.[97]

General Kenney's attack on Wewak in August 1943, was a superb counterair campaign designed to protect his bases in the Markham Valley from destruction by Japanese air forces. He well understood that the Japanese could overwhelm his forces with a concentrated and focused aerial campaign. Kenney's solution was typical of the man. He destroyed his enemy before his enemy attacked him.[98] Kenney's relentless pursuit of Japanese bases and shipping kept his opponent short of the supplies and reinforcements he would need for a counterair campaign. The Japanese forces lacked the broad range of equipment required for a large scale base contruction program while the Allied air engineers could rapidly carve out an airfield even when transport squadrons had to fly in the equipment and men to do the job, as at Kokoda, Wanigela, Dobodura, and the Markham Valley. The American air-warning system, so faulty and problematic at the start, was far better than any the Japanese deployed by late 1943. Nevertheless, in the

257

**Low Level Operations in New Guinea.** (*Clockwise from above*) **Japanese emplacements suffer the attention of Fifth Air Force B–25s, (2) American A–20 in low level pass over Japanese Betty parked in grass field at Lae, Spring 1943; partially disassembled fighters are beneath trees, (3) B–25s sew para-frag bombs among Japanese aircraft at Wewak on the northeast coast of New Guinea in early February 1944. (4) Fuel truck blazes as Fifth Air Force raids a seaside strip where unfinished camouflage frames reveal aircraft positions. (5) A–20 works over Japanese planes parked in the open at Hollandia.**

process of organizing air defenses in an army unprepared to deploy huge forces overseas, the Allies suffered heavy losses. American inexperience could not be overcome by industrial production; the commanders had to apply themselves to solving problems, training their men, and determining the best ways to use the firepower at their disposal.

Allied antiaircraft gun battalions, mostly American, began appearing in large numbers in New Guinea in 1943. Plagued by seemingly endless organizational problems and an unfamiliarity with aerial warfare, they eventually outclassed the Japanese AA units in number of guns and quality of equipment. Even so, the amount and effectiveness of antiaircraft guns did not tilt the balance in favor of one or the other side's air forces.

Japanese use of air power in New Guinea and the Solomons was faulty. Although in numbers they often held the preponderance of force, especially in 1942 and 1943, they failed to develop a coherent scheme of operations to overwhelm their enemy. Japanese air commanders repeatedly brought large numbers of reinforcements to face the Allies and then expended them in small attacks on a variety of targets. Their failure to attempt destruction of Kenney's air forces puzzled him. For many months, Kenney was uncertain he could stop a concerted counterair campaign. Knowing that his air force was vulnerable and that if it were destroyed the Allies could not hold New Guinea, Kenney chose an aggressive course of action that was facilitated by an enemy who diluted his forces or could not sustain them.[99]

After 1942 the quality of Japan's pilots deteriorated. As many as 10,000 pilots may have been lost in the Southwest Pacific Area during 1942 and 1943. Both Japanese Army and Navy training schools expanded in 1942, but pilots entering combat had progressively less flying experience. Advanced training of Japanese pilots was severely reduced as attempts were made to speed the flow to front line organizations.[100] Similar problems beset the U.S. Army Air Forces early in the war. In 1942, for example, the need for fighter pilots was so urgent that they were sent overseas with only 40 hours of training in their combat aircraft. During 1943, combat training was increased, but still rarely exceeded 80 hours. Japanese Army and Navy pilot production in 1941 was 2,700; in 1942 and 1943 this rose to 5,000 and 5,400 respectively with the Navy's effort peaking at a total of about 1,200 in April 1943. In contrast, the American goal for 1941 was 30,000; for 1942 it was 50,000. The AAF turned out 70,000 in 1943. To these figures must be added training by the Allies. Even allowing for the needs of fighting in Europe and Asia simultaneously, this dwarfed the Japanese effort.[101]

As is usual in war, a combination of factors led to Japan's inability to defend her air bases adequately or to destroy those of the Allies in the Southwest Pacific. Not only were the Allies able to outproduce the Japanese in virtually all types of war material, but Allied aircraft and weapons were superior. Japanese planes normally were not armored, and although they were often faster and more maneuverable than those of their opponents, they lacked resiliency under fire. Thus the Allies scored a higher ratio of victories in air to air combat, suffered lower replacement costs, and kept a higher level of experienced pilots on duty.

The few Japanese radars in the Solomons and New Guinea were technically inferior to American and British sets. Japan's inability to detect approaching formations retarded base defense. At Munda, where Japanese commanders relied on ground observers, they suffered repeated heavy damage to aircraft and air base facilities. Similar problems existed at Wewak in 1943 and 1944 where exceptionally high losses resulted.

Japanese antiaircraft weapons in the SWPA used obsolete sighting and aiming mechanisms. The inability to track enemy aircraft was one of the reasons for inaccurate fire by Wewak's defenders, and the problem was seen elsewhere in the Southwest Pacific. The Japanese could put up heavy but wasteful and inaccurate fire.

Both sides excelled at repairing airfield damage. At Guadalcanal, bomb damage repairs kept the base operating after repeated attacks. Japanese airfield battalions performed well at Munda and in New Guinea, but the immense, continuing firepower brought to bear by the Allies in the end overwhelmed Japan's airmen and air base crews. At the same time, the Allies demonstrated superiority in air base construction by airlifting aviation engineers to isolated sites, where they built new fields within striking distance of Japanese bases. From the newly built fields, Allied airpower struck progressively heavier blows at Japanese Army and Navy air installations, bringing defeat when the flying units could no longer be sustained.

# Part 3
# The Cold War Era

# Chapter VIII

# Two Limited Wars: Korea and Southeast Asia

Slightly more than a decade separated aerial fighting in Korea and Vietnam, but the two conflicts had much in common. The United Nations in Korea from 1950 to 1953 and the Allies in Southeast Asia during the years 1964 to 1973 almost always held air superiority. In both instances, the communist opponents fielded air forces designed for defense. Air base attackers encountered heavy antiaircraft fire that threatened their attempts to destroy enemy air operations. At the same time, the communist air forces in Korea and Vietnam made extensive use of geographic and political sanctuaries as a means of air base air defense, (*Map 23*) venturing out to fight at the times and places they chose. Both conflicts offer examples of limited wars involving air forces of unequal size. Nevertheless, the air base air defense experiences, especially in Southeast Asia, found application not only in the 1973 October War in the Middle East, but also in examining the general conduct of counterair warfare.

In both conflicts, communist airfields were the target of repeated attacks. In Korea, however, United Nations' bases were rarely struck, and in Southeast Asia air attacks on Allied bases in South Vietnam and Thailand were unknown. Both North Korean and North Vietnamese defenders relied heavily on ground based antiaircraft weapons. Neither communist force had enough fighter interceptors, and neither could contest the air for extensive periods of time with their enemies. On the other hand, keeping communist bases closed required repeated strikes followed by frequent aerial reconnaissance. Often, the effort needed to attack an airfield was better used on other targets, and bases themselves became secondary considerations in planning the air war.[1]

**EAST ASIA**

**Map 23**

## Dominating the Air in Korea

As a former Japanese possession, Korea was occupied after World War II by the Americans in the south and the Russians in the north. Hostile governments were established in each tier of the country, each claiming to represent the whole. By June 1950, the North Korean People's Army (NKPA) consisted of about 89,000 well equipped combat soldiers and a border constabulary of 18,000 men. The North Korean Air Force (NKAF) possessed some 145 World War II Russian Yak fighters, twin engine bombers, and a variety of trainers. In contrast, the Republic of Korea's Army (ROKA) numbered 65,000 lightly armed troops intended for internal and border security use. The ROK Air Force (ROKAF) had just 16 noncombat airplanes. Such a military organization, although useful for maintaining internal order, lacked the strength, training, and equipment for defense against a modern army, let alone the protection of air bases. In June 1950, a small American advisory group working with the ROK forces was the only other military presence in South Korea.[2]

During the predawn hours of June 25, 1950, North Korean military forces invaded the south. Within two days, the United States entered the fighting under the auspices of the United Nations (UN). Americans flew air support for the ROK forces from bases in Japan, then shifted to main fields at Taegu, Pusan, and Pohang in Korea, and smaller satellite fields such as Taejon. On June 27, Maj. Gen. Earle E. Partridge, Fifth Air Force Commander, and at the moment acting as Far East Air Forces Commander for Lt. Gen. George E. Stratemeyer, who was returning from Washington, secured permission from Maj. Gen. Doyle O. Hickey, Deputy Chief of Staff, U.S. Far East Command, to transfer to Korea U.S. Army AA units attached to Fifth Air Force wings in Japan. At the direction of the Joint Chiefs of Staff, General MacArthur, Commander-in-Chief, Far East Command, had prohibited use of American ground forces in Korea on the day of the attack, but Hickey readily assented, and AA automatic weapons teams quickly deployed to Suwon AB, south of Seoul.* There they engaged attacking NKAF Yaks on the 29th.[3]

As the US Air Force enlarged its position in Korea, antiaircraft detachments accompanied the combat and support units from other Fifth Air Force bases. In Japan the AA attached to an air base fell under the operational control of the base commander; this practice continued in Korea.[4]

There was no American radar in Korea before the conflict. On July 20, to provide an aircraft warning and tactical air-control system, Fifth Air Force activated the 6132nd Tactical Air Control Group. The unit was immediately sent to Taegu, arriving on July 23, where it joined Detachment 1, 620th Aircraft Warning and Control Squadron, which had already come from Johnson AB, Japan. The 620th possessed one AN/TPS–1B radar, the only such set in Korea. A Tactical Air Control Center (TACC) was set up, but it lacked other radar equipment and a full set of radios. In addition, although the TACC was given an air warning mission, its primary job was

---

* Hickey's decision was contrary to the JCS's instructions. President Harry S Truman did not authorize use of ground troops in Korea until June 30, 1950. Hickey no doubt authorized the move to cover USAF cargo planes using Suwon and to protect MacArthur, who landed there on the 29th to view the fighting near Seoul first hand.

**F–80s roll past 40–mm gun emplacement. Guns and crews were hastily transferred from Japan to Korea in June 1950 to protect American bases.**

close air support of ground forces, not air defense. A further impediment was confusion as to the intended location of the TACC. On July 28 most of the center moved to K–3 airfield at Pohang. A small TACC and the Tactical Air Control Party section remained at Taegu with Partridge. On July 30, the tactical air-control element at Pohang, threatened by the NKPA pushing south along Korea's east coast, moved to Pusan, where it had a month's respite to get organized.[5] Newly arriving personnel were still found to be untrained and additional electronics gear arrived without technical instructions. Not only were skilled USAF radar operators and repairmen rare in 1950, but so few were being trained that Fifth Air Force's demands quickly absorbed all available men. Instruction of new arrivals by the 6132nd began at Pusan in late August. For some time this was the only source of qualified technicians.[6]

As electronic techniques and equipment improved, so too did the success of the aviators. U. S. Air Force fighters and fighter bombers quickly reduced the NKAF and turned to support the UN's ground forces, which the North Koreans had pushed into a defensive perimeter around Pusan by late summer of 1950. The NKAF had not expected serious opposition, apparently assuming that no foreign defense of the South would develop. As a result, Russian and Chinese advisors had not equipped North Korea with large quantities of antiaircraft equipment. Most of the AA fire encountered by UN fliers came from light and medium automatic weapons. In October 1950, after General MacArthur's forces landed at Inchon, the Americans captured Soviet made 37-mm and 85-mm guns from NKPA units in the Seoul and Wonju areas. At the same time, Far East Command intelligence analysts noted an increase in air defenses of the northern capital of Pyongyang. American airmen judged them quite accurate.[7]

From the start of the war, camouflage and concealment was the hallmark of North Korean air defense. In general, the North Koreans were very effective at hiding their war materiel from attacking pilots. Fifth Air Force's Office of Tactical Air Research and Survey noted that "the continued scarcity of targets, which minimizes the effectiveness of our air potential, is a tribute to the enemy's performance in camouflage." The NKAF, however, did not disguise its resources to the extent of the NKPA, preferring instead to rely upon dispersion and deception. Wrecked or destroyed aircraft were camouflaged, giving the appearance of an attempt to conceal operational airplanes. Dummy planes appeared in and around airfield parking areas. These decoys proved successful, repeatedly drawing attacks by Allied pilots.[8] At Wonson airfield, the North Koreans sheltered aircraft in underground structures, hiding them while at the same time protecting them from blast or splinter damage. On October 29th, after the UN occupied the base, General Partridge inspected the runways and facilities. He observed two underground hangars of heavily reinforced concrete construction with steel blast doors, covered with sod and planted with grass and shrubs. Inside one hangar were eight Ilyushin Il-10 twin engine bombers; seven more were in the other. None appeared damaged from air attack; instead, they had been burned by the retreating North Koreans.[9]

The Manchurian sanctuary for the communist air forces bedeviled the UN Command from the war's beginning. As early as July 1950, General Stratemeyer concluded that the North Korean Air Force operated, at least in part, from Manchuria. He also thought the NKAF was being reequipped from there, as reconnaissance revealed new reserves of twenty-six airplanes at Pyongyang and sixty-eight at Yonpo AB, both in North Korea. When he sent bombers to destroy them, they had disappeared and were not to be found at any of the NKAF's four serviceable bases. On August 25, aircraft reconnoitering communist airfields along the Yalu River, separating Korea and Manchuria, drew heavy caliber AA fire, some of which was believed to have come from the Chinese side of the border, although this could not be established conclusively. Stratemeyer continued efforts to destroy enemy air power, concentrating on bombing the few usable fields.[10]

**South Korean military policemen inspect stripped Yak–9 discovered at Wonsan by advancing U.N. forces, October 1950.**

The heady success of the American invasion at Inchon in September 1950 tended to offset the possibility of new troubles ahead. Late in November, the UN Command began an offensive from positions in mountainous North Korea near the Manchurian border in hopes of achieving complete victory by Christmas. Especially severe weather put an icy surface on the roads and hindered the amassing of an adequate level of supply for the advancing army. The Chinese struck with an estimated half million men infiltrated into Korea since October. General MacArthur faced what he now called a whole new war. Quickly it became apparent that a retreat to Seoul would be necessary to avert destruction of the United Nations' army.

The Chinese had organized air support on their side of the Yalu River. Antung, just across the border and north of the Korean town of Sinuiju, became a major Chinese air base with new concrete runways, radar, and AA defenses. UN intelligence services came to the conclusion that MiG–15s based there were apparently being supplied in large numbers by Russia. Worse, the Chinese Air Force's MiGs soon demonstrated themselves better fighters than any of the types used in the UN Command. Although the communist fliers were inexperienced in combat and gave little close air support to their ground forces, they challenged the UN's fighters and bombers. In the hands of skilled and experienced pilots, a large force of MiGs could have swept the skies clear of opposition. Until better fighters arrived, General Partridge's fliers had to develop defensive tactics to protect their older, slower aircraft; the superior performance of the MiGs and their limited use close to sanctuary bases prevented an immediate UN counterair offensive. Also, Allied bombers, such as the B-26 and B-29, needed protection during daylight operations near the Yalu River, further draining Fifth Air Force's offensive ability. During this time, Partridge concentrated on protecting the retreating army. Air superiority, so easily won from the NKAF, now appeared threatened.[11]

Fortunately for the UN Command, its air bases faced almost no threat from Red air attacks, and it continued to contest the skies over North Korea. By the end of January 1951, UN forces were holding a line south of Wonju and Suwon. Allied air forces moved south to bases at Taegu and Pusan or in Japan; from there they carried out intensive air-to-ground attacks which finally helped stop the communist advance.[12] UN reconnaissance and attack aircraft flew daily to the Yalu, observing activity, bombing bridges, and interdicting targets even when MiG defenders outnumbered them ten or twelve to one. Through the early part of 1951, the Chinese and Korean pilots lacked confidence enough to raid UN bases. Their aircraft could not strike the South from Yalu bases, and they never developed airfields closer to the front lines. Only two small raids on Kimpo AB in October were exceptions to the rule and indicated a communist intent to strike if they could muster the force. Neither raid caused much damage.[12]

Some believed the Chinese may also have made a calculated decision to avoid attacking air bases to avert possible retaliation on their installations in Manchuria. General Omar N. Bradley, Chairman of the Joint Chiefs of Staff, referred to what he believed was the UN's "privileged sanctuary," citing the fact that communist forces "are not bombing our ports and supply installations, and they are not bombing our troops." With the equipment available and the state of training of the Chinese and North Korean Air Forces, such a sanctuary existed only in the fact that the enemy was incapable of launching telling attacks to the south.[13]

American leaders, lacking a full understanding of the relations between the communist powers and facing a largely unknown military organization, had to assume a Red counterair capability and a continuing need to suppress it. They focussed on the far northwest corner of Korea containing the bases at Sinuiju, Sinanju, Uiju, and Chang-ju, the temporary preserve of communist fliers that took the nickname "MiG Alley." Here, air defense was formidable because of large numbers of fighters and their proximity to bases in Manchuria. The Joint Chiefs of Staff, however, cautioned that attacks on air bases had to be confined to Korea.[14]

Apprehensive of widening the war by provoking the Russians or Chinese, the UN forces avoided air strikes on Manchuria, though they did occur.* The Russians were known to occupy large parts of Anju airfield in Manchuria. There were numerous reports of Russian ground units in North Korea, and Soviet air elements were reported at other bases in Manchuria. The North Korean port of Rashin (now Chongjin) also was off limits to bombers because Russian ships often used it as an alternate when Vladivostok was icebound.[15]

A USAF Air Staff assessment of May 1951 discounted the possibility of a wider war as a result of limited raids on Manchurian airfields, but predicted a propaganda effect, especially among America's western allies. The report judged that the most likely Soviet reaction would be to augment Chinese and North Korean air strength to gain air superiority progressively farther south. Lacking any authorization from Washington for proscriptive strikes north of the Yalu, Stratemeyer and Partridge believed they had to attack the increasingly better defended North Korean air bases to prevent the enemy from infiltrating aircraft southward, extending his fighting range.[16]

During April 1951, mounting evidence pointed to just such an extension of communist air forces southward. Early in the month reconnaissance reported repair activities on at least thirteen airfields. New antiaircraft defenses appeared on reconnaissance reports with greater frequency. Some areas became heavily protected. Pyongyang City, for example, had 80 heavy guns and 151 automatic weapons—most were located on or around Pyongyang East airfield. Chinese Air Force MiG activity also increased dramatically early in 1951. As many as seventy-five of the fast communist jets operated from Antung. Other bases in MiG Alley were repaired with revetments and AA gun emplacements. The communist fighter pilots struck hard at UN bomber formations, especially the American B–29s.[17]

In mid-December 1950, Fifth Air Force received the first of its new F–86 Sabrejets, which had the speed and performance needed to defeat the MiG–15 in aerial combat. The initial gain was short lived as Red Chinese advances south of Seoul during January 1951 forced the Sabres out of Kimpo AB and back to Japan. Supported by a heavy air interdiction campaign, General Matthew B. Ridgway, newly appointed Commander of the U. S. Eighth Army, began an effort to recapture lost territory—and airfields. Early in 1951 the UN retook Suwon, returning the F–86s to a field from which they could again operate over MiG Alley and protect bomber formations bent on keeping airfields out of action. In a series of air battles between April 17 and 23, F–86s of the 4th Fighter-Interceptor Wing fended

---

* Soviet intentions and their reactions to these attacks remained an enigma. On October 8, 1950, two American pilots mistook a Russian airfield at Vladivostok for a North Korean base and strafed it, causing an unknown amount of damage. Russia's public reaction was subdued; Partridge relieved the responsible group commander. Other border violations by UN aircraft, especially while in combat, apparently caused little problem.

off MiG–15s while Japan based B–29s made repeated airfield attacks. The UN pilots inflicted heavy losses on the Chinese and North Koreans and forced them to regroup. On May 9, 312 US Air Force and Marine jets attacked aircraft and defending AA at Sinuiju airfield. There was little resistance by MiG–15s, and with fighter-bombers on AA supression attacks, the base was quickly destroyed.[18]

Stung by their inability to defeat the American "invaders," the Chinese Air Force apparently sought to revise its operating doctrine. The Russian aircraft the Chinese had were interceptors, lacking in range and principally useful for air defense. They wanted air power that could attack and carry the fight to enemy bases, supply lines, and reinforcement marshalling areas. Recognizing their failings, the Chinese wanted to obtain aircraft similar in performance and capability to those used by the United States. All of this, though, would take time and Russian agreement to provide long range aircraft. The relentless UN attacks gave the Chinese little flexibility. Even using Russian and Eastern European pilots for training and combat did not alleviate the problem. These "international volunteers" were not used in an air superiority campaign against air bases in the south, but their influence was seen in the slow but steady increase in communist proficiency and in their participation in air to air fighting over the northern part of Korea.[19]

Unable to compete with the United Nations air forces in the air outside of MiG Alley, the communists continued to increase the number and types of AA weapons in North Korea. In September 1950, North Korean forces had an estimated 70 guns and automatic weapons. By June 1951, there were at least 300 heavy AA guns, 500 lighter automatic weapons, and large numbers of machine guns, almost all of Russian or Chinese origin. Airfields of sufficient size (*Map 24*) to support jet fighter operations were stoutly defended. On the 34 largest fields (those with a runway length exceeding 3,000 feet) there were 598 revetted aircraft parking spaces. There were, however, no communist jets stationed in Korea and few conventional aircraft made use of the sites; UN bombing continued with the object of keeping them unserviceable. If nothing else, the bases were magnets, drawing bombers away from other targets.[20]

At the end of October 1951, aerial reconnaissance disclosed twenty-six MiG–15s on Uiju in MiG Alley. Some were parked on alert at the end of the runway. This was the first confirmed instance of communist jets operating from bases south of the Yalu River. During the last week of October eleven Soviet built Tu–2 twin-engine medium bombers attacked a UN radar station and airstrip on Cho-do, an island off North Korea's Yellow Sea coast. Although the raid caused casualties, radar operations continued. These two incidents were seen as further indications of the enemy's intent to exert his influence in the air and possibly begin using bases farther to the south. Uiju AB was promptly attacked and by the end of November the MiGs had

**Fifth Air Force reconnaissance photo designates area of extensive repairs to Sunan airfield in North Korea.**

departed. The bombers, on the other hand, probably came from Mukden, China, and the sanctuary regulations quashed any inclination on the part of the UN generals to destroy their bases.[21]

During 1952, the Chinese and North Koreans attempted unsuccessfully to use 3 airfields at Pyongyang, where as many as 2,000 people filled and repaired bomb craters. The inexperienced communist airmen launched a few night raids on Kimpo and Suwon using old Po–2 biplanes flying from Sariwon and other sites, but were unable to mount an effective attack. Anticipating air attacks, the United Nations troops placed AA guns at each of their installations. A radar warning net gave some surveillance, but the mountainous country prevented effective electronic observation, and the AA guns were ineffective in the dark. To end the nighttime incursions, night fighters went on alert and scrambled when a plane was heard. One North Korean Po–2 met an abrupt end when a U.S. Navy jet flew into the slower aircraft. A result of the raids was a tendency of the UN's AA gunners to fire at anything flying at night slower than 100 knots. Throughout the course of the war, the North Korean, Chinese, and Russian air commanders used the northern sanctuary to their great advantage, training aircrews and venturing into or withdrawing from combat when the situation suited them. Meanwhile, the United Nations' forces continued to attack each airfield in North Korea that showed signs of use.[22]

**Hits by 307th Bomb Wing put Sunan out of action again.**

The numbers of MiG–15 fighters continued to grow during 1952, reaching a peak of about 7,000 aircraft by midyear. Over 1,100 were at Manchurian bases, the rest in China proper and Siberia, close enough to provide ready reinforcement. Air defense technology kept pace with the growing number of planes. Excellent, modern radar came into greater use, although definite problems existed in employment. Communist defenders lacked enough sets to provide full coverage; at several air bases in North Korea they doubled the number of guns controlled by one unit and aiming efficiency dropped off. In the absence of radar equipped night fighters, searchlight teams used radar plots to try and pinpoint and illuminate bombers so that day fighters could attack out of the darkness. Flak continued to be intense.[23]

By early 1953, Fifth Air Force intelligence counted an alarming total of 823 heavy guns, 31 gun control radar sets, and 902 medium caliber automatic weapons in North Korea. Most were in the western or northwestern part of the country, protecting supply routes, storage areas, and airfields. Communist AA regiments moved the weapons frequently. Consequently, it was difficult to keep close watch over all known firing positions. The number of weapons, while fluctuating, remained high as each successive count was made. Almost daily airfield and AA suppression attacks continued. At the same time, the communists again started a major airfield rehabilitation project that coincided with renewed promise in the Panmunjom truce talks. A stipulation in the still unsigned armistice document prohibited introduction of forces in excess of those already in Korea when the truce became

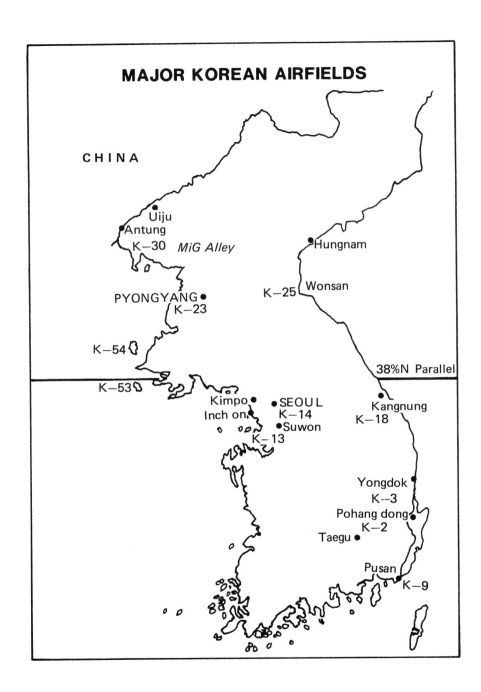

# MAJOR KOREAN AIRFIELDS

CHINA

Uiju
Antung
K—30    *MiG Alley*

Hungnam

PYONGYANG
K—23

K—25    Wonsan

K—54

38%N Parallel

K—53

Kimpo    SEOUL    Kangnung
Inch on    K—14    K—18
Suwon
K—13

Yongdok
K—3

Pohang dong
K—2

Taegu

Pusan
K—9

**Map 24**

**Fifth Air Force Intelligence outlined the limits of a dummy field constructed in North Korea in December 1951.**

effective. Neutral observers were to police the peace terms, but Allied commanders feared the enemy would bring in as many airplanes as possible at the last moment, especially during the final twelve hours of combat between the signing of the terms and the cease fire. To forestall this, they began an intense interdiction campaign with very heavy airfield attacks.[24]

Between March and July 1953, no more than two North Korean airfields were rated as fully operational by Far East Air Forces intelligence. A small number of bases were partly serviceable from time to time. Constant pressure was necessary as a MiG–15 could land on a 2,400-foot strip of turf, easily returned to service after a raid. The North Koreans also resorted to increasingly clever camouflage and deception. At Namsi airfield, the North Koreans painted false craters on the runway that may even have fooled one MiG–15 pilot, who overshot the adjacent sod area, crashed, and burned.[25]

The North Koreans accelerated repairs of the bases. Pyongyang Main airfield, out of use since December 1950, was ready by the end of June. Bad weather during the final weeks of the conflict restricted visibility over these targets, and poststrike photoreconnaissance was even more difficult. Nevertheless, the UN air force pressed home the campaign. On July 27, the last day of hostilities, only Uiju was operational.[26]

During three years of fighting in Korea, air base air defense was not a major part of the air war on the UN side. No United Nations base ever suffered significant damage. The combined communist air forces were unable to exert air power adequate to challenge successfully the largely American UN force. The United Nations pilots, on the other hand, kept most bases in North Korea closed, forcing their enemies to use the safe Manchurian airfields. While the UN's AA guns remained silent during much of the three years, communist gun crews shot down 550 aircraft, but most of these losses occurred over targets other than air bases. Radar directed guns accounted for substantial American losses, especially among B–29s. The heavy guns could not cope with the low level attacks favored by UN fighter bomber pilots. Of the various types of AA weapons used in defending North Korea, the most effective by far were the automatic weapons, especially when used against targets flying below 3,000 feet. Even so, ground guns could not influence the outcome of the fighting. To continue operation of their airfields, the communists resorted to massive efforts at repair, mobilizing large groups of laborers to fill bomb craters and level runway and taxiway surfaces. The most significant defense the communists had was the freedom to base aircraft in Manchuria. Although UN pilots at times violated the border in hot pursuit of an aerial enemy, they did not as a rule attack bases on the other side of it. The desire to avoid a wider war on the Asian continent led to specific restrictions that allowed air bases to operate largely unmolested north of the Yalu River.[27]

## Success and Frustration in Vietnam: 1964–1973

At the conclusion of World War II, France returned to Indo-China to restore its prewar control. The communist Viet Minh, however, refused to accept French colonial rule. Failing to achieve a political settlement, the Viet Minh began a military revolution lasting several years. Following the French defeat at Dien Bien Phu and the subsequent departure of French military forces in 1954, the United States began supporting the interim government of South Vietnam, pending a national plebiscite called for in the 1954 Geneva agreement. Fearing the large population of North Vietnam would vote for national reunification under Ho Chi Minh, their leader and a long established nationalist and communist, the United States supported the new Republic of Vietnam (RVN), established in the south on October 26, 1955, and headed by President Ngo Dinh Diem. To counter the strong military forces of the north, South Vietnam began to expand the small armed force initially organized by the French. Air bases were built or expanded at Saigon, Da Nang, and other locations formerly used by France or Japan. A U.S. Military Assistance Advisory Group provided training and materiel support to the RVN.[28]

The North Vietnamese, using their Viet Cong subordinates in the south, began a campaign of guerrilla warfare designed to destroy the Diem government. Many Viet Cong were southerners who went north and then returned. At the same time, the growing aggressiveness of North Vietnam caused the government of Thailand increasing concern. In mid-1961, the U. S. Air Force established a detachment of F–102 air defense fighters at Bangkok's Don Muang Airport, where it remained almost continuously until 1970. The American presence in Southeast Asia grew as both sides escalated the struggle for control of the Republic of Vietnam. By midyear 1964, two American A–1E squadrons operated from Bien Hoa airfield near Saigon, training South Vietnamese crews. In Thailand, USAF and Royal Australian Air Force (RAAF) units were found at Don Muang Airport and Korat, Takhli, and Udorn Royal Thai Air Force bases after 1962. Although the risk of air attack was small, these aircraft were exposed to serious ground attacks that on occasion caused heavy damage. [29]

As the Americans and South Vietnamese built their air capability, the North Vietnamese, with Chinese and Russian assistance, did the same. Ho Chi Minh's government rapidly rebuilt several old French and Japanese airdromes. Four air bases—Phuc Yen, Kep, Gia Lam (Hanoi), and Kien An (Haiphong)—became the main fields for jets in North Vietnam. Nine other airfields were able to handle propeller driven military and civil aircraft. Because of North Vietnam's growing air threat and the uncertain position of the Chinese Communists, the Americans and their allies installed an air defense system covering several bases in Thailand and the RVN within range of North Vietnamese MiGs. [30]

The rapid American buildup at Da Nang in 1965 quickly outpaced the field's ability to handle the number of aircraft assigned. This overcrowding left choice targets for North Vietnamese airmen, had they wanted to strike. U. S. Air Force interceptors supported by Army and Marine Hawk missile* battalions formed what Headquarters, Pacific Air Forces (PACAF), described as a "heavy defense system." The PACAF planners postulated the loss of two-thirds of any force sent against Da Nang, but feared the survivors could do extensive damage to parked aircraft on unrevetted hardstands, exposed fuel tanks, a large bomb storage area which greatly exceeded its maximum safe explosive content, and support facilities. Fortunately, no air attack on Allied bases materialized then or later in the course of the war. None of the American air defenses was tested in battle. [31]

North Vietnam's air defense system, by contrast, was heavily exercised. Beginning in 1964 the North Vietnamese government organized and trained an air force oriented largely to defending its homeland. From almost nothing, the North Vietnamese Air Force grew until, in late 1966, Pacific Air Forces saw it as having "appreciable success in harassing our aircraft." The PACAF staff officers also believed they now had to revise an earlier judge-

---

\* A surface to air, radar guided, antiaircraft missile able to hit targets from 100 feet to about 38,000 feet above ground. Its maximum slant range was 22 miles. The Hawk became operational in 1960, and was deployed with U.S. forces and allies.

**American F–102s shelter behind gravel filled prefabricated steel revetments at Da Nang, South Vietnam, July 1966.**

ment that the MiG activity would be "operationally tolerable."[32] American and South Vietnamese attacks had been made on North Vietnam's air bases in the narrow southern panhandle below 19°N latitude and at Dien Bien Phu in 1965, but these were minor installations where no sizable air force unit operated. The Allies encountered little defensive fire, and all the bases were put out of action. The North Vietnamese attempted repairs, but follow up strikes discouraged them and the bases remained dormant for some time. The North Vietnamese did not give up, however. They still harassed American tactical fighter bomber pilots attacking targets in North Vietnam, a danger to continued air interdiction. Although losses to MiGs in aerial combat were few, the approach of the communist fighters often forced the heavily laden, less maneuverable American F–105s to jettison their ordnance.[33] Between August 15, 1966, and the end of the year, 119 American Air Force sorties jettisoned bomb loads to evade MiGs, and the PACAF staff began to pay more attention to the problem.

On the heels of earlier intermittent retaliatory strikes in the north, the major air campaign against North Vietnam, Operation ROLLING THUNDER, began in March 1965. It continued until November 1, 1968, when President Lyndon B. Johnson declared a halt, hoping to achieve peace through negotiations. ROLLING THUNDER, however, was not a single campaign in the fashion of World War II or the Korean conflict. (*Map 25*) Rather, it was an on again, off again affair of fifty-seven different phases over a period of three and a half years. Each portion of the campaign and the targets to be hit were individually approved by the United States Joint Chiefs of Staff, the Secretary of Defense, or the President. The intent of the incremental attacks was to convince North Vietnam to cease hostilities in the south by threatening ever increasing damage. Specific areas were excluded from bombing—a 25 to 35 mile wide buffer zone along the Chinese border, an area around the capital city of Hanoi up to 35 miles wide, and the a smaller zone five miles in depth around the major port city of Haiphong. The border buffer zone was established to prevent inadvertent bombing of China, which the Johnson Administration feared might trigger extensive Chinese intervention in the fighting. American spokesmen publicly emphasized the restraint implicit in observing these restricted zones.[34]

Three of the five largest North Vietnamese airfields—Kien An, Cat Bai, and Gia Lam—lay within areas where strikes were often prohibited. Air bases outside the sanctuaries, such as Phuc Yen and Kep, were near population centers and were thus kept off the authorized target list for some time, providing them immunity from attack. The Americans first attacked Phuc Yen in October 1967. The American policy of incremental bombing increases and prohibited targets, while politically attractive, provided the defenders an inestimable advantage: air defense systems could be acquired and installed with minimal interference. Hundreds of Russian and Chinese guns, missiles, and radar units appeared at critical places. At the same time, the North Vietnamese enlarged the bases so that by the end of 1966, there were 253 revetted parking spaces on the bases and 412 open parking spots. Still, the growth of the NVNAF was slow, its training held back by the complexity of aircraft and their support systems.[35]

In addition to the advantages conferred on their defense by American bombing limitations, the enemy in the north also used several Chinese air bases to shelter scarce aircraft. The Chinese had well developed radar early warning and ground controlled intercept systems connected to those of North Vietnam. The GCI operations of each country supplemented the other; both were modern and staffed by trained, competent people. The Chinese air bases themselves had formidable and active defensive systems, and an attack upon them could provoke Red Chinese participation in the war.[36]

North Vietnam's radar systems were located so as to protect the vital portions of the country and served several purposes. Radar installation, begun in the early 1960s, accelerated; a variety of Russian or Chinese types were copied from American designs of the World War II period, and some were of East bloc origin. By 1965 the North Vietnamese had thirty-three electronic warfare and ground control intercept sets and nine fire control sets in use. They installed radar sets to aim and control the Russian built SA–2 surface to air missiles introduced into Southeast Asia in 1965 and to aim antiaircraft guns: Russian 100-mm, 85-mm, and sometimes 57-mm weapons. Warning of impending air attacks also came from Russian ships which followed U. S. Navy carriers in the Gulf of Tonkin. By the end of 1966

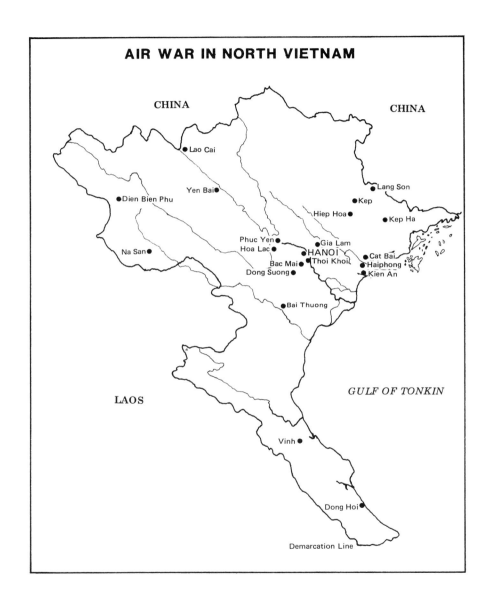

# AIR WAR IN NORTH VIETNAM

CHINA

CHINA

● Lao Cai

Yen Bai ●

● Dien Bien Phu

● Lang Son

● Kep

Hiep Hoa ●

● Kep Ha

Phuc Yen ●

Gia Lam ●

Na San ●

Hoa Lac ●

HANOI ●

● Cat Bai

Bac Mai ●

Thoi Khoi

● Haiphong

Dong Suong ●

Kien An

● Bai Thuong

LAOS

GULF OF TONKIN

Vinh ●

Dong Hoi ●

Demarcation Line

**Map 25**

**SAM site photographed in North Vietnam, May 1966.**

there were thirty electronic warfare sites feeding four filter centers which in turn supported an air defense headquarters in Hanoi. Radar control operations were dispersed with redundant communications. The North Vietnamese frequently moved radar sites, greatly complicating targeting problems. Additionally, putting one filter center out of operation, as the U. S. Navy did in 1966, did not reduce effectiveness; other centers assumed the workload. As in World War II and Korea, attacking pilots had great difficulty in locating radar sets. Lacking jamming equipment and radiation homing weapons at first, American fliers were slow in disrupting the fire control mechanisms for the SA-2s.[37]

After their first success in destroying an American fighter in July 1965, the North Vietnamese used SA-2 antiaircraft missiles widely. The missile had a range of about 17 miles, and was effective against airplanes flying between 3,000 and 60,000 feet. The missiles could be used below that altitude, but often aircraft flying so low were not detected rapidly enough for the crews to fire. Each missile battalion had from 4 to 6 mobile missile launchers, 8 to 12 missiles, and radar sets operating from prepared sites.

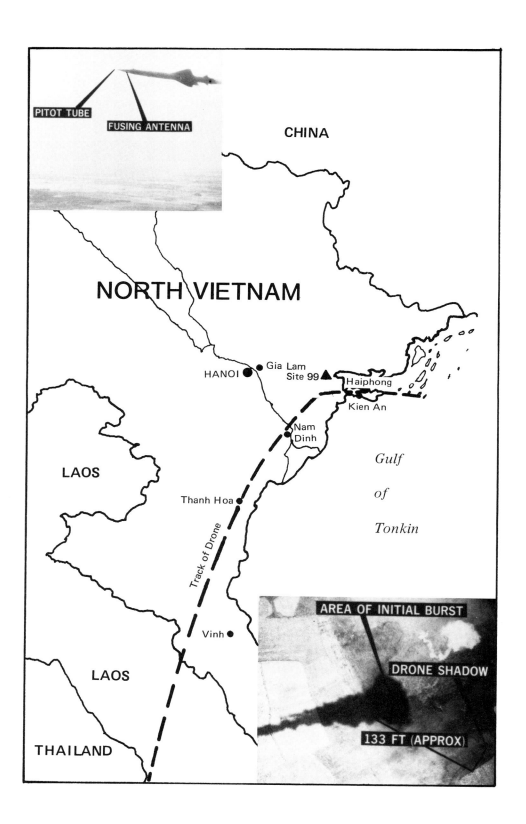

PITOT TUBE

FUSING ANTENNA

CHINA

NORTH VIETNAM

Gia Lam
Site 99

HANOI

Haiphong

Kien An

Nam
Dinh

LAOS

Gulf

of

Tonkin

Thanh Hoa

Track of Drone

Vinh

LAOS

AREA OF INITIAL BURST

DRONE SHADOW

133 FT (APPROX)

THAILAND

North Vietnamese engineers built more than 190 launch areas between 1965 and 1968, 40 of which were normally occupied. Battalions moved rapidly from site to site after firing a weapon or suspecting that they had been observed by reconnaissance flights. The SA-2 was an area defense weapon, but the North Vietnamese used it for defense of small sites such as air bases as well. Kep airfield, for example, was the headquarters of a regiment controlling 5 battalions, 1 of which was always within range of the installation.[38]

Joining radar, MiG fighters, and ground to air missiles in the North Vietnamese defenses was yet another, and by far the most potent, defense element: antiaircraft gunfire. To the Americans the intent of the defense system quickly became clear. MiG fighters harassed the attacking fighter-bombers, and SA-2s kept the hostile aircraft flying low into the area where the gunners could aim potentially devastating fire. Before the Southeast Asian conflict, the United States Air Force and Navy apparently concluded that AA was obsolete and not a serious threat to a low flying, quick striking, tactical nuclear attack force. American pilots were not mentally prepared for the ferocious barrage which met their low level flights over North Vietnam. In 1967, the Pacific Air Forces staff estimated that throughout North Vietnam there were 9,000 AA weapons, many of medium caliber (37-mm and 57-mm), some as large as 100-mm.[39] Reconnaissance was not adequate to provide a correct count, especially of light guns which could easily be concealed. As intelligence gathering improved, the estimate declined to a more realistic 2,000 by the end of 1969. After the bombing ceased in November 1968, large numbers of North Vietnamese weapons were moved to Laos to protect the supply routes to the south and west; many more guns went to repair shops and storage areas. Ground gunfire accounted for more than eighty percent of all American aircraft combat losses in Southeast Asia.[40]

During its more than seven years of operation, North Vietnam's air defense system was the most thoroughly tested in the history of aerial warfare. Designed primarily to protect the nation's capital city and main port, it encompassed airfields near Hanoi, Haiphong, and in the southern panhandle. Five air surveillance sectors covered the country; three were in the most important northern portion. Reports of intruders went from any of several air surveillance sites to initial screening at radar reporting stations, then to the sector filter center which prepared a composite picture and sent it to the weapons operations center at Bac Mai airfield. The entire process took less

**In May 1969 North Vietnamese air defense forces at Site 99 attacked an unmanned USAF reconnaissance drone flying toward Haiphong and Kien An, a nearby airfield. The drone's cameras photographed the missile's pass and, seconds later, its detonation.**

TABLE 28

## North Vietnamese Antiaircraft Artillery
## September 1967

|                | Machine Guns* | Medium** | Heavy§ |
|----------------|---------------|----------|--------|
| Number of Guns | 692           | 3,079    | 1,330  |
| Active Sites   | 138 †         | 671      | 236    |
| Total Sites    | 706           | 1,581    | 537    |

\* 12.7-mm or 14.5-mm machine guns. Optically aimed. Usually 4–6 guns per site.

\*\* Medium antiaircraft, 37-mm or 57-mm automatic weapons. In this category, only the 57-mm was capable of accepting and using radar fire control data for aimed fire. Both were capable of optically aimed fire. Usually 4–6 guns per site.

§ Heavy antiaircraft, 85-mm and 100-mm guns. Both capable of optically aimed fire, although estimates indicated that all batteries in North Vietnam were associated with a fire control radar. Usually 6–8 guns per site.

† Calculated using an average of 5 guns per site.

**Sources:** Hq. USAF Combat Target Task Force Report, October, 1967

than three minutes. While reports were made up the chain, SAM and AA sites were alerted as was an alternate operations center twenty or thirty miles from Bac Mai. In 1974 the U. S. Air Force's Project Red Baron air to air combat analysts at Nellis AFB, Nevada, concluded that the North Vietnamese air defense system, was "one of the best defense systems in existence."[40]

Geography and climate gave North Vietnam other advantages. The country was small, and important targets were relatively few. As a result, air commanders bent on attack could not count on surprise as the North Vietnamese knew where, and approximately when, to expect raids. They concentrated AA weapons at significant points. The monsoon rains between November and March caused severe problems during the early war years. The Americans lacked an all weather bombing system in Vietnam and could not reach targets obscured by rain or heavy clouds. Sometimes weeks passed between raids. During the slack periods, North Vietnam's leaders recruited the population into massive repair efforts.[41]

**Amid destruction on and around the field, the North Vietnamese have accomplished repairs to the runway at Hoa Loc airfield** (squares). **They have also painted false craters on the surface to simulate additional damage** (circles).

The bristling North Vietnamese defenses protected far more than air bases. Their major responsibility was shielding supply and transport facilities, industrial operations, and electric power production facilities. Air bases received AA weapons protection, including SAMs, but they often benefitted from bombing prohibitions and proximity to other heavily defended locations.

Throughout 1966, there was debate within the Pacific Air Forces staff about the significance the northern bases as targets. Many did not consider air base attacks of prime importance, although North Vietnam's interceptors forced the Americans to tailor tactics to protect their fighter bombers. Only 3 percent of the aircraft losses were to enemy interceptors, and this could be controlled by F–4 fighter escort. Attacking the bases at the same time implied accepting losses. Phuc Yen and Kep could probably claim five to six percent of the sixty fighter bombers and seventeen percent of the B–52s. Furthermore, any inkling of a pending attack on major air bases would send the communist aircraft to China or other dispersal areas; and even if North Vietnamese bases were hit and greatly damaged, they could be repaired quickly. Eliminating the NVNAF entirely was out of the question, since the source of supply in China and Russia could not be cut off. Finally, the Americans believed, perhaps unjustifiably, that at the large number of U. S. airfields and with improved revetments, American air defenses, although untested, would stop any enemy air raid. Concentrating on industrial and interdiction targets instead of airfields seemed potentially more profitable since it promised to have a greater impact on the course of the war.[43]

Intelligence estimates also evaluated the more passive measures the North Vietnamese used to protect their aircraft. Phuc Yen airfield had many revetted parking spaces away from the base. All of the storage and support areas were well dispersed, and camouflage was skillfully used to hide guns and vital equipment. At Phuc Yen and elsewhere, the North Vietnamese buried or partly buried fuel storage tanks. Runways, taxiways, and parking ramps could be easily repaired should bombs crater them. U. S. Pacific Command experts believed the North Vietnamese also used helicopters to lift fighters and carry them to and from hidden parking areas some distance from Kien An airfield. Although cumbersome, helicopter movement would have been quite practical for an air force that did not plan to contest every attack. For the Americans, locating the aircraft in the surrounding country was all but impossible.[44]

North Vietnamese bases could not escape indefinitely. In April 1967, as the United States increased pressure on Ho Chi Minh's government, Pacific Command and the Joint Chiefs designated air bases for attack. Only Gia Lam, Hanoi's international airport, remained inviolate. Phuc Yen was finally attacked in October. Experience and new AA suppression weapons enabled the Americans to cope with the defense. They dealt heavy blows to their opponent's air force, destroying twenty-four MiGs on the ground in April and May 1967. Coupled with sixty-one more shot down by U. S. Air Force and Navy fighters in the same two-month period, these losses forced the NVNAF to reduce combat flying for some months while reassessing tactics.[45]

American attackers developed a variety of techniques to overcome the defense. Airborne radar warning equipment and visual observation of missiles in flight allowed American fighter pilots to evade SAMs with radical maneuvers. Electronic jamming reduced missile accuracy significantly. Flying above 3,000 feet to avoid the heaviest fire from the AA guns, and diving on targets from a formation protected by jamming reduced aircraft losses. Missile and AA hunter killer groups, known as Iron Hand or Wild Weasel, attacked defense sites, especially the radar sets, with a variety of weapons, including Shrike missiles. The Shrike was designed to lock onto a radar signal and follow it to its source, but American pilots tended to distrust it for its erratic performance. Because its detonation could not be seen, they never knew immediately if it had destroyed enemy radar transmitters. It did force defenders to use the radars only intermittently to avoid becoming targets. Radar suppression rather than destruction became the principle mission for these missiles. In March 1968, the improved the AGM–78 or Standard ARM (for antiradiation missile), arrived in Southeast Asia. The

After October 1967, Phuc Yen airfield in North Vietnam was struck repeatedly until the bombing halt. The symmetrical clusters below the airstrip are 57-mm antiaircraft gun emplacements.

Standard ARM, however, was used only seventy times before the President ordered the 1968 bombing restrictions, and its success could not be accurately judged. Another new type of weapon was the laser guided bomb which, like the Standard ARM, arrived too late for a full evaluation in combat during ROLLING THUNDER. How effective the new weapons would be was not clear, although they gave promise of more destructive attacks on defenses.[46]

By trial and error and by carefully studying defenses, the Americans learned the least dangerous routes to targets. Airfields at Kep, Kien An, Hoa Lac, Cat Bai, and Phuc Yen were bombed repeatedly. North Vietnamese crews flew most of the jet aircraft to Chinese bases at Peitun–Yunnani. By the end of March, 1968, only seven MiG–21s and six MiG–15s or –17s

289

remained in the country. On March 31st, however, President Johnson restricted bombing to areas south of 19° N latitude in North Vietnam's panhandle. Immediately repairs began on the major bases in the north and by October all jet airfields were again in service; most were, in fact, being improved, and two new fields neared completion. After November 1, when President Johnson extended the bombing prohibition to all of North Vietnam, Vinh and Dong Hoi airfields in the southern panhandle were also restored to use.[47]

Between November 1, 1968, and April, 1972, the United States did not allow bombing of North Vietnam except under certain very restrictive circumstances. During this time reconnaissance flights frequently crossed the country and adjacent territories and waters. In some instances, the North Vietnamese tried to destroy the intruding airplanes. When such attempts occurred, the American command allowed immediate protective reaction strikes. At times these strikes were directed at air bases, but neither the strikes nor the AA fire encountered were militarily significant.[48]

The North Vietnamese, however, continued to improve their national defenses. Before the bombing halt they learned that radar discipline—turning on the set just before firing—reduced exposure to American attacks. The North Vietnamese also fitted optical sights to both SAM launchers and 57-mm and 85-mm guns, again to reduce the need for radar, at least in clear weather. The North Vietnamese also learned that they could link electronic warfare and ground control intercept radar missile sites. By doing so, they launched SA-2s without the tell tale electronic emissions that the Americans had learned to associate with the SAM fire direction system, thus catching pilots by surprise.[49] To protect his crews from this danger, the Seventh Air Force Commander, General John D. Lavelle, permitted attacks on four airfields, associated radar, and missiles in transit, beginning in November 1971. (These attacks, some of which allegedly violated the American rules of engagement, resulted in Lavelle's relief in early March and subsequent retirement in April 1972.) On March 30, 1972, when North Vietnam launched its attack across the Cambodian and Laotian borders and the Demilitarized Zone separating the two Vietnams, the air forces called upon to stem the tide faced a much more hazardous situation than they did in 1968 when the bombing campaign against North Vietnam ceased.[50]

As the response to North Vietnam's 1972 offensive took shape, the rules of engagement were much different from those in effect during ROLLING THUNDER. With certain exceptions, such as populated areas, the Chinese border buffer zone, religious shrines, hospitals, and POW camps, field commanders had far greater authority to launch air attacks against targets as the need arose—if the target was on the JCS approved list. The use of laser or electro-optical guided munitions allowed the U.S. to strike when necessary, in an air campaign of significantly different character nicknamed

LINEBACKER. Military airfields in North Vietnam could be attacked except when aircraft of a third nation were present. As before, antiradar missiles could be used against the sites unless the missile could hit Chinese territory. Like the earlier ROLLING THUNDER effort, LINEBACKER's targets were primarily North Vietnam's transportation and supply distribution systems.[51]

In the panhandle in 1972, there were 5 airfields and about 15 MiGs, 28 batteries of surface to air missiles, and more than 1,000 AA weapons, mostly machine guns and light or medium guns. To the north there were 4 main airfields: Phuc Yen, Yen Bai, Kep, and Gia Lam. Each kept 4 to 6 MiGs on alert. In addition, Phuc Yen had about 30 fighters in caves or covered revetments; the base's maintenance facilities were in tunnels and caves of Tam Dao mountain, 3 miles north of the runway. Yen Bai airfield had about 60 aircraft (40 of which the Americans believed to be in storage or reserve) protected by extensive tunnels and caves in nearby limestone hills. Gia Lam had facilities for 6 to 10 fighters; Kep's commander dispersed his 20 fighters in covered parking or underground hangarettes. The additional bases of Kien An, Dong Suong, Hoa Loc, and Bai Thuong accommodated jets and at times served as dispersal sites. Between 1968 and 1972 warning and ground control radar sets throughout North Vietnam increased from 33 to 49.[52]

North Vietnam's alert fighters remained dispersed and under cover unless an imminent threat arose. Once a warning sounded, the North Vietnamese pilots were on "condition one" alert; they and their aircraft moved to ready positions on the airfield. If an attack did not materialize within a short time, the fighters then returned to protected dispersal parking. If attacking aircraft arrived undetected, reaction times to get fighters airborne averaged seven to eight minutes, leaving the interceptors vulnerable on the ground. Apparently the North Vietnamese used the alert system to avoid a repetition of earlier losses to American and South Vietnamese air raids. Night fighter defense was limited to a few qualified pilots flying MiG-21s from Phuc Yen who often refrained from attacking while relaying altitude, speed, and heading information to SAM batteries.[53]

Between April 14 and 20, 1972, the Allies attacked bases in the panhandle and along the coast heavily. Reconnaissance flights reported extensive runway and taxiway damage. A MiG-15 was destroyed at Bai Thuong; two MiG-17s were destroyed at Kien An, and two damaged. Large amounts of fuel burned at Cat Bai airfield. Defensive fire was light and ineffective, but several new weapons were noted by American Navy and Air Force pilots. The MiG-21J, with improved internal guns and armed with air to air missiles, appeared. In addition, a new radar gun control system, called GUN DISH, came into use. Both the MiG-21J and GUN DISH used radar frequencies for which the Americans had no jamming equipment. The Americans countered with a variety of tactics and the new AIM-9J air to air missile,

TABLE 29

**North Vietnamese Air Threat**

| Date | MiG–15/17 | MiG–21 | Il–28 |
|---|---|---|---|
| August 1964 | 36 | | |
| December 1964 | 53 | | |
| May 1965 | 56 | | 8 |
| December 1965 | 62 | 7 | 6 |
| December 1966 | 50 | 16 | 6 |
| December 1967 | 28 | 12 | 8 |
| December 1968 | 111 | 34 | 6 |

| Location | May 65 | April 66 | April 67 | Dec 67 | Dec 68 |
|---|---|---|---|---|---|
| Phuc Yen | 56 MiG–15/17 | 53 MiG–15/17 | 26 MiG–15/17 | 11 MiG–15/17 | 27 MiG–21 |
| | 15 MiG–21 | 16 MiG–21 | 6 MiG–21 | | |
| | 8 Il–28 | 8 Il–28 | 6 Il–28 | 8 Il–28 | 3 Il–28 |
| Cat Bi | none | none | 14 MiG–17 | 2 MiG–17 | none |
| Kep | none | 10 MiG–17 | 4 MiG–17 | 9 MiG–17 | 4 MiG–15/17 |
| Gia Lam | none | none | 31 MiG–17 | 6 MiG–17 | 18 MiG–15/17 |
| | | | | | 6 MiG–21 |
| Peitun– | | | | | |
| Yunnani (China) | | | | | 7 MiG–21 |
| | | | | | 89 MiG–15/17 |
| | | | | | 3 Il–28 |

**Sources:** Seventh Air Force Weekly Intelligence Summary, 14 December 1968
SEAsia Counterair Alternatives; CINCPAC Command History 1964, 1965, 1966
TAC Intelligence Consolidated Order of Battle,
Communist SEA, Jan 1968, Vol 3A, Part I

which brought down several MiGs after its debut in August 1972. The AIM–9J, an improved Sidewinder intended for close air to air combat, gave good results in Southeast Asia.[54]

The renewed airfield attacks soon demonstrated the utility of laser guided bombs. On July 26, 1972, a small formation from the 8th Tactical Fighter Wing, stationed at Ubon Royal Thai Air Force Base, hit Dong Hoi.

In less than two minutes the accurate ordnance cratered the runway. Defensive fire damaged none of the attacking aircraft. Dong Hoi and the other bases were closely watched, and the Navy and the Air Force regularly assailed those south of the 20th parallel to keep them unserviceable. Few MiGs flew over the panhandle area.[55]

Over the North's heartland, however, the situation was not so clear for the Americans. The highly refined and compact air defense system detected raids before they entered North Vietnam's airspace, and launched interceptors or missiles. By July 1972, the MiG pilots had improved so much that for the first time during the war the North Vietnamese fighters were shooting down more attackers than they themselves lost. The Americans reacted quickly, stressing the use of flying tactics best suited to the F–4s, and using more experienced pilots to teach those newly arrived in Southeast Asia. The American intercept warning system centered in Thailand was the most significant change. American Air Force and Navy commanders now could guide their escort fighters toward the MiGs and warn other aircraft of danger. The situation quickly reverted to the Americans' favor. After August 1972, claims for aircraft kills rose to four to one in favor of the United States.[56]

The bombing of the North continued into October 1972. On October 10, believing that North Vietnam was interested in peace, President Richard M. Nixon prohibited attacks within ten nautical miles of Hanoi. On the 23rd of the month, the President halted attacks north of the 20th parallel. Yet despite the heavy bombardment and increased accuracy of guided bombs, the North Vietnamese were reluctant to reach agreement at the peace table. They were aware of the approaching elections in America and the limited United States forces in Southeast Asia. The return of fighters and B–52s to combat as a result of the spring invasion of the south in 1972 did not restore the levels of aircraft which existed before the President began to reduce American military forces in Southeast Asia. Furthermore, the heavy air defenses of North Vietnam forced the Americans to provide large support elements for the tactical bomber forays. Fighter escorts, tankers, search and rescue aircraft, Navy and Air Force Iron Hand hunter killer flights, and others meant that for every attacking airplane approximately four more were in the air as auxiliaries. The North Vietnamese seemed convinced they were making their enemy sacrifice too many aircraft and crews to continue.[57]

Believing they would have to fly into the Hanoi-Haiphong area again in the near future, American military leaders in the Pacific prepared for that eventuality. Admiral Noel Gayler, Commander-in-Chief, Pacific, told his subordinate commanders on October 26 to be ready to resume interdiction bombing in the north. By October 29 the Navy's Task Force 77 and Seventh Air Force, in conjunction with the Strategic Air Command, prepared a plan to use B–52s along with tactical fighters to "destroy as much as possible of the NVN tactical [air order of battle] within a 48 hour period." The plan called for a surprise attack by B–52s on the most heavily used North Vietnamese bases at night, when their defenses were weakest. This would be followed by a fighter bomber strike against dispersal bases soon after daybreak.[58]

To force the issue in Paris, President Nixon decided to resume bombing the Hanoi-Haiphong area. The series of new air attacks, designated LINEBACKER II, continued from December 18 to December 29 with a one day stand down on Christmas. The Americans directed LINEBACKER II against all major target complexes in the main part of the country. Many had already been bombed, but repairs were under way. The first three days of LINEBACKER II saw 314 B–52 sorties directed against 11 target areas, 3 of them air bases. B–52s from the 307th Strategic Wing at U-Tapao, Thailand, hit Hoa Loc, Kep, and Phuc Yen airfields on the night of December 18.[59]

F–111s made additional air base attacks, approaching the targets at night at altitudes of 200 and 500 feet and flying at nearly 500 miles per hour. The use of terrain following radar (TFR) allowed the 474th Tactical Fighter Wing's planes to dart across Southeast Asia from their Thai bases. Although the F–111s were too few to be decisive, they harassed the enemy airmen and defenses and occasionally caused severe damage. The F–111's ability to jam defense electronics and find the precise target as it flew at very low altitude made its bombing so accurate that it caused operations at Yen Bai to cease for a day. At Yen Bai, the American bombs hit within fifty feet of the intended impact point. Elsewhere, the fighter bombers struck Hoa Lac, Kep, Bac Mai, and Phuc Yen with almost as much success. The F–111s continued the strikes for several days, often with great accuracy. Despite the heavy bombing and significant damage at some fields, especially Bac Mai, the Yen Bai attacks of the 18th were the only instance when the Americans succeeded in completely closing an airfield. Nonetheless, North Vietnam's airfield defenses were completely inadequate. No SAMs hit the low flying attackers, and light to moderate AA fire from small arms, 23-mm, and 57-mm weapons was very poorly aimed. F–111s suffered no damage by airfield defenses during LINEBACKER II. On other attacks in North Vietnam during the same time, two F–111s were shot down. Four others received slight damage.[60]

In contrast to the accuracy achieved by the F–111s, four F–4s and forty A7s failed to do much damage at Yen Bai on December 19 and 20. Craters were scattered as a result of these raids; the damage not as effective as that of the more accurate F–111s. Even though each B–52 strike hit its assigned airfield targets with high explosives and caused severe cratering, none of the SAC bombardments caused operations to cease for more than a few hours. Cluster bombs and other fragmentation weapons were not used as often as necessary to disable airplanes, equipment, and personnel. The accuracy of

B–52s at high altitude was not equal to what F–111s had achieved. Aircraft parking, shops, and areas where people congregated could not be hit with as much certainty and effect. The slightest wind drift or bomb release inaccuracy at 35,000 feet put the hits off the aiming point.[61]

Coincident attacks on antiaircraft positions (both SAMs and guns) suppressed fire for short periods, but did not destroy the North Vietnamese capability. Nevertheless, the AA suppression effort allowed the bombers to reach their targets. The effectiveness of North Vietnam's airfield defenses varied greatly. Against low level night attacks they were useless. High altitude bomber and daylight fighter-bomber air raids, however, received a much hotter and more effective welcome. The geographical area was so small that overlapping radar and weapons complemented each other. During the day, the gunner's aim was easier, but not decisive. Air bombardment caused heavy damage and forced the North Vietnamese once again to remove MiG fighters to China. Unlike the preceding LINEBACKER I, where communist fighters accounted for twenty-two of thirty-six USAF aircraft lost over the Hanoi–Haiphong region, MiG interceptors were not the most prominent threat during LINEBACKER II. Surface to air missiles caused more damage to the attackers, although they were ineffectual in preventing or reducing the pressure brought to bear. At the start of LINEBACKER II, B–52s approached target areas on predictable flight paths, and SAMs shot down eleven in four days. SAC commanders quickly changed tactics, but the most dramatic reduction in bomber losses came from electronic suppression of gun and SAM control radar, the use of deception, such as chaff, and most important, destruction of the main SAM assembly facility in Hanoi.[62]

The loss of eleven B–52s prompted SAC to eliminate SAM production in North Vietnam. Poor weather and the inability of B–52s to hit a small target without damage to the surrounding civilian population brought a denial of the Strategic Air Command's first request to attack the assembly buildings. The JCS finally approved an attack by sixteen F–4s using a Long Range Navigation (LORAN) beacon that guided attackers to the target and allowed great accuracy. American pilots attacked the heavily defended target from above an overcast at 20,000 feet. Dodging forty-eight SAMs, the single attack succeeded in destroying the facility. Subsequent SAC bombardment of SAM storage and distribution areas beginning on December 26 further restricted the North Vietnamese air defense efforts.[63]

During LINEBACKER II, surface to air missiles were most effective against the B–52s, bringing down 15 for 996 missiles known to have been launched. SAMs were least effective against tactical aircraft, shooting down 2 for 225 missiles fired. MiGs and AA accounted for 7 more American tactical aircraft. But the inability of the defenders to regroup after their own heavy losses was most important. The large numbers of SAMs fired during the first three days and the loss of their missile assembly and distribution capability left the North Vietnamese with no supply for the launch battalions. Mining ports and road and rail interdiction curtailed import and delivery of the weapons. Subsequent to the large numbers of launches during the first few days of LINEBACKER II and destruction of the assembly building, missile firings were so few and so poorly aimed that they lost effectiveness as a serious threat. Although North Vietnam's air defense commanders removed guns and SAMs from southern North Vietnam to protect Hanoi and Haiphong, the weapons either arrived too late or were destroyed *en route*. The freedom of the American field commanders to vary target strike times and methods and to attack as soon as a menace was recognized meant the defenders could no longer count on stereotyped approach patterns.[64]

The LINEBACKER II attacks appear to have achieved their limited goals and were especially effective in shutting down air bases. They drove the North Vietnamese Air Force out of the country. By depriving the North Vietnamese SAM system of missiles, the Americans choked off the enemy's air defense system. The North Vietnamese resumed peace talks, the campaign ended on December 29, and a cease fire went into effect by mid-January 1973.

## Comparison of the Campaigns: Korea and Vietnam

Combat over North Korea and North Vietnam was similar in many respects. In both conflicts an enemy air force had varying degrees of sanctuary. In the Korean War, Manchurian bases were inviolate. In Southeast Asia, Chinese bases remained so even while American attackers continually shifted their policies toward bases within North Vietnam itself. Communist air forces made immediate and continuing use of the restrictions to protect their forces. Sanctuaries in North Vietnam created by the bombing prohibition allowed the enemy to install heavy defenses. Once they had emplaced guns or missiles in or near a prohibited bombing zone, defenders could move them quickly, and often fought with minimal risk of destruction. Aerial fighting over North Korea and North Vietnam took place largely within compact geographical areas: in Korea's MiG Alley and North Vietnam's Red River delta. Defenders in the two countries had the advantage of being able to concentrate antiaircraft weapons in small areas. This allowed effective control and a very intense volume of fire. Large numbers of guns appeared in both North Korea and North Vietnam. Most effective were the medium sized automatic weapons, that is, the 23-mm, 37-mm, and 57-mm guns.

Self imposed rules of engagement were stricter in Southeast Asia than in Korea. Target lists governed air attacks in North Vietnam, many requiring almost daily approval from Washington. Except during the LINEBACKER operations at the end of the Southeast Asia war, American commanders needed specific approval to strike a target in North Vietnam, even if it was already validated by the JCS. By contrast, only the port of Rashin and the hydroelectric dams were off limits in Korea. The theater commander attacked targets within that country at his discretion.

North Vietnam's defenders had ample time to shift guns and missiles among many prepared sites. This mobility made American reconnaissance and target development much more complex. Attackers faced unexpected and heavy ground fire, surface to air missiles, and fighter interceptors, often all three on the same sortie. Support aircraft required to suppress defenses often outnumbered the attackers trying to destroy a target in the Red River delta.

The U. S. Navy and the U.S. Air Force did not expect the heavy fire encountered below 3,000 feet over Vietnam. American aircraft designed in the 1950s for a short nuclear war relied on speed and penetration during an intense conflict. Only the American F–111 had the equipment to detect radar signals and to counter radar directed fire in Vietnam. Thus, until mid-1967, losses were higher than they might otherwise have been. Imperfect weapons and political restraints placed on both bombing intensity and targets allowed the North Vietnamese to develop a proficient defense. The North Vietnamese commanders directed an able corps of MiG interceptor pilots flying from bases that were only infrequently out of action. When American forces could freely operate in Vietnam on the basis of intelligence information, they reduced defenses and forced the enemy into temporarily abandoning airfields. In both cases, the defenders had the use of abundant civilian and military manual labor to repair damage and rehabilitate essential services. As in World War II, keeping a flying field out of action required continuous and accurate strikes.[65]

Dissimilarities in the experiences gained in operations against North Korean and North Vietnamese defenses were many and profound. Most significant was the fact that the North Vietnamese prosecuted the war themselves. In Korea large Chinese formations fought UN forces; Russian pilots engaged in aerial combat, and Russian gunners manned AA batteries. Between 1950 and 1953, communist fliers used bases in Manchuria, often to the exclusion of those in Korea. In contrast, foreign regular military units were absent in Vietnam. North Vietnamese generals conducted the war and wherever possible operated the North Vietnamese Air Force from bases within their own country. Radar coverage in North Vietnam was far more extensive, and the equipment had advanced another generation beyond that used in Korea up to twenty-five years before. The Soviet Union and the Chinese supplied enough to support the defender's needs. North Vietnam's radar controlled a highly sophisticated and numerous array of weapons in Vietnam, including surface to air missiles that bedeviled American pilots even after they learned how to avoid or deflect them. The Vietnamese enemy made much more efficient use of underground structures for command and control facilities, aircraft parking areas, and maintenance shops.

Both conflicts saw decisions oriented toward keeping the conflicts strictly local and limited affairs. Yet the sharpest contrast on the American side of the war was in the increased political restrictions imposed upon American field commanders in Vietnam. Militarily, the decisions in both cases greatly benifitted defenders and frustrated those charged with achieving decisive results.

# Chapter IX

# The Middle East: 1948–1973

During the first thirty years of its existence, Israel fought her neighboring Arab states four times; the 1947–1949 War for Independence, the 1956 Suez Crisis, the Six Day War of June 1967, and the 1973 Yom Kippur War. One can also include a fifth conflict, the so called War of Attrition of 1967–1970, a much more limited engagement, consisting mostly of air and artillery duels near the Suez Canal. These clashes were an outgrowth of long standing mutual distrust dating from the early 20th century when Jewish Zionists sought a homeland in Palestine. The largely Moslem Arabs, however, viewed the Zionist movement and the growing Jewish population with great suspicion, fearing loss of lands they had owned for generations, disruption of their cherished family and community ties, and a threat to their rights within one of the holiest places of Islam, the city of Jerusalem. That Jerusalem was also holy to Jews and Christians was secondary. The Arabs believed that Arabic law and Koranic tradition gave them an unbroken right to the land from before the seventh century Islamic conquest of Jerusalem. Expelled from the city by the Roman Emperor Hadrian (A.D. 78–138) in the year 135, after the last Jewish revolt, Jews were allowed by Constantine to visit Jerusalem but once a year, on the anniversary of the destruction of the last Temple. Arab researchers insisted that the ban was not further modified, that it was continued by Islamic authorities, and that the Zionists had no valid claim to Palestine.[1]

The post-World War II influx of Jewish settlers fleeing the disaster of the Holocaust greatly exacerbated hostility evident from 1922 when Great Britain became the League of Nation's Mandatory Power in Palestine. Arab riots in 1922, 1929, and 1936 protesting Jewish emigration were fomented by the Mufti of Jerusalem, Haj Amin el-Husseini. The Mufti, an influential leader, played upon the popular fear that Jews were arriving in great numbers and supplanting Moslems with the intent of taking control of the holy shrines. After World War II, immigration increased as displaced persons from Europe sought a new home. Friction between the peoples grew and on November 29, 1947, the United Nations voted to partition Palestine between Arabs and Jews with Jerusalem designated an international territory. The Palestinians, supported by the neighboring Arab governments, rejected the proposal, seeing Palestine as part of a Greater Syria. Great Britain, suffering from the cost of World War II, relinquished control in May 1948. It could no longer afford to keep a 100,000 man army in Palestine. The Jews in Palestine created the state of Israel on May 8, 1948, and since that time security of the state has been a prime consideration for Israel's political leaders.[2]

The 1948 war pitted a newly formed Israeli Air Force (IAF), or *Chel Ha'Avir*, against the Egyptian Air Force (EAF). Both were equipped with World War II aircraft, but air operations were a small part of the fighting. In the main, the IAF was able to achieve two things during the War of Independence. First, it stopped Arab pilots from attacking Jewish territory and even undertook some limited bombing of Arab lands. Second, the IAF organized an effective air transport operation that supplied settlements and ground forces in the Negev Desert, which comprises most of southern Israel. The early difficulties of the *Chel Ha'Avir* were compounded by arguments between its first commander, Brig. Gen. Aharon Remez, and the Israel Defense Force's Chief of Staff, Yigal Yadin. Remez's RAF background led him to seek a fully independent air force, something Yadin opposed, believing the nature of the war and the forces fighting it did not require complete service autonomy. Yadin won. Remez's legacy, however, was an excellent training establishment to support the emerging *Chel Ha'Avir*.[3]

An armed force organized originally from the Haganah, Irgun, and Lehi underground partisans that fought the Arabs for possession of Palestine in the early 1940s, the Israeli Defense Force of 1948–49 suffered from lack of manpower, outdated equipment, and the need to fight on several fronts at one time. The constant demands of battle caused the Israeli military to develop a philosophy of flexibility, surprise, and innovation often missing in the armies of their Arab foes. Geography gave the Israelis another great advantage once the State of Israel was established: they were able to operate along short internal lines of communication, shifting forces when or where needed to protect various borders.[4]

After an early flirtation with an air force designed along functional lines, having both tactical and strategic units, it became apparent to Israel's leaders that such an organization was too expensive. Brig. Gen. Dan Tolkovsky, the IAF's commander between 1953 and 1958, promoted the idea originated by his predecessor, Haim Laskov, of centralized control of air operations and use of one type of aircraft for many different missions.

Laskov, in turn, drew inspiration from the Desert Air Force of World War II. Tolkovsky believed it necessary to "compensate for our small numbers [of aircraft] by emphasizing high serviceability and quick turnaround [of planes being serviced after a sortie]." He knew the Egyptians had serious problems in centralizing control of their air force, since they had to defend their bases and major cities along the Nile River while carrying on a war in the Sinai. The large size of the EAF, however, made it a potentially deadly enemy and Tolkovsky firmly believed that, as the IAF's major threat, it had to be destroyed immediately on a resumption of the conflict.[5]

Egypt's Air Force, part of its military legacy from British colonial days, began modernizing in 1955. Unable to obtain enough arms from the United States, Egypt's leader, Gamal Abdul Nasser, turned to the Russians. Striking a bargain with the Soviet Union's proxy, Czechoslovakia, Nasser obtained MiG–15 and –17 fighters, Ilyushin Il–28 light bombers and Il–14 transports, which began to arrive late in the year. Russia also provided flying and maintenance instructors who worked at the large number of formerly British airfields between the Nile and the Negev. American intelligence estimates credited the EAF with 442 pilots, however, the Americans believed only 87 to be qualified for combat; of that number, 46 were jet pilots. Furthermore, the EAF's command and logistic support structures were weak because of the lack of trained, experienced people. The Israeli Air Force, on the other hand, had an excellent training, maintenance, and command arrangement which supported 16 fighter and fighter-bomber squadrons, 3 transport squadrons, and liaison aircraft. It operated from 8 major airfields and was generally considered the best air service in the Middle East.[6]

In 1955, Israel felt itself threatened when Nasser blockaded the Gulf of Aqaba at Sharm el-Sheikh, commanding the narrow Straits of Tiran at the southern tip of the Sinai, thus cutting Israel's port of Eilat from its access to the Red Sea. For several years, attacks by Arab guerrillas (*Fedayeen*) on Israeli territory had originated largely in Egypt and were a constant source of trouble between the countries. By 1956, Israel faced an Egyptian-Jordanian-Syrian military coalition threatening it from all sides save along the short demarcation line with Lebanon. Israeli political and military leaders concluded they had to use force to resolve their country's precarious situation. The British and French joined in the action as a result of Nasser's nationalizing the Suez Canal, formerly controlled by those two countries. Both Britain and France believed the canal vital not only to their worldwide mercantile and defense interests, but also to general international trade. In addition, both European powers had other axes to grind with Nasser: France because of open and rather shrill Egyptian support for Algerian rebels seeking independence from France; Britain because of repeated terrorist attacks on her nationals in Egypt and Nasser's violently anti-British propaganda in the Middle East.[7]

Although the Israelis realized the importance of a first strike at an enemy's air bases, the IAF did not attack Egyptian airfields during the Suez Crisis of 1956. (*Map 26*) The plan for the Suez operation, drawn up during October 1956, called for an initial Israeli thrust into the Sinai Peninsula, engaging Egyptian forces there and ostensibly threatening the canal. Britain and France would then use the fighting as a pretext to seize the canal under the guise of enforcing peace and separating the belligerents. The two European allies would assume the task of neutralizing the Egyptian Air Force. The IAF was only to protect ground forces and transport army units to key positions in the Sinai. It would not attack airfields in the hope the Egyptians would not realize immediately what was happening, and then, when they did, exercise restraint in retaliatory attacks. Just to be on the safe side, however, French fighters would be stationed at Tel Aviv's Lod airfield. The recent installation of Israel's first modern radar at Lod made the employment of French fighters possible.[8]

The Israeli operation began late on October 29. To confuse the Egyptians, four Israeli F–51 Mustangs (acquired from the surplus of various countries) flew at low level across the Sinai and cut telegraph and telephone lines on twelve foot poles with their propellers This daring feat was followed by an air drop of a parachute battalion, commanded by Col. Ariel Sharon, that was to seize the Mitla Pass, near the Suez Canal. Egypt quickly found itself at war.[9]

True to the plan, France and Britain presented their previously agreed upon ultimatum, ordering Israel and Egypt to withdraw forces from the canal. As anticipated, Egypt refused. The British and French then entered the fighting, bombing the EAF's airfields on the night of October 31. Unlike the Israelis, Britain and France intended to strike from Malta, Cyprus, and aircraft carriers to destroy the EAF at the outset of fighting, thus gaining air superiority immediately and protecting their convoys approaching Port Said. Using night high altitude bombing tactics developed during World War II, and bombs no larger than 1,000 pounds to limit civilian casualties, the bombers struck twelve airfields. Because of the darkness and altitude, accuracy was not good and the bombs caused little damage to aircraft and installations. Several of the EAF's bombers and fighters escaped to bases in the south. Egyptian air interception was minimal, the AA gunfire wildly inaccurate, and aircraft on the ground had no protective revetments. On November 1, the RAF, Royal Navy Fleet Air Arm, and French Air Force fighter-bombers began daylight raids on air bases to finish off the Egyptians. Altogether, forty-four British and French squadrons assembled for the campaign. Most were initially directed against the bases, and by morning of November 2 the EAF had been largely destroyed on the ground, never having struck inside Israel.[10]

302

**Map 26**

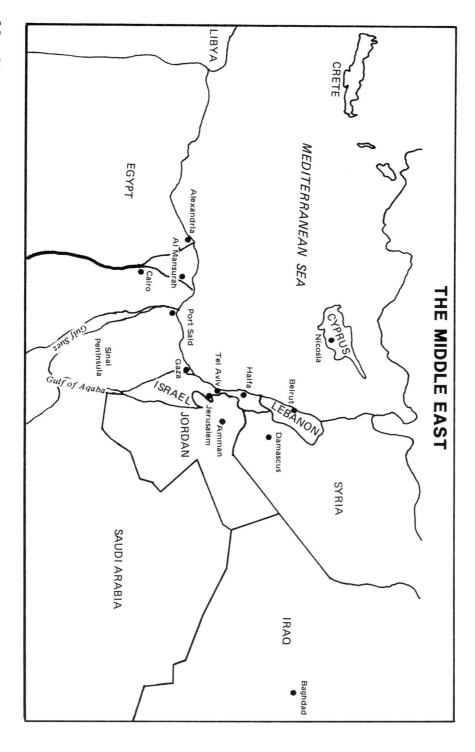

THE MIDDLE EAST

LIBYA

CRETE

EGYPT

MEDITERRANEAN SEA

Alexandria

Al-Mansurah

Cairo

Port Said

CYPRUS

Nicosia

*Gulf of Suez*

Sinai
Peninsula

Gaza

Tel Aviv

Haifa

Beirut

*Gulf of Aqaba*

ISRAEL

Jerusalem

Amman

LEBANON

Damascus

JORDAN

SYRIA

SAUDI ARABIA

IRAQ

Baghdad

## TABLE 30

## Comparative Strengths
## Egyptian and Israeli Air Forces
## 1956

### Egyptian Air Force

| Type | No. of Aircraft | |
|---|---|---|
| Light Bombardment | | 2 Squadrons |
| Il–28 | 49 | |
| Fighter and Fighter-Bomber | | 6 Squadrons |
| MiG–15, –17 | 126 | |
| Vampire | 78 | |
| Meteor | 29 | |
| Transport | | 2 Squadrons |
| Il–14 | 43 | |

In addition, the Egyptians had one light liaison squadron

### Israel Air Force

| Type | No. of Aircraft | |
|---|---|---|
| Fighter and Fighter-Bomber | | 16 Squadrons |
| Ouragon | 50–60 | |
| Gloster Meteor VIII | 24 | |
| F–51D | 25 | |
| Mosquito | 50–60 | |
| Mystere IVA | 50 | |
| Transport | | 3 Squadrons |
| C–46 & C–47 | 40–50 | |
| B–17G | 6 | |

At least one French F–84F squadron operated from Lod Airfield, Tel Aviv
The Israeli Ministry of Defense cites figures slightly lower than those shown here.

**Source:** Goldberg, "Air Operations in the Sinai Campaign—1956"

TABLE 31

## British and French Aircraft Strength, 1956

### Royal Air Force/French Air Force

| Base | Valiant | Canberra | Hunter | Venom | Mystere | F–84F | Recon |
|------|---------|----------|--------|-------|---------|-------|-------|
| Hal Far, Malta | – | 16 | – | – | – | – | – |
| Luqa, Malta | 28 | 16 | – | – | – | – | |
| Akrotiri, Cyp. | – | – | – | 64 | – | 18 | 26 |
| Nicosia, Cyp. | – | 48 | 32 | – | – | – | – |
| Haifa, Israel | – | – | – | – | 36 | – | – |
| Lod, Israel | – | – | – | – | – | 18 | – |
| Total | 28 | 80 | 32 | 64 | 36 | 36 | 26 |

### Royal Navy/French Navy

| Carrier | Sea Venom | Sea Hawk | Wyvern | Corsair | Avenger |
|---------|-----------|----------|--------|---------|---------|
| HMS Albion | 24 | 24 | – | – | – |
| HMS Bulwark | – | 16 | – | – | – |
| HMS Eagle | 16 | 8 | 16 | – | – |
| Arromanches | – | – | – | 24 | – |
| Lafayette | – | – | – | – | 12 |
| Total | 40 | 48 | 16 | 24 | 12 |

**Source:** BDM Corporation: "Air Superiority and Airfield Attack: Lessons from History"

Some scattered Egyptian aircraft still had to be dealt with. Twenty Russian built Ilyushin Il–28 jet bombers remained at Luxor. Twenty more, along with 10 Il–14 transport aircraft, fled to bases in Saudi Arabia where they were protected by Saudi neutrality. On November 4, American built F–84Fs of the French Air Force, each fitted with two 450-gallon external fuel tanks, flew from Lod airfield to strafe the planes at Luxor. Two attacks met no opposition; the bombers were destroyed on the ground. For the remainder of the campaign, Egypt's Air Force was no threat. Estimates of Egyptian losses ranged up to 260 aircraft destroyed with 7 British and French planes shot down. The Egyptian Army fought on for a few more days, but, demoralized by air attacks and broken up by the rapid Israeli advance, it could not continue. On November 6, a United Nations arranged truce went into effect.[11]

The 1956 Sinai Campaign ended in frustration for the British and French, who were forced by Russian-American opposition to give up their military gains, withdraw within a few months, and be replaced by a United Nations Emergency Force (UNEF). Although air base attack and defense were not an important part of the action, the air campaign foretold future operations. Lacking protection by a competent air defense and adequately trained pilots, the EAF fell easy victim to an overwhelming British and French force even though the attackers carried out an imperfect plan. The UNEF separated the Israelis and Egyptians, but the warring parties continued to eye each other warily. As part of the supervised truce, Israel regained shipping rights past Sharm el-Sheikh through the Straits of Tiran; the UNEF's presence ended the *Fedayeen* raids from Egypt, although the guerrillas soon moved to Jordan to continue their depredations. The threat of an Egyptian-Syrian-Jordanian alliance against Israel subsided temporarily with the UN ceasefire.[12]

For the IAF, air defense of Israel remained the top priority. Air defense to the Israelis, however, did not mean that they would fight only to defend the airspace over their country. No enemy aircraft could be left with the potential to attack Israel. The destruction of the EAF by Britain and France in 1956 seemed to reinforce the IAF's faith in its own operating doctrine. Although untried, Israel's conception of attacking Egyptian airfields had been validated by the Franco-British success in destroying the Egyptian aircraft on the ground. IAF commanders kept their plans for preemptive first strikes current over the next decade.

## The Six Day War: 1967

Subsequent to the UN truce arrangements, both Egypt and Israel began to rebuild and modernize their forces. Syria, Jordan, and Iraq, which refrained from entering the 1956 war, also improved their armies. Of Israel's potential foes, Egypt's Air Force remained the largest and best. By 1960, the Soviet Union provided Egypt a billion dollars in equipment and sent a military mission that taught strategy and tactics, equipment operation, and maintenance. Egypt rebuilt almost its entire Air Force with Soviet supplied aircraft and, in 1967, it consisted of about 450 planes flying from some 25 bases. The EAF had an especially well developed airlift capability, able to transport 3,000 paratroops at one time, and a dangerous bomber force composed of some 30 Tupolev Tu–16 medium bombers and 40 Il–28s. The bomber force presented a threat to any of Israel's cities or military installations.[13]

Training standards in the EAF were fairly high, although the service had only about 500 pilots—not enough to allow for everyday flying of all operational aircraft. For various reasons, the EAF usually had about 20 percent of its aircraft nonoperational, and the Egyptians were unfamiliar with some of the new types of aircraft and equipment just arrived from Russia. Beginning in 1962, Nasser committed his military to support of the revolutionary faction in Yemen's civil war. About 60 fighter-bombers were thus occupied on the Arabian peninsula attacking Royalist troops in the mountainous interior of Yemen. Since they did not face a Yemeni air force, the Egyptians did not have to fear an attack on their bases and therefore learned nothing about base defense.[14]

Other Middle Eastern air forces varied widely in ability. Like its Egyptian counterpart, the Syrian Air Force was Soviet equipped. The Syrians had about 120 aircraft, mostly MiG–21s, –19s, –17s, but also 6 Il–28 bombers. It, too, was short of pilots. Training and pilot procurement had been hampered by political instability in the country, but Syrian air bases lay within easy striking range of Israel. The Iraqi Air Force was about twice the size of Syria's, although it had only one base (designated H–3) near enough to Israel to pose a threat. Iraq's Air Force was composed of a mixture of British and Russian airplanes. The Jordanian Air Force, having but 22 Hawker Hunter fighters and 16 pilots, was of uncertain fighting capability.[15]

In 1967, the IAF was made up almost entirely of French built Mystere and Mirage fighters. It also had some obsolescent Ouragons and Vautours. To beef up the service, the Israelis fitted Fouga Magisters, trainers built in Israel under license from France, with rockets and used them for close air support. Israel faced the same Arab threats as it did in 1956, and it still did not have transit rights in the Suez Canal. The Syria-Jordan-Egypt military combination, however, was now more potent and included the support and participation of Iraq. Additionally, Arab guerrilla raids were more frequent and lethal and emanated more from Syria, supporter of the Palestine Liberation Army (PLA), than from Egypt. Continuing to tolerate *Fedayeen* or PLA attacks was possible, but politically difficult for any Israeli govern-

TABLE 32

## Comparative Strengths
## Arab and Israeli Air Forces
## 1967

### Israeli Air Force

| Type | No. of Aircraft |
|---|---|
| Fighter and Fighter Bomber | |
|   Super Mystere* | 40 |
|   Mystere IV A | 40 |
|   Mirage III J | 64 |
|   Ouragon | 48 |
|   Vautour II A | 25 |
| Training | |
|   Fouga Magister** | 60 |
| Transport | |
|   Noratlas and Boeing Stratocruiser | 20 |
| Helicopter | |
|   (Super Frelon, Sikorsky H–34, H–55, Alouette) | 25 |
| Total | 322 |

*   Twenty were on loan from France for training and were returned after the fighting. Official Israeli figures vary slightly.
** Fitted with rockets for ground attack.

### Arab Air Forces

| Type | Egypt | Syria | Iraq | Jordan |
|---|---|---|---|---|
| Fighter and Fighter Bomber | | | | |
|   MiG–21 | 120 | 20 | 60 | – |
|   MiG–19 | 80 | 20 | 30 | – |
|   MiG–15,–17 | 180 | 60 | – | – |
|   Su–7 | 20 | – | – | – |
|   Hawker Hunter | – | – | 50 | 22 |
| Bomber | | | | |
|   Tu–16 | 30 | – | 6 | – |
|   Il–28 | 40 | 6 | 10 | – |
| Transport | | | | |
|   Il–14 | 60 | – | – | |
|   An–12 | 25 | – | – | – |
|   Helicopters | 60 | – | – | 26 |
|   Mixed types | | | | 40 |
| Training and Miscellaneous | 120 | – | 20 | – |
| Total | 735 | 106 | 176 | 88 |

**Sources:** O'Ballance, *Third Arab-Israeli War*
        Weizman Briefing

ment. A lost war, the Israels were certain, meant annihilation of the country.[16]

The Arabs, however, perceived their own position quite differently. Bitter at the loss of land to Israel in 1948–49 and rankled by the destruction of Egypt's Air Force in 1956, Syria and Jordan were also aggrieved by a squabble with Israel over rights to the waters of the Jordan River. In Syria the Ba'ath regime, installed by a 1966 *coup de etat*, was convinced Israel intended to destroy it. This fear grew in part from Israel's large scale military retaliation for guerrilla raids. Then on April 7, 1967, Israeli aircraft shot down six Syrian MiGs in a single encounter and overflew Damascus, Syria's capital, as if to celebrate the victory. Humiliated by the loss of its jets, in May 1967 Syria's government became increasingly concerned that it was soon to face a serious attack. (*Map 27*) These fears were fed by Russian reports to both Egypt and Syria that Israel had massed some eleven brigades on Syria's border and planned an invasion. On May 12 an unidentified senior Israeli official reportedly remarked that Israel planned to carry out military operations against Syria to overthrow its government. Whether or not the statement was ever made, its quotation in a speech by Nasser on May 23 increased tensions.[17]

A Syrian appeal to Nasser for help was followed by a rapid deterioration in Israel's already tenuous relations with the Arabs. Although Arabs and Israelis were hostile to one another, many informal contacts, as well as those through the UNEF, existed. The United States Ambassador to Egypt believed the slide toward war was probably neither anticipated nor desired by any of the countries directly involved. Nevertheless, on May 16, Nasser put his military on alert and ordered the UNEF out of the country. Two days later, U Thant, Secretary General of the United Nations, acceded to this, and, in a controversial act, removed the peacekeeping force. Nasser moved his army into the Sinai, and on May 19 Israel announced its intent to fight if he closed the Gulf of Aqaba to Israeli shipping, which Nasser did on May 22. On May 30, fearing his shaky position as Jordan's monarch would weaken if he did not support his Arab brothers, King Hussein agreed to participate in a combined military force under Egyptian leadership.[18]

Surrounded by numerically superior enemies, Israel saw its position as extremely perilous. On June 1 Prime Minister Levi Eshkol, who had no military background, appointed Moshe Dayan Israel's Minister of Defense. Except for two short periods during 1953 and 1955, the defense portfolio always had been retained by the Prime Minister. Dayan's appointment was a clear indication of how seriously Israel now viewed the situation. The new Defense Minister was an extremely able leader, Chief of Staff during the 1956 war, and a man not disposed to await an attack on his country. The Israeli Air Force commander was Brig. Gen. Mordechai Hod, who continued the policies of his predecessor, Brig. Gen. Ezer Weizman, in keeping the

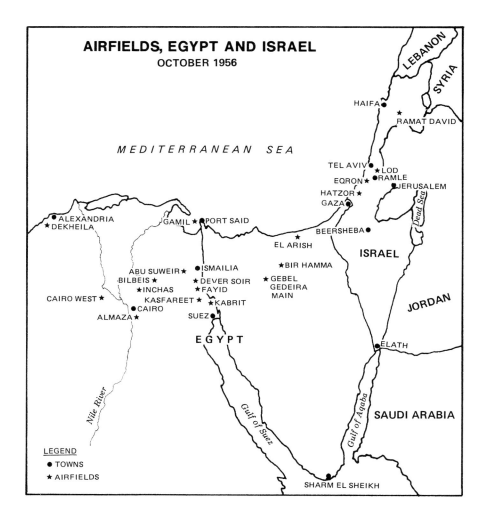

**Map 27**

force aggressive and trained to a high degree of fighting skill. Both Weizman and Hod kept the plan of attack on Egypt's air bases continuously up to date; the pilots' target folders held the latest reconnaissance photographs of the objective sites. Dayan now ordered the IAF to ready its pilots for a preemptive strike on Egyptian air bases.[19]

Remembering the Anglo-French assault of eleven years earlier, President Nasser may have anticipated the impending strike. That at least was the opinion of Anwar el-Sadat, a long time colleague of Nasser's and, at the time of the Six Day War, Speaker of the Egyptian National Assembly. In 1977, Sadat, who succeeded Nasser as President of Egypt, related a meeting of June 2, 1967, during which Nasser supposedly warned General Sidqi Mahmoud, the EAF's commander, of the threat of a strike by Israel in the next few days. Mahmoud replied, nervously, that defenses were in place and only ten percent losses should be expected from such an eventuality. According to Sadat, Nasser expected war to begin not later than Monday, June 5.[20]

The Egyptian Air Force used about 22 main flying fields (*Map 28*), most of them less than 300 nautical miles from Israel. Two bases were 400 nautical miles distant. Four were in the Sinai. A radar system gave warning of approaching aircraft to the military command center near Cairo. The command center was, in turn, linked to Egypt's major military installations including some 25 SA-2 missile sites. Egypt deployed her surface to air missiles as area defense weapons; each unit was laid out similarly to those encountered in North Vietnam and protected by AA guns. At the airfields, Egypt placed varying numbers of 12.5-mm, 14.7-mm, 37-mm, and 57-mm AA guns. Antiaircraft protection for the bases was deficient, however. A large proportion of the AA guns sent by the Russians had been assigned to the Army to protect field units. The Israelis believed there were few radar controlled guns protecting each base.[21]

MiG fighters were normally on air defense alert. Egypt protected its parked aircraft with World War II-style open earthen revetments. These revetted parking places, however, were not hardened with concrete or steel, making the planes vulnerable to air attack. MiG fighters on airborne patrols normally stayed aloft for several hours each morning to defend against Israeli incursions during the postdawn hours. Egypt's military staff believed this to be the time of greatest danger.[22]

The Israelis selected ten of the Egyptians' most important bases for the first attack. General Hod intended to "destroy the air power of Egypt." To do this he wanted "to catch them on the ground and [keep] them on the ground." Some of Hod's colleagues believed the planned attack was a tremendous gamble, the odds against its success great. Precision flying was absolutely necessary. Almost all the IAF's fighter-bombers had to be used; virtually none could stay behind to guard Israel. The reactions of Syria and Jordan could only be estimated. If they brought their air forces to bear before the Israeli attackers returned home they could ambush the planes when they were short of fuel and out of ammunition.[23]

To prepare for a future war, the IAF had for years kept training standards high, stressing accurate gunnery and precision bombing. Simulated airfields in the Negev served as exercise targets several times yearly. Each of the sites had runways, dispersal areas, and dummy aircraft. After the war, General Weizman estimated that each attacking IAF pilot had made be-

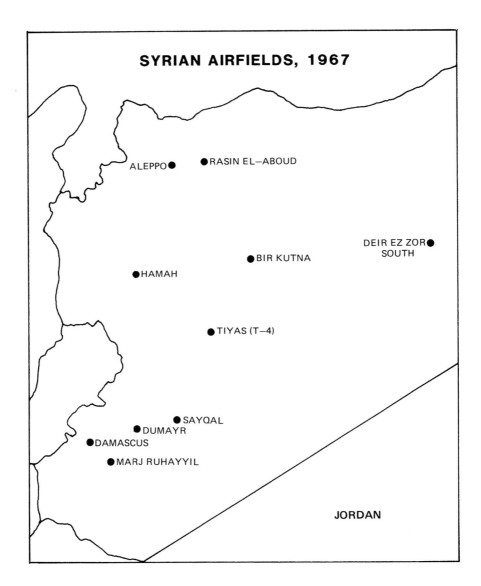

**SYRIAN AIRFIELDS, 1967**

ALEPPO● ●RASIN EL—ABOUD

DEIR EZ ZOR●
SOUTH

●BIR KUTNA

●HAMAH

●TIYAS (T—4)

●SAYQAL
●DUMAYR
●DAMASCUS
●MARJ RUHAYYIL

JORDAN

**Map 28**

tween fifty and one hundred practice attacks in the five to seven years before 1967. Israel's intelligence estimates were superb. They contained virtually all their enemies' aircraft dispositions and the flying schedules of the opposition units. Deception, too, played an important part. For some months before June 5, the IAF's pilots had repeatedly flown training missions out to sea after taking off, knowing they were being tracked on Egyptian radar. Some of the attack force would follow the same route part way, and it was important to lull the Egyptians into a false sense of security and avoid last minute suspicions.[24]

General Hod knew the critical importance of his timing. He expected to accomplish Israel's war aims before the great powers imposed a UN sponsored cease fire. He had to destroy the Egyptian Air Force and then recover to face Syria and Jordan, if necessary. He calculated that he had about 3 hours: a half hour for Egypt to understand what had happened; a half hour for Egypt to explain to Syria, one hour for the Syrians to think about it, and at least a half hour for Syria to react. In effect, he was gambling that Syria would help "protect" his bases by its confusion and subsequent reticence to enter battle.

The Israeli government almost shelved Hod's plan for political reasons. Some key cabinet members participating in the decision for war did not believe that total air superiority over Egypt could be gained in less than a day, and they feared the risks of leaving Syria's air force intact for that long a time. There was no choice but to gamble, however. Israel had only 200 fighter-bombers, and massing that small force was the only way to succeed. Furthermore, the design of the aircraft severely limited the types and amount of weapons that could be carried. The attack had to destroy the main enemy at the first blow. As this became clear to the Ministerial Defense Committee of Israel's cabinet on June 4, they approved Moshe Dayan's motion to establish H-hour as 0745 (0845 Cairo time) the next morning. At H-hour, Israeli pilots would be over their targets, and the morning ground fog would have cleared. The early Egyptian patrols would have landed—the EAF habitually did not replace them—and the senior Egyptian officers would be on their way to work from breakfast.[25]

Each section of the Israeli first wave took off from its base in time to allow all to arrive at their targets at 0845. The strikes operated under a set of simple rules: no overt act that might warn of an impending blow to the airfields; each airfield to be hit initially by four fighter-bombers; and absolutely no radio transmissions for any reason by the attackers until after they struck. Some of the sections flew out to sea—as had the previous training flights; some traveled south across the Sinai. All were at very low altitude, often no more than thirty feet—so low that they raised spray and steam from the Mediterranean's smooth surface and dust from the desert floor. Shortly after take off, those over water turned south and began navigating toward

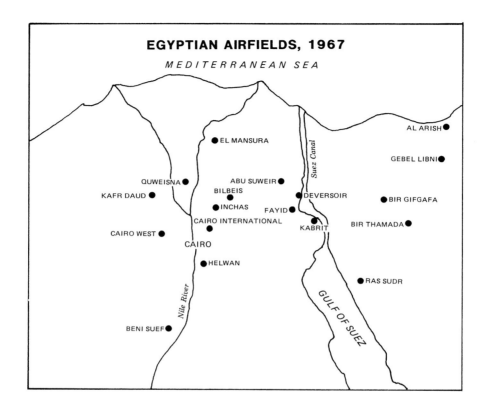

**EGYPTIAN AIRFIELDS, 1967**

MEDITERRANEAN SEA

AL ARISH ●

GEBEL LIBNI ●

EL MANSURA ●

Suez Canal

QUWEISNA ●
KAFR DAUD ●
ABU SUWEIR ●
BILBEIS ●
● INCHAS
● DEVERSOIR
● BIR GIFGAFA
FAYID ●
CAIRO INTERNATIONAL ●
KABRIT
BIR THAMADA ●
CAIRO WEST ●
CAIRO
● HELWAN

Nile River

GULF OF SUEZ

● RAS SUDR

BENI SUEF ●

**Map 29**

their targets. (*Map 29*) Contrary to some commentators' initial opinions, the IAF's flights that morning did not swing far out to sea and circle to approach the enemy bases from the south; few of their aircraft had the fuel capacity for a roundabout route to the target.[26]

To add to the defenders' confusion, the Israelis broadcast tape recordings of routine radio transmissions. They filled the airwaves with the chatter of pilots to create the illusion of a day of ordinary flying for their listeners along the Nile and in Damascus. In another deception, Israel announced on June 4 the impending release of some reserve troops, hoping to allay fear of imminent war.[27]

On the approach to the targets, the IAF ignored Egypt's defenses. Egyptian radar was useless because of the attackers' low altitude, and the IAF left it intact to avoid warning the Egyptians. These locations, however, the Israelis attacked on the flight home as targets of opportunity. Because

314

the Israelis did not fully understand the SA-2s, they were somewhat apprehensive of them and avoided the missiles. When the first wave of airplanes arrived over their targets, the base defense gunners were surprised and rarely fired. It is possible that some MiGs took off or were airborne when the Israelis arrived; they may have shot down two attackers. Otherwise, the interception attempt was ineffectual. Each wave of Israeli fighter-bombers stayed over their targets for five to seven minutes, the first series of attacks lasting eighty minutes in all. In a twenty minute break, the first returning planes were refueled, reloaded, and given new pilots.[28] The scenario repeated itself in another eighty minute period of attacks.

After the first assault, AA gunfire increased and was sometimes heavy, but the gunners apparently suffered considerable confusion and often failed to coordinate their fire. Some of Egypt's defenses simply were inadequate. SA-2 surface to air missiles launched at the Israelis were ineffective at low altitude. The SAMs failed to score a hit and taught the Israelis not to fear them. The Israelis lost only nine aircraft with six damaged in the first series of attacks.

The Egyptians used dummy airplanes at many places. Some estimates say as many as forty percent of those seen by Israeli pilots were fakes, but they were often set in unlikely places. Too, the Egyptians failed to simulate fuel and exhaust stains normally associated with aircraft and made the dummies yet more recognizable. Few of the false targets drew fire.[29]

Fortuitous circumstances also played a role in the surprise. In the summer of 1966 a Christian Iraqi pilot, believing he suffered religious discrimination at home, defected to Israel flying a MiG-21 fighter. Possession of this aircraft gave the IAF a chance for mock aerial combat against their enemy's best equipment, a tremendous advantage in actual air fighting. In a curious turn of affairs, given Nasser's apparent belief the war would start on or before June 5, Egypt's Chief of Staff, Field Marshal Abdel Hakim Amer, and the Air Force's commander, Lt. Gen. Mahmoud, were in a plane bound for Thamed when the attack began. Because they were in the air, AA gunners were restricted in their freedom to fire at aerial targets. Out of touch with the situation on the ground, the commanders could give no orders. Apparently those in charge on the scene were unwilling or unable to act decisively in their stead. It is possible the absence of Amer and Mahmoud was critical in the failure of the Egyptian defenses to recover after the first attack. If so, lack of competent action by subordinates was a disastrous failure on the part of the entire Egyptian command.[30]

In his autobiography, Anwar Sadat described the scene at military headquarters as news of the magnitude of Israel's victory became clear to Egypt's leaders. Sadat seemed to distrust Amer because of the latter's constant desire to encroach on political power by exerting increasing military control over the country. Sadat found a dazed Field Marshal Amer in his office at the command center. He seemed not to recognize Sadat and apparently was unable to act decisively. Nasser was stunned, and he too could not react effectively, even to remove any of his inept his subordinates. As the war progressed, it became ever more apparent that the military leadership was faltering badly. Amer was finally removed from office in August 1967 and died the next month in detention near Cairo.[31]

As the Israelis readied the second wave, they had to adjust their targets to account for the initial damage—which well exceeded expectations. They now directed attacks at other bases not yet hit, where some of the EAF's planes had sought refuge. The Egyptian losses continued and, even though fields at Luxor, Bilbeis, and Hughada were not bombed until noon or later, by late morning the ability of Egypt to wage aerial war was gone. Eighteen air bases were strafed and bombed in Egypt on the first day to destroy airplanes on the ground; almost 300 aircraft were reduced to wreckage.[32]

Many Egyptian bases experienced the effects of a new weapon. The final pass made by the first sections of attackers released what came to be called the "concrete dibber bomb." Conventional high explosive bombs delivered by fast moving aircraft at low altitude tended to ricochet, bouncing like a stone skipping over a pond. The French first experimented with a device that used retrorockets to slow itself down in flight. The Israelis improved upon the idea further and added a parachute to stabilize the bomb in its descent at a 70- to 80-degree angle incident to the ground. Launched about 100 meters over any runway, the ordnance proceeded through this sequence until rockets in its tail propelled the 365-pound warhead through the concrete runway surface to explode deep in the ground below it and leave a crater with badly cracked concrete around it. Delay fuzes could be set to catch enemy jets landing on the field in the aftermath of a raid and to complicate long term repair work.[33] Hod believed that only a few craters would disrupt the take off of Egyptian jet fighters and keep them out of action.[34]

Brigadier Hod's calculations of Arab reaction times were accurate, erring only in favor of Israel. Like Sadat's description of Egypt's headquarters scene on June 5, Moshe Dayan's was probably colored too, although it was a fair account of the IAF commander's reactions. Hod sat tensely in the IDF command post with the Chief of Staff, Yitzhak Rabin, and Defense Minister Dayan, the three scanning operational reports and waiting for the flights to reach their targets. After the first strikes, the pilots broke radio silence to report amazing successes. As the possibility of failure disappeared, Hod's mood shifted first to relief, and then elation. He changed targeting for later flights to avoid objectives already destroyed. Just before noon, Jordan's Air Force attacked the town of Netanya and the IAF's airfield at Kefar Syrkin, ten miles east of Tel Aviv. One Noratlas transport was destroyed on the ground. The Syrian Air Force joined the fray, bombing without much effect the oil refinery at Haifa and a small airfield in the Jezreel valley, where Israeli gunners shot down one of the attacking Syrian aircraft. Hod quickly ordered his staff to prepare instructions for attacks on Syrian, Jordanian, and Iraqi tactical bases. The results were devastating.[35]

Israel's apparent intent was to ignore the threat of Arab countries other than Egypt until they opened hostilities. Responding to attacks from the north and east, a third wave of Israeli fighter-bombers was in the air by 1215. Fifty-one sorties hit Jordan's Mafrak and Amman airdromes (*Map 30*), destroying all Jordan's Hawker Hunters. Syria lost 53 planes at Damascus and 3 other locations while the Iraqis lost 10 at H–3. Now fully alert, the Syrians mounted a stiff defense. The Israelis lost 10 aircraft in aerial fighting with 5 pilots killed and 2 taken prisoner. Nevertheless, the air war was virtually over with 451 Arab airplanes destroyed in the first 2 days, only 58 of which were shot from the sky in dog fights; almost all of the rest were caught on the ground on the first day. The seizure of air superiority allowed Israel to shift its air operations to support of the Army and underwrite the speed of the drive to the Suez Canal.[36] Israel's successful stroke against Egypt was its most productive air defense. By eliminating two-thirds of its opponent's aerial combat capability, the IAF secured its own bases.

Even without this initial stroke, Israeli bases had a line of defense. These bases possessed complex, although not always heavy, ground defenses. Many aircraft parking spots were hardened and partly underground. Each had fuel and electric power; often they were camouflaged. Antiaircraft guns and a few American built Hawk missiles, highly regarded by General Weizman, were in evidence. The commander of the IAF's antiaircraft unit at each base was also the base commander's assistant for air defense, advising and acting for him in all AA matters. However highly Israel may have regarded its ground weapons, it was unable to match those of its enemy in number and, therefore, relied on seizure of air superiority to protect its air bases and the country. For instance, Israel had just six batteries of Hawks, of which five were operational. Israel's defense policy concentrated AA weapons at air bases and a few other highly sensitive fixed installations. Ground units received only those considered essential. The hundreds of AA guns lost by Egypt in the Six Day War were nowhere equalled in the IDF's ground units. Although important to defense, AA weapons had a secondary place in Israeli thinking. As General Weizman put it, "if we lose air superiority it won't make a difference [how many guns we had at the bases]." One other factor governed Israel's deployment of its limited number of weapons, both guns and Hawks, and reduced their density at air bases: the nuclear plant at Dimona was a priority resource requiring heavy defense. It was inconceivable that such a location would have been left with light protection.[37]

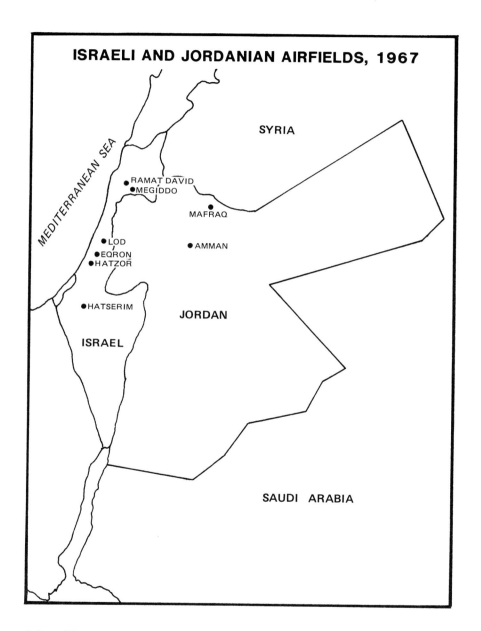

ISRAELI AND JORDANIAN AIRFIELDS, 1967

SYRIA

MEDITERRANEAN SEA

● RAMAT DAVID
●MEGIDDO

● MAFRAQ

●LOD
●EQRON
●HATZOR

● AMMAN

●HATSERIM

JORDAN

ISRAEL

SAUDI  ARABIA

**Map 30**

In any event, there was almost no call for the IDF's air defense weapons to be used. The Arabs paid the price of overconfidence and of being surprised. For all of their superior manpower, they lacked the flexibility of doctrine and the unity of purpose exhibited by the Israelis. On the first day of fighting, the Arabs lost almost 400 aircraft destroyed at 25 bases. Egyptian ground defenses, described by General Weizman as heavy, but much less severe than expected, were not overcome; they were ignored. In any event, suppression of AA defense was not possible as the attacking aircraft were fully loaded with the fuel and ammunition needed to destroy the force they hoped to catch on the ground. No aircraft could be spared from attacks on parked planes and runway cratering to engage defenses.[38]

Command and control of the Egyptian defenses failed. Faced by the surprise attack and with the principal air and ground commanders isolated from the fight, others who might have assumed responsibility for air base defense could not or would not do so. Even though the airfields were repairable in a day or two, sometimes within hours, the initial disaster in Egypt had been too heavy to overcome. During the six days of fighting, Israel lost ten percent of its pilots and twenty percent of its planes while imposing aircraft losses of up to two-thirds on the enemy. For the *Chel Ha'Avir,* outnumbered on June 4 by three to one, this was a stunning victory.

## War of Attrition: 1967–1970

During the 1977 peace talks, an Egyptian general approached Israel's Defense Minister Ezer Weizman and asked him if he knew "what offended us most [in 1967]? That newspaper photograph showing your women soldiers standing guard over our soldiers, who lay face downward on the sands of Sinai."[39] The remark illustrated the bitter humiliation suffered by the Egyptians as a result of the swift defeat. That memory made the war of 1973 almost inevitable. One of the Egyptians' prime concerns, a subject of constant thought, was how to achieve air superiority in the next battle. After Nasser's death in September 1970, his successor, Anwar el-Sadat, found himself in an increasingly more difficult position. Many expected him, as the leader of the most important Arab nation, to deal successfully with Israel, yet Israel occupied a large portion of Egypt's territory, the Sinai, and there seemed little prospect of voluntary return. Most of the world, including America and Russia, believed Egypt and the other Arab states powerless to contest Israel's military position. Frustrations continued to mount as time passed. Egypt, the ostensible leader of the Arab world, seemed unable to direct itself toward restoring its prestige and territorial integrity.[40]

At the end of the Six Day War, Israel's land included large new portions in the north, along the Golan Heights. In the east, Jerusalem and the West Bank had been seized from Jordan; to the south Israel held the Sinai Peninsula. Many people believed the Jewish state could now achieve peace on favorable terms; the Arabs, however, did not agree. Within a month the first clash along the Suez Canal between Egypt and Israel heralded the start of what was called the "War of Attrition." Between 1967 and August 1970 the conflict continued with varying intensity. The resulting actions, especially by Egypt, would change the style of fighting in the area.[41]

The 1967 campaign had hardly ceased before Arab and communist nations began a massive resupply effort. On June 9 forty MiG–21 fighters arrived in Egypt from Algeria; sixty more came from Czechoslovakia. Other east European nations sent additional aircraft, and Egypt withdrew some of its own from Yemen. On June 10 and 11, forty military cargo flights landed in Cairo from Russia and a shipload of tanks reached Alexandria. Some of the equipment was in transit when the 1967 war began, but these and many other deliveries were accelerated.[42]

Nasser sacked Egypt's senior Air Force leaders. Over the next two years several commanders sought to resurrect the service, aided by the fact that most Egyptian pilots survived the surprise attack and were able to fly. The EAF's pilots were told by their new commander, " . . . forget about the disaster of June 5. We are going to build a new Air Force and we are going to do to Israel what they did to us."[43] Under the influence of Russian advisers, a major organizational change created the Air Defense Command, responsible to the Chief of Staff, who was also Minister of War. Not a separate service, ADC comprised Army and Air Force units. It functioned separately and controlled all surface to air missiles and fighter-interceptors. Antiaircraft guns not specifically assigned to deployed ground units also came under ADC's control. Early warning and fire control radars, communications, and command functions were centralized under General Mohammed Ali Fahmi, the ADC commander.[44]

The Russians intended their resupply of the Arabs immediately following the war to replace losses, rebuild capability, and restore confidence in Arab armed forces. Static defenses received special attention as improved radar and surface to air missiles arrived. Almost overnight Egypt began an intensive effort to build reinforced, covered concrete revetments. On July 27 an Israeli reconnaissance flight over Egypt brought back photographs of an air base being reconstructed. The Egyptians were using the terrain to mask resources from approaching planes and conceal the new facilities. Aircraft parking areas were being built into the ground and were enclosed by heavy concrete covers. At a briefing for senior American officials in September 1967 in the Pentagon, General Weizman expressed concern about Israel's need to consider the new defenses in planning air attacks if war should start anew.[45]

The hardened shelter construction discovered by the IAF in July was the start of an extensive new program. Over the next few years, Egypt built about 1,000 such covered revetments, more than enough for her entire Air Force. Further, the Egyptians created protected bunkers for SA-2 and SA-3 missile launch sites and regional radar command centers. Israeli opinion was divided on whether the designs were Russian inspired or domestic, but the effect was the same: far greater protection for the EAF and associated defense units.[46]

The hard shelters were of several basic types. Many were above ground and large enough to hold one or two fighters. Another sort was completely underground, covered with sand or dirt, camouflaged, and difficult for an attacking pilot to see. Most of the shelters had sliding doors made of steel reinforced concrete. Although the workmanship appeared crude and unsophisticated, the structures could withstand considerable blast pressure. A direct hit by a heavy, penetrating weapon was needed to damage or destroy aircraft within. Israel did not have such ordnance. Bunkers protecting equipment and crews at SAM sites, both SA-2 and SA-3, were of steel reinforced concrete and either partly or wholly below ground. Radar antennas were placed on the roofs of the structures. The missiles themselves were located nearby on their launchers. Some new SAM sites took the form of drive through bunkers so that radar and launch vans could be moved rapidly from place to place, yet be protected when at the launch sites. The design of the missile launch sites allowed dispersal and redundancy of equipment. Each had its own electric generators, further protecting the location from the effects of air attack elsewhere. However, the missiles themselves were often in the open and exposed to attack when they were on their launchers.[47]

The Egyptians took great care in constructing their regional radar command centers. The radar center at Fayid air base, for example, was air conditioned and fitted with electricity and connections to support a complex computer system. It had sturdy blast doors, was camouflaged, and revealed modern design techniques. In October 1973, it had not yet been put into service. Throughout the country, other air base facilities were protected equally well. Beginning in 1967 jet fuel storage tanks were buried. The tanks were connected by pipelines in reinforced, underground ducts. Cut off valves were underground, and other equipment was secured in reinforced masonry buildings.[48]

In 1967, Syria, Jordan, and Iraq started similar hardening programs. Aircraft parking, maintenance, arming, and refueling areas received protection. The Egyptians and Syrians widened taxiways to serve as auxiliary runways. Additional runways were built at some bases, and the Arabs began research aimed at developing runway destruction bombs. Egyptian construction crews widened and strengthened highways in various places; aircraft shelters built along the roadside gave added dispersal capability.[49]

As the Arabs proceeded with construction, the War of Attrition became progressively more severe. Most of the fighting centered on the Suez Canal and involved artillery and aerial bombardment and raids by each side on enemy installations. Heavy exchanges of fire were more or less continuous between March 1969 and August 1970. On occasion, Israel's aircraft and commandos penetrated far into Egypt, accomplishing such feats as blowing up electric transmission lines near the Aswan Dam. In December 1969, a team of Israeli commandos flew by helicopter to Ras-Arab where it captured and removed a Russian built radar set. Throughout, the Egyptians used their very considerable artillery superiority to try to exhaust the Israelis, who replied with ever greater air attacks on a variety of installations and facilities. Newly delivered American built F–4s and A4s made their appearance with the IAF in 1969. These aircraft quickly became the mainstay of the *Chel Ha'Avir.*[50]

Egypt's dependence upon the Soviet Union for planes and antiaircraft weapons gave the Soviets a progressively greater stake in Egypt's military affairs. It was a situation not welcomed by all Arabs, and frictions arose between the often arrogant Russian teachers and their Egyptian and Syrian students. Nevertheless, between 1968 and 1973, Russia and her east European allies delivered between $2.4 and $3.5 billion worth of military goods to the Arabs. This was double or triple the amount supplied to Israel by the United States, depending on the method of calculating relative values. Israeli combat aircraft increased 82 percent; Egyptian and Syrian 137 percent, although the Arabs received a diverse mixture not always easily maintained. As the War of Attrition intensified, public reaction in Egypt to Israeli incursions forced the Egyptian military command to activate its surface-to-air missile defenses. The IAF promptly attacked the sites causing great damage to the missile complexes. Between July 1967 and January 1970, the Israelis shot down forty-eight Egyptian aircraft in air combat. Israel did not admit losses, but few, if any of its aircraft were lost. Concern grew in Moscow that some sort of action was needed to reverse the trend and protect the reputation of Russian weapons.[51]

Early in 1970, faced with an increasingly grave situation along the canal, President Nasser sought more Soviet help. The Soviet Union replied by sending 1,500 personnel to man some 40 to 50 SA–3 batteries. The SA–3, a two stage, mach-2, radio controlled weapon with a slant range of about 12 miles, could reach an altitude of 49,000 feet and was roughly equivalent to the IAF's American made Hawks. The SA–3s quickly appeared around air bases near Alexandria and Cairo as well as other locations such as the Aswan Dam. The Israelis matched base defense efforts by continuing to build hardened parking shelters at their bases. Guns were either 40-mm radar directed Bofors or captured Russian built 37-mm and 57-mm cannons. Camouflage was skillful, and some hangarettes were partially concealed in palm groves.[52]

In April 1970, Soviet pilots began to fly air defense missions over the Nile, freeing Egyptian fighters and improved SA-2s for duty along the canal. To avoid confrontations with the Russians, Israel ceased its attacks on targets deep inside Egypt. Israeli security, always good, became tighter. Pilots' names were not made public; their air bases were not indentified in information releases, and censors restricted news interviews with aircrews. The Israelis refused to discuss techniques of air operations. The scene of fighting shifted to the Suez Canal area where intense air and artillery battles were common. The EAF's pilots, emboldened by new aircraft and improved training, made repeated strikes in the Sinai. Air bases were among the targets, and Israel reported shooting down two Il-28s over occupied Al Arish airfield. In a surprise move late on the night of June 29, the Russians moved operational SA-2 and SA-3 missile batteries to positions near the Suez Canal. The sites had been prepared in secret, at night, in anticipation of the move. As the SA-2 and SA-3 missiles moved into place, 23-mm guns were ready to give low level protection. The IAF's pilots responded with attacks on the new sites. Israeli spokesmen claimed heavy damage was inflicted.[53]

Fearing the outcome of an escalating conflict, the Soviet Union and the United States arranged a cease fire that became effective on August 8, 1970. The cease fire terms included a "standstill" line thirty-two miles west of the canal. Egypt was to refrain from placing additional AA missiles between the line and the canal. Almost immediately, however, the Israelis claimed Russo-Egyptian violations. Late in 1970, General Aharon Yariv, Israel's chief of intelligence, pointed out that before the cease fire there were fifteen occupied SAM sites in the area. Yariv added that reconnaissance aircraft photographed new ones on August 16 and 19, and that by early November forty to sixty such sites existed. The interlocking fields of fire of the guns and missiles made the IAF's penetration attempts very hazardous.[54]

During the week before the cease fire took effect, the IAF tried American supplied ECM pods, first used in Vietnam, to allow F-4s to avoid the missiles. Five of the IAF's aircraft were shot down in two days, although Israel made no public announcement at the time. Well after the fact, Maj. Gen. Binyamin Peled, the IAF's commander from 1973 to 1977, said he lost the aircraft because of poor tactics and reliance on ECM pods not suited to the radar frequencies found in the Middle East. Nevertheless, once the cease fire was in effect, Israel discontinued its heavy bombing, and large scale penetrations of Egyptian air space stopped. Consequently, the IAF's harsh experience in that one week could not be countered by mounting a successful mission to prove to pilots, politicians, and observers that the newly installed, heavy belt of missiles was not impenetrable. According to Peled, far too many myths about the new AA weapons grew between late 1970 and the beginning of the October War. In Peled's view, the reality of dealing with surface to air missiles was clouded by what he called needless fears of "an idiot . . . senseless snake." By October 1973, Peled believed, "Ezer Weizman and many others [were] as scared of [SAMs] as my wife is scared of a cockroach."[55]

In Egypt, friction between the Russians and Egyptians, especially President Sadat, continued to grow, in part because of slow delivery of new weapons. Sadat was determined to renew the war since he could see no other way to reclaim Egypt's land. Israel showed no inclination to return any of the occupied Sinai, and Sadat had come to believe that only by breaking the military deadlock could there be any hope of great power support for finding an answer to the Arab-Israeli bitterness. Renewal of the conflict, even with limited aims, might precipitate negotiations. In addition, Sadat thought an attack on Israel's occupation forces would relieve growing political pressure at home. Arab humiliation continued to fester, and in Egypt Sadat was under increasing pressure to act. As ostensible leader of the Arab coalition, he was looked to for leadership. To accomplish something significant, however, Sadat needed offensive as well as defensive weapons but the Soviet Union was perhaps not willing to provide a long term attack capability it could not control directly. Then too, the Soviet Union was unwilling to jeopardize its developing detente with the United States by appearing to foment renewed strife. On July 17, 1972, a frustrated Sadat ordered over 4,000 Russian military advisers out of his country within a week. The Israelis, not believing Egypt able to organize a war without outside help, thought chances of conflict greatly reduced, an end that Sadat had at least partly contrived. Russia, not wanting to lose the influence and investment it had in the Arab world, responded by sending some of the war material Sadat wanted. New Sukhoi Su-20s and SA-6 and SA-7 surface to air missiles appeared, as did additional batteries of SA-3s and improved SA-2s. Syria and Iraq also received Russian supplies.[56]

When Sadat ousted the Russians, he renewed his ties with the Arab world's leaders and enlarged his plan of strategic deception, relying on earlier Russo-Egyptian planning. There were many elements to his illusion. Since Syria and Egypt had large standing armies posted along the cease fire lines, a reserve mobilization was not necessary to renew the conflict. The Egyptian Second and Third Armies took extensive training in canal crossing over several years, often along the Nile in Lower Egypt. Egypt held at least forty-one military exercises near the canal between 1967 and the October 6 attack. Secrecy was close. Although Sadat and Syrian President Hafez al-Assad spurred general war preparations, the Egyptian and Syrian leaders held information about the intended date of attack to a very few senior leaders.[57]

Field army commanders knew the attack date just ten days in advance. Sadat and Assad told the Russian ambassadors to their respective countries of their intentions on October 3 and 4, and battalion commanders learned of the advance on the morning of October 6. On the political front, the Arabs disguised or concealed indications of intent. Sadat laid plans to attend an October UN meeting in New York and discreetly passed this information to East European leaders in the belief it would find its way to other countries, which it did. Most important of all, Israeli leaders misjudged the information they had. Believing it would take until 1975 for the Egyptian and Syrian Air Forces to reach peak capability, the Israelis were reluctant to judge them ready for combat. The departure of Russian advisers left Israel and others convinced the Egyptians could not install and use the complicated radar and missile equipment they had, some of it still in shipping crates. In fact, the Egyptians were quite ready to set it up and integrate it into the command and control structure in a short time—and they did with the help of about 1,000 Russians who quietly returned.[58]

Israeli intelligence assessments failed to take into account several items of information available to them. The Syrians had reinforced their divisions facing the Golan Heights, but two of their armored divisions could not be located by Israeli intelligence analysts. Live ammunition was being widely issued during an early October "exercise." Egyptian soldiers wore chemical resistant clothing, usable only once. Egyptian and Syrian forward air bases were reinforced and other Arab nations strengthened the two countries' military units. Israel's self imposed restrictions on reconnaissance overflights after the 1970 cease fire and the installation of the SAM belt near the canal precluded their gaining extensive in depth photography of enemy troop movements. The result of careful Arab preparations and Israel's errors gave Sadat and Assad an important advantage.[59]

## The October War: 1973*

At two o'clock on the afternoon of October 6 the Arabs struck. The day was Yom Kippur, the Jewish Day of Atonement, and most Israelis were in synagogues or at home. The surprise was not total, however. Suspicious of the Arabs' intentions, Defense Minister Dayan had sent one of Israel's best armored brigades to reinforce the Golan Heights three days before, but the Army, while on alert, had not mobilized its reserves and had only about twenty-five percent of its manpower on duty. The Air Force and the Navy were on alert and did not need to call up reservists as they were both largely composed of regulars, even in peacetime. Much has been made of the Israe-

---

* Israelis refer to the war as the Yom Kippur War as it began on October 6, the Yom Kippur holy day in 1973. The Arabs, in turn, call it the Ramadan War since it began during the Islamic religious period of Ramadan. The term October War, used in this study, encompasses both references.

**Israeli Gun Crew with 40–mm Bofors in the Sinai, October 1973.**

lis' intelligence failures in the face of Arab moves, but there is little reason to suppose that they could have predicted events with complete accuracy. Israel had faced such developments previously, and war did not always come as a consequence of singular Egyptian activity. Many of the misunderstood indicators later cited by critical analysts were of only partial validity. Since 1967 most Syrian and Egyptian troops were on the front lines, but a short distance from, and always threatening, the IDF. Additionally, Israeli political leaders, headed by Prime Minister Golda Meir, were reluctant to strike a preemptive blow. For the benefit of world opinion, and especially that of the United States, they believed it better to be in the position of the injured party.[60]

On the afternoon of October 6, Anwar el-Sadat sat in his military control center, talking to his commanders and awaiting reports from his pilots. At two o'clock his armies sent the first assault wave across the Suez Canal in small boats. When they seized positions on the far side, engineers quickly moved pontoon bridges into place. Tank and truck traffic could now cross. Fighters and fighter-bombers from half a dozen bases flew low, just clearing the high sand banks each side built along either side of the canal. At

326

fifteen minutes past two, the radio began revealing results of years of planning. Approaching Ras Nasrani air base, MiG–17s climbed quickly, then dove toward the runways releasing their bombs, while MiG–21s flew top cover. Two of the IAF's Phantoms roared down the runway and rose to intercept, shooting down several intruders. Israeli gunners ran to their Bofors guns and began firing. Captured Russian 37-mm and 57-mm guns, used by the IAF for base defense, also opened fire, but the Israeli fusillade could down no Egyptian airplane. At Bir Gifgafa air base Su-7s dropped enough bombs on the field to dig five craters in the runways; then they turned to destroy the control tower. Elsewhere, Egyptian jets attacked radar stations, destroying two early warning sets. At least two other bases suffered moderate damage to runways and some facilities. Israeli fighters landing at Ras Nasrani after combat had to dodge craters and debris; the landing gear of one F–4 was damaged. Bir Gifgafa was not operational for four hours as understrength repair crews worked feverishly to clear the runways. (*Map 31*) Sadat was pleased. He believed the EAF had redeemed the failure of 1967. In fact, the Egyptian fliers helped alter the balance of power in the Middle East for a time.[61]

Israeli fighters could not retaliate. Earlier that day, General Peled, as a result of the government decision against a preemptive strike, ordered offensive weapons on the IAF's aircraft replaced with air defense munitions. The IDF believed the Arabs would strike late that afternoon, too late for Israel to mount an air assault on the SAM belt. Lacking current photographic coverage of the enemies' bases and missile sites, Peled could only send up air combat planes and fighter-bombers to help relieve the beleaguered Army forces near the canal as daylight slipped away. (*Map 32*) Protecting from air attack the two Arab armies, one crossing the canal, the other assaulting the Golan Heights, were about 172 SAM battalions (each the rough equivalent of an American battery), most of which were along the canal or near the Syrians' front lines. Ten Egyptian and 15 Syrian battalions had the new SA–6 missiles, unfamiliar to the IAF. All the SA–6s were close to the forward edge of the battle area, not protecting airfields, but this was no help to Israel's pilots who were forced to learn quickly how to avoid the lethal weapons. The SA–6 was a mach-2.8, low altitude weapon not susceptible to jamming by Israel's ECM equipment. Because of its small flame and lack of smoke, it was very difficult for pilots to see once launched. Lacking enough daylight and information to carry out a complex defense suppression operation, the Israelis waited until the next day to respond.[62]

On the afternoon of the sixth, the IDF quickly found itself in trouble on the Golan Heights. A strong Syrian armored assault pushed the Israelis back, and only the fiercest resistance prevented a breakthrough to the Sea of Galilee. The IAF's fighter-bombers, flying to the aid of the defenders, faced a SAM belt along the Syrian lines almost as heavy as the Egyptians installed

**EGYPTIAN AIRFIELDS, 1973**

MEDITERRANEAN SEA

Al Manzila

Al Rahmaiya

Bahiq    Jiyanklis    El Mansura

Suez Canal

Birma    Zalahia

Quweisna    Az Zaqaziz

Kafr David    Abu Suweir

Bilbeis Northeast

Tukh Highway Strip    Bilbeis 2    Fayid

Cairo West    Bilbeis    Kabrit

Inchas

Cairo International

Cairo    Wadi Al Jandali    Sinai

Helwan

Al Fayyum

Nile River

Beni Suef    GULF OF SUEZ

Wadi Abu Rish

Al Minya

Hurghada

## Map 31

west of the canal. Syrian missiles began taking a heavy toll of the IAF airplanes, and had to be suppressed. General Peled told his men to entice the Syrian missilemen to fire repeatedly at their planes, which dodged the salvoes. Aircraft flying behind friendly lines located the SAM sites which were then bombarded by artillery. This tactic was especially effective against the mobile SA–6s, the 18-mile range of which was less than that of Syria's improved SA–2. When Syria's missiles were exhausted temporarily, Peled's men turned on the airfields (*Map 33*) and attacking ground forces, blunting the enemy's armored thrust and stalling a hastily organized Russian aerial

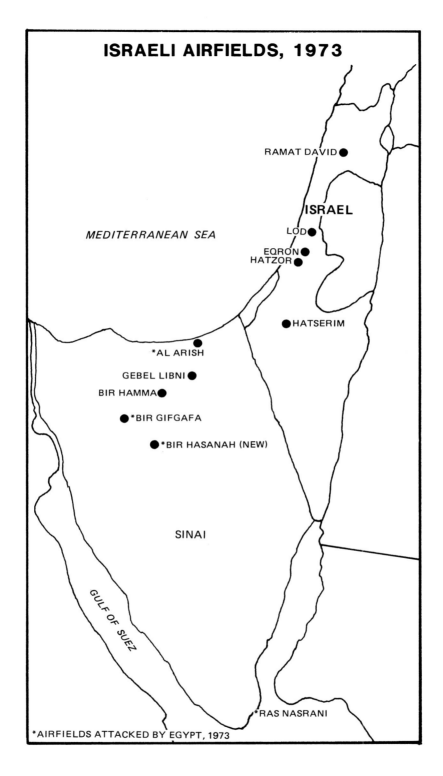

**ISRAELI AIRFIELDS, 1973**

*MEDITERRANEAN SEA*

RAMAT DAVID ●

**ISRAEL**

LOD ●

EQRON ●
HATZOR ●

● HATSERIM

*AL ARISH ●

GEBEL LIBNI ●

BIR HAMMA ●

● *BIR GIFGAFA

● *BIR HASANAH (NEW)

SINAI

*GULF OF SUEZ*

*RAS NASRANI ●

*AIRFIELDS ATTACKED BY EGYPT, 1973

**Map 32**

resupply effort. Syrian bases were attacked throughout the first two weeks of fighting, but by October 9 the Israelis began a drive toward Damascus. The outcome of the fight in the north was already clear.[63]

After deflecting or eliminating the immediate threat from Syria, the IDF turned its full attention to a more determined adversary, Egypt. In all, Israel attacked between seventeen and twenty-four bases during October. On October 7, the Arabs' forward missile batteries and air bases came under attack. On that day 44 sorties of F–4s, with Mirages for top cover, hit seven Egyptian bases, the most concentrated Israeli assault on airfields in a single day to that point in the war. On the 10th, some 130 sorties delivered bombs on 5 Syrian and 2 Egyptian installations. The most pressing problem was to wrest the initiative from the Arabs. Without a mobilized army the burden fell on the IAF, which responded at the expense of counterair and interdiction operations, its main missions.[64] The effort expended was about the same as that of the Six Day War, but the results were far less dramatic. Disruption of Arab air operations was not as pronounced as in the earlier conflict. Because of the pressing need to help the Army, the *Chel Ha'Avir* found itself having to battle the attacking ground force and the enemy's protective AA cover, the latter a target far down on its list of mission priorities. In attacking the Arabs' air bases, especially those in Egypt, the IAF found the resistance much different than before. The Arabs abandoned the idea of forward air cover for the battle area and kept their air defense planes patrolling the rear area. Although not trained to a degree sufficient to compete with Israel's pilots, the Arab fighters were a distraction that had to be faced in order to penetrate to the bases.[65]

The most important question for Israel became what bases to bomb and when. Defenses were a consideration, although according to General Peled not a major one. His prime concern was to obtain current aerial photographs of targets, then have his pilots briefed as to what was to be attacked and how to avoid the air defenses. Defended less heavily than the canal or the Syrian front facing the Golan, many Arab air bases were protected by four to six missile sites and AA guns of varying caliber—hardly easy targets. Peled maintained, however, that with the degree of accuracy of the IAF's weapon navigation system, his aircraft could release conventional general purpose unguided bombs from 7,500 feet altitude and hit any target 10,000 feet away. The important point was to use the advantages accruing to an attacker by confusing the defenders with drone decoy aircraft, chaff, electronic countermeasures, varying approach patterns and times, and firing stand off antiradiation weapons such as the heavily used Shrike. Once the attack was made, the pilots got their planes out quickly, reducing exposure to surviving AA weapons. In contradistinction with the American experience in Vietnam, Peled found the Shrike very effective. He noted, however, that the weapon had to be used in conjunction with deception and in tactics

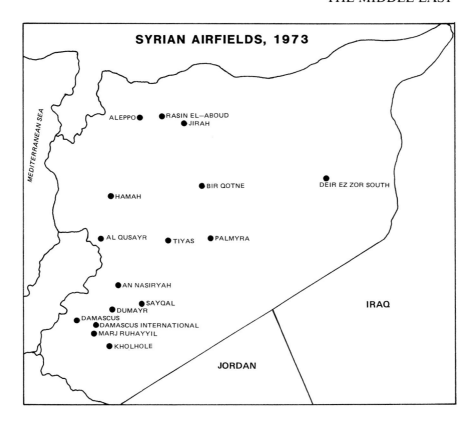

**SYRIAN AIRFIELDS, 1973**

MEDITERRANEAN SEA

ALEPPO

RASIN EL—ABOUD
JIRAH

BIR QOTNE

DEIR EZ ZOR SOUTH

HAMAH

AL QUSAYR   TIYAS   PALMYRA

AN NASIRYAH

SAYQAL
DUMAYR
DAMASCUS
DAMASCUS INTERNATIONAL
MARJ RUHAYYIL

KHOLHOLE

IRAQ

JORDAN

**Map 33**

employing far more planes than the U. S. Air Force two aircraft Wild Weasel team. Peled preferred to use enough antiradiation weapons to force the enemy to shut down an entire area's SAM radar operation, whereupon he could deliver telling blows on the exposed SAMs themselves, which he considered "one of the softest targets on the face of the earth." Once the defenses were overcome or bypassed, the IAF could then deal with the enemy's air bases or other targets.[66]

The IAF found that the numerous Arab concrete reinforced hangarettes gave excellent protection from 500-pound bombs (the normal weapon) and Maverick air to ground guided rockets. Neither weapon alone could penetrate the structures and demolish the contents. The Israeli Air Force destroyed only one hangarette during the war. Next, the Israelis tried cratering runways. An early cratering tactic was to have the bombing planes preceded by attack aircraft releasing cluster bomb units. The CBUs suppressed AA

TABLE 33

## Comparative Strengths
## Arab and Israeli Air Forces
## 1973

### Israel Air Force

| Type | No. of Aircraft |
|---|---|
| Fighter and Fighter-Bomber | |
| F–4 | 101 |
| A4 | 162 |
| Mirage | 67 |
| Super Mystere (SMB–2) | 20 |
| Assault Helicopters | 40 |
| | 309 |

### Arab Air Forces

| Type | Egypt | Syria | Total |
|---|---|---|---|
| Fighter and Fighter-Bomber | | | |
| MiG–21D | -- | 20 | 20 |
| MiG–21F | 20 | 16 | 36 |
| MiG–21J | 180 | | 212 |
| MiG–21 | -- | 34 | 34 |
| MiG–15 | 16 | -- | 16 |
| Su–7 | 50 | 39 | 89 |
| Su–20 | 15 | -- | 15 |
| MiG–21C & E | 60 | 4 | 64 |
| MiG–17 | 90 | 84 | 174 |
| Reconnaissance | | | |
| Su–7 | 6 | -- | 6 |
| MiG–21 | 6 | 4 | 10 |
| Bomber | | | |
| Tu–16 | 26 | -- | 26 |
| Additional Probable | | | |
| Modified Su–20 | 30 | 30 | 60 |
| Hawker Hunter | 37 | -- | 37 |
| Mirage | 27 | -- | 27 |
| Probable Maximum | 563 | 263 | 826 |

**Source:** Weapon System Evaluation Group, Paper P–1007, "Preliminary Assessment of the Effectiveness of Weapon Systems Used by the Opposing Forces in the October 1973 Middle East War."

TABLE 34

## Comparative Strengths
## Arab and Israeli Air Defenses
## 1973

### Israel Air Defense Systems

| Type | Number |
|---|---|
| 20-mm Mk I Polsten (UK) | 180 |
| 20-mm HSS–804 (Swiss) | 420 |
| 37-mm (Italy) | 50 |
| 37-mm (USSR) M1939 | Undetermined |
| 40-mm (W. Ger.) | 54 |
| 40-mm (UK) | 15 |
| 40-mm Bofors L/70 (Swiss F/C) | 150 |
| 57-mm S60 (USSR) | Undetermined |
| 3.7 in. (UK) | Undetermined |
| Total | 869 + |
| Hawk Missiles | 400 |
| Hawk Launchers | 72 |

### Egyptian Air Defense Systems

| Type | Number |
|---|---|
| 12.7-mm Quad. Barrel (Czech) | 363–441 |
| 14.5-mm ZPU 2/4 (USSR) | 306–334 |
| 23-mm ZU 23 (USSR) | 379–457 |
| 20-mm M53–M–57 (Yugoslavia) | 400 |
| 37-mm M1939 (USSR) | 435–513 |
| 57-mm S60 (USSR) | 225 |
| 85-mm KS–12 and M1944 (USSR/Czech) | 180 |
| 100-mm KS–19 (USSR) | 362 |
| 23-mm ZSU/23 SP (USSR) | 6 or 7 battalions |
| 57-mm ZSU/57 SP (USSR) | 263 |
| Total | 2886–3148 + |
| SA–2 Missiles (Estimates) | 1700 |
| Launchers | 420 |
| SA–3 Missiles | 1400 |
| Launchers | 200 |
| SA–6 Missiles | 300 |
| Launchers | 20 |
| SA–7 Missiles (128 Platoons) | 15–20,000 |

**Source:** US Army Combined Armed Center, "Analysis of Air Combat Data, 1973 Mideast War" Vol. II.

fire by making the gunners seek shelter, but the main effect was to warn the defenders that an attack was coming. After the runway bombardment, very efficient repair crews went to work filling the holes. At the more important bases the work took two hours; the average closure was five to six hours, enough to allow attacking formations to reach other targets, but not enough to keep the enemy air force on the ground in a continuing conflict. Some Israeli pilots observed MiG–21s landing on 3,000 foot sections of cratered runways.[67]

The most effective counterair tactic was the one Israeli air commanders liked least: air to air combat. Believing that the need for dogfighting signified a failure to lay waste an enemy air force's operating bases, the Israelis now had to shoot their foe from the sky. In the first 2 weeks of fighting, the Arabs lost 334 airplanes in combat; Israel lost 3. Israel's effort at base attack yielded just 22 planes destroyed on the ground, while Arab defensive fire accounted for 7 F–4s, a 3 to 1 ratio which did not please the IAF's leaders. The air superiority gained by combat victories, however, allowed the IAF to attack the heavy flow of tanks and reinforcements headed for both active fronts. In attacking the reinforcements, the Israelis also struck the air defense belts west of the canal and along Syria's border. The IAF's fighting was desperate. By far the greatest number of its losses came during close air support and SAM suppression missions.[68]

While Israel carried the battle far beyond its borders, its airfields suffered little damage in return after the first day. The IAF's air defenses, centrally controlled either at the air headquarters or one of the three territorial force operating centers (south, covering the Sinai; central, protecting the West Bank; north, the Golan Heights), prevented air attacks from reaching targets inside Israel. While the IAF's gunners shot down 101 aircraft attacking Israel's ground forces, they hit none over their own air bases.[69]

The Arabs' Russian built planes lacked radar warning, night attack instruments, and ECM self protection devices. Egypt had barely enough pilots to fly its combat planes, and many Syrian and Egyptian pilots lacked flying proficiency. For these reasons, the Arabs did not intend to pursue a sustained campaign of counterair attacks; they tried very little defense suppression. Moreover, many of their bombs were duds. In one air base raid ten Egyptian bombs fell, but eight failed to explode. Egyptian Tu–16 bombers launched about twenty-six Kelt air to ground missiles. The Kelts, some with an antiradiation capability, destroyed one warning and ground controlled intercept radar and badly damaged another. Five fighter bomber attacks made with bombs and rockets damaged two Hawk sites. The poor quality of the Arab pilots and their inadequate aircraft, when matched against the Israeli's superior force and excellent flying, made a significant difference. In an attempt to fend off Israel's air attacks, Syria tried another weapon: Russian built FROG–7 ground to ground battlefield support missiles armed

TABLE 35

### Syrian Air Defense Systems, 1973

| Type | Number (all figures are estimates) |
|---|---|
| 12.7-mm Quad Barrel (Czech) | 425 |
| 14.5-mm Quad ZPU4 (USSR) | 195 |
| 20-mm Single and Triple mount (Swiss) | 255 |
| 30-mm HSS-831 (Swiss) | 32 |
| 37-mm M1939 (USSR) | 290 |
| 40-mm Bofors 4/70 (Spain) | 30 |
| 57-mm S60 (USSR) | 225 |
| 85-mm M1944 (Czech) | 100 |
| 85-mm KS–12 (USSR) | 40 |
| 100-mm KS–19 (USSR) | 170 |
| 130-mm KS–30 (USSR) | 74 |
| 23-mm ZPU 23/4 SP (USSR) | 80–100 |
| 57-mm ZPU 57/2 SP (USSR) | Undetermined |
| Total | 1916 + |
| | |
| SA–2 Missiles | 200 |
|     Launchers | 70 |
| SA–3 Missiles | 100 |
|     Launchers | 20 |
| SA–6 Missiles | Undetermined |
|     Launchers | 60 |
| SA–7 Missiles (64 platoons) | 10,000 |

**Source:** US Army Combined Arms Center, "Analysis of Air Combat Data, 1973 Mideast War" Vol. II

with high explosive warheads. A few of these single stage rockets (perhaps three to five) hit in the vicinity of Ramat David airfield in northern Israel. The projectiles buried themselves in the ground where they exploded, causing the surface to collapse creating a line of small craters, but no substantial damage.[70]

Table 36

# Probable Aircraft Losses, October War

## Israel

| Cause of Loss | F–4 | A–4 | Mystere | Mirage | Helicopter | Misc |
|---|---|---|---|---|---|---|
| SA–2, –3, –6 | 9 | 27 | 1 | 2 | 1 | – |
| AAA | 9 | 12 | 2 | 4 | 3 | 1 |
| SA–2, –3, –6 and AAA | 1 | 1 | 1 | – | – | – |
| SA–7 | – | 2 | 1 | – | – | 1 |
| SA–7 and AAA | 1 | 2 | – | – | – | – |
| Tech. Failure | 4 | – | 1 | 3 | 1 | – |
| Interception | 3 | – | – | – | – | – |
| Unknown | 3 | 6 | – | 1 | – | – |
| Other | 2 | 3 | – | 1 | – | – |
| Total | 32 | 53 | 6 | 11 | 5 | 2 = 109 |

| Loss on Type of Mission | F–4 | A–4 | Mystere | Mirage | Helicopter | Misc |
|---|---|---|---|---|---|---|
| SAM Suppression | 8 | 6 | – | – | – | – |
| Interception | 3 | – | – | 3 | – | – |
| Patrol | 2 | – | – | 8 | – | – |
| Strategic | 2 | – | – | – | – | – |
| Airfield Attack | 7 | – | – | – | – | – |
| Close Support | 8 | 47 | 6 | – | – | – |
| Other | 2 | – | – | – | 5 | 2 |
| Total | 32 | 53 | 6 | 11 | 5 | 2 = 109 |

## Egypt and Syria

| Cause of Loss | | |
|---|---|---|
| Air-to-Air Combat | 334 | (destroyed by IAF fighters) |
| Airfield Attack | 22 | (Destroyed on ground) |
| Army Ground Weapons | 36 | |
| Hawk SAM | 23 | (18 aircraft + 5 helos.) |
| 20-mm AA | 42 | |
| Unknown | 59* | |
| Total | 516 | (480 fixed-wing + 36 helicopters) |

* Most thought to have been shot down by friendly AA fire.

**Sources:** US Army Combined Arms Center, "Analysis of Combat Data—1973 Mideast War"

After destroying much of the enemy air forces in aerial combat, the IAF turned its attention to SAM and AA suppression and continued close air support of the Army. The fierce battle raging in the desert brought high casualties to each side. Egypt, however, failed to capitalize on its advantage from the first assault. On the 14th, responding to pleas for help from her now hard pressed ally, Syria, Egypt began a renewed drive which faltered short of the Gidi and Mitla Passes. Worse, by abandoning their initial limited aim of seizing land just east of the canal, Egypt's Army left the protection of the AA umbrella, most of which remained on the west bank of the canal. Now Israeli air and ground units could counterattack more freely, and they did so with devastating effect. On October 16, Israeli Maj. Gen. Ariel Sharon sent part of his division across the Suez Canal north of the Great Bitter Lake. After two days of intense fighting, Sharon's men placed an armor-infantry wedge between Egypt's Second and Third Armies. Israeli heavy artillery crossed the canal and began to shell SAM sites, destroying several and allowing the capture of others. Free of the SAM threat in this area, the IAF could support the Army and expand its antimissile campaign. The first week of fighting taught the *Chel Ha'Avir* many lessons in how to deal with the enemy AA. On the canal's west bank, it now added to the Army's achievements and employed all its deceptive and destructive resources to further neutralize the Egyptian defenses.[71]

The bulk of Israel's aircraft losses came during the first six days of the conflict. During this time, the IAF's close air support helped repulse the initial Arab attack. Antiaircraft sites covering the Golan and the east bank of the canal shot down sixty-seven Israeli planes. Beginning with the seventh day of fighting, October 12, 1973, the loss rate declined markedly. By then the Syrians were retreating, and the IAF could turn most of its attention to the Egyptians. By the ninth day of fighting, Egypt's tanks and infantry were fully exposed in the Sinai. Strike sorties increased on that day, and remained high. Only on October 17 and 18, as Sharon's troops, with air support, pushed between the Second and Third Armies, did the Israeli air losses increase, and then only slightly. The Israelis had learned how to cope with the air defense problem; their combined land-air assault on the AA belt succeeded.[72]

Once the breach opened, mutual self protection between the Egyptian gun and missile sites declined, and Peled's men could exploit the inherently soft missiles as targets. On October 19, Fayid air base fell to Sharon's men. Wishing to preserve his armies, Sadat agreed to a United States-Soviet Union sponsored cease fire. After an initial attempt to end the fighting failed on the 22nd, a cease fire took effect on October 24, thus protecting some of the Arabs' gains, preventing possible collapse of the Egyptian Army, and laying the groundwork for a later disengagement of forces.[73]

TABLE 37

**Israeli Air Force
October 1973 War
Daily Loss Summary**

| Day | Date | A/C Lost | Daily Sorties Egypt | Syria | Remarks |
|-----|------|----------|---------------------|-------|---------|
| 1 | Oct 6 | 6 | 197 | 25 | Yom Kippur |
| 2 | 7 | 22 | 241 | 247 | |
| 3 | 8 | 9 | 434 | 188 | |
| 4 | 9 | 17 | 442 | 168 | |
| 5 | 10 | 3 | 296 | 230 | |
| 6 | 11 | 10 | 69 | 353 | |
| 7 | 12 | 5 | 172 | 197 | |
| 8 | 13 | 6 | 96 | 133 | |
| 9 | 14 | 2 | 229 | 48 | 2d Egyptian Offensive |
| 10 | 15 | 3 | 246 | 62 | |
| 11 | 16 | 2 | 283 | 30 | Sharon's Counterattack |
| 12 | 17 | 5 | 213 | 18 | |
| 13 | 18 | 6 | 263 | 0 | |
| 14 | 19 | 0 | 375 | 2 | Fayid AB Falls |
| 15 | 20 | 3 | 376 | 4 | |
| 16 | 21 | 3 | 327 | 55 | |
| 17 | 22 | 0 | 532 | 24 | |
| 18 | 23 | 0 | 354 | 42 | |
| 19 | 24 | 0 | 315 | 4 | Cease Fire |

## Mideast Air Warfare in Perspective

The four major wars fought by the Arabs and Israelis between 1948 and 1973 saw tactical changes brought about by improved aircraft and a variety of new offensive and defensive weapons. Attacks on airfields received little emphasis in 1948; the installations on both sides were too small and too primitive to warrant much attention. The air forces of 1948 were not important enough to draw attention to themselves. In 1956, during the Suez Crisis, the British and French realized the need to disable Egypt's Air Force. They did so using World War II tactics and against a force not prepared to defend itself. Egypt's pilots lacked training. Their command and control system was ineffective; poor marksmanship and inadequate range made their AA guns useless.

The wars of 1967 and 1973, however, when viewed together, present fascinating contrasts. In June 1967, Israel destroyed the large, modern air forces of the three main Arab contestants, Egypt, Syria, and Jordan in less than five hours; that of Iraq was badly damaged. The loss of any chance at contesting air superiority came about because the Arab nations, having learned little from the aerial attacks in 1956, were completely unprepared to defend their air bases. The air commanders failed to anticipate both the probability of a blow directed against their units and the devastation such an aggressive strike would cause. Protection for parked aircraft was negligible; antiaircraft gun defenses failed to deter the Israelis from attempting the attack or to deflect it once it came. An attempt at using SA–2s during the Six Day War failed completely. The weapon's radar was not able to lock onto a low flying target, and the missiles were left pointed toward the sky. The disruption caused by the surprise IAF raid kept most major Egyptian bases out of operation until the ground battle was decided. While the attacks on Syria, Iraq, and Jordan were not a surprise, coming as they did several hours after the destruction of the EAF, they were just as effective.

The contrast in air base defense in 1973 was significant. Immediately after the 1967 war the Arabs began building steel reinforced concrete hangarettes, each containing important service facilities such as fuel, compressed air, spare parts, and electric power. Additional runways and taxiways were built at existing bases and some twenty new installations were constructed. The project also included protected command posts, fuel storage, and air defense control facilities. Work of such a magnitude had guidance from Russian advisers, but was possible because of the large Arab populations, making ample labor available for the effort. More intense Soviet involvement could be seen in the development of an integrated air defense system that featured numerous interlocking, radar directed surface to air missiles and AA gun sites. Each site gave a measure of protection to nearby positions. All were linked by a modern command and control network using telephone cables to prevent jamming.

Before the Arabs began the October War, Israel's Air Force had prepared a series of plans to deal with renewed fighting. Based upon the experience of 1967, the first thrust by the IDF would have been a preemptive strike against enemy airfields. Because of the protection given the aircraft at Egyptian and Syrian bases, and Israel's apparent failure to develop suitable ordnance, it was questionable how successful such a blow would have been. In any event, for a variety of political and economic reasons, the plan miscarried in 1973. Prime Minister Golda Meir's government prohibited early attack by the IAF and restricted the reserve mobilization. The situation facing Israel's defenders on October 6 could not have been worse. Immedi-

**Israeli bombs strike main runway at Zalakieh Airfield, Egypt, October 1973.**

ately, they had to fend off a well planned, two front Arab offensive protected by the heaviest air defense screen yet seen in warfare. Syria's armored forces and the Egyptian tanks and infantry seized the initiative, forcing the IAF to act as flying artillery, concentrating on close air support for the ground units desperately trying to fend off opponents of nearly overwhelming size. Only when the IDF's reserves arrived to block the Syrians' passage down from the Golan to Galilee and that of the Egyptians further into the Sinai, could the *Chel Ha'Avir* turn its full attention to air superiority.

A clear distinction must be drawn between Arab ground based air defenses along the two front lines and the defenses found around airfields. It was along the front lines that the Arabs staked their hopes for victory, and there they ultimately lost. For a few days, until overcome by the Israelis' combined air ground assaults, the defenses along the Suez Canal and, to a lesser degree, along the Syrian side of the Golan, stymied the IAF. The situation was not the same at Arab air bases where active defenses were less evident and where the IAF, between October 7 and 20, regularly sent some of its fighter-bombers. While expending about the same amount of effort attacking bases in 1967 and in 1973, Israel lost fewer planes on such missions

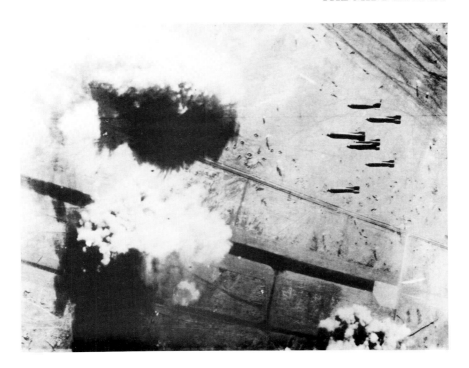

**Syrian airfield at Nassarieh suffers the same fate in the October war.**

throughout the latter conflict than on the air base raids of June 5, 1967. During the October War, the important factor in protecting aircraft and facilities was the dispersed, hardened structures. The IAF's main problem was not missiles or gunfire, but the failure either to develop or use weapons able to penetrate walls and destroy materiel and aircraft.

Because neither Syria nor Egypt had forged air arms competent enough to cope with the IAF, they had to content themselves with an initial air attack, after which their air forces acted as defensive patrols or stayed on the ground in isolated shelters. That their base defenses were greatly improved and very effective in 1973 can be seen by a comparison of losses. In 1967, 450 Arab aircraft burned at their bases without firing a shot. In 1973, however, only 22 fell victim to Israeli raiders. The heavy close air support demands placed on the IAF detracted from its ability to attack bases. Consequently, it is speculative to judge how well the Arabs' base defenses would have worked had Israel turned its full attention to them at the outset of fighting on October 6. General Peled was initially hard pressed to overcome the problems of contesting the AA shield while giving the Army close air support. Once he found the ground war stabilized, however, he was able to come to grips with the heavy SAM and AA threat along the Suez Canal. Israeli Army advances to the west bank of the canal broke the continuity of the missile belt. That opening allowed the IDF to expand its air and artillery attacks on the air defenses with both antiradiation missiles and conventional weapons, and ultimately to defeat them.

It mattered little what Israel knew or predicted of Arab intentions. The IAF was superior in all respects save size, and firm in its belief that the best way to defend its air bases was to defeat the enemy air force. For this reason, Israel's base defenses were never thoroughly tested. Although the Arabs protected their bases markedly better in 1973 with the hardened structures, the IAF carried the fight to enemy air space. Had Israel prepared a weapon capable of destroying an airfield's hardened installations, the outcome in the air could well have been hastened by several days.

# Chapter X

# Conclusion

A host of factors has intruded upon the art and science of air base air defense since the earliest aviators attempted to carry out attacks on enemy airdromes. Only rarely has there been a successful defense in isolation from the events on the remainder of a battlefront, and the defense can never be considered outside the context of air superiority. The defense has seldom prevailed with earthbound weapons alone. This was not clearly understood during World War I; airplanes were still too fragile and lacked the range to carry destructive attacks to enemy installations reliably, and the concepts underpinning such an offensive air doctrine were still developing. The squabbles between the American antiaircraft service and airfield commanders likewise resulted more from their failure at the time to comprehend the principles of an integrated air defense than any other factor. Doctrine on air war was still in its infancy during the 1920s, and air commanders in different countries continued to argue its application, even as a new conflict heavily tested Allied and Axis airfield defenses. The need for air superiority for successful air base air defense became starkly clear during World War II, however. Between 1939 and 1945 there were many major defensive battles involving air bases, but few where the winning side did not hold or gain control of the air.

In one of the most celebrated air base air defense actions, the Battle of Britain, the RAF faced a *Luftwaffe* which initially held superiority, sought to destroy RAF's Fighter Command, but lacked the long range bombers and fighters needed to do the job. In addition, the Germans had only one fighter, the Me109, that could protect the attacking force from the Hurricanes and Spitfires. The bombers themselves were very vulnerable. The German attack plan was flawed and inexperienced leaders failed to make that up with corrective tactical decisions. Ultimately, Germany's Air Force lost the struggle for control of Fighter Command's bases.

Admittedly, the fight for Malta was an example of successful air base defense *without* defensive air superiority. The struggle for this mid-Mediterranean island was, in fact, one of the only instances where defenders relied almost exclusively on ground based gunfire, dispersal, and shelter. Closer examination, however, reveals a far more complicated picture. The Axis successfully swept the RAF's fighters from the sky several times, but failed to destroy the air base complex when Hitler declined to seize the island with an air and seaborne invasion. Failing to capture Malta meant that Great Britain could reestablish flying operations and resume interdiction of the supply lines to North Africa. The consequences for Germany were enormous. When the German-Italian Army surrendered at Tunis in 1943, the heavy losses of men and equipment diminished the ability of the Axis to defend itself in the West while facing the growing power of the Red Army in the East. The struggles over Great Britain and Malta pointed out an inherent disadvantage of air power: an air force can reduce an enemy's ability to fight and even temporarily neutralize air bases, but the bases can recover quickly as attention shifts away from them to other targets.

Understanding an air base's vulnerability, and its inherent resilience, did not come easily for either air or army commanders during the early years. The end of the First World War left most of the major nations aware of the potential for airfield attacks in future conflicts. That awareness, however, was something gained over a period of several years of combat. Initial measures to protect air bases had been just as haphazard as were attempts to destroy them from the air. The limited range and ability to carry only small bomb loads meant that early aircraft were not a serious threat to ground installations more than a few miles behind the lines. This was fortunate for the defenders, who were equally handicapped, it seems, by the ineffective early AA guns and their own small aircraft. As airplanes developed in size and sophistication, however, they were used to attack an opponent's landing grounds and other sensitive targets more frequently. By 1916, responding to the new weapon, antiaircraft gunners learned to fire at high altitude, moving targets. Fuzes and projectiles were redesigned to accommodate the peculiarities of antiaircraft artillery. As a result, the ratio of aircraft downed per rounds fired in 1918 was significantly higher than that of two years earlier. By war's end, base defenses, including camouflage and light and heavy AA weapons, proliferated. Both sides organized special air defense units, designed to protect army troops and air fields. Most important, the idea that air superiority was needed for adequate defense emerged in the plans and operations of the Allies and Germany.

After the Armistice, aircraft development continued, especially during the late 1920s and the 1930s. Bombers were larger, faster, and better protected. Tactical attack aircraft able to strike at airfields appeared in the air forces of many nations. Numerous technical and organizational problems remained through the interwar years, however. The most persistent air defense difficulty was that of detecting approaching aircraft early enough to mount a counterblow, either in the air or from ground fire. Increasing speed and lethality of aircraft made acoustic detection devices obsolete, and the abilities of human observers on the ground remained limited by bad weather and darkness. Yet, the lack of money for design and production of newer, more advanced detection systems during the lean budgetary years of the Great Depression left these outdated listening devices and ground observers still in wide use in 1940.

Development of fighter or pursuit aircraft, including their integration into tactical defense systems, received little peacetime priority despite the World War I accomplishments of such aviation in the RAF and other air services. Even the persistent arguments of a few visionaries like the U.S. Army Air Corps' Maj. Claire L. Chennault received little attention. The difficulty of bringing relatively slow fighters close enough to a bomber to allow shooting it down helped foster the idea in some countries that armed bombers would be able to penetrate to the heartland of an enemy nation relatively unscathed.

Changes during the late 1930s held great promise for air defense, however. The British built a radar screen to protect their islands, then produced transportable radar sets for tactical use. Outside Great Britain, however, radar did not find as receptive an audience. The U.S. Army kept its small radar force a secret confined largely to Signal Corps circles. Army planners did not integrate it into tactical air defense plans. Similar delays among the Germans, Russians, and Japanese in adopting radar also negated the potential value of this new electronic medium for the first two years of World War II.

Wartime events forced a greater investment in radar technology. Warning was absolutely essential to base defense, and radar production contracts were quickly let. Ground observers supplemented small sets with the information fed to a central control point. Concomitant development of IFF transponders and better radios increased a defense force's ability to fend off an attack in a coherent fashion. The improved ability to detect and to discriminate partially reduced the attackers' advantages of speed, surprise, and lethality. At the same time, prewar ideas that equated air base defense only with guns at an airfield gave way to the integrated use of weapons, camouflage, decoy aircraft, dummy airfields, and damage repair.

The air doctrine and the aircraft technology of the interwar period also militated against the development of a coherent concept of air base defense. Air leaders thought more about attack than they did air base defense; thus defense preparations proved generally inadequate when conflict once more erupted. At first sight, this seemed an anomaly since one is just the reverse of the other. Someone planning to raid an opponent's landing fields and destroy his planes should surely have expected and prepared for the same treatment to be given his aircraft and ground installations. In the 1930s, the U. S. Army had only reluctantly accepted air defense participation in major exercises such as the First Army maneuvers. The reports issued on completion of the exercise did not address serious questions of deficient equipment and command and control. One reason for the Americans' lack of emphasis on defense lay in the evolving nature of air bases themselves. Light planes used between the wars could land and take off on virtually any level field. If one patch of ground was unusable, another would do just as well. The airplanes of the time required little in the way of service facilities. Consequently, the term "air base" did not always refer to a single landing field. Sometimes it meant a general geographic area, often fifty miles or more across, containing many landing grounds. Protecting such an expanse of real estate obviously was impractical for a small army concerned with the safety of the continental United States and its territories and restrained fiscally by the depression bound economy. It was not until the general use of heavy or high performance aircraft, such as four engine British and American bombers, that hard runways and taxiways and the need for complex service facilities concentrated an "air base" within a relatively small area.[1] By then, war spending greatly increased the flow of weapons and fostered improved defense organization.

During World War II, air base air defense became part of the broader effort to gain air superiority. More than air combat was involved in the protection of bases, however. After Germany's conquests of continental air forces in 1939 and 1940 and the retreat of the RAF from France, a greater array of warning services, antiaircraft gun deployment, and base recovery efforts appeared. Moreover, close cooperation between several types of units were common to successful base defense.

Interservice cooperation and the need for joint or combined operations was vital to air base air defense in most theaters. The greatest success was probably that of the British in Egypt and Libya in 1942 and 1943. A comparable achievement was seen also in the Southwest Pacific. Service cooperation, however, often flourished as a function of the personal philosophies of individual commanders rather than as recognized battle doctrine. In the Western Desert, Tedder, Coningham, and Montgomery forged a superb working arrangement, but only after some trying times. Conversely, Rommel and several of the *Luftwaffe*'s commanders in North Africa often failed to agree on cooperation between air and ground elements. The German Air Force's bases and its ability to support the Axis army in the desert suffered. Halfway around the world, the natural trust of Douglas MacArthur and George Kenney contributed to the construction of a string of crucial air bases in Australia and New Guinea. From these bases Kenney's raiders delivered repeated, devastating blows on Japanese installations.

World War II brought rapid changes in the use of antiaircraft guns. Before the war, planners often viewed employment of AA guns as separate from the command of flying operations. The number of guns needed for adequate base protection was generally misunderstood and underestimated, or procurement was severely constrained by the effects of the world economic depression. A forced parsimony of the Exchequer in the mid-1930s left the British Expeditionary Force in France in 1939 with just one light AA regiment for the Air Component's air base air defense. The British Army alloted about the same number of guns for defense of the independent Advanced Air Striking Force's airdromes. Allied warning services were completely inadequate, and the two regiments mounted only a token defense. At most, the warning services made for a false sense of security. The collapse of the Allies in France in 1940 brought about a reevaluation of the meager gun allowances and a recognition that more weapons were required. Even so, production could not approach the needs of global warfare for several years. Until 1944, AA guns were a scarce commodity in the Allied forces. The Mediterranean Command's Anti-Aircraft and Coast Defense Committee spent at least as much time wrestling with questions of gun allocation as it did with policy and command problems.[2]

The importance of recovery efforts to operation of an air base and the base's continued use by a flying force was soon emphasized. After devastating raids during the Battle of Britain, the RAF restored several of its bases to operation only through the most exemplary efforts of leadership and diligence. Fighters could operate largely because of the repeated efforts of military and civilian crews who repaired bomb damage. Elsewhere, American and Japanese commanders in the Solomon Islands went to great lengths to repair bomb damage and keep airfields serviceable. The Americans succeeded at Guadalcanal; the Japanese lost at Munda and had to abandon their important airfield there.

On the Eastern Front, the Red Air Force viewed base recovery in a different light. In the Russian forests and on the steppes, there was ample space for building crude airfields used by a few planes serviced at a main base some miles away. The easily concealed fields were so simple that bomb damage was readily repaired or the runway abandoned; operations could simply move elsewhere. Viewed by some as primitive, the Red Air Force's system proved as effective in terms of *VVS* doctrine as that of any other combatant. After the initial period of retreat and disorganization in 1941, the Russians began to use the thousands of landing fields and an extensive observation and warning system to great advantage. The multiplicity of sites presented incredible targeting problems for Axis commanders and the Red Air Force's mobility meant that once warned they had an excellent chance to escape destruction. The ability to move quickly to a base, and to employ nearby decoy fields was one of the keys to the Red Air Force's survival.

Changes in the nature of bases to meet new and heavier aircraft led to evolution in their construction. By 1943, Allied forces were able to lay out a flying field, grade the surface, and cover it with perforated steel planks, crushed rock, or coral in a matter of days. This ability did not come easily. In the Southwest Pacific, for example, a great deal of learning and many organizational changes were needed before George Kenney could airlift engineers to build a base in remote New Guinea.

Training, too, became an integral part of air base air defense. The proficiency of radar operators in Britain in 1940 and of Malta's gunners in 1941 and 1942 were prime examples. A more subtle result could be seen later in the war. A report by the American Army's AA Command on July 6, 1943, quoted a British Royal Artillery officer, who said that it was "a fallacy [to believe] that the highest standard of [AA gunnery] training is attained purely by frequent engagement with the enemy." . . . The "best chance of a hit is on the opening round and . . . the utmost accuracy of these rounds must be stressed."[3] Shooting of that sort demanded concentrated practice before the fighting. Such training had to be made as realistic as possible. The use of live ammunition fired at moving targets was almost axiomatic. These comments, however, carried with them the incisive and painful reminders of the Royal Artillery's inability to find training targets at Singapore in 1941. American Brig. Gen. Lyman Lemnitzer* severely criticized poor radar maintenance, and the inability of American radar to work as it should in North Africa. Many and varied resources had to be molded into one command to achieve the training and operational coordination needed for successful tactical air defense. Theater air commanders, gun crew chiefs, and the leaders of teams that located unexploded ordnance or filled bomb craters all had to be proficient at their jobs. Only in the last two years of the war did the Allies achieve strong working relationships among the various services. By then, the German and Japanese air forces were debilitated by several years of fighting.

Even on the verge of victory, interservice rivalry threatened to undo the American military's attainments. Worse, the problems which surfaced continued into the postwar years. In World War II, the growth of tactical air defense differed, as would be expected, in each major theater. The disturbing factor was that the differences stemmed more from the theater commanders' wishes than thoughtful application of air-ground warfighting

---

* At the time, Lemnitzer commanded the 34th AA Brigade in North Africa. Later, he was Chief of Staff to the Allied Supreme Commander, Mediterranean. After the war, he was Chief of Staff of the U.S. Army, 1959–1960, Chairman of the Joint Chiefs of Staff, 1960–1962, and Commander of NATO forces from 1962 to 1969.

doctrine. Capable commanders such as MacArthur and Kenney did well, but even in MacArthur's Southwest Pacific, confusion in the Allied air defense control system continued into early 1944. Less experienced men, inheriting forces equally inexperienced in battle, fared correspondingly worse.

By mid-1944, American air-ground coordination problems in air defense appeared solved with the general recognition that air defense warning, command, and combat elements had to be grouped under a single organization, but this was only a surface gloss. Increasingly, special interests of Army and Air Force leaders surfaced, jeopardizing much of the cooperation learned over several years. A report completed in May 1945 by the General Board, United States Forces, European Theater, was replete with examples of the services' inability to decide how to integrate AA into theater air defense operations.[4] As a matter of course, such conflict affected air base air defense practices. The United States Army, and after 1947, the Army and Air Force together, seemed determined to misjudge the needs of base defense.

The confusion and the conflict was due in part to interservice rivalry and an argument over the definition of roles and missions. World War II also left varying views of the relative importance of AA guns. Early in the war, the *Luftwaffe* earned a reputation for highly effective and lethal AA fire against inadequately armed and armored aerial opponents. Because the Germans had more such weapons, and used them so well, they lent to AA an inflated reputation in air base defense. Certainly, antiaircraft artillery fire could be deadly, especially at altitudes below 3,000 feet, and pilots rightly feared it. On the other hand, AA guns could fire at a low and fast aerial target for only a short time. In addition, AA suppression measures, like machine gun fire and bombs, could be very effective. Only a highly disciplined gun crew functioned well under the stress of heavy attack. Even under ordinary circumstances, AA gun crews reacted differently according to degrees of nervousness, excitement, or training.

After World War II, many nations demobilized their military forces. Among them were those of the United States. At the same time, deterrence and retaliation received much more thought because of nuclear weapons. The United States spent much of the available defense money on the Strategic Air Command. By 1950, the USAF's tactical force had shrunk, and collateral training of such specialties as radar operators was greatly reduced. When the Korean War began, Fifth Air Force commanders assumed air superiority would protect their advanced bases, and subsequent experience showed Generals Partridge and Stratemeyer to be right. Defense of UN bases was rarely tested; when attacks came, they were not serious.

A decade after the Korean War, the U.S. military found itself embroiled in Southeast Asia. Again, the Americans assumed correctly that air superiority would protect their overcrowded bases. The North Vietnamese Air Force did not venture south of the military demarcation line, and one can only speculate about the result of an air attack on a base such as Da Nang. A survey of the results of a sapper attack on July 5, 1965, and subsequent stand off attacks there and at other installations might cast doubt upon how much damage the American air defenses would have been able to prevent had they been tested.[5] American attacks on the NVNAF's airfields were sporadic, largely because the Americans did not wish to risk losses while hitting targets of doubtful value. Only late in the conflict, during LINE-BACKER I and LINEBACKER II, were such attacks pursued seriously. Results were mixed. North Vietnam's air base defense system scattered and sheltered its flying squadrons, but when U. S. Air Force, Navy, and Marine airpower attacked in force, defense proved inadequate and the NVNAF withdrew temporarily to China. Although the bases, with one exception, were not closed for more than a few hours, North Vietnamese sorties were reduced drastically for a time, thus reducing the danger from fighter interception. Throughout the post-World War II period, the American military, while occasionally losing planes to aerial assault, lived a charmed existence. It has not faced in combat an enemy determined to destroy it, so there was no compelling need to resolve differences of opinion as to base defense responsibility. Meanwhile, the Middle East wars of 1967 and 1973 showed new possibilities for air base attack and defense.

The Arab air forces were a significant threat to their enemy, Israel. The Israelis clearly recognized this. In World War II, future Israeli air commanders learned well from the RAF. Later, in 1956, they saw again what air power did to Egypt's Air Force. The 1967 attack on the EAF was a direct outgrowth of the French-British success at neutralizing the Egyptians during the Suez Crisis. Geography, which limited the number of Israeli airfields, combined with a sense of desperation among IAF commanders to promote a belief in the necessity for a first strike. Lacking the political limitations the Americans accepted in Southeast Asia, the Israelis were more aggressive in planning and weapon development. The resulting low level attacks of June 5, 1967, destroyed for a time the Arabs' air capability. The shock to Arab pride was great, but it did not preclude their devising better ways to protect airplanes.

In the 1967 conflict, the Israelis' sudden strike, including the use of special "concrete dibber bombs," left the EAF paralyzed. Aircraft losses were heavy, and runway damage repair was slow. Some bases were out of operation for long periods. This was not the case in October 1973 when adequate advance preparation of hardened structures protected most aircraft, and expertly trained repair crews restored bases to use in hours. Protected aircraft parking areas and other facilities (such as ammunition dumps, fuel storage, and power generation units) increased the difficulty of destroying an air base. When the Israelis struck at Egyptian and Syrian bases in 1973 and found they had no weapon to penetrate hardened hangarettes, they realized what the *Luftwaffe* learned at Malta in 1942, and before that over England in 1940: successful attacks on bases require proper weapons to overcome the passive as well as the active protective measures encountered. Nevertheless, in 1973, the Arabs lacked the skills to contest air superiority. The result was that even with inadequate air base attack weapons, Israel was able to dominate her enemies' flying fields.

The experience of the October 1973 war also suggested the use of modern technology to create an almost impenetrable air defense. A first look at the results of that war seems to support such a possibility. The Arabs, with Soviet support, built a heavy belt of missiles and AA guns. When fighting began, the Israelis were forced to battle the missile belt to give their Army close air support. In turn, the IAF suffered severe losses in three weeks of combat. However, the conclusion by some observers that heavy fields of AA gunfire and surface to air missiles kept the Israelis away from Arab air bases was false. From October 7, the second day of fighting, to the end of the conflict, Israeli fighter-bombers struck at will at Egyptian and Syrian airfields. In doing so, they lost fewer aircraft than during the series of air base attacks on the single day of June 5, 1967. General Peled's airmen knew how to do the job. In not wholeheartedly contesting air superiority, the Arabs tacitly recognized this. Why the IAF's leaders were not better prepared to destroy targets whose characteristics they were fully aware of is difficult and speculative to answer. Overconfidence growing out of the 1967 war and the subsequent ability to shoot down Arab aircraft in aerial combat are the most probable answers.

Syrian and Egyptian antiaircraft weapons on the front lines caused most of the IAF's losses in 1973. Along both the Golan and Canal fronts, the Israelis defeated the AA systems by combining ingenious air tactics, guile, aircraft modification (like extending the tailpipes of jets to reduce damage from small air to ground missiles), and air ground cooperation, including artillery and armor penetration. Certainly, the ability to provide an impenetrable air defense was not proved by the Arabs. Israel won because her forces were better trained, better equipped, and abler than those of her opponents. However, the short duration of the conflict, the mismatch in quality of fighting equipment, and Arab inability to contest control of the air makes tentative any attempt to form general conclusions about the changed nature of tactical air warfare and vulnerability that might apply to a longer and more general conflict.

Methods and doctrines employed by various air forces to achieve dominance have differed greatly. Air superiority and the ensuing requirements of air base air defense had to be defined anew not only for World War II, but also for the different theaters within that war, and for each conflict since.

Because modern aircraft have become such powerful and flexible fighting tools, air superiority in a tactical campaign had to be won day by day. Bases attacked once could not be considered out of action; often they were returned to use overnight. Furthermore, there were campaigns in which air superiority and air base air defense failed to fit a preconceived notion. Commanders who could not adapt their thinking to new circumstances quickly found their units in trouble and often lost the battle.

New weapons developed since 1945 have changed the style of fighting and of defending landing grounds. Design evolution produced guns and missiles able to follow a target more rapidly than before, be aimed more precisely, and fire faster. At the same time, costs for such weapons and their accompanying control systems have risen, more skillful servicing has become necessary, and crews have to be better trained. Offensive weapons also improved. Bases have been struck by faster planes with weapons able to be more effectively aimed and of greater destructive capacity. The practical use of remotely piloted aircraft and stand off weapons has just begun. Thus far, remote control has been limited largely to deception and reconnaissance, but offers the promise of even greater application to truly offensive weaponry. The mere presence of weapons, however, has proved little. Success emerged only when a commander had guns, missiles, or fighters in adequate numbers, with well trained crews, and used them according to the needs of battle.

Paradoxically, since 1940 air bases have been difficult to defend, but they have also proven to be very hard to destroy. Neither the defense of Malta nor the Arabs' success in 1973 at protecting aircraft and restoring their bases set a standard of achievement that allowed the separation of air base air defense from questions of theater air capability, deftness of command, or interservice cooperation. That so few examples of base defense without air superiority exist does not mean it has not been achieved. Rather, the question must be viewed in the light of overall air and air-ground operations. In base defense there has not yet been found a substitute for destruction of the enemy's air force by a strong, well planned counterair campaign.

# Appendices

## Representative Major Fighter Aircraft of World War II

| Type | Max. Speed | Cruising Range (miles) | Service Ceiling | Armament | | Initial Rate of Climb (ft/min) |
|------|-----------|------------------------|-----------------|----------|--|--------------------------------|
| **Germany** | | | | | | |
| Me109e | 357 mph at 12,000 ft | 413 | 36,000 | 2 | 20-mm cannon | 3,100 |
| | | | | 2 | 7.9-mm machine guns | |
| Me109f | 390 mph at 22,000 ft | 440 | 37,000 | 1 | 20-mm cannon | 3,320 |
| | | | | 2 | 7.9-mm machine guns | |
| Me110 | 360 mph at 22,000 ft | 680 (external tanks) | 32,810 | 2 | 20-mm cannon | 2,250 |
| FW190 | 395 mph at 17,000 | 525 | 37,000 | 4 | 20-mm cannon | 3,050 |
| | | | | 2 | 7.9-mm machine guns | |
| **Italy** | | | | | | |
| Macci MC 202 | 372 mph at 18,000 ft | 475 | 37,700 | 2 | 12.7-mm machine guns | 3,600 (approx.) |

| | Speed | | Ceiling | No. | Armament | |
|---|---|---|---|---|---|---|
| **Britain** | | | | | | |
| Hurricane I | 320 mph at 20,000 ft | 460 | 33,200 | 8 | .303 machine guns | 2,300 |
| Hurricane II | 339 mph at 22,000 ft | 460 | 35,600 | 4 | 20-mm cannon | 2,500 |
| Spitfire MkI | 362 mph at 18,500 ft | 500 | 37,200 | 8 | .303 machine guns | 2,850 |
| Spitfire MkII | 357 mph at 17,000 ft | 500 | 37,200 | 8 / 2 | .303 machine guns / 20-mm cannon | 2,850 |
| Spitfire MkV | 374 mph at 13,000 ft | 470 | 37,000 | 8 / or / 4 / 2 | .303 machine guns / .303 machine guns / 20-mm cannon | 3,000 (approx.) |
| | | | | | | |
| **France** | | | | | | |
| Dewoitine 520 | 326 mph at 19,685 ft | 615 | 36,090 | 1 / 4 | 20-mm cannon / or 5 7.5-mm machine guns | 2,362 |
| | | | | | | |
| **Japan** | | | | | | |
| Mitsubishi 96–2a (Navy) | 250 mph at 9,000 ft | 440 | 31,000 | 2 | 7.7-mm machine guns | (obsolete 1942) |
| Nakajima Ki–43 (Army) | 329 mph at | 1,095 | 36,250 | 2 | 7.9-mm machine guns | 3,250 |
| Mitsubishi A6M2 (Zero) | 340 mph at | 1,900 | 34,000 | 2 | 20-mm cannon | 4,500 |

*Appendix 1 (continued):*

**Soviet Union**

| | Speed | | Ceiling | Armament | | Range |
|---|---|---|---|---|---|---|
| Yak–1 | 360 mph at 16,400 ft | 528 | 32,810 | 1 | 20-mm cannon | 3,950 |
| | | | | 2 | 12.7-mm machine guns | |
| LaGG–3 | 354 mph at 16,400 ft | 345 | 31,495 | 2 | 7.62-mm machine guns | 2,953 |
| | | | | 1 | 12.7-mm machine gun | |
| Yak–3 | 410 mph at 16,400 ft | 559 | 35,425 | 1 | 20-mm cannon | 4,265 |
| | | | | 2 | 12.7-mm machine guns | |
| La–5 | 403 mph at 16,400 | 475 | 31,160 | 2 | 20-mm cannon | 3,600 |
| P–39Q | (see under United States) | | | | | |

**United States**

| | Speed | | Ceiling | Armament | | Range |
|---|---|---|---|---|---|---|
| P–38F | 395 mph at 25,000 ft | 1,500 | 39,000 | 4 | .50 cal machine guns | 2,850 |
| | | | | 2 | 20-mm cannon | |
| P–39Q | 385 mph at 11,000 ft | 650 | 35,000 | 1 | 37-mm cannon | 4,000 |
| | | | | 4 | .50 cal machine guns | |
| P–40E | 354 mph at 16,000 ft | 700 | 29,000 | 6 | .50 cal machine guns | 2,050 |
| P–47D | 428 mph at 30,000 ft | 475 | 42,000 | 8 | .50 cal machine guns | 2,800 |
| P–51D | 437 mph at 25,000 ft | 950 | 41,900 | 6 | .50 cal machine guns | 3,475 |
| F4F–4 | 318 mph at 19,400 | 770 | 34,900 | 6 | .50 cal machine guns | 2,000 |

# Representative Antiaircraft Weapons, World War II

| Weapon | Projectile Weight (pounds) | | Muzzle Velocity | Rate of Fire (per minute) | Effective Range (feet) |
|---|---|---|---|---|---|
| **United States** | | | | | |
| 37-mm | 1.4 | lbs | 2,600 | 120 | 10,500 |
| 3-in M3 | 12.9 | lbs | 2,800 | 25 | 28,000 |
| 3-in M4 | 12.9 | lbs | 2,800 | 25 | 29,000 |
| 90-mm | 23.4 | lbs | 2,700 | 27 | 33,800 |
| 105-mm | 32.8 | lbs | 2,800 | 15 | 37,000 |
| 120-mm | 50.0 | lbs | 3,100 | 12 | 47,400 |
| **Great Britain** | | | | | |
| 40-mm Bofors | 2.0 | lbs | 2,700 | 120 | 5,000 |
| 3-in | 16.5 | lbs | 2,000 | 25 | 25,200 |
| 3.7-in Mk3 | 28.0 | lbs | 2,600 | 25 | 32,000 |
| 3.7-in Mk6 | 28.0 | lbs | 3,425 | 19 | 45,000 |
| 4.5-in | 54.0 | lbs | 2,400 | 8 | 34,500 |
| **Japan** | | | | | |
| 7.7-mm | .47 | oz | 2,700 | 250 | 2,000* |
| 13.2-mm | 1.8 | oz | 2,722 | | 8,400* |
| 20-mm | 4.8 | oz | 2,720 | 120 | 7,500* |
| 25-mm | 8.2 | oz | 2,850 | 190 | 7,500 |
| 75-mm | 14.3 | lbs | 2,450 | 15 | 21,250 |
| | | | | | *estimated |
| **Germany** | | | | | |
| 20-mm Flak 38 | 4.2 | oz | 2,950 | 700 | 3,500 |
| 37-mm Flak 36 | 1.4 | lbs | 2,690 | 80 | 3,000 |
| 40-mm Bofors | (See under Great Britain) | | | | |
| 88-mm Flak 18, 36, 37 | 20 | lbs | 2,690 | 15–20 | 26,250 |
| 88-mm Flak 41 | 20.7 | lbs | 3,280 | 20 | 35,000 |
| 105-mm | 33.2 | lbs | 2,890 | 10–15 | 31,000 |

**Soviet Union**

| | | | | | | |
|---|---|---|---|---|---|---|
| 37-mm | M39 | 1.6 | lbs | 2,700 | 160 | 12,000 |
| 76-mm | M38 | 14.5 | lbs | 2,700 | 20 | 26,000 |
| 85-mm | M39 | 20.2 | lbs | 2,650 | 20 | 25,000 |
| 85-mm | M14 | 20.2 | lbs | 2,950 | 20 | 31,000 |
| 105-mm | M34 | 33.0 | lbs | 3,050 | 12 | 38,000 |

# Glossary

| | |
|---|---|
| AA | Antiaircraft, antiaircraft guns |
| ABDA | American-British-Dutch-Australian Command, 1942 |
| ACTS | Air Corps Tactical School (U.S.) |
| *Aeronautique Militaire* | The French Air Service of World War I |
| Air Army (Japanese) | Early in World War II, the major Japanese Army air commands were known as air forces or air groups. As the air arm gained a greater measure of independence from the ground force, the Japanese reorganized their forces and groups as air armies. There was one air general army with six air armies, the latter assigned to specific theaters of operations. |
| Air Brigade (Japanese) | One or two air regiments with intelligence, (Japanese) signal, or reconnaissance units as required. |
| Air Division (Japanese) | Two to Four air regiments, two to four airfield battalions, one independent air squadron (reconnaissance), plus intelligence and signal units. |
| Air Fleet (Japanese) | Two or more aircraft carriers with cruiser or destroyer escort. |
| Air Flotilla (Japanese) | Land based naval air unit. |
| Air Regiment (Japanese) | Twenty-five to forty fighter planes. A bomber regiment had as few as twelve medium or heavy bombers. |
| Air Sector Command (Japanese) | Usually about eight airfield battalions, all operating within the same general area. |
| Altitude | The vertical distance to a point in space from a reference plane, usually the horizontal plane containing an AA battery or radar station. |
| A.M.E.S. | British. Air Ministry Experimental Station; a cover name for radar, see also RDF |
| Area Army (Japanese) | Two or more armies or other combat units with necessary line of communication units. Conducted general field operations. |
| Army (Japanese) | Two or more divisions with added combat units with necessary line of communication units. Conducted general field operations. |
| Battery | A group of two or more artillery or AA guns. Generally three or four guns. |
| Bn | Battalion |
| CAP | Combat Air Patrol |
| CCF | Chinese Communist Forces |
| Chance of Damage | The summation of the chances of being hit by AA fire when passing along a crossing course within range of gun batteries. See also effectiveness. |
| *Chel Ha'Avir* | Israel Air Force |
| Continuous Following | A method of director fire control in which the fire control devices are kept on the target and the data vary continuously with the position of the target. |

| Crossing Course | The horizontal course of an airplane which is within range of an AA battery, but which does not pass vertically over the battery. |
|---|---|
| Dead Zone | The area directly above a gun position into which the gun cannot fire because the quadrant elevation mechanism cannot raise the gun muzzle any higher. This is usually 80 degrees. The diameter of the zone, in which a directly approaching plane is safe, increases in proportion to increasing altitude. |
| Director | A predicting instrument used to determine the firing data pertaining to the future position of the target aircraft. |
| EAF | Egyptian Air Force |
| Effective Ceiling | The maximum vertical range at which an AA gun or missile can accurately engage an approaching aircraft. |
| Effectiveness | The product of the number of shots fired along any crossing course and the mean probability of the shots. |
| EW | Early Warning |
| FEAF | Far East Air Forces, United States |
| Flak | German acronym derived from the word *Fliegerabwehrkanone,* antiaircraft gun |
| GAF | German Air Force, *Luftwaffe* |
| GCI | Ground controlled intercept, a method of guiding fighters toward approaching aircraft. Usually by means of radar. |
| *Geschwader* | A flying unit of the *Luftwaffe* made up of 3-4 *Gruppen.* The approximate equivalent of a USAAF wing. |
| GL | Gun laying |
| G.O.R. | Gun Operations Room |
| *Gruppe* | A flying unit of the *Luftwaffe* made up of 2 to 4 *Staffeln.* About the equivalent of a USAAF group or an RAF wing. Pl., *Gruppen.* |
| Heavy AA | Antiaircraft guns of a caliber greater than 50-mm. |
| *Hikojo Daitai* | World War II Japanese air base battalion |
| HMSO | Her Majesty's Stationary Office |
| IAF | Israel Air Force |
| IDF | Israel Defense Force |
| IFF | Identification Friend or Foe |
| IIS | Informational Intelligence Summary (USAAF) |
| *Jagdgeschwader* | A fighter *Geschwader* of the *Luftwaffe* |
| JATO | Jet assisted take off |
| JOC | Joint Operations Center |
| *JG* | See *Jagdgeschwader* |
| *Kampfgeschwader* | A bomber *Geschwader* of the *Luftwaffe* |
| *KG* | See *Kampfgeschwader* |
| *Lehrgeschwader* | A training or demonstration *Geschwader* of the GAF |
| LC | Library of Congress, Washington, DC |
| *LG* | See *Lehrgeschwader* |
| Limiting Envelope | Points in space, representing the maximum gun or missile ranges for all altitudes, connected by a continuous line. The curved line is called the limiting envelope. The maximum range for any altitude for heavy and medium AA guns is limited by the muzzle velocity and the maximum fuze time. For AA missiles the maximum range is determined by the engine burn time and thrust generated. Mathematically, the limiting envelope is the locus of all points on trajectories for the time of flight of maximum range. |

| | |
|---|---|
| Light AA | Small caliber antiaircraft guns. In this study, weapons of .50 caliber, 25-mm or less are considered light AA. During World War II, however, the British Army considered 40-mm to be light AA. |
| *Luftflotte* | German. Air Fleet, a German World War II unit roughly comparable to an American numbered air force or RAF group. |
| LORAN | Long Range Aid to Navigation |
| MAAF | Mediterranean Allied Air Force |
| MAG | Marine Air Group |
| MAW | Marine Air Wing |
| Maximum Ceiling | The greatest vertical range of a projectile. |
| Medium AA | Antiaircraft guns of 37-mm, 40-mm, or 50-mm. |
| M.R.U. | British. Mobile Radio Unit, mobile radar. |
| MS | Manuscript |
| M.T. | British. motor transport, mechanical transport |
| NAAF | Northwest African Allied Air Force |
| NATAF | Northwest African Allied Tactical Air Force |
| NK | North Korea |
| NKAF | North Korean Air Force |
| NKPA | North Korean Peoples' Army |
| NVN | North Vietnam |
| NVNAF | North Vietnamese Air Force |
| PRO | Public Record Office, London |
| Probability | The chance of a single shot being a hit. |
| *PVO Strany* | The national air defense forces of the Soviet Union during World War II. Separate from the tactical air force (see *VVS*). |
| RAAF | Royal Australian Air Force |
| Radar | American and British acronym for radio detecting and ranging. A device for determining electronically the distance, speed, or altitude of an approaching object. The determination is made by measuring the time of echo of a radio wave. |
| RAF | Royal Air Force |
| RDF | British. Radio direction finding, a cover name for radar. |
| *Regia Aeronautica* | Italian Air Force, World War II |
| Regt | Regiment |
| RG | Record Group, U.S. National Archives |
| SCR | Signal Corps Radio, used to designate various types of equipment, such as the SCR–270 long range warning radar. |
| *SG* or *STG* | *Stukageschwader,* a dive bomber *Geschwader* of the *Luftwaffe* |
| Slant Range | The distance from a gun or missile site to the position of the target airplane. |
| Sortie | One aircraft flying one mission |
| *Staffel* | The *Luftwaffe's* smallest operational flying unit. Roughly comparable to, but smaller than, an American or RAF squadron, usually 9 aircraft. |
| TACP | Tactical air control party |
| USAAF | United States Army Air Forces |
| USSBS | United States Strategic Bombing Survey. The survey was conducted after World War II and is reported in separate sections for Europe and the Pacific. |

*VVS*               *Voyenno-Vozdushniye Sily,* during World War II, or in Soviet terms the Great Patriotic War, the tactical air arm of the Red Army.

W.O.U. (British)    Wireless Observation Units

Y-Service           Tactical radio intercept and decryption units. The term is commonly applied to the British and American military of World War II, but all countries had such organizations.

*Zerstörergeschwader*   Squadron of Me110 "Destroyer" fighters of the *Luftwaffe.*

# Notes

## Introduction

1. Derek Wood and Derek Dempster, *The Narrow Margin, The Battle of Britain and the Rise of Air Power 1930–40* (New York, 1961), p 229, Appendices 6, 13, and 18; Hugh P.

Lloyd, *Briefed to Attack, Malta's Part in African Victory* (London, 1949), Chapters XII and XIII, *passim*.

## Chapter I

### Air Base Defense in World War I

1. James T. B. McCudden, *Flying Fury, Five Years in the Royal Flying Corps,* edited by Stanley M. Ulanoff (Garden City, 1968), pp 21–57.

2. H. A. Jones and Walter Raleigh, *The War in the Air*, 6 vols (Oxford, 1922–1934), Vol I, p 327; McCudden, *Flying Fury,* pp 54–55.

3. Maurer Maurer, ed. *The U.S. Air Service in World War I,* 4 vols (Washington, DC, 1978), Vol II, p 148.

4. Table of Engineer Data on Construction of Production Center No 2, Weekly Rpt, 11 Nov 1918, Air Service, AEF, in "History of the Air Service, American Expeditionary Force," compiled by Col Edgar S. Gorrell. 280 vols, RG 120, NA. The Gorrell History is also in National Archives Microfilm Group M–990, 58 rolls.

5. Jones and Raleigh, *War in the Air,* Vol I, pp 395–400.

6. McCudden, *Flying Fury,* pp 46–47;

Jones and Raleigh, *War in the Air,* Vol I, p 327.

7. S. W. Roskill, ed. *Documents Relating to the Naval Air Service, 1908–1918* (London, 1969), pp 167–171, 181–183; Jones and Raleigh, *War in the Air,* pp 375–390; George H. Quester, *Deterrence Before Hiroshima, The Airpower Background of Modern Strategy* (New York, 1966), pp 35 and 52.

8. William Manchester, *The Arms of Krupp, 1587–1968* (Boston & Toronto, 1968), p 126; Otto-Wilhelm von Renz, *The Development of German Antiaircraft Weapons and Equipment of all Types up to 1945,* USAF Hist Study 194 (Maxwell AFB, 1958), pp 1–4; Ian V. Hogg, *Anti-aircraft: A History of Air Defence* (London, 1978), pp 13–14. Hogg gives the caliber of the Krupp Balloon Gun as 25-mm, von Renz as 37-mm.

9. Manchester, *Krupp,* p 263; Hogg, *Anti-Aircraft,* pp 19–29; von Renz, *Development of German Antiaircraft,* Ch 2, p 14. Antiair-

craft guns were available and produced before the war, however, given their relative scarcity in August 1914 Manchester's assertion that they were "bought furiously" may not be an accurate description.

10. Jones and Raleigh, *War in the Air*, Vol I, pp 168, 268; Roskill, *Naval Air Service*, pp 139, 148 and 167.

11. Jones and Raleigh, *War in the Air*, Vol II, pp 168–171; Hogg, *Anti-Aircraft*, pp 39–43.

12. Hogg, *Anti-Aircraft*, pp 41–42.

13. *Ibid*, pp 35, 65–67; Extracts from Conference on Anti-Aircraft Defense, Paris, December 26, 1923, M.I.D. Report No. 6312, USAF Collection 145.91–534, pp 1–4.

14. Hogg, *Anti-Aircraft*, pp 44–47.

15. *Ibid*.

16. Jones and Raleigh, *War in the Air*, Vol II, pp 149–150, 183, 283–285, 320–321, Appendices VI and IX; Malcolm Cooper, "The Development of Air Policy and Doctrine on the Western Front, 1914–1918," *Aerospace Historian* 28 (Spring 81), p 43.

17. Jones and Raleigh, *War in the Air*, Vol II, pp 281–297, 324–326, 442–445; Cooper, "Air Policy and Doctrine," pp 42–45.

18. Jones and Raleigh, *War in the Air*, Vol III, pp 319–320, Vol IV, pp 115–117.

19. *Ibid*, Vol II, Appendix VIII, Vol III, Appendix XI.

20. Jones and Raleigh, *War in the Air*, Vol VI, p 162–163; U.S. Department of the Army, *United States Army in World War I, 1917–1919*, 17 vols, (Washington: 1948), Vol I, Report of Baker Mission, pp 55ff; Washington, DC, National Archives, Navy and Old Army Branch, "Report on Anti-aircraft Defense," 5 March 1918, Correspondence of the Anti-Aircraft Service, RG 120, entry 741.

21. Raymond H. Fredette, *Sky on Fire, The First Battle of Britain 1917–1918 and the Birth of the Royal Air Force* (New York, 1966), photographs pp 102–103; Jones and Raleigh, *War in the Air*, Vol VI, pp 158–164.

22. *Ibid*.

23. "History of 17th Aero Sq," in History of Organization of Aero Squadrons, Vol I, pp 16–17, USAF Collection, 167.401–14.

24. Washington, D.C., National Archives, Correspondence of the Anti-Aircraft Service, AEF, RG 120, entry 741.

25. *Ibid*.

26. *Ibid*.

27. Ltr., Wheeler to GHQ, AEF (G–3), Issue of Anti-Aircraft Machine Guns, May 14, 1918, HQ, AEF Records, RG 120, entry 741.

28. *Ibid;* Records of the 2nd Antiaircraft Machinegun Battalion, AEF Records, RG 120, NA.

29. Correspondence of the Anti-Aircraft Service, AEF, RG 120, entry 741.

30. History of the 1st Air Depot at Colombey-les-Belles, Gorrell History, roll 31; Maurer, *U.S. Air Service in World War I*, Vol IV, pp 1–10.

31. Maurer, *U.S. Air Service*, Vol I, p 175; Gorrell Hist, roll 31.

32. Maurer, *U.S. Air Service*, Vol I, pp 284–308; AEF Memorandum No. 1, Composition of Anti-Aircraft Radio Net, in *ibid*, Vol IV, pp 100–102.

33. *Ibid*, Vol IV, p 42.

34. *Ibid*, p 37–38; Air Corps Tactical School (ACTS) Air Force (Antiaircraft Defense) Course, March 1940, section AF–16–C, RG 18, entry 273.

35. William C. Sherman, *Air Warfare*. (New York, 1926), p 36.

36. Cooper, "Policy and Doctrine," pp 43, 45–46.

37. Hogg, *Anti-Aircraft*, p 67; Report of the Baker Mission, pp 64–65.

38. Jones and Raleigh, *War in the Air*, Vol VI, p 158ff.

39. Maurer, *U.S. Air Service*, Vol I, p 175; Baker Mission Rept, U.S. Army in World War I, pp 64–65.

## Chapter II

### Interwar Doctrine and Technology Changes

1. Richard Suchenwirth, *The Development of the German Air Force, 1919–1939*, USAF Hist Studies 160 (Maxwell AFB, 1968), Ch 1, *passim*.

2. Christopher Thorne, *The Limits of Foreign Policy; The West, The League and the Far East Crisis of 1931–1933* (New York, 1973), Ch 1.

3. Sherman, *Air Warfare,* p 116; Robert F. Finney, *History of the Air Corps Tactical School, 1920-1940,* USAF Hist Study l00 (Maxwell AFB, 1955), p 12; Maurer, *U. S. Air Service* Vol II, pp 313ff.

4. Claire L. Chennault, The Role of Defensive Pursuit, [privately published monograph] 1933, *passim.*

5. *Ibid,* pp 6-12.

6. *Ibid,* pp 15-17.

7. Intv, author with Lt Gen Devol Brett, USAF, Ret, Washington, D.C., Feb. 15, 1985; Thomas A. Sturm, "Henry Conger Pratt: First Air Corps Permanent General Officer," *Aerospace Historian* 22 (June 1975), p 72; Air Corps Newsletter, "The GHQ Air Force Concentration in Florida," 15 January 1936, pp 11-15; Richard H. Kohn and Joseph P. Harahan, eds, *Air Superiority in World War II and Korea* (Washington, DC, 1983), pp 14-46; John F. Shiner, *Foulois and the Army Air Corps, 1931-1935* (Washington, D.C., 1983), pp 45-48; Robert F. Futrell, *Ideas, Concepts, Doctrine: A History of Basic Thought In The United States Air Force 1907-1964* (Maxwell AFB, 1971), p 35, 76-77.

8. Wood and Dempster, *Narrow Margin,* pp 126ff, 170; Edward L. Safford, *Modern Radar: Theory, Operation and Maintenance* (Blue Ridge Summit, Pa., 197l), pp 19-20.

9. Wood and Dempster, *Narrow Margin,* pp 279-285; Ronald W. Clark, *Tizard* (Cambridge, Mass., 1965), pp 114-116; Air Corps Tactical School (ACTS), Air Force (Antiaircraft Defense) Course, 1939-1940, Papers of Lt Col Fenton G. Epling, RG 18, entry 273; Intv, General Earle E. Partridge, Apr 23-25 1974, USAF Collection K239.0512-729, pp 272-273.

10. Samuel Eliot Morison, *The Rising Sun in the Pacific, 1931 - April 1942* [History of United States Naval Operations in World War II] (Boston, 1968, pp 31-33; David O. Woodbury, *Builders for Battle, How the Pacific Naval Air Bases were Constructed* (New York, 1946), pp 39-42; Charles Updegraph, *Special Marine Corps Units of World War II* (Washington, D.C., 1972), pp 54, 61-63; Futrell, *Ideas, Concepts, Doctrine,* pp 72, 81.

11. ACTS, Antiaircraft Course, section AF-17-C.

12. *Ibid.*

13. *Ibid,* section AF-16-C.

14. Fina! Rept, Blue Army, 25 August 1940, Epling Papers, RG 18, entry 273.

15. U.S. War Dept, *The New Army of the United States,* Aug 1, 1941, p 27; *Coast Artillery, A Complete Manual of Technique and Material* (Harrisburg, 1941), pp 441-468; William J. Wuest, *History of Heavy AA Fire Control and Materiel* (Ft. Bliss, 1951), p 126; "History of Air Defense," *Air Defense Magazine,* July-Sept 1979, pp 38-40.

16. Report on Development of Aircraft Warning Service, Nov 6, 1941, HQ, AF Combat Cmd, RG 18, entry 270.

17. U.S. War Dept, *Training Regulation 435-30,* 16 April 1928, pp 4ff.

18. U.S. War Dept, The Engineer School, Second Research Course, March 1, 1940, Defense of Air Bases, USAF Collection, 248.82-75R; The Air Corps Board, Study No 5, 8 January 1936, USAF Collection 169.7032-70.

19. U. S. War Dept, Coast Artillery School, AAA Defense Against Glide and Dive Attack, 1940. USAF Collection, 248.712-8.

20. Rept, Air Staff, Post-Hostilities Intelligence Requirements on the German Air Force, HQ, AAF, Nov 22, 1944, Sect IV, Tactical Employment, *Luftwaffe* Directive 16, "The Conduct of Aerial Warfare," paras. 16-19, 26, USAF Collection 519.601B; Williamson Murray, "The Luftwaffe Against Poland and the West," draft study for AF/CHO, 1985.

21. *Luftwaffe* Directive 16, paras 4, 55.

22. Horst Boog, "The *Luftwaffe* and Technology," *Aerospace Historian* 30, September, 1983, pp 200-206; An excellent discussion can also be found in Boog's "Higher Command and Leadership in the German Luftwaffe, 1935-1945," *Air Power and Warfare* (Proceedings of the Eighth Military History Symposium, USAF Academy, 1978), Washington, D.C., 1979, pp 128-158. Williamson Murray, *Strategy for Defeat The Luftwaffe 1933-1945* (Maxwell AFB, 1983), Chap 1, covers the topic in broader terms.

23. Suchenwirth, "Historical Turning Points", Ch 1.

24. *Ibid,* p 108; Hogg, *Anti-Aircraft,* p 81; Alfred Price, *Luftwaffe Handbook, 1939-1945* (New York, 1977), p 65; Hogg, *Anti-Aircraft,* pp 84, 108ff.

25. Memorandum, 1939, Brig Gen B. K. Yount, Asst Chief of the Air Corps, Spaatz Papers, LC, Manuscript Div.

26. Wood and Dempster, *Narrow Margin,* p 57; Clark, *Tizard,* p 168-169.

27. "History of Air Defense," *Air Defense Magazine,* (Jan-Mar 78), pp 18-26, and (Jul-Sept 78), pp 17-24; U.S. Navy Photographic

Intelligence Center, "Japanese Antiaircraft and Coastal Defense Weapons," Washington,[nd], pp 2ff, USAF Collection 180.6042A.

28. U.S. Navy Dept, "Japanese Radar Equipment" *U.S. Navy COM-ONI Technical Intelligence Bulletin* 2, May 1945, USAF Collection 180.6023-2; "Japanese Air Weapons and Tactics," *United States Strategic Bombing Survey, Pacific* pp 1-7, 65-67. Hereafter *USSBS, Pacific*; Interrogation No. 476, Kanjo Takiyanagi, Nov. 29, 1945 in *Ibid*.

29. London, Air Ministry, Directorate of Intelligence, "Airfield Battalions (Hikojo Daitai) of the Japanese Army Air Force." June 1944, p 18. USAF Collection 512.63144-1; Hogg, *Anti-Aircraft*, pp 174ff.

30. Saburo Sakai, with Martin Caidin and Fred Saito, *Samurai* (New York, 1957), pp 25-31; Interrogation No. 602, Yoshimori Terai, November 28, 1945, *USSBS, Pacific*.

30. Interrogation No. 473, Minoru Genda, November 27, 1945, "Japanese Air Weapons and Tactics, *USSBS, Pacific,* pp 3-4, 64.

32. *Ibid,* pp 3-4, 33-41.

33. Von Hardesty, *Red Phoenix, The Rise of Soviet Air Power, 1941-1945* (Washington, DC, 1982), pp 42-50.

34. Roy A. Medvedev, *Let History Judge, The Origins and Consequences of Stalinism* (New York, 1971), pp 12-13.

35. Robert Conquest, *The Great Terror, Stalin's Purge of the Thirties* (New York, 1970), pp 484-492; Alexander Boyd, *The Soviet Air Force Since 1918* (New York, 1977), pp 114-115.

36. *Ibid;* Hardesty, *Red Phoenix,* pp 52-58.

37. John T. Greenwood, "The Great Patriotic War, 1941-1945," *Soviet Aviation and Air Power,* ed by Robin Higham and Jacob W. Kipp (Boulder, 1978), pp 72-73; M.N. Kozhevnikov, *The Command and Staff of the Soviet Army Air Force in the Great Patriotic War 1941-1945* (Moscow, 1977), translated and published by the U.S. Air Force, Ch 2, *passim*.

38. U.S. War Dept, U. S. Army Air Intelligence Rept No 100-45-34, An Analysis of the Soviet Air Force, 19 June 1946, USAF Collection 142.048-45; Walter Schwabedissen, *The Russian Air Force in the Eyes of German Commanders,* USAF Hist Study 175 (Maxwell AFB, 1960), p 35.

39. John Erickson, "Radio-location and the Air Defence Problem: The Design and Development of Soviet Radar 1934-1940," *Science Studies* (1972), pp 241-263.

40. Schwabedissen, *Russian Air Force,* p 35; Klaus Uebe, *Russian Reactions to German Airpower in World War II,* USAF Hist Study 176 (Maxwell AFB, 1964), p 34ff.

41. S. Woodburn Kirby, *The War Against Japan,* 2 vols (London, 1957), Vol I, p 21ff.

42. Frederick Pile, *Ack-Ack, Britain's Defence Against Air Attack During the Second World War* (London, 1949), pp 60-92.

43. *Ibid;* Hogg, *Anti-Aircraft,* pp 90-92, Appendices 3 & 4.

44. Clark, *Tizard,* pp 149-163.

45. Wood and Dempster, *Narrow Margin,* pp 140-181, 205.

46. *Ibid,* pp 154-155.

47. Rept, Study of Air Defense Problems, Oct 30, 1940, Office of the Chief of the U.S. Army Air Corps, RG 18, box 183; Wood and Dempster, *Narrow Margin,* pp 154-155, 170-181, 197-214.

48. Denis Richards and Hilary St. George Saunders, *Royal Air Force 1939-1945,* 3 vols (London, 1953), Vol. I, pp 17-18; Robin Higham, "The RAF and the Battle of Britain," draft study prepared for AF/CHO, pp 6-8.

49. Intv, Lt Gen Elwood R. Quesada, May 12-13, 1975, Sect VI, p 6, U.S. Air Force Oral History Collection; Kohn and Harahan, eds, *Air Superiority,* pp 14-16.

# Chapter III

## *Blitzkrieg* and the Battle of Britain

1. Michael Alfred Peszke, "Pre-War Polish Air Force: Budget, Personnel Policies, and Doctrine," *Aerospace Historian* 27 (Fall 81), 186-189; Michael A. Peszke, "Poland's Preparation for World War Two," *Military Affairs* 18 (Feb 79), 18-24.

2. *Ibid.*

3. Peszke, "Pre-War Polish Air Force," p 188.

4. Cajus Bekker, *The Luftwaffe War Diaries* (Garden City, New York, 1968), p 23; Berlin, German Air Historical Branch (8th Section), "The *Luftwaffe* in Poland, September 1939," July 11, 1944, translated in Air Ministry, UK July 12, 1947, as German Translation VII/33, USAF Collection 512.621.

5. Wilhelm Speidel, *The German Air Force in the Polish Campaign of 1939,* U.S. Air Force Hist Study 151 (Maxwell AFB, 1965) Part 1, p 36; Jerzy B. Cynk, *History of the Polish Air Force, 1918-1968* (Reading, 1972), p 272.

6. Cynk, *History of the Polish Air Force,* pp 99-155; Jerzy B. Cynk, *Polish Aircraft, 1893-1939* (London, 1971), pp 158-172; German Translation VII/33.

7. Peszke, "Pre-War Polish Air Force," pp 186-188; Peszke, "Poland's Preparation for World War Two," p 19-20; Speidel, *GAF in Poland,* Part 1, pp 38-39; German Translation VII/33, Luftwaffe in Poland.

8. Cynk, *History of the Polish Air Force,* pp 121-122; German Translation VII/33, Luftwaffe in Poland.

9. Speidel, *GAF in Poland,* Part 1, p 38; Peszke, "Poland's Preparation for World War Two," p 22.

10. Speidel, *GAF in Poland,* Part 1, pp 21-22; German Translation VII/33, Luftwaffe in Poland.

11. Cynk, *Polish Air Force,* pp 125ff; Rept, "Air Attacks of Airfields," Air Ministry, UK, 1943, pp 7, 9, USAF Collection 512.549-3.

12. Bekker, *Luftwaffe,* pp 30-38; Cynk, *Polish Air Force,* pp 126-130.

13. *Destiny Can Wait, The Polish Air Force in the Second World War* (London, 1949), pp 8-20.

14. *Ibid;* Cynk, *Polish Air Force,* pp 128, 133-135, 152-155; Bekker, *Luftwaffe,* p 364.

15. Suchenwirth, "Historical Turning Points," Chapter 1, *passim;* Killen, *History of the Luftwaffe,* p 101; Albert Kesselring, *Kesselring, A Soldier's Record* (New York, 1954), pp 39-40; Speidel, *GAF in Poland,* Part 2, pp 30-31, 128-129; German translation VII/33, Luftwaffe in Poland.

16. *Ibid.*

17. von Renz, *Development of German Antiaircraft Weapons,* pp 229, 278a-282.

18. *Ibid,* p 283a.

19. Jeffrey A. Gunsburg, *Divided and Conquered, The French High Command and the Defeat of the West, 1940* (Westport, 1979), pp 46-51, 106-108; Richards and Saunders, *Royal Air Force,* Vol I, p 123; Faris R. Kirkland, "The French Air Force in 1940," *Air University Review,* Sept-Oct 1985, pp 101-102. Kirkland cites Gunsburg's belief that the French operated the six radar sets. They did not. The sets were British with some French officers in training. See RAF Draft Narrative, The Campaign in France and the Low Countries, pp 98-104.

20. RAF Draft Narrative, The Campaigns in France and the Low Countries, pp 12-18.

21. *Ibid;* Robert Jackson, *Air War Over France, May-June 1940* (London, 1974), p 16; Walter Grabman, *German Air Force Air Defense Operations,* USAF Hist Study 164 (Maxwell AFB, 1959), p 278a.

22. David A. Griffin, "The Role of the French Air Force, The Battle of France, 1940," *Aerospace Historian* 21 (Fall 74), pp 144-146; RAF Draft Narrative, The Campaign in France and the Low Countries, pp 95-96.

23. Jackson, *Air War Over France,* p 46; Wilhelm Speidel, *The German Air Force in France and the Low Countries, 1939-1940,* USAF Hist Study 152 (Maxwell AFB, 1958), (Unpublished) Pt 3: p 103; Alistair Horne, *To Lose A Battle, France 1940* (Boston, 1966), p 199.

24. Jacques Benoist-Mechin, *Sixty Days that Shook the West, The Fall of France: 1940* (New York, 1963), p 67; Gunsburg, *Divided and Conquered,* pp 107-108; Horne, *To Lose a Battle,* pp 210-213; Killen, *History of the Luftwaffe,* pp 113-114.

25. Jackson, *Air War Over France,* pp 41-47; Bekker, *Luftwaffe,* pp 113-114; Fritz Morzik, *German Air Force Airlift Operations,* USAF Hist Study 167, (Maxwell AFB, 1961) pp 106-108; Air Ministry, UK, German Translation VII/83, German Aircraft Losses September 1939-December 1940 (Except Poland). USAF Collection 512.621.

26. Jackson, *Air War Over France,* p 47; Benoist-Mechin, *Sixty Days,* pp 67-93; Horne, *To Lose A Battle,* pp 127-132.

27. Jackson, *Air War Over France,* p 51; Air Ministry, UK, Air Attacks of Airfields, p 17; Speidel, *GAF in France and the Low Countries,* Part 3, p 355; Richards and Saunders, *Royal Air Force,* Vol 2, pp 111-115.

28. Speidel, *GAF in France and the Low Countries,* Part 3, pp 190ff, 290ff.

29. Horne: *To Lose A Battle,* p 229;

Bekker, *Luftwaffe,* pp 114–115; RAF Narrative, pp 200; Richards and Saunders, *Royal Air Force,* Vol I, pp 120–123.

30. Speidel, *GAF in France and the Low Countries,* Part 3, p 81; Richards and Saunders, *Royal Air Force,* Vol I, pp 120–121, 130–134; Murray, The Luftwaffe Against Poland and the West, pp 30–33, and Table I.

31. *Ibid,* pp 349ff; Jackson, *Air War Over France,* pp 82–84ff. General Speidel's claim of 450 French losses to 9 German is overstated and undoubtedly distorted by propaganda. Few German records of this period survived the war and, while Jackson's information is not totally reliable, it is based on better sources. The German claim of 350 aircraft destroyed on the ground exceeded the total ground losses of the *Armée de l'Air* for all of May and June. The German claim of 22 French aircraft downed by antiaircraft fire is hardly plausible. Paris was too far from the German lines for this to be so and there is no evidence of friendly fire being so misdirected.

32. Jackson, *Air War Over France,* pp 83, 136; Speidel, *GAF in France and the Low Countries,* Part 3, p 130.

33. Jackson, *Air War Over France,* pp 93ff, 135.

34. Peter Chamberlin and John Milsom, *Self-Propelled Anti-Tank and Anti-Aircraft Guns* (New York, 1975), pp 34–58.

35. Peter Townsend, *Duel of Eagles* (New York, 1970), p 433.

36. Wood and Dempster, *Narrow Margin,* pp 25–31, 81–100; Richard Collier, *Eagle Day* (New York, 1966), p 269; Alan L. Gropman, "The Battle of Britain and the Principles of War," *Aerospace Historian* 18 (Fall 71), pp 138–142.

37. Leonard Bridgman, comp and ed, *Jane's All The World's Aircraft, 1942* (New York, 1943), pp 93c–97c.

38. Wood and Dempster, *Narrow Margin,* pp 25–31, 81–100; Collier, *Eagle Day,* p. 269; Gropman, "The Battle of Britain," pp 138–142.

39. Wood and Dempster, *Narrow Margin,* pp 170–181.

40. Pile, *Ack-Ack,* pp 108–110; Wood and Dempster, *Narrow Margin,* pp 170–181.

41. Report, Study of Air Defense Problems; Wood and Dempster, *Narrow Margin,* pp 174–178.

42. Air Ministry, UK, *The Origins and Development of Operational Research in the Royal Air Force* (London, 1963), p 20; Wood and Dempster, *Narrow Margin,* pp 144,

174–175; Townsend, *Duel of Eagles,* pp 173–174.

43. Air Ministry, *Operational Research,* p 10–20; Wood and Dempster, *Narrow Margin,* pp 174–181; Basil Collier, *Defence of the United Kingdom* (London, 1957), pp 168–169.

44. Air Ministry, *Operational Research,* pp 10–20.

45. F. W. Winterbotham, *The Ultra Secret* (New York, Evanston, 1974), pp 7–16, 40–55; F.H. Hinsley, *et al, British Intelligence in the Second World War, Its Influence on Strategy and Operations,* 3 vols. (New York, 1979), Vol I, pp 161–182, Appendices 1 and 9.

46. Collier, *Defence of the U. K.,* p 245; Rept, Study of Air Defense Problems; Gropman, "Battle of Britain," p 144.

47. Pile, *Ack-Ack,* pp 113–116.

48. *Ibid,* pp 111–116; Collier, *Defence of the U.K.,* pp 153–154; Air Ministry, UK, Air Attack of Airfields, p 13.

49. Collier, *Defence of the U. K.,* pp 448–449, 479–481; Pile, *Ack-Ack,* pp 113, 131; Hq U.S. Army Air Forces, Information Intelligence Summary No. 35, July 6, 1942, (Hereafter cited as IIS No—and date); Hugh C.T. Dowding, "The Battle of Britain," Sup No 37719 (10 September 1946), *The London Gazette,* p 4543.

50. Pile, *Ack-Ack,* p 136–137; Wood and Dempster, *Narrow Margin,* p 205.

51. Guy Hartcup, *Camouflage, A History of Concealment and Deception in War* (New York, 1980), p 133ff.

52. *Ibid,* pp 99ff.

53. Graham Wallace, *R. A. F. Biggin Hill* (London, 1957), p 101; Hartcup, *Camouflage,* p 65; Air Ministry, UK, "A German Account of the Air War Against Great Britain," translation of a lecture by Capt. Otto Bechtle given at Berlin-Gatow, Feb. 2, 1944, USAF Collection 512.62512 TE-53, p 5. Hereafter cited as Bechtle Lecture.

54. Wallace, *Biggin Hill,* pp 107, 121.

55. Gropman, "Battle of Britain," p 142; Wallace, *Biggin Hill,* p 104.

56. Wood and Dempster, *Narrow Margin,* pp 101–107, 282–285; Bechtle Lecture; Bekker, *Luftwaffe War Diaries,* pp 145–147.

57. Gropman, "Battle of Britain," p 141; Wallace, *Biggin Hill,* pp 158ff.

58. Wood and Dempster, *Narrow Margin,* p 312; Wallace, *Biggin Hill,* pp 171–180; Winterbotham, *Ultra,* pp 5–58; Pile, *Ack-Ack,* pp 136–138; Air Ministry, UK, Air Attack on Airfields, p 16.

59. *Ibid.*
60. Harry T. Sutton, *Raiders Approach. The Fighting Tradition of Royal Air Force Station Hornchurch and Sutton's Farm* (Aldershot, 1956), pp 100–101.
61. *Ibid,* pp 102–103, 132–133.
62. *Ibid,* p 115.
63. *Ibid,* p 120.
64. Quester, *Deterrence before Hiroshima.* (New York, London, Sydney, 1966), pp 117–120; Bullock, *Hitler,* p 596; Winston S. Churchill, *The Second World War,* 6 vols, Vol II, *Their Finest Hour* (New York, 1962), p 283.
65. Wood and Dempster, *Narrow Margin,* pp 409–419; Gropman, "Battle of Britain," p 143.

66. Hartcup, *Camouflage,* p 69; John Bushby, *Air Defence of Great Britain* (London, 1973), pp 156–166; Air Ministry, UK, Air Attack on Airfields, p 16; Bechtle Lecture.
67. Wood and Dempster, *Narrow Margin,* pp 468, 472–473; Air Ministry, "Air Attacks of Airfields," pp 15–16.
68. Griffin, "French Air Force, 1940," pp 144–149; Benoist-Mechin, *Sixty Days,* pp 28–42; Horne, *To Lose a Battle,* pp 182–204.
69. Wood and Dempster, *Narrow Margin,* pp 215–216; Gropman, "Battle of Britain," pp 139, 143; Bechtle Lecture, pp 7–8.
70. Richards and Saunders, *Royal Air Force,* Vol I, pp 145–157.

## Chapter IV

## Malaya and Malta: 1941–1942

1. S. Woodburn Kirby, *et al, History of the Second World War, The War Against Japan,* 5 vols (London, 1957), Vol I, *The Loss of Singapore,* Appendix 3; I.S.O. Playfair, *History of the Second World War, the Mediterranean and Middle East* 4 vols (London, 1956), Vol I, pp 29, 119.
2. Kirby, *The Loss of Singapore,* pp 6–7; Paul Maltby, "Report of the Air Operations During the Campaigns in Malaya and Netherland East Indies from 8th December 1941 to 12th March 1942," Third Supplement to *The London Gazette,* 20 February 1948, p 1349; Robert Brooke-Popham, "Operations in the Far East from 17th October 1940 to 27th December 1941," supplement, *The London Gazette,* 22 Jan 1948, p 536.
3. Kirby, *The Loss of Singapore,* pp 14–16.
4. Maltby, "Report on Air Operations in Malaya," p 1349; Stanley L. Falk, *Seventy Days to Singapore,* (New York, 1975), pp 45, 48; Kirby, *The Loss of Singapore,* pp 153–175, 467; Air Ministry, Draft RAF Narrative, *The Campaigns in the Far East* 2 vols, Vol I, p 41, AF/CHO.
5. Maltby, "Report on Air Operations in Malaya," p 1349.
6. Brooke-Popham, "Operations in the Far East," pp 536–538.
7. Morison, *The Rising Sun in the Pacific,* pp 51–56.
8. Maltby, "Report on Air Operations in Malaya," pp 1349–1350.
9. *Ibid,* pp 1350–1351.

10. *Ibid,* pp 1347, 1351.
11. *Ibid;* Air Ministry, UK, *The Far East,* Vol I: pp 41–42.
12. Maltby, "Rept on Air Operations in Malaya," pp 1348, 1356.
13. *Ibid,* pp 1351, 1359–1360; Kirby, *The Loss of Singapore,* p 183; Air Ministry, UK, *The Far East,* Vol I, pp 41–42.
14. *Ibid;* Falk, *Seventy Days,* pp 44–45; Kenneth Attiwill, *Fortress, The Story of the Siege and Fall of Singapore* (New York, 1960), pp 24–25; U.S. War Dept, HQ Army Air Forces, IIS No. 35, 6 July 1942.
15. Masanobu Tsuji, *Singapore, The Japanese Version,* trans by Margaret E. Lake (Sidney: 1960), pp 44–52; Interrogation No. 278, Lt Gen Saburo Endo, 3 and 28 Nov 1945, *USSBS, Pacific.*
16. Shin Ishikawa, Katsumi Dozone, and Minoro Miyako, "Southeast Asia Air Operations Record, Phase I, Nov 1941 to Feb 1942," trans and edited by U.S. Army Far East Command, Japanese Monograph No 55, Aug 1946; Shiro Yamaguchi, "Malay Invasion Naval Operations," trans and edited by U.S. Army Far East Command, Japanese Monograph No. 107, Oct 1952.
17. Kirby, *The Loss of Singapore,* pp 76–79, 170–175.
18. Richards and Saunders, *Royal Air Force,* Vol II, pp 14–17; Kirby, *The Loss of Singapore,* pp 180–181.
19. Brooke-Popham, "Operations in the Far East," p 556; Maltby, "Report on Air

Operations in Malaya," pp 1348–1356, 1359–1360; Air Ministry, *The Far East,* Vol II, pp 17–20.

20. Richards and Saunders, *Royal Air Force,* Vol II, pp 14–17; Kirby, *The Loss of Singapore,* pp 180–181; Maltby, "Report on Air Operations in Malaya," p 1366.

21. Ltr, Brigadier B.W. Key to Captain Wilfrid Miles, 18 February 1948, Public Record Office (PRO), Air 20/209; Ishikawa, Dozone, and Miyako, Japanese Monograph No. 55, p 46.

22. Maltby, "Report on Air Operations in Malaya," p 1367; South African Air Ministry, *Tactical and Technical Notes,* No 26, Apr 17, 1942, p 4, USAF Collection, 512.5496.

23. Yamaguchi, Japanese Monograph No 107, p 14; Maltby, "Report on Air Operations in Malaya," pp 1367, 1413.

24. Air Ministry, *The Far East,* Vol II, pp 62–63.

25. "Hawaii–Malaya Naval Operations," Enemy Publications No 6, trans by Allied Translator and Interpreter Section, South West Pacific Area, pp 12–19, RG 407; Maltby, "Report on Air Operations in Malaya," p 1368; Endo Interrogation, *USSBS, Pacific.*

26. Kirby, *The Loss of Singapore,* pp 238–241.

27. Tadaka Numaguchi and Katsugi Akiyama, "Report on Installations and Captured Weapons, Java and Singapore," May 1942, translated and edited by U.S. Army Forces Far East, as Japanese Monograph No. 68, 1958, pp 53–61; Maltby, "Report on Air Operations in Malaya," p 1371.

28. Maltby, "Report on Air Operations in Malaya," p 1374; Richard L. Watson, Jr., *Army Air Action in the Philippines and Netherlands East Indies, 1941–1942,* USAF Hist Study 111, (Maxwell AFB, 1945) pp 101–104.

29. Msg, Air Ministry to AOC Far East, 19 Jan 1942, PRO Air 20/209; Maltby, "Report on Air Operations in Malaya," p 1375; Kirby, *The Loss of Singapore,* p 241; Endo Interrogation.

30. Maltby, "Report on Air Operations in Malaya," p 1376; Numaguchi and Akiyama, Japanese Monograph No. 68, pp 53–61.

31. Maltby, "Report on Air Operations in Malaya," pp 1377–1379.

32. *Ibid,* pp 1374–1378; Attiwill, *Fortress,* p 76; Kirby, *The War Against Japan,* Map 18.

33. Maltby, "Report on Air Operations in Malaya," pp 1379–1380.

34. *Ibid,* pp 1380–1382.

35. *Ibid,* pp 1382–1383. See Japanese Monograph No 55. Total Japanese losses from all causes were not insignificant during the Malay Campaign. The report cites several instances of Japanese aircraft lost in combat well before the arrival of the Hurricanes. Neither this report nor Maltby's estimate of losses provide information on specific causes of Japanese air casualties. The obscurity of information makes an assessment of antiaircraft effectiveness versus fighter interception very difficult.

36. Maltby, "Rept on Air Operations in Malaya," pp 1379–1380; Both Masanoubu Tsuji's account of the preparation and conduct of the Malay operation and the air operations plan in Japanese Monograph 55 clearly illustrate the singleness of purpose of the Japanese. Tsuji's observations on the conduct of the fighting should be read to gain a balanced viewpoint.

37. Maltby, "Rept on Air Operations in Malaya," p 1374; Brooke-Popham, "Operations in the Far East," p 563; Air Commodore L. E. O. Charleton, *Britain at War, The Royal Air Force,* 5 vols (London, 1941–1945), Vol. 2, pp 224–250. Charleton's comments on the Allied setbacks in the Pacific contain descriptions of Japanese abilities typical of the prewar and wartime attitudes. American and British intelligence reports of World War II sometimes reported the presence of German aircraft and pilots in Japanese air formations (See, for example, Ltr, Office of the Commander, 7th Air Force, 29 Dec 1942, 730.310B. See also, Tac. and Tech. Notes 57, 26, and 54, all of which cite "verified" reports of Japanese use of German aircraft). So far as is known, there was only limited Axis cooperation of this sort in the Pacific. The Japanese and Germans conducted some exchanges of technical information, but the Japanese did not use German planes, nor did they build copies of the Ju87, Me109, or other aircraft. A single Me109 was delivered from Germany for tests. See René J. Francillon, *Japanese Aircraft of the Pacific War,* (New York, 1970) p 498.

38. Brooke-Popham, "Operations in the Far East," pp 536–538.

39. Playfair, *The Mediterannean and Middle East,* Vol II, pp 43–44; William G. S. Dobbie, "The Siege of Malta," 1940–1942," *Royal Engineers Journal* (Jan–Mar 43), pp 1–8.

40. *Ibid.*

41. Playfair, *Mediterranean and Middle East,* Vol II, pp 44–45; H. E. C. Weldon,

"The Artillery Defence of Malta," *Journal of the Royal Artillery,* LXXIX (Jan 52), pp 15–27.

42. Playfair, *Mediterranean and Middle East,* Vol II: pp 46–58.

43. *Ibid,* pp 47–48; HQ, Italian Air Force, Memorandum, "The Air and Naval Bases of Malta," 31 Oct 42, Translation VII/43, trans Air Ministry, UK, 1947; "Agreement reached on the operational activity of the Italian and German Air Forces in the Central and Eastern Mediterranean and bordering areas," July 18, 1941, Air Ministry [UK] translation, Document No G 181132. Both in USAF Collection 512.621.

44. Basil Embry, *Mission Completed* (New York, 1958), pp 228–233.

45. Playfair, *Mediterranean and Middle East,* Vol II, p 53.

46. *Ibid,* p 45; Hugh Lloyd, *Briefed to Attack, Malta's Part in African Victory* (London, 1949), pp 33–35.

47. *Ibid,* pp 62–70; Air Ministry, *RAF in the Second War: Works Services* (London, 1956), pp 408–419; Lloyd, *Briefed to Attack,* pp 67–70, 136–138, 174–177.

48. *Ibid.*

49. *Ibid,* p 70; Embry, *Mission Completed,* pp 230–231.

50. Lloyd, *Briefed to Attack,* Ch V–VII; Albert Kesselring, *Kesselring: A Soldier's Record* (New York, 1954), pp 117, 123–124; Arthur William, Lord Tedder, *With Prejudice* (Boston, 1966), p 245.

51. Air Historical Branch, *Luftwaffe* (8 Section) Study, "German Air Force Activities in the Mediteranean, Tactics and Lessons Learned 1941–1943," 30 Oct 1944, Air Ministry, UK, Translation VII/2, 1946; "Agreement on Operational Activity," 18 July 1941; Kesselring, *Soldier's Record,* p 115.

52. HQ, Italian Air Force, "Memorandum on the Malta Situation," 10 May 1942, Air Ministry, UK, Translation VII/57, December 1947; HQ, Italian Air Force, "Italian Air Operations in Anticipation of an Attack on the Island of Malta and Plan for the Occupation of that Island," [nd, but 1942], Air Ministry, UK, 1946, both in USAF Collection, 622.661–5; Weldon, "Artillery Defence of Malta," pp 21–22.

53. Kesselring, *Soldier's Record,* p 118.

54. Helmuth Felmy, "The German Air Force in the Mediterranean Theater of War," USAF Hist Study 161 (Maxwell AFB, 1955) p 237; Lloyd, *Briefed to Attack,* pp 161–162, 164–165; Hq RAF Middle East, Rept on RAF Operations in the Western Desert and Eastern Mediterranean, Appendix B, 18 Nov 1941 to 19 May 1942, USAF Collection 512.421B.

55. *Ibid,* pp 132, 142; Tedder, *Prejudice,* p 245.

56. Lloyd, *Briefed to Attack,* pp 118–121; RAF in Western Desert and Eastern Mediterranean, App B.

57. *Ibid;* Kesselring, *Soldier's Record,* p 124; Playfair, *Mediterranean and Middle East,* Vol III, p 189.

58. Weldon, "Artillery Defence of Malta," p 24; Playfair, *Mediterranean and Middle East,* Vol III, p 179; Joseph Attard, *The Battle of Malta* (London, 1968), pp 55, 176.

59. Weldon, "Artillery Defence of Malta," p 24.

60. *Ibid,* pp 23–25.

61. Lloyd, *Briefed to Attack,* pp 186–187; Felmy, *GAF in the Mediterranean Theater,* p 239; Attard, *Battle of Malta,* p 165; Playfair, *Mediterranean and Middle East,* Vol III, p 179; Weldon, "Artillery Defence of Malta," p 22.

62. Lloyd, *Briefed to Attack,* pp 160–169, 174–177; Italian Air Force, "Air and Naval Bases of Malta," p 3.

63. Attard, *Battle of Malta,* pp 187–188; Kesselring, *Soldier's Record,* p 140.

64. Embry, *Mission Completed,* pp 230–232; Felmy, "GAF in the Mediterranean Theater," p 236; Lloyd, *Briefed to Attack,* pp 147, 165–166; Tedder, *Prejudice,* p 245, 426; Kesselring, *Soldier's Record,* p 132.

65. *Ibid;* Kesselring's Plan for the Invasion of Malta, German Translation VII/141, May 1955, Air Ministry, UK, in USAF Collection K512.621-141.

66. Hinsley, *et al, British Intelligence in the Second World War,* Vol 2, pp 291–323, 346–348.

67. Playfair, *Mediterranean and Middle East,* Vol III, pp 179, 185; RAF, Report on Operations in the Western Desert and Eastern Mediterranean, App B.

68. German Air Force, "Tactics and Lessons Learned; Tedder, *Prejudice,* p 267; Lloyd, *Briefed to Attack,* p 157, Chapter XIV.

69. Lloyd, *Briefed to Attack,* pp 184–188.

70. Kesselring, *Soldier's Record,* pp 140–141; Felmy, *GAF in the Mediterranean Theater,* p 231; Tedder, *Prejudice,* p 106; HQ, Italian Air Force, "Plan for Invasion of Malta," 1942; "German Air Force Policy During the 2nd World War," German translation VII/153, Air Ministry, UK, April 1956, p 16, USAF Collection, K512.621-153.

71. HQ, Italian Air Force, "Plan for the Invasion of Malta," 1942; Suchenwirth, *Historical Turning Points in the German Air Force War Effort,* pp 93–97.

72. Maltby, "Report on Air Operations in Malaya," p 1376, 1380–1381; Weldon, "Artillery Defence of Malta," p 21–24; Numaguchi and Akiyama, Japanese Monograph No. 68.

73. See Orders of Battle for Malaya and Malta; Lloyd, *Briefed to Attack,* p 229; Weldon, "Artillery Defence of Malta," pp 25–26.

74. James Leasor, *Singapore, The Battle That Changed the World* (Garden City, 1968), Ch 7; Attiwill, *Fortress,* Ch 11–13, *passim;* Kirby, *The Loss of Singapore,* pp 238–241, 457, Ch 24; Norman F. Dixon, *On the Psychology of Military Incompetence* (New York, 1976), pp 130–144.

75. Lloyd, *Briefed to Attack,* Chapter XVII; Tedder, *Prejudice,* pp 264–270.

76. Lloyd, *Briefed to Attack,* pp 145, 161; RAF, Report on Operations in the Western Desert and Eastern Mediterranean, App. B.

77. Ishikawa, Dozone, and Miyako, "Southeast Asia Air Operations Record," Japanese Monograph No 55.

78. *Ibid;* Deichman and Marquard, "Luftwaffe Methods in the Selection of Offensive Weapons," part 2; Felmy, *GAF in the Mediterranean Theater,* pp 232–242; Munitions and Supply Charts, in Ishikawa, Dozone, and Miyako, "Southeast Asia Air Operations Record," Japanese Monograph No 55, pp 94–97; Joe G. Taylor's "Analysis of Pre-Invasion Air Operations, Pacific Area, November-December 1943," USAF Hist Study 125 (Maxwell AFB, 1954), contains an excellent comparison of the factors governing bombing effectiveness during some concentrated efforts of relatively short duration.

## Chapter V

## Campaigns in Africa

1. Correlli Barnett, *The Desert Generals* (New York, 1960), pp 13–58.

2. Tedder, *Prejudice,* pp 52–59; Erwin Rommel, *The Rommel Papers,* edited by B. H. Liddell Hart (New York, 1953), pp 99–101; Air Ministry, UK, Air Attacks of Airfields, p 29.

3. Rommel, *Papers,* pp 99–101.

4. Tedder, *Prejudice,* pp 71, 97–99; Rommel, *Papers,* pp 120–129; Felmy, *GAF in the Mediterranean Theater,* Sect III, pp 55–56.

5. *Minutes, OKW Conference with the Italian General Staff, June 2, 1941,* German Translation VII/128, Air Ministry, UK, USAF Collection K512.621; Tedder, *Prejudice,* pp 76–77, 100–107; Rommel, *Papers,* pp 120–129.

6. *Ibid;* War Department, U.S. Military Attache Cairo Rept No 2361, Apr 2, 1942, AA Defense of Tobruch Fortress, USAF Collection 170.2278-16.

7. Tedder, *Prejudice,* pp 76–82; Msg, Col Bonner Fellers to War Dept, June 2, 1941, USAF Collection 170.2278-16.

8. *Ibid;* Intv, Lt Col Cornelius V. Whitney, Apr 6, 1943, USAF Collection 616.101; Rept, Royal Air Force Operations in the Western Desert and Eastern Mediterranean, 18 Nov 1941 to 19 May 1942, Hq RAF Middle East, [nd, but 1942] USAF Collection 512.421B.

9. Tedder, *Prejudice,* pp 170–175; Whitney Intv.

10. Tedder, *Prejudice,* pp 170–175

11. *Ibid;* Rept, Experiences in Employment of AA Units, GHQ Middle East, [nd, but 1942] USAF Collection 248.712-68; RAF Middle East Review No 4, July–Sept 1943, pp 77–81.

12. Tedder, *Prejudice,* pp 105, 121, 171–178; RAF in the Western Desert and Eastern Mediterranean, 18 Nov 1941 to 19 May 1942, p 4.

13. Tedder, *Prejudice,* pp 170–175; Whitney Intv.

14. RAF in the Western Desert, 1941–1942, pp 30–31; Tedder, *Prejudice,* pp 198, 210–213.

15. RAF in the Western Desert, p 29.

16. Rept, Experiences in the Employment of AA Units; RAF Middle East Review No 4, July -Sept 43, pp 77–81.

17. Tedder, *Prejudice,* pp 234–244; Whitney Intv, pp 4–9; RAF in the Western Desert, 1941–1942, p 45; Air Ministry, UK, RAF Draft Narrative, *The Middle East Campaigns,* Vol III, pp 39–43.

18. *Ibid.*

19. Rept, Controlled Interception (Air Raid Warning) in the Western Desert and Associated Problems, Maj David H. Likes,

Dec 29, 1942, pp 14–15, USAF Collection 168.605–24; Air Ministry, UK, *Middle East Campaigns,* pp 39–42; Rept, Development of the Organization of Fighter Defence in the Middle East, Oct 1942–10 Jan 1943, Hq. Middle East Air Force, in the Mediterranean Allied Air Forces file, Reel No. 7, USAF Collection 622.011. Hereafter cited as "MAAF Reel" with appropriate reel number.

20. Hinsley, *British Intelligence in the Second World War,* Vol 2, pp 375–380; Development of Fighter Defence in the Middle East, p 2; Ralph Bennett, *Ultra in the West: The Normandy Campaign 1944–45* (New York, 1980), Ch 1, *passim.*

21. Wesley F. Craven and James L. Cate, editors, *Europe: Torch to Pointblank* [The Army Air Forces in World War II] (Chicago, 1950), pp 8–12, 28–36; Whitney Intv, pp 9–10; Development of Fighter Defence in the Middle East, p 3.

22. Hist, 57 Ftr Gp; Tedder, *Prejudice,* pp 357–360; Rommel, *Papers,* pp 317–326, 335; War Diary, *Panzer Armee Afrika,* 28 July to 23 Oct 1942, entries for 20–23 Oct 42, German Translation VII/105, Air Ministry, UK, USAF Collection K512.621.

23. Operations Records, No 2 Armoured Car Company, RAF, Nov 1942, PRO, Air 29/55; Air Ministry, UK, *Middle East Campaigns,* Vol IV, pp 415–417.

24. Air Ministry, UK, *Middle East Campaigns,* Vol IV, pp 415–417; 21st *Panzer* Division Rept, 23 Oct–20 Nov 1942, German Translation VII/112, Air Ministry, UK, p 17, USAF Collection K512.621.

25. War Diary, *Panzer Armee Afrika,* entries for 20–23 Oct 42, German Translation VII/105, Air Ministry, UK, USAF Collection K512.621; Rommel, *Papers,* pp 317–326,335; Tedder, *Prejudice,* pp 357–360.

26. Rommel, *Papers,* p 134.

27. *Ibid,* pp 218, 266–268; Felmy, *GAF in the Mediterranean Theater,* Sect III, pp 53–56, 84; U.S. War Dept, Air Staff, Post Hostility Rept, Sect IV, p 22; Albert Kesselring, "The War in the Mediterranean," in *World War II German Military Studies,* 24 vols, Donald S. Detwiler, Charles B. Burdick, and Jürgen Rohwer, eds (New York, 1979), Vol 14, pp 7–9; A Tactical Appreciation of the War in Tunisia, German Translation VII/6, Air Ministry, UK, p 11; Signals and Directives Concerning Axis Problems of Supply and Co-operation, Apr–June 1941, German Translation VII/128, Air Ministry, UK; Fuehrer HQ Memo, Subj: German Afrika Corps, 20 May 1941, and HQ *Fliegerkorps X,* Corps Order, USAF Collection 512.621 and K512.621.

28. Air Staff Post Hostility Rept, Sect IV, A–3, pp 12–14, 29–30; Felmy, *GAF in the Mediterranean Theater,* pp 53–56, 84.

29. Felmy, *GAF in the Mediterranean Theater,* p 53; Air Staff Post Hostility Rept, Sect IV, A–3,–6 (Tactical Employment) which includes *Luftwaffe* Directive 16 and interviews of Lt Gen Karl Koller.

30. Interrogation of Maj Gen Adolf Galland and Field Marshal Erhard Milch, in Air Staff Post Hostility Rept, Sect IV–C; Tactical and Technical Notes, No 56, pp 8–9.

31. Gebhard Aders, *History of the German Night Fighter Force, 1917–1945* (London, 1979), pp 42, 52; Ltr, von Waldau to *Luftwaffe* Operations Staff, April 28, 1941, German Translation VII/128, Air Ministry, UK; Hq RAF Middle East, Enemy R.D.F. in the Mediterranean, Report No 3, Sept 23, 1942, USAF Collection 533.650.

32. Felmy, *GAF in the Mediterranean Theater,* pp 53–56, 84; Air Staff Post Hostility Rept, Sect IV, pp 14–22, 29–30.

33. Interrogation of Maj Gen Galland and Lt Col Bar, Mobility of Fighter Units, Sept 4, 1945, Air Staff Post Hostility Rept; Felmy, *GAF in the Mediterranean Theater,* p 224.

34. Felmy, *GAF in the Mediterranean Theater,* pp 54–55, 83; Air Staff Post Hostility Rept, Intv of Karl Koller; Tactical and Technical Notes No 27, Enemy Camouflage and AA in the Western Desert, June 25, 1942; Air Attacks of Airfields, p 31; IIS No 67, Notes on Axis North African Tactics, Oct 21, 1942; Hogg, *Anti-Aircraft,* p 94.

35. Tactical and Technical Notes No 27; IIS No 77, Camouflage of Enemy Aircraft, Nov 12, 1942; Combined Services Detailed Interrogation Center (CSDIC), Report No 578, The German Air Force in Italy, July 12, 1945, USAF Collection 512.619C–7C.

36. CSDIC Rept No 578.

37. George F. Howe, *Northwest Africa; Seizing the Initiative in the West* [United States Army in World War II] (Washington, 1957), pp 13–31, 185–191; Winston S. Churchill, *The Hinge of Fate* (Boston, 1950), pp 432–451.

38. Howe, *Northwest Africa,* pp 13–31; Craven and Cate, *Torch to Pointblank,* pp 77–78, 115–120.

39. Rept 48295, Rept of Commander, Task Force 34, Torch Operation Repts; Rept 44607, Report of Air Operations Task Group 34.10;

Rept 44041, Ltr, Dwight D. Eisenhower, Report of Operation Torch. Cited reports are in U. S. Center for Naval History, Operational Archives.

40. *Ibid;* See also: Howe, *Northwest Africa,* pp 189-191, and Craven and Cate, *Torch to Pointblank,* pp 77-78

41. Hist, 14 Ftr Gp.; Memo, Proposed New Fighter Airdrome, Feb 11, 1943, MAAF Reel 277.

42. Hist, XII Ftr Cmd, USAF Collection 654.906; Hq, U.S. Army Antiaircraft Command, Intelligence Memorandum No. 138, Antiaircraft Artillery Organization, Equipment and Operations in the North African Campaign, 1942-1943, July 26, 1943; Intv, Capt August W. Mysing, [nd, but 1943] USAF Collection 248.532-4; SRH-037, "Use of Ultra in the European Theater, World War II," pp 9-10, AF/CHO.

43. Ltr, Group Capt D.F.W. Atcherly to Welsh, Special Rept on the Unsatisfactory R.D.F. and Signals Situation, Nov 21, 1942, MAAF reel 10, sec. 120; Hist, XII Ftr Cmd, Radar Organization, Jan 1943 to Sept 1944; War Diary, XII Ftr Cmd, Hq and Hq Co, AWS, USAF Collection 654.901.

44. Msg., Operational Control of Air Defences Overseas, Jan 29, 1943, MAAF reel 277; War Diary, XII Fighter Cmd, Hq and Hq Co, AWS.

45. Craven and Cate, *Torch to Pointblank,* p 127; Memo on the Defence of Airfields Against Attack, Apr 25, 1943, MAAF reel 1; Ltr, AA Defence of Aerodromes, Feb 28, 1943, MAAF reel 1.

46. Tedder, *Prejudice,* pp 400-404; Ltr, Brig Gen Laurence S. Kuter to General H. H. Arnold, Organization of American Air Forces, May 12, 1943, USAF Collection 614.201-1.

47. Craven and Cate, *Torch to Pointblank,* pp 161-162.

48. Tedder, *Prejudice,* pp 396-400; Speech, Air Vice Marshal Coningham to senior Torch Officers, Tripoli, Feb 16, 1943, USAF Collection 614.201-1.

49. HQ Northwest African Air Forces, GO No 1, Feb 18, 1943.

50. AAA Cmd Intel Memo No 138; Mysing Intv; Memo, Group Capt. J.A. Tester, Maintenance of R.D.F. in Mediterranean Air Command, June 24, 1943; Ltr, Air Vice Marshal G.G. Dawson to Air Vice Marshal Hugh P. Lloyd, July 1, 1943; Ltr, Col Davis D. Graves, Personnel of 588 Platoons, June 9, 1943; Memo, Wing Cdr E. Swinney, Ameri-

can RDF Stations-SCR 588, July 24, 1943, MAAF reel 10, sec. 120, 121.

51. Ltr, HQ, Northwest African Strategic Air Force to Spaatz, Aircraft Warning Service, Mar 31, 1943, USAF Collection 652.661; Ltr, Doolittle to Spaatz, Fighters for Airdrome Defense, Apr 1, 1943, USAF Collection 652.661; Ltr, HQ. Northwest African Coastal Air Force to Spaatz, R.D.F. Policy, Apr 19, 1943, MAAF reel 283.

52. Mysing Intv; Hist XII Bmr Cmd, USAF Collection 652.667; Ltr, AA Defence of Airdromes.

53. Air Ministry, UK, Rept of a Committee on the Future of the RAF Regiment, 1945, USAF Collection 512.15-1; U.S. Military Attache Rept No 46660, The Royal Air Force Regiment, Mar 10, 1942, USAF Collection 142.04-12; RAF Mediterranean Review No 10, Jan to May 1945, pp 142-147.

54. Air Mininstry, UK, Rept of a Committee on the Future of the RAF Regiment, 1945.

55. Ltr, Lt Col H. R. Salmon, RAF Regiment NAAF to Air Commodore G. R. Beamish, Feb 26, 1943, MAAF reel 1.

56. *Ibid.*

57. HQ, NAAF Organization Memo No 28, Formation of Light AA Squadron, R.A.F. Regiment, May 11, 1943, MAAF reel 7.

58. Ltr, Allied Force HQ, Establishment of "Inner Artillery Zones" (IAZ), "Gun Defended Areas" (GDA), and "Special Areas" in the North African Theater, Feb 15, 1943; Ltr, HQ, NATAF, Flying Discipline, Mar 31, 1943; Ltr, HQ NATAF, Aircraft Recognition, Mar 25, 1943, all in MAAF reel 1.

59. Ltr, HQ, Northwest African Coastal Air Force to Spaatz, R.D.F. Policy, Apr 19, 1943, MAAF reel 283; Hist, XII Ftr Cmd, Radar Organization; Northwest African Strategic Air Force, Three Significant Days (April 4, 5, 6), USAF Collection 615.308-1.

60. Felmy, *GAF in the Mediterranean Theater,* pp 534-588; CSDIC Report No 579, July 14, 1945, USAF Collection 512.619-C; Hinsley, *British Intelligence in World War II,* Vol 2, pp 487-492.

61. Northwest African Tactical Air Force, Special Intelligence Report No 4, Axis Landing Grounds in N. Tunisia, [nd, but 1943], USAF Collection 614.323-2; Felmy, *GAF in the Mediterranean Theater,* pp 635-640, 725, 740; The *Luftwaffe* in the Battle for Tunis, October 17, 1944, German Translation VII/5, Air Ministry, UK.

62. Felmy, *GAF in the Mediterranean Theater,* p 640; Hq, RAF Middle East, En-

emy R.D.F., Report No 5, Dec 14, 1942, and Enemy R.D.F., Rept No 11, May 12, 1943, MAAF reel 286.

63. Rept, Northwest African Strategic Air Forces, Three Significant Days, May 16, 1943; German translation VII/6, Air Ministry, UK.

64. Hinsley, *British Intelligence in World War II*, Vol 2, pp 494–495, 575–576, 605–608, 729; The Mediterranean Campaign, with attached reports of 1941 relating to supply deliveries, German Translation VII/63, Air Ministry, UK; see also German Translation VII/128 for signals detailing supply problems.

65. German Translation VII/5, Air Ministry, UK, p 3; U.S. Military Attache Rept No 2418, German Equipment, July 27, 1943, USAF Collection 142.646–1; Felmy, *GAF in the Mediterranean Theater*, pp 692–695; Tactical and Technical Notes No 56, Aug 17, 1943, pp 4–8.

66. Felmy, *GAF in the Mediterranean Theater*, p 644, and appendices to this work found in the German language manuscript; AAF Statistical Digest WWII, Dec 1945, p 160; The Course of the War in the Mediterranean Theater of Operations, Jan 1–May 13, 1943, German Translation VII/72, Air Ministry, UK, July 29, 1944, p 1.

67. Felmy, *GAF in the Mediterranean Theater*, pp 736, 752–753a; German Translations VII/5, p 4, and VII/25, p 21, Air Ministry, UK.

68. *Ibid;* Hinsley, *British Intelligence in World War II*, Vol 2, p 612.

69. Rommel, *Papers*, pp 241–242.

70. RAF in the Western Desert, 1941–1942, Appendix I; HQ. XII Bmr Cmd, Information About the Enemy, Dec 24, 1942, p 1, USAF Collection 533.650.

71. Coningham Speech

72. *Ibid;* Memo, Maj Gen H. R. Oldfield to General H. H. Arnold, Dec 24, 1943, Simpson Collection 248.712–41; Kuter Ltr, Org of the AAF, May 12, 1943, USAF Collection 614.201–1

73. Rommel, *Papers,* p 282; Coningham Speech and excerpt of remarks by General Bernard L. Montgomery, Feb 1943, USAF Collection 614.201–1; AAF Statistical Digest WW II, p 256, 264.

74. Kuter Ltr, Org of the AAF, May 12, 1943, p 1.

75. *Ibid,* p 5.

76. *Ibid.*

77. War Dept, FM 100–20, Command and Employment of Air Power, July 1943.

## Chapter VI

### The Eastern Front: 1941–1944

1. Ray Wagner, ed, *The Soviet Air Force in World War II, the Official History, Originally Published by the Ministry of Defense of the USSR,* trans by Leland Fetzer (New York, 1973), p 35; Bekker, *Luftwaffe War Diaries,* pp 180–181; John Erickson, "The Soviet Response to Surprise Attack: Three Directives, 22 June 1941," *Soviet Studies,* 23 (April 1974) pp 519–553; Hardesty, *Red Phoenix,* pp 11–15.

2. Conquest, *The Great Terror,* pp 484–492; Erickson, "The Soviet Response to Surprise Attack," pp 534, 544–545.

3. Boyd, *The Soviet Air Force,* pp 88–107; Greenwood, "The Great Patriotic War, 1941–1945," pp 75–80; Solzhenitsyn, *Gulag,* Vol I, p 80.

4. Hermann Plocher, *The German Air Force versus Russia, 1941,* ed by Harry R. Fletcher, USAF Hist Study 153, (New York, 1965) p 38. There are three volumes to this work covering 1941, 1942, and 1943 respectively. They are USAF studies No. 153, 154, and 155 and will hereinafter be cited as Plocher, *GAF vs Russia,* with appropriate year.

5. Karl Heinz Seiss, "The German Attack Cannot be Stopped," *Frankfurter Zeitung,* June 22, 1941, cited in *Masterpieces of War Reporting,* ed by Louis L. Snyder, (New York, 1962), pp 113–114; Franz Halder, *Private War Journal,* Vol III, USAF Collection 171.38–3, pp 161–166; Boyd, *The Soviet Air Force,* pp 113–114; Erickson, "The Soviet Response to Surprise Attack," *passim.*

6. Plocher, *GAF vs Russia, 1941,* pp 40–41; Halder, *Private War Journal,* vol VIII, p 161.

7. Bekker, *Luftwaffe War Diaries,* pp 218–219.

8. *Ibid,* p 221; Diary of Herbert Pabst,

June 22, 1941, translation in AF/CHO, German text in USAF Collection, K113.407–3.

9. Hans-Ulrich Rudel, *Stuka Pilot,* trans by Lynton Hudson (Dublin, 1952), p 19; Walter Schwabedissen, *The Russian Air Force in the Eyes of German Commanders*, pp 116–119; Bekker, *Luftwaffe War Diaries,* p 221; Kozhevnikov, *Command and Staff of the Soviet Army Air Force,* pp 46–49, 55.

10. Medvedev, *Let History Judge,* pp 12–13; Erickson, "The Soviet Response to Surprise Attack," pp 349–350.

11. Nathan Leites, *Soviet Style in War* (New York, 1982), pp 230–265; William Craig, *Enemy at the Gates, the Battle for Stalingrad* (New York, 1973), pp 71–78; Medvedev, *Let History Judge,* pp 12–13, 406; Erickson, "The Soviet Response to Surprise Attack," pp 550–552; Svetlana Alliluyeva, *Twenty Letters to a Friend* (New York, 1967), p 185; Solzhenitsyn, *Gulag,* pp 25, 81–83.

12. Bekker, *Luftwaffe War Diaries,* p 222.

13. Plocher, *GAF vs Russia, 1941.* Ch 4 and 6, *passim.*

14. Bekker, *Luftwaffe War Diaries,* pp 222–223; Wagner, *Soviet Air Force in World War II,* p 161; Washington, Dept of the Air Force, *Air Intelligence Digest,* Feb 1953, pp 6–9.

15. Robert A. Kilmarx, *A History of Soviet Air Power* (New York, 1962), pp 200–213; Craven and Cate, *Men and Planes,* pp 350–354; For Russian losses see: "The Part Played by the GAF on the Eastern Front," Supreme Headquarters Intelligence Party Rept No 31, USAF Collection 512.62512M–31.

16. Klaus Uebe, *Russian Reactions to German Air Power in World War II,* USAF Hist Study 176, (New York, 1964), p 7.

17. Kozhevnikov, *Command and Staff of the Soviet Army Air Force,* pp 43–45.

18. Leon Gouré and Herbert S. Dinerstein, "Political Vulnerability of Moscow: A Case Study of the October 1941 Attack" (Santa Monica, 1952), Ch 3, *passim;* Paul Carell, *Hitler Moves East 1941–1943* (New York, 1966), pp 329–365, 396; CSDIC (Air) Report No A585, Aug 3, 1945, USAF Collection 512.619C–7C.

19. Carell, *Hitler Moves East,* pp 329–365; Rudel, *Stuka Pilot,* p 46; Schwabedissen, *Russian Air Force in the Eyes of German Commanders,* pp 16, 148; Ministry of Defence, UK, "Soviet Airfield Policy and Development," JIB 5/118/1616, Nov 1948, USAF Collection, 512.6111–I; P. N. Pospelov, *et al, History of the Great Patriotic War of the Soviet Union,* 6 vols, trans and reproduced as bound typescript by Office of the Chief of Military History, U. S. Army, 1965–1970, vol II, p 21.

20. Rept, "Air Staff Post Hostilities Intelligence Requirements on German Air Force," Sect III, Tactical Employment, 519.601 B–4; Col Ye. Simakov, "Camouflage of Air Force Operations," *Soviet Military Review,* April 1982, pp 26–27. Simakov's article is an excellent summation of the Soviet Air Force's camouflage and deception tactics at its World War II airfields. It was reprinted by the U. S. Air Force in AFRP 200–1, *Soviet Press,* July–August 1982.

21. *Ibid;* Uebe, *Russian Reactions to German Air Power,* pp 34–50.

22. HQ, USAF Air Intelligence Rpt No 100–45–34, 19 June 1946, USAF Collection 142.048–45; IIS No 13, Comments on German and Soviet Air Forces, Apr 16, 1942; Plocher, *GAF vs Russia, 1942,* pp 214–217; Air Intelligence Rept No 100–45–34.

23. *Ibid.*

24. Plocher, *GAF vs Russia, 1942,* pp 214–217.

25. U.S. War Dept, Intelligence Bulletin No 5, January 1, 1942, Employment of German Antiaircraft Artillery in Russia, USAF Collection 170.2252–5; IIS No 24, The German Air Force, Its Mobility, Airdrome Commands, Maintenance and Supply Organization, Nov 2, 1942, USAF Collection 142.034–2.

26. Air Staff Post Hostilities Report, Sect III, Tactical Employment and Conduct of Aerial Warfare; IIS No 24; Plocher, *GAF vs Russia, 1942,* pp 216–217.

27. Air Staff Post Hostilites Rept; Conduct of Aerial Warfare; Employment of German Antiaircaraft Artillery in Russia; IIS No 24; Air Ministry, Notes on Defense of GAF Airfields, Apr 18, 1944, USAF Collection 512.645–1.

28. *Ibid;* Pospelov, *History of the Great Patriotic War,* Vol III, *pp 439–446.* Although it is not possible to substantiate all of the Soviet allegations of forced labor, deportation, and other crimes by German occupation forces, it is clear that civilians were often forced to work at military construction projects.

29. Plocher, *GAF vs Russia, 1942,* p 139–142; *See also* John F. Kreis, Air Base Ground Defense, Draft Manuscript in AF/CHO.

30. IIS No 77, Camouflage of Enemy Aircraft, Nov 12, 1942. Air Force General

Information Bulletin (Hereafter AFGIB), No 20, Feb 1944, pp 18–22.

31. Carrell, *Hitler Moves East,* pp 618–631; Craig, *Enemy at the Gates,* p 378.

32. Plocher, *GAF vs Russia, 1942,* pp 272, 306; Uebe, *Russian Reaction to German Air Power,* p 21; Morzik, *GAF Airlift Operations,* pp 185.

33. Plocher, *GAF vs Russia, 1942,* pp 259, 261–262, 279–308, 351; AFGIB No 20, Feb 1944, pp 18–22 and MID Rept No 5, 13 Dec 1943, NARA.

34. AFGIB No 20, pp 18–22; Plocher, *GAF vs Russia, 1942,* p 293; Morzik, *GAF Airlift Operations,* p 195; Von Hardesty, *Red Phoenix, the Rise of Soviet Air Power, 1941–1945* (Washington, 1982), pp 105–119.

35. Plocher, *GAF vs Russia, 1942,* pp 259–262, 279–308, 351; AFGIB No 20, 18–22 and MID Rept No 5, 13 Dec 43.

36. Morzik, *GAF Airlift Operations,* pp 191–192, 195; Hardesty, *Red Phoenix,* pp 114–118.

37. Plocher, *GAF vs Russia, 1942,* pp 292–306, 315, 329.

38. Erich von Manstein, *Lost Victories* (Chicago, 1958), Ch 13, *passim;* Plocher, *GAF vs Russia, 1943,* pp 26–27, 365.

39. Plocher, *GAF vs Russia, 1943,* pp 44–45; AFGIB No 20, p 18.

40. Plocher, GAF vs Russia, 1943, pp 49–50; AFGIB No 5, Soviet Fighter Tactics, Oct 1942, pp 10–13; Y. Veraksa, "Fighters Attack an Airfield," *Soviet Military Review,* July 1971, pp 39–41.

41. Erickson, *The Road to Berlin,* p. 97; Plocher, *GAF vs Russia, 1943,* pp 72–74.

42. Plocher, *GAF vs Russia, 1943,* pp 78–83; Hinsley, *British Intelligence in the Second World War,* Vol 2, pp 615–627, 767–765.

43. Wagner, ed, *Soviet Air Force in World War II,* pp 166–171; IIS No 43–41, 20 Aug 1943; Air Intelligence Rept No 100–45–34; Erickson, "Soviet Radar," pp 255–263; Schwabedissen, *Russian Air Force,* p 256; E. Simakov, "Camouflage of Air Force Operations," pp 26–27.

44. Wagner, ed, *Soviet Air Force in World War II,* p 167–169; Plocher, *GAF vs Russia, 1943,* pp 57–65.

45. Plocher, *GAF vs Russia, 1943,* pp 60–66.

46. AFGIB No 15, Oct 42, Soviet Fighter Tactics; Veraksa, "Fighters Attack an Airfield," pp 39–41.

47. Plocher, *GAF vs Russia, 1943,* pp 82–83.

48. *Ibid,* pp 83–84.

49. *Ibid,* pp 83–86, 100; Manstein, *Lost Victories,* p 449.

50. Hardesty, *Red Phoenix,* p 165.

51. Albert Speer, *Inside the Third Reich* (New York, 1970), pp 278–291, 332–333, 346–350. See also: Charles Webster and Noble Frankland, *The Strategic Air Offensive Against Germany 1939–1945* 4 vols, (London, 1961) II: *passim.*

52. Churchill, *Closing the Ring,* pp 292–333; Glenn B. Infield, *The Poltava Affair, A Russian Warning: An American Tragedy* (New York, 1973), pp 1–14.

53. John R. Deane, *The Strange Alliance* (New York, 1947), Ch II, *passim.*

54. Memo, Harriman-Molotov Meeting, 5 Feb 1944, History of the Eastern Command, United States Strategic Air Forces, Europe, USAF Collection 522.01 to 522.161; Deane, *Strange Alliance,* pp 108–109.

55. Eastern Command History, Rept of 5 Mar 1944; FRANTIC Plan, 22 May 1944.

56. Repts of Meetings, Red Air Force Headquarters, 5 and 17 Mar 1944, in Eastern Command History; Kenneth R. Whiting, ed and trans, "Bulganin's Summary of Soviet Military Art and Science," in *Readings in Soviet Military Theory,* (Maxwell AFB, 1952), pp 67–80; George F. Kennan, *Soviet-American Relations, 1917–1920,* 2 vols, Vol 2, *The Decision to Intervene, passim.*

57. Deane, *Strange Alliance,* pp 114–120.

58. Memo, Harriman-Molotov Meeting, 5 Feb 1944; Rept of Proceedings of Board of Officers, 2 Aug 1944; Eastern Command History, Ch 6, Airdrome Operations.

59. Eastern Command History, Ch 6; Intv, Brig Gen Alfred A. Kessler, 5 July 1944, in Eastern Command History.

60. *Ibid.*

61. Report on Shuttle Mission to Russia, Col Archie J. Old, Jr, 6 July 1944, in Eastern Command History; Infield, *Poltava Affair,* pp 138–139.

62. Old, Rept on Shuttle Mission; Rept of Board of Officers.

63. Ltr, Lt Col William M. Jackson, 24 June 1944, in Eastern Command History.

64. Rept of Board of Officers

65. Old, Rept on Shuttle Mission.

66. Infield, *Poltava Affair,* Ch 11, 12, 15, *passim.*

67. Old, Rept on Shuttle Mission; Deane, *Strange Alliance,* p 122; IIS 44–31, 15 Oct 1944.

68. Kessler Intv.

69. Infield, *Poltava Affair,* p 145–154.

70. Pospelov, *History of the Great Patriotic War,* vol III, p 597.

71. Leites, *Soviet Style in War,* p 243.

72. *Ibid,* pp 237–252.

73. Infield, *Poltava Affair,* p 171.

74. Leites, *Soviet Style in War,* pp 237–252; Greenwood, "The Great Patriotic War," p 98; Craig, *Enemy at the Gates,* pp 71–78.

75. Boyd, *Soviet Air Force Since 1918,* p 102; Historical Research and Evaluation Organization, *The Development of Soviet Air Defense Doctrine and Practice* (Dunn Loring, Va, 1981), pp 2–25 to 2–31.

76. Greenwood, "The Great Patriotic War," p 131; J.I.B.5/118/1616, Soviet Airfield Policy and Development.

77. *Ibid,* p 104.

Chapter VII

## The Solomons and New Guinea
## 1942–1944

1. John Miller, Jr., *Guadalcanal: The First Offensive* [United States Army in World War II] (Washington, 1949), Ch 1; Cdr Masatake Okumiya, Interrogation No 75, October 12, 1945, pp 5–6, *USSBS, Pacific.*

2. *Ibid.*

3. Frank O. Hough, Verle E. Ludwig, and Henry I. Shaw, Jr., *Pearl Harbor to Guadalcanal* [History of U. S. Marine Operations in World War II] (Washington, 1958), pp 210–213.

4. Miller, *First Offensive*, Chapter 1.

5. *Ibid;* Hough, Ludwig, and Shaw, *Pearl Harbor to Guadalcanal*, p 243.

6. *Ibid.*

7. Hough, Ludwig, and Shaw, *Pearl Harbor to Guadalcanal*, pp 247, 259, 264.

8. General George C. Kenney Papers, entries for August 7–8, 1942, in AF/CHO; Hist, 28th and 93rd Bomb Sqdns. General Kenney's papers, actually a diary kept during World War II, were typed after the war and organized into eleven loose leaf binders. Interspersed throughout are letters to and from President Franklin D. Roosevelt, General Douglas MacArthur, General H. H. Arnold, and Kenney's subordinate commanders in the SWPA.

9. Hough, Ludwig, and Shaw, *Pearl Harbor to Guadalcanal*, pp 259–260; Division Commander's Final Rept on Guadalcanal Operation, May–July 1943 (Vandegrift Rept), Phase III, Annexes B, D, and G, Records of the First Marine Division, Box 4, U. S. Marine Historical Archives.

10. Miller, *First Offensive*, Ch 1.

11. Rept, Third Defense Battalion Operations at Guadalcanal, Mar 1943, Col Robert H. Pepper, First Marine Division Records, Box 6, A 32–1, U S Marine Historical Archives.

12. Charles L. Updegraf, *U. S. Marine Corps Special Units of World War II* (Washington, 1972), pp 61–77; Rept on Fighter Direction at Cactus, 8 October 1942–1 Jan 1943, Lt Lewis C. Mattison, Jan 1, 1943, AF/CHO.

13. Rept, Third Defense Bn Operations at Guadalcanal, Mar 1943.

14. *Ibid;* Intv, Ens W. A. Noll, USNR, 25 Mar 1943, USAF Collection, 730.310B; Mattison, Fighter Direction at Cactus.

15. Third Defense Bn Operations, pp 13–16.

16. *Ibid,* p 4; Rept on Marine Antiaircraft at Guadalcanal, Solomon Islands, Oct 28, 1942, Lt Col Robert H. Totten, Box 6, A 32–2, U.S. Marine Historical Archives.

17. Gordon Swanborough and Peter M. Bowers, *United States Navy Aircraft since 1911* (Annapolis, 1976), p 210; Hist, 67 Ftr Sqn, Part I; Noll Intv; IIS No 43–5, Jan 8, 1943.

18. Vandegrift Rept, Phase III, Annex B; Phase IV, p 14.

19. Eric A. Feldt, *The Coastwatchers* (New York, 1946), pp 83–95.

20. Vandegrift Rept, Phase IV, Annex A, Phase V, Annex N; IIS No 43–8, Jan 23, 1943; Totten, Rept on Marine Antiaircraft at Guadalcanal, pp 2–5; Noll Intv; Mattison, Fighter Direction at Cactus.

21. Feldt, *Coastwatchers*, pp 92–96; Robert Sherrod, *History of Marine Corps Aviation in World War II* (Washington, 1952), p 86.

22. Vandegrift Rept, Phase IV, Annex D, Phase III, Annex B; Rept on Radar Operation at Cactus, Master Technical Sergeant Der-

mott H. MacDonnell, Dec 16, 1942, AF/CHO.

23. Noll Intv; Mattison, Fighter Direction at Cactus; Intv, author with Lewis C. Mattison, Washington, DC, Oct 7, 1983; MacDonnell, Radar at Cactus; Intv, Maj Joseph N. Renner, July 17, 1943, USAF Collection, 180.451-7.

24. *Ibid.*

25. Noll Intv; Hist, 67 Ftr Sqn, part 1.

26. Mattison, Fighter Direction at Cactus; IIS No 73, Nov 26, 1942; IIS 43-5.

27. Pepper, Rept of Third Defense Bn; Mattison, Fighter Direction at Cactus, p 7.

28. Vandegrift Rept, Phase III, Annex B; Noll Intv; Rept of Maj Thomas F. Riley, 1st Aviation Engineer Bn (USMC), Box 6, A 31-1, U. S. Marine Corps Historical Archives.

29. Noll Intv; William F. Halsey, *Admiral Halsey's Story* (New York, 1947), p 116; Mattison Intv.

30. Noll Intv; IIS No 73; IIS No 43-8.

31. Hist, 67th Ftr Sqn.

32. Noll Intv; Hough, Ludwig, and Shaw, *Pearl Harbor to Guadalcanal*, pp 308-330.

33. Mattison, Fighter Direction at Cactus, pp 5-9.

34. Vandegrift Rept, Phase V; Hough, Ludwig, and Shaw, *Pearl Harbor to Guadalcanal*, pp 324, 354-358; Interrogation No. 475, Masatake Okumiya, Nov 29, 1945. *USSBS, Pacific.*

35. *Ibid.*

36. Mattison Intv; Ltr, Mattison to author, Oct 24, 1983.

37. Pepper, Rept of Third Defense Bn, Encl A; Mattison, Fighter Direction at Cactus, Appendix B. Mattison's report contains a day by day listing of aircraft of both sides shot down. The list is not definitive, but was prepared by Lt. Mattison from the best information he could find. Although not wholly authoritative, it tends to confirm Miller's assessment of Japanese losses.

38. Sherrod, *Marine Aviation in World War II*, p 128; Miller, *Cactus Air Force*, p 209; Samuel Eliot Morison, *The Struggle for Guadalcanal, August 1942-February 1943* [History of United States Naval Operations in World War II] (Boston, 1950), pp 223-224.

39. National Security Agency, *Special Research Histories* 136, "Radio Intelligence in World War II," 188, "U. S. Navy Strategic Radio Direction Finder Station Guadalcanal," 197, "U. S. Navy Communication Intelligence Organization, Liaison and Collaboration, 1941-1945."

40. First Marine Division Records, Daily Intelligence Summaries, entries for Oct 5-13, Nov 8, and Dec 5 and 9, 1942, Box 8, C4-3, U. S. Marine Historical Archives; Feldt, *Coastwatchers*, pp 117-118.

41. *Ibid.*

42. First Marine Division Records, Intelaries, entries for December 1942, Box 8, C2-1; Okumiya, Interrogation No 75, p 6, *USSBS, Pacific.*

43. Lt Cmdr S. Yunoki, Interrogation No 195, October 27, 1945, *USSBS, Pacific;* Hist, 67 Ftr Sqn, part II, p. 63, 69.

44. Rept, Commander South Pacific Area (COMSOPAC), Guadalcanal Escorted Bomber Missions During Month of Dec 1942 through Febr 24, 1943, Mar 15, 1943; Yunoki Interrogation, *USSBS, Pacific.*

45. IIS No 43-15, Feb 13, 1943.

46. Yunoki Interrogation, *USSBS, Pacific;* Hist, 67 Ftr Sqn, part II, pp 63, 69.

47. *Ibid;* Rept, COMSOPAC, Guadalcanal Escorted Bomber Missions, Dec 1942 through Feb 24, 1943, Mar 15, 1943, USAF Collection.

48. Rept, Air Aspects of the Munda Campaign, U.S. Pacific Fleet, Intelligence Division, Aug 15, 1943, USAF Collection 180.204A; Memo, Munda Campaign Statistical Analysis, HQ, Thirteenth Air Force, Oct 14, 1943, USAF Collection, 750.308-10.

49. Halsey, *Admiral Halsey's Story*, p 161; Louis Morton, *Strategy and Command: The First Two Years* [The United States Army in World War II] (Washington, 1962), pp 505-512.

50. Samuel Milner, *Victory in Papua*, [The United States Army in World War II] (Washington, 1951), pp 39-44.

51. Wesley F. Craven and James L. Cate, eds, *The Pacific: Guadalcanal to Saipan* [The Army Air Forces in World War II] (Chicago, 1950), pp 5-10.

52. Milner, *Victory in Papua*, pp 39-44.

53. *Ibid*, pp 65-71.

54. *Ibid*, pp 71-76.

55. *Ibid*, pp 88-96; Kenney Papers, entries for Sept 1942.

56. Hist, V Ftr Cmd, Ch 1, USAF Collection 731.01; Army Air Forces School of Applied Tactics (AAFSAT), Intelligence Rept No 25, Mar 1944, USAF Collection 248.535-25.

57. Kenney Papers, Aug 2, 30, 1942; Ltr, Whitehead to Kenney, Jan 18, 1943, Kenney Papers.

58. Craven and Cate, *Guadalcanal to Saipan*, pp 97-108; Milner, *Victory in Papua*, pp

26–27; Antiaircraft and Air Warning Unit Files, U.S. Army Center of Military History Organizational History Files; Ltr, Whitehead to Kenney, Oct 24, 1942, Kenney Papers; George C. Kenney, *General Kenney Reports* (New York, 1949), pp 210–215.

59. Hist, V Ftr Cmd, p 109; Kenney Papers for 1942, *passim*; Antiaircraft and Air Warning Unit Files, Org Hist Files, U.S. Army; History of U. S. Aircraft Warning System in SWPA, USAF Collection, 731.663.

60. General Headquarters, SWPA, Standing Operating Procedure No 7, June 26, 1943, USAF Collection, 710.301A; Hist, V Ftr Cmd, pp 105–117; Ltr, C of S, Fifth Air Force, to Commanding General, V Ftr Cmd, 28 Sept 1943 and reply dated 24 Oct 1943, USAF Collection, 731.152-1.

61. Ltr, Capt Ross C. Baker, V Ftr Cmd, Asst A–3 to Commanding General V Ftr Cmd, 18 Apr 1944, in Kenney Papers; Hist, 8th, 35th, and 49th Fighter Control Squadrons.

62. *Ibid;* History of Aircraft Warning in SWPA; AAF Training Standard 30-4-1, May 14, 1943.

63. Antiaircraft and Air Warning Unit Files; Ltr, Maj Gen William F. Marquat, Air Defense Commands, 30 June 1944, USAF Collection, 730.3812; Rept of Activities of Separate Airborne Coast Artillery Batteries, USAF Collection, 248.712-91.

64. Kenney Papers, Sept 1, 1942.

65. *Ibid, passim.*

66. *Ibid*, Aug 3, 1942 and *passim.*

67. *Ibid;* Ltr, Kenney to MacArthur, Feb 4, 1943, Kenney Papers; Kenney, *Kenney Reports*, pp 101–103; Douglas MacArthur, *Reminiscences* (New York, 1964), p 157; George A. Meidling, ed, *Organizations, Troops, and Training* [Engineers of the Southwest Pacific 1941–1945], Office of the Chief Engineer, Army Forces Pacific, 1951, pp 95–96, Appendix IV.

68. Kenney Papers, *passim.*

69. Kenney, *Kenney Reports*, pp 101–103; MacArthur, *Reminiscences*, p 157; Meidling, *Organizations, Troops, and Training*, pp 95–96.

70. Ltrs, Whitehead to Kenney, Feb 10 and May 29, 1943, Kenney Papers.

71. *Ibid;* Ltrs, Whitehead to Kenney, June 18 and 20, 1943, and Marquat to Whitehead, June 15, 1943.

72. Hist, 14th Antiaircraft Command, Antiarcraft and Air Warning Unit Files, U.S. Army Center of Military History.

73. Ltr, Capt Ross C. Baker, Asst A–3, VFtr Cmd, to Commanding General, V Ftr Cmd, 18 Apr 1944, in Kenney Papers.

74. Hist, V Ftr Cmd, Ch 1, pp 97–98, and 8th Ftr Ctl Sqn; Hist, 85th Air Defense Wing, Dec 1943–June 1944.

75. Kenney Papers, Aug 7, 25, and 26, Dec 10, 1942, and Jan 9, 18, and May 7, 1943; SWPA Allied Translator and Interpreter Section, Information Bulletin No 1, Nov 23, 1943, USAF Collection, 710.625; Col Rinsuka Kaneko, Interrogation No. 440, Nov, 21, 1945, *USSBS, Pacific.*

76. Hist, V Bomber Command; History of Flakintel, SWPA, May 1, 1944, USAF Collection, 732.646.

77. IIS 43–38, July 30, 1943, "Japanese Antiaircraft Installations," pp 10–21.

78. History of Flakintel, "Trends of Japanese Antiaircraft Tactics."

79. IIS 43–43, Sept 10, 1943, "Destruction of Enemy Planes at Wewak," p 2; David Kahn, *The Codebreakers, The Story of Secret Writing* (New York, 1967), pp 578–579.

80. Ltr, Col Harry F. Cunningham, ACofS A–2, Advance Echelon Fifth Air Force, to Kenney, 26 Dec 1943, Kenney Papers. In November 1945, Col. Kaneko (Interrogation No 440) told a Bombing Survey interviewer that only about 120 operational aircraft were lost. The remainder were derelicts because of lack of parts and maintenance problems.

81. History of Flakintel; "Operational History of Naval Communications," Japanese Monograph No 118, U.S. Army Forces Far East, 1953, pp 109–113; Capt H. Komoto, Interrogation No 360, Nov 12, 1945, and Col Rinsuka Kaneko, Interrogation No 440, Nov 21, 1945, *USSBS, Pacific.*

82. Sigeru Sugiyama and Kengoro Tanaka, "18th Army Operations," 3 vols, Japanese Monographs No. 37, 38, and 39, Oct 1957, U.S. Army Far East Command, Vol. I, pp 29–31; Ltr, Whitehead to Kenney, May 5, 1943; Kenney Papers, entry for May 7, 1943; Kenney, *Kenney Reports*, p 233.

83. History of Flakintel, Japanese AA Installations map.

84. SWPA Air Evaluation Board, Rept No 21, Airdrome Neutralization, intv with Col Rinkai Kaneko, Oct 18, 1945, pp 82–86, USAF Collection 138.8-21.

85. SWPA Air Evaluation Board, Rept No 23, Neutralization of Wewak, USAF Collection 138.8-23; Ltr, Wewak Air Blockade, ACofS, A–2, Fifth Air Force Advance Echelon, Mar 29, 1944, Kenney Papers.

86. SWPA Air Evaluation Board, Rept No 23.

87. *Ibid*; See also Kenney Papers for January through March 1944; Ltrs, Whitehead to Brig Gen Paul B. Wurtsmith, Feb 11 and 21, and Mar 6, 1944, and Whitehead to Kenney, Feb 11, 1944, in Kenney Papers.

88. SWPA Air Evaluation Board, Rept No 21; Airdrome Neutralization; SWPA Air Evaluation Board, Rept No 25, Neutralization of Wewak; Ltr, ACofS, A-2, Fifth Air Force Advance Echelon, Mar 29, 1944, Wewak Air Blockade, Kenney Papers.

89. *Ibid*; See especially bomb squadron mission reports in SWPA Rept No 23.

90. Neutralization of Wewak, pp 36–50.

91. *Ibid;* Airdrome Neutralization, pp 15–22, 53.

92. *Ibid;* Craven and Cate, *Guadalcanal to Saipan*, p 590.

93. *Ibid;* Intvs No 388, 483, and 486, Lt Col Koji Tanaka, Nov–Dec 1945, *USSBS, Pacific.*

94. ACofS Ltr, Wewak Air Blockade; Kenney Papers, Mar 27, 1944; Craven and Cate, *Guadalcanal to Saipan*, p 589.

95. Kenney Papers, Mar 29 and Apr 1, 1944; Msg, COMAFADVON 5 to Kenney, Mar 31, 1944; Sugiyama and Tanaka, "18th Army Operations," Vol III, Japanese Monograph No 39, pp 36–42.

96. *Ibid;* Craven and Cate, *Guadalcanal to Saipan*, pp 592–598.

97. IIS No 44–31, Oct 15, 1944; Kenney Papers for 1942, *passim;* Morton, *Strategy and Command*, p 357; Kenney, *Kenney Reports*, p 241; Tanaka Intvs, *USSBS, Pacific.*

98. Kenney, *Kenney Reports*, pp 251–253, 262, 276–277.

99. *Ibid*, pp 225–226, 241, 245, 259, 303.

100. *USSBS, Pacific, Japanese Airpower*, pp 35–40; Lt Cdr Takeda Shigeki, Interrogation No 354, Nov 4, 1945, *USSBS, Pacific.*

101. Natalie Grow, "Procurement of Aircrew Trainees," USAF Hist Study 15, p 9; Jerry White, "Combat Crews and Unit Training in the AAF, 1939–1945," USAF Hist Study 61 pp 29–36; Shigeki Interrogation, *USSBS, Pacific.*

## Chapter VIII

### Two Limited Wars
### Korea and Southeast Asia

1. Roy E. Appleman, *South to the Naktong, North to the Yalu*, [United States Army in the Korean War] (Washington, 1961), pp 8–12, 394; Rept, Principles for the Selection of Targets for Air Attack in Korea, Hq, Far East Air Forces, Aug 25, 1953, USAF Collection K720.323A.

2. James F. Schnabel and Robert J. Watson, *The Joint Chiefs of Staff and National Policy, The Korean War* [History of the Joint Chiefs of Staff], Vol III, Part I (hereafter: *JCS, The Korean War)*, (Washington, 1978), pp 41–42; Robert F. Futrell, *The United States Air Force in Korea, 1950–1953*, rev ed (Washington, 1983), p 17.

3. Diary, Maj Gen Earle E. Partridge, 1950–1951, entries for June 25–29, 1950, USAF Collection 168.7014–1; Schnabel and Watson, *JCS, The Korean War*, pp 115–122; P. LeR. Loomis, "Antiaircraft at Suwon," *Antiaircraft Journal*, Sept–Oct 1950, pp 2–5.

4. Hist, 5AF, July–December 1950, Vol III, pp 33–39, USAF Collection K730.01.

5. *Ibid;* Partridge Diary, July 1950; Hist, 5AF, Jan–June 1953, Vol VI, p 363.

6. Hist, 5AF, July–Dec 1950, Vol III, pp 33–39, 42; Ltr, Ivan J. Getting to John L. McLucas, 12 Mar 1974, AF/CHO.

7. Futrell, *USAF in Korea*, pp 98–101; Far East Air Forces Weekly Intelligence Roundup, 8–14 Oct 1950 (hereafter: FEAF Wkly Intel Rdp), USAF Collection K720.600; Partridge Diary, Oct 2, 1950.

8. Rept, Enemy Use of Camouflage in the Korean Campaign, HQ, 5AF Office of Tactical Air Research and Survey Special Rept No 32, Jan 22, 1951 (hereafter: Enemy Use of Camouflage in Korea), USAF Collection K730.01–25.

9. Partridge Diary, Oct 11, 1950; FEAF Wkly Intel Rdp 8–14 Oct 1950.

10. FEAF Wkly Intel Rdp, 8–14 Oct 1950; Partridge Diary, Oct 14, 1950; Diary, Lt Gen George E. Stratemeyer, entries for July 2–19, 25 Aug 1950, USAF Collection K168.7018.

11. Futrell, *USAF in Korea*, pp 239–246,

255, 277; Appleman, *South to the Naktong, North to the Yalu*, pp 770–776.

12. Futrell, *USAF in Korea*, pp 239–246, 255, 277; FEAF Wkly Intel Rdp, 8–14 Oct 1950; Partridge Diary, Oct 14, 1950.

13. Schnable and Watson, *JCS, The Korean War*, p. 555.

14. Remarks of General Bryce Poe II to author; FEAF Wkly Intel Rdp, No 69, 22–28 Dec 1951; Futrell, *USAF in Korea*, p 286; Intel Production Memo No 8; Rept, Soviet Activity in North Korea and Nearby Manchuria, HQ, 5AF, Nov 21, 1951, USAF Collection K730.600.

15. Schnabel and Watson, *JCS, The Korean War*, pp 452–455; HQ, USAF, Air Intelligence Production Memo No 8, Soviet Reaction to United Nations Air Attack on Chinese Communist Air Bases in Manchuria, May 2, 1951, USAF Collection K142.0303–8; Partridge Diary, Oct 8, 9, 12, 1950; Intv, Lt Gen Devol Brett with author, Feb 1985.

16. Schnabel and Watson, *JCS, The Korean War*, pp 454–455; Rept, Soviet Reaction to United Nations Air Attacks.

17. FEAF Wkly Intel Rdp., 29 April–5 May 1951; Futrell, *USAF in Korea*, pp 293–300.

18. Futrell, *USAF in Korea*, pp 278–279, 293–300, 301–306.

19. FEAF Wkly Intel Rdp, 22–28 Dec 1951; Soviet Activities in North Korea and Nearby Manchuria.

20. Hist, 5AF Jan–June 1951, Vol I, Appendix 3, Air Intelligence Estimate, June 19, 1951, pp 366–372.

21. FEAF Wkly Intel Rdp, 4–10 Nov 1951; Futrell, *USAF in Korea*, pp 307–310, 506–507.

22. *Ibid;* Remarks of General Bryce Poe.

23. *Ibid*.

24. Fifth Air Force Monthly Intelligence Summaries, Mar-July 1953, USAF Collection K720.607A.

25. *Ibid*.

26. FEAF Wkly Intel Rdp, 12–27 July 1953.

27. USAF Statistical Summary for 1953, p 56; HQ, 5AF Operations Analysis Memo No 64, A Study of Ground Fire Attrition in the Korean Theater, June 17, 1953.

28. Robert F. Futrell, *The Advisory Years to 1965* [The United States Air Force in Southeast Asia] (Washington, 1981), pp 3–40.

29. *Ibid*, pp 221–225; Guyman Penix and Paul T. Ringenbach, *Air Defense in Southeast Asia, 1945–1971*, Project CHECO Rept (Hickam AFB, Hawaii, 1973) p 31.

30. *Ibid;* Hist 7AF, Jan–June 1970, Status of Airfields in NVN, USAF Collection K740.01–25.

31. Rept, Southeast Asia Counter Air Alternatives (SEACAAL) HQ, Pacific Air Forces, Dec 31, 1966, USAF Collection K717.310-1; Penix and Ringenbach, *Air Defense in SEA*.

32. SEACAAL, pp I-1 – I-2, Appendix J.

33. SEACAAL, pp III-1 – III-7.

34. *Ibid;* Melvin F. Porter, *Linebacker: Overview of the First 120 Days*, Project CHECO Rept (Hickam AFB, Hawaii, 1973) pp 1–11; Melvin F. Porter, *Air Tactics Against NVN Air/Ground Defenses*, Project CHECO Rept (Hickam AFB, Hawaii, 1967) p 26; Washington *Post*, May 22, 1967, p 1.

35. *Ibid;* U. S. Grant Sharp, *Strategy for Defeat, Vietnam in Retrospect* (San Rafael, 1978), pp 202, 209.

36. SEACAAL, Appendix K.

37. *Ibid*, pp IV-1 to IV-7; "Expansion of NVN Radar Systems Continues," *Defense Intelligence Digest*, Vol 5, No 2, Feb 1967, p 32.

38. John C. Pratt, *Air Tactics Against NVN Air Ground Defenses, Dec 66-1 Nov 68*, Project CHECO Rept, (Hickam AFB, Hawaii, 1969) pp 1–10; Monte D. Wright, *USAF Tactics Against Air & Ground Defenses in SEA, Nov 68–May 70* Project CHECO Rept, (Hickam AFB, Hawaii, 1970); Rept, SA-2 Deployment and Tactics in North Vietnam, HQ, 7AF, June 23, 1966; Seventh Air Force Weekly Air Intelligence Summary (7AF WAIS), Dec 14, 1968, pp 5–8, USAF Collection K740.3072.

39. SEACAAL, *passim;* Rept, Anti-Aircraft Threat in SEA, Joint Anti-Aircraft Effectiveness Conference, 1–8 Nov 1966, USAF Collection K417.0372-11; Weapons System Evaluation Group Rept No 128 (WSEG 128), Apr 1968, Analysis of Combat Aircraft Losses in Southeast Asia, Part II, Vol I, Enclosure B, USAF Collection K160.804-116.

40. WSEG 128, Part II, Vol I, p 61; Bernard C. Nalty, *Tactics and Techniques of Electronic Warfare, Electronics Countermeasures in the Air War Against North Vietnam, 1965-1973*, [The Air Force in Southeast Asia] (Washington, 1977), pp 10–11; Institute for Defense Analyses, Selected Topics in Air Defense Suppression, IDA Study No S-369, p 19, USAF Collection K160.8041-369.

41. Red Baron III, Air-to-Air Encounters in Southeast Asia, Vol III: Analysis, pp 6–12, 94–97.

42. "Tactical Lessons of Vietnam," *Aviation Week and Space Technology*, May 21, 1973, p 7; Porter, *Linebacker: Overview of the First 120 Days*, pp 57–58.

43. SEACAAL, Appendix B; SEACAAL, Appendix L, pp I–1 to I–16; WSEG 128, Part I: Summary and Conclusions.

44. *Ibid;* Pacific Command (PACOM) Intelligence Digest, May 1970, pp 31–38.

45. Porter, *Air Tactics Against NVN Defenses, 1967*, pp 14–24.

46. Nalty, *Tactics and Techniques of Electronic Warfare*, pp 53–66; Sharp, *Strategy for Defeat*, pp 177–185, 202; Rept, Rolling Thunder-Linebacker, A Preliminary Comparative Analysis, July 1972, USAF Collection K168.06; US Air Force Tactical Fighter Weapons Center, Interim Rept No 7 (Project Red Baron), U. S. and Enemy Air-to-Air Tactics in SEA: Part II, July 1972, pp 50–51, USAF Collection K417.0735–1; IDA Study S–369, pp 7–11, 65.

47. *Ibid;* 7AF WAIS, Dec 14, 1968.

48. Hearings before the Armed Services Investigating Subcommittee of the Committee on Armed Services, House of Representatives, *Unauthorized Bombing of Military Targets in North Vietnam*, 92nd Cong, 2nd sess (Washington, 1972), *passim;* Hearings before the Committee on Armed Services, Senate, *Nomination of John D. Lavelle, General Creighton W. Abrams, and Admiral John S. McCain*, 92nd Cong, 2nd sess (Washington, 1972), *passim*.

49. *Ibid*.

50. *Ibid*.

51. Rolling Thunder–Linebacker Preliminary Comparative Analysis; Porter, *Linebacker: Overview of the First 120 Days*, pp 44–48, 62–63.

52. *Ibid;* Rolling Thunder–Linebacker, Preliminary Comparative Analysis.

53. *Ibid*.

54. HQ, PACAF, Summary, Air Operations Southeast Asia Apr 1972, pp 4–3 to 4–8, USAF Collection K717.306–1; Rept, Summary of Air Opertions in SEA, Center for Naval Analyses (Arlington, 1972), pp 4–1 to 4–13, USAF Collection K180.0481–6; John W. Seemann, *Combat Snap (AIM-9J Introduction to SEA)*, Project CHECO Rept (Hickam AFB, Hawaii, 1974) pp 29–31.

55. Calvin R. Johnson, *Linebacker Operations, September–December 1972*, Project CHECO Rept (Hickam AFB, Hawaii, 1978) p 21; Msg, CINCPACAF to 7AF (Gen Vogt), 112151Z Aug 72, subj: Linebacker Operations; Msg, 7AF/DO to CINCPACAF/DO, 060301 Aug 72, subj: Paveway System Delivery Techniques, in USAF Collection K744.312, and CHECO microfilm.

56. Porter, *Overview of the First 120 Days*, pp. 45–47, 67–69.

57. Johnson, *Linebacker Operations*, pp 9–11, 19.

58. Msg, CINCPAC to Adm Clarey, Gens Clay, Weyand, and Meyer, 260332Z Oct 72, subj: Air Operations Message Number Two; Msg, CINCPACFLT to CINCPAC, 291520Z Oct 72, subj: Taxi Road; Msg, CINCPACFLT to CINCPAC, 291852Z Oct 72, in K744.312.

59. Johnson, *Linebacker Operations*, p 55; McCarthy, James R., and Allison, George B. *Linebacker II: A View From The Rock*, [USAF Southeast Asia Monograph Series, vol VI: monograph 8] (Maxwell AFB, 1976), p 41; HQ, PACAF, Linebacker II Operations Rept, July 2, 1973, Lessons Learned Summary, Airfields, USAF Collection K186.06–232 and–233.

60. Msg, CINCPACAF/DO, Talbott, to 7AF/DO, Blesse, 230330Z Dec 72, subj: F–111 Operations, in K744.312; Msgs, 474 TFW to NMCC, 190455Z Dec 72, 200640Z Dec 72, 210530Z Dec 72, 220335Z Dec 72, 240320Z Dec 72, 270347Z Dec 72, and 7/13 AF to TAC/DO, 100850Z Jan 73, all in AFCHO; Oral History Intv, General John W. Vogt, Aug 8–9, 1978, USAF Collection K239.0512–1093, pp 86–99.

61. PACAF, Linebacker II Operations Rept, p 3–4, and Lessons Learned Summaries on Airfields and LORAN Strikes.

62. *Ibid;* PACAF, Air Operations Summary Southeast Asia, Jan 1973, pp 4–B–1 to 4–B–48; Vogt Intv, pp 86–89.

63. Vogt Intv, pp 90–92; McCarthy and Allison, *Linebacker II: A View From The Rock*, pp 97–98.

64. Linebacker II Operations Rept, pp 3–4; Lessons Learned Summaries on Airfields and LORAN Strikes.

65. Project Red Baron III, Vol III, Part I, pp 50–51.

## Chapter IX

### The Middle East: 1948–1973

1. Paul A. Jureidini, *et al, The Middle East, A Study of Conflict* (Washington, 1969), pp 23–36; Chaim Herzog, *The Arab-Israeli Wars* (New York, 1982), pp 11–21; A. L. Tibawi, "Jerusalem, Its Place in Islam and Arab History," in *The Arab-Israeli Confrontation of June 1967: An Arab Perspective*, ed by Ibrahim Abu-Lughod (Evanston, 1970), pp 10–48.

2. *Ibid.*

3. Intv, Brereton Greenhous with General Dan Tolkowski, Jan 13, 1984, p 2, AF/CHO.

4. Herzog, *Arab-Israeli Wars*, pp 106–108.

5. Tolkowski Intv, pp 2–6.

6. Alfred Goldberg, *Air Operations in the Sinai Campaign* (Washington, 1959), pp 5–8.

7. Ibrahim Abu-Lughod, "Israel's Arab Policy," *The Arab-Israeli Confrontation*, pp 73–75; Abba Eban, *An Autobiography* (New York, 1977), pp 204–205; Moshe Dayan, *Story of My Life* (New York, 1976), pp 184–199.

8. Eban, *Autobiography*, pp 204–205; Roy Fullick and Goeffrey Powell, *Suez: The Double War* (North Pomfret, Vt, 1979), pp 2–3; Tolkowski Intv, p 4; Dayan, *My Life*, p 272.

9. Dayan, *My Life*, p 195–199.

10. *Ibid;* Fullick and Powell, *Suez*, pp 109–122.

11. *Ibid;* Goldberg, *Suez Campaign*, pp 26–27.

12. Dayan, *My Life*, pp 216–217.

13. Edgar O'Ballance, *The Third Arab-Israeli War* (Hamden, 1972), pp 56, 90–96.

14. *Ibid.*

15. *Ibid*, pp 60–62.

16. *Ibid*, pp 50–52; Charles W. Yost, "The Arab-Israeli War, How It Began," *Foreign Affairs*, Jan 1968, pp 304–320; Hisham Sharabi, "Prelude to War: The Crisis of May-June 1967," *The Arab Israeli Confrontation*, pp 49–65; Ezer Weizman, Arab-Israeli War Briefing [to the U. S. Department of Defense], Washington, Sept 11–12, 1967, Sec. I, p 4, AF/CHO.

17. Weizman Briefing.

18. *Ibid;* Dayan, *My Life*, pp 361–368.

19. Dayan, *My Life*, pp 402–417; Memo, Meeting with Brig Gen Mordecai Hod, HQ USAF/XO, Jan 12, 1968, USAF Collection K239.0512-913.

20. Anwar el-Sadat, *In Search of Identity* (New York, 1977), pp 173–174.

21. Weizman Briefing, Sec. I, pp 19, 26, Sect II, pp 10, 15; USAF Hod Memo; "Mock Dogfights Sharpened Israeli Pilots," *Aviation Week and Space Technology*, July 3, 1967, p 24–27.

22. Weizman Briefing, Sect II, p 21.

23. Intv, Brereton Greenhous with General Mordecai Hod, Jan 16, 1984, pp 1–2; Weizman Briefing, Sect I, pp 19–24.

24. Weizman Briefing, Sect I, pp 27–28; Hod Intv, pp 2–3; Warren C. Wetmore, "Israel's Air Punch Major Factor in War," *Aviation Week and Space Technology*, July 3, 1967, p 20.

25. Hod Intv, pp 1–2; Dayan, *My Life*, pp 410–415.

26. *Ibid.*

27. USAF Hod Memo; Dayan, *My Life*, pp 416–420; Weizman Briefing, Sect I pp 18–24.

28. Wetmore, "Israel's Air Punch," p 19.

29. *Ibid;* Weizman Briefing, Sect I, pp 20–25, Sect II, p 11; Dayan, *My Life*, pp 416–422; O'Ballance, *Third Arab-Israeli War*, p 65; Intv, Brereton Greenhous with Col Yoash Tsiddon-Chatto, Jan 14, 1984, p 2.

30. Tsiddon-Chatto Intv; Wetmore, "Israel's Air Punch."

31. *Ibid.*

32. O'Ballance, *Third Arab-Israeli War*, pp 55, 63–68; Sadat, *Identity*, p 174.

33. Sadat, *Identity*, pp 173–180.

34. O'Ballance, *Third Arab-Israeli War*, pp 66–68; Weizman Briefing, Sect I, pp 20–25.

35. John W. R. Taylor, ed, *Jane's All The World's Aircraft, 1968–1969*, p 503; Robert R. Rodwell, "Three Hours—And Six Days," *Air Force*, Oct 1967, p 58; Hod Intv, pp 1–2.

36. Dayan, *My Life*, pp 418–427.

37. *Ibid;* "Mock Dogfights Sharpened Israeli Pilots," *Aviation Week*, July 3, 1967, pp 18–22; Wetmore, "Israeli's Air Punch," pp 24–27.

38. Weizman Briefing, Sect II, pp 13–22.

39. Ezer Weizman, *The Battle for Peace* (New York, 1981), p 52.

40. Sadat, *Identity*, pp 205–231; Mohamed Heikal, *The Road to Ramadan* (New York, 1975), pp 167–168.

41. Herzog, *Arab-Israeli Wars*, pp 195-197.

42. "Massive Resupply Narrows Israeli Margin in Air Power," *Aviation Week and Space Technology*, June 19, 1967, pp 16-19.

43. Weizman Briefing, Sect II, pp 5-6.

44. Richard F. Nyrop, *et al, Area Handbook for Egypt* (Washington, U.S. Dept of the Army, 1975), pp 362-363; Heikal, *Ramadan*, p 238.

45. Rept, SecDef to Congress, The Effectiveness of United States Military Aid to Israel, Dec 1974, p 14; Weizman Briefing, Sect II, p 22.

46. Rept, Weapons Systems Evaluation Group, Data from the October 1973 Middle East War, Vol IV: Structural Engineering (Aircraft Shelters) Report (WSEG Report 237), Jan 1975, pp 95-112, 226.

47. *Ibid;* Edward H. Kolcum, "Soviets Accelerating Mideast Drive," *Aviation Week and Space Technology*, May 18, 1970, pp 14-18.

48. WSEG Rept 237, Vol IV, pp 111-122.

49. *DIA Digest*, Jan 1970, p 2; "Airfield Attack: Lessons of the Mideast Wars," *Born in Battle: Defence Update*, Oct 1982, pp 38-42.

50. Herzog, *Arab-Israeli Wars*, pp 205-210; A. J. Barker, *Arab-Israeli Wars* (London, 1980), p 105.

51. Herzog, *Arab-Israeli Wars*, pp 212-217; SecDef Rept, Effectiveness of US Military Aid, pp 8-15.

52. Edward H. Kolcum, "Soviets Shifting Mideast Balance," *Aviation Week and Space Technology*, May 11, 1970, pp 18-21; Edward H. Kolcum, "Vietnam Lessons Helped Israel Build Mideast Air Superiority," *Aviation Week and Space Technology,* May 25, 1970, pp 18-21.

53. "Russians Fly Defense Missions for Egypt in Middle East Conflict," *Aviation Week and Space Technology,* May 25, 1970, May 4, 1970, p 27; "Soviets Deploy New Suez Defenses," *Aviation Week and Space Technology,* July 13, 1970, pp 14-16.

54. "New Missile Sites Threat to Israeli Air Supremacy," *Aviation Week and Space Technology*, Aug 24, 1970. p 20; Edward H. Kolcum, "SAM Changes Force New Strategy on Israelis," *Aviation Week and Space Technology*, Nov 16, 1970, pp 16-21.

55. Intv, Brereton Greenhous with General Binyamin Peled, Jan 13, 1984, AF/CHO.

56. Sadat, *Identity*, pp 225, 231-238; SecDef Rept, Effectiveness of US Military Aid; Insight team of the London Sunday Times, *Insight on the Middle East War* (London, 1974), pp 29-31; Hiam Bar-Lev, "Surprise and the Yom Kippur War," *Military Aspects of the Israeli-Arab Conflict*, ed by Louis Williams (Tel Aviv, 1975), pp 262-263.

57. Sadat, *Identity*, pp 232-240; Rept, Joint Chiefs of Staff, US Military Operational Survey Team Visit to the Israeli Defense Forces (IDF), Israel, Dec 1973, pp 2-17, USAF Collection K178.203-17.

58. *Ibid;* Janice Gross Stein, "'Intelligence' and 'Stupidity' Reconsidered: Estimation and Decision in Israel, 1973," *Journal of Strategic Studies*, Sept 1980, pp 147-167; Edgar O'Ballance, *No Victor, No Vanquished, The Yom Kippur War* (San Rafael, 1978), pp 19, 42-44, 284.

59. Rept, US Mil Visit to IDF, pp 20-21.

60. Dayan, *My Life*, pp 572-575; Rept, US Mil Visit to IDF, pp 1-20; Stein, "'Intelligence' and 'Stupidity' Reconsidered;" Janet G. Stein, "Military Deception, Strategic Surprise, and Conventional Deterrence: A Political Analysis of Egypt and Israel, 1971-73," *Journal of Strategic Studies*, March 1982. pp 94-118.

61. Sadat, *Identity*, p 249; "Airfield Attack," *Born in Battle*, pp 37-38; Rept, US Mil Visit to IDF, p 25.

62. Rept, US Army Combined Arms Center, Special Readiness Group, ACN 22216, Analysis of Combat Data—1973 Mideast War, Vol. IV, Appendix E, June 1974, p E-6; Peled Intv. Speaking ten years after the war, General Peled gave his views on the inadequacies of Israeli combat intelligence assessments in 1973 and on the misconceptions he thought his critics and other observers had formed of his policies. He contended that the IAF did not have access to air reconnaissance that would have made SAM suppression along the coast easier. Peled's remarks show signs that he was still exercised and somewhat defensive about these subjects in 1984. His remarks were clearly colored by his experiences, and some of his recollections are erroneous. He is nevertheless quite revealing of the way the IAF dealt with the Arab threat.

63. Peled Intv, pp 6-7, 14; Rept, US Army CAC, Special Readiness Group, Analysis of Combat Data—1973, Vol IV, p E-6; Matmon Information File, tables 13, 14, and 17, USAF Collection K178.203-18.

64. *Ibid.*

65. Rept, Naval Weapons Center, NWC TP 5885, The Yom Kippur War, Analysis of Weapon Implications, July 1976, pp 33-35.

66. Peled Intv, pp 3, 9–18.

67. NWC TP 5885, pp 91–92; WSEG Rept 237, Vol IV, Ch 3, *passim*.

68. U.S. Army, Combined Arms Center, ACN 22216, pp E–11 to E–13.

69. *Ibid*, pp E–11 to E–21.

70. *Ibid*.

71. *Ibid;* WSEG Rept 237, Vol IV, pp 152–153; NWC TP 5885, p 106.

72. Peled Intv; Herzog, *Arab-Israeli Wars*, pp 262–284, *passim*.

73. Herzog, *Arab-Israeli Wars*, pp 259–261.

74. Peled Intv; Herzog, *Arab-Israeli Wars*, pp 262–284, *passim*.

# Chapter X

## Conclusion

1. Air Corps Tactical School, Course AF–16–C, Antiaircraft Defense of an Air Base, Mar 8, 1940, Headquarters Air Forces Combat Command, Epling Papers, RG 18; Ltr, Clarification of the Term "Air Base," HQ, GHQ AF to Commandant, ACTS, Aug 5, 1939, USAF Collection 248.12615.

2. RAF Draft Narrative, *The Campaign in France and the Low Countries*, pp 105–113; MAAF reel no 31, Records of AA and CD Section.

3. U.S. Army Antiaircraft Artillery Command, Intelligence Memo No 35, July 6, 1943, USAF Collection 248.712–88.

4. War Dept, Rept, Command, Staff, and Administration of Antiaircraft Artillery Units, United States Forces, European Theater, May 1945, USAF Collection 502.101–37. *See also*: John T. Correll, "Air Defense from the Ground Up," *Air Force*, July 1983, pp 38–43.

5. Roger Fox, *Air Base Defense in the Republic of Vietnam, 1961–1973* (Washington, DC, 1979), pp 40–48.

# Bibliographic Note

Original sources used for these case studies came largely from the U.S. Air Force Historical Research Center's collection at Maxwell Air Force Base, Alabama, and the National Archives and Records Service in Washington, DC, and at the Office of Air Force History in Washington, which retains on microfilm much of the record collection in the repository at Maxwell AFB. The specific locations of the files cited are provided in the footnotes by reference to the major collection titles and their respective repositories. For files in collections at the U.S. National Archives and Records Administration (NARA), record group and file numbers are supplied; files located at the USAF Historical Research Center carry the designation "USAF Collection" with appropriate alpha-numerical cataloging data. British Public Record Office files show the designation "PRO." Where they are used the Inferential Retrieval Index System (IRIS) file designators are also cited.

Of surpassing interest among these materials are the records of the Mediterranean Allied Air Forces. The original papers of this command are held in the NARA collections at the Washington National Records Center, Suitland, Maryland. A microfilm made at the end of World War II is also at the USAF Historical Research Center, but is of uneven quality. A general index of subject files exists, but research requires diligent effort. A copy of the extensive report titled "Air Staff Post-Hostility Intelligence Requirements on the German Air Force," begun in 1944, is now held by AF/CHO. Not well indexed, it nevertheless contains many interviews, translations, and analytical statements not available elsewhere or scattered through other records collections.

Japanese sources derive from the U. S. Army's Japanese Monograph series, the interrogations conducted after World War II in conjunction with the United States Strategic Bombing Survey, and the records of the Allied Interpreter and Translator Section, Southwest Pacific Theater. In addition, General George C. Kenney kept an extensive and rather frank diary during the war. After Japan's surrender, he had most of the material typed, although some original handwritten pages remain. These documents, along with chronologically interspersed letters, reports, and memoranda are collected at AF/CHO as the Kenney Papers. Kenney used the material as the basis for his book, *General Kenney Reports,* which contains extensive comment by one of the leading American air commanders of the Pacific war and a man who was a close confidant of General of the Army Douglas MacArthur. When the diary was transcribed, Kenney frequently added notes containing postwar information developed by the USSBS teams, discovered in Japanese records, or gathered in his direct conversations with individual Japanese soldiers and airmen.

Records of the U.S. Marine Corps are available at the U.S. Marine Corps Historical Center in the Washington Navy Yard. Certain special studies, particularly those related to the Arab-Israeli Wars of 1967 and 1973 are from the Technical Library of the U.S. Air Force Assistant Chief of Staff, Studies and Analysis. Transcriptions of interviews conducted specifically for these case studies are retained in the author's files in AF/CHO; some restrictions still attach to their use.

The following are the principal secondary sources used in this work.

## Books

Abu-Lughod, Ibrahim, editor. *The Arab-Israeli Confrontation of June 1967: An Arab Perspective,* Evanston: Northwestern University Press, 1970.

Aders, Gebhard. *History of the German Night Fighter Force, 1917–1945.* London: Jane's, 1979.

Air Ministry, UK. *The Origins and Development of Operational Research in the Royal Air Force.* London: HMSO, 1963.

Alliluyeva, Svetlana. *Twenty Letters to a Friend,* translated by Priscilla Johnson McMillan, New York: Harper and Row, 1967.

Allison, David Kite. *New Eye for the Navy: The Origin of Radar at the Naval Research Laboratory.* Washington: Naval Research Laboratory, 1981.

Appleman, Roy E. *South to the Naktong, North to the Yalu* [United States Army in the Korean War], Washington: Office of the Chief of Military History, 1961.

Ashmore, Edward B. *Air Defense,* London: Longmans, Green and Co., 1929.

Attard, Joseph. *The Battle of Malta,* London: William Kimber, 1980.

Attiwill, Kenneth. *Fortress, The Story of the Siege and Fall of Singapore,* Garden City: Doubleday and Co., 1960.

Badri, Hassan al-, Taka-el Magloub, and Mohammed Dia el-din Zahdy. *The Ramadan War, 1973,* Dunn Loring, Va.: T.N. Dupuy Associates, 1978.

Barker, A. J. *Arab-Israeli Wars,* Shepperton: Ian Allen, Ltd., 1980.

Barnett, Corelli. *The Desert Generals,* New York: Berkley Publishing Co., 1960.

Bekker, Cajus. *The Luftwaffe War Diaries,* edited and tralsated by Frank Ziegler, Garden City: Doubleday and Co., 1968.

Bennett, Ralph. *Ultra in the West: The Normandy Campaign, 1944–45.* New York: Charles Scribner's Sons, 1980.

Benoist-Mechin, Jacques. *Sixty Days that Shook the West, The Fall of France: 1940.* New York: G. P. Putnam's Sons, 1963.

Bidwell, Shelford, and Dominick Grahame. *Fire-Power: British Army Weapons and Theories of War, 1904–1945,* London: George Allen and Unwin, 1982.

Boyd, Alexander. *The Soviet Air Force Since 1918,* New York: Stein and Day, 1977.

Bullock, Alan. *Hitler, A Study in Tyranny,* Torchbook edition, London: Harper and Row, 1964.

Bushby, John. *Air Defence of Great Britain,* London: Ian Allen, 1973.

Carrell, Paul, *pseud.* [Paul K. Schmidt]. *Hitler Moves East 1941–1943,* New York: Bantam Books, 1966.

Chamberlain, Peter, and John Milsom. *Self-Propelled Anti-Tank and Anti-Aircraft Guns,* New York: Arco Publishing Co., 1975.

Charleton, L. E. O. *Britain at War, The Royal Air Force,* London: Hutchinson and Co., Ltd., 1941–1945. 5 volumes.

Chennault, Claire Lee. *Way of a Fighter,* edited by Robert Hotz, New York: G. P. Putnam's Sons, 1949.

_____ . The Role of Defensive Pursuit, privately published, 1933.

Churchill, Winston S. *The Second World War,* New York: Houghton Mifflin Co., Bantam edition, 1961, 6 volumes.

Clark, Ronald W. *Tizard,* Cambridge: The M.I.T. Press, 1965.

Clausewitz, Carl von. *On War,* edited and translated by Michael Howard and Peter Paret, Princeton: Princeton University Press, 1976.

*Coast Artillery, A Complete Manual of Technique and Material,* Harrisburg: Military Service Publishing Co., 1941.

Collier, Basil. *The Defence of the United Kingdom.* London: HMSO, 1957.

Collier, Richard. *Eagle Day, The Battle of Britain, August 6 – September 15 1940,* New York: E. P. Dutton and Co., 1966.

Conquest, Robert. *The Great Terror, Stalin's Purge of the Thirties,* New York: Macmillan Co., 1970.

Craven, Wesley Frank, and James Lea Cate, editors. *The Army Air Forces in World War II,* Chicago: University of Chicago Press, 1948–1958. 7 volumes.

Cynk, Jerzy B. *History of the Polish Air Force, 1918–1968,* Reading: Osprey Publishing, 1972.

_____ . *Polish Aircraft, 1893–1939,* London: Putnam and Co., 1971.

Dayan, Moshe. *Story of My Life,* London: Weidenfeld and Nicolson, 1976.

Deane, John R. *The Strange Alliance,* New York: Viking Press, 1957.

Detweiler, Donald S., and Charles B. Burdick, editors. *War in Asia and the Pacific, 1937–1945,* New York: Garland Publishing Co., 1980, 15 volumes.

Detweiler, Donald S., Charles B. Burdick, and Jürgen Rohwer, editors. *World War II German Military Studies,* New York: Garland Publishing, 1979, 24 volumes.

Dixon, Norman F. *On the Psychology of Military Incompetence,* New York: Basic Books, Inc., 1976.

Eban, Abba. *An Autobiography,* New York: Random House, 1977.

Ellis, Lionel F. *The War in France and Flanders, 1939–1940,* London: HMSO, 1953.

Embry, Basil. *Mission Completed,* New York: Frederick A. Praeger, Inc., 1958.

Erickson, John. *The Road to Berlin,* Boulder: Westview Press, 1983.

Falk, Stanley. *Seventy Days to Singapore,* New York: G. P. Putnam's Sons, 1975.

Feldt, Eric A. *The Coastwatchers,* New York: Oxford University Press, 1946.

Fetzer, Leland, editor. *The Soviet Air Force in World War II, The Official History, Originally Published by the Ministry of Defense of the USSR,* translated by Ray Wagner, Garden City: Doubleday and Co., 1973.

Fredette, Raymond H. *The Sky on Fire, The First Battle of Britain, 1917–1918, and the Birth of the Royal Air Force.* New York: Holt, Rinehart and Winston, 1966.

Fullick, Roy, and Geoffrey Powell. *Suez, the Double War,* North Pomfret, Vt.: Hamish Hamilton, 1979.

Futrell, Robert F. *The United States Air Force in Korea, 1950–1953,* revised edition, Washington: Office of Air Force History, 1983.

Futrell, Robert F. *Ideas, Concepts, Doctrine: A History of Basic Thinking in the United States Air Force, 1907–1964,* Maxwell Air Force Base: Air University, 1971.

Greenfield, Kent Roberts. *American Strategy in World War II: A Reconsideration,* Westport, Ct.: Greenwood Press, 1963.

Gouré, Leon, and Herbert S. Dinerstein. *Political Vulnerability of Moscow: A Case Study of the October 1941 Attack.* Santa Monica: Rand Corporation, 1952.

Gunsburg, Jeffrey A. *Divided and Conquered, The French High Command and the Defeat of the West, 1940,* London: Greenwood Press, 1979.

Gunston, Bill. *The Encyclopedia of the World's Combat Aircraft,* New York: Chartwell Books, Inc., 1976.

Halsey, William F. *Admiral Halsey's Story,* New York: McGraw-Hill Book Co., 1947.

Hardesty, Von. *Red Phoenix, The Rise of Soviet Air Power, 1941–1945,* Washington: Smithsonian Institution Press, 1982.

Hartcup, Guy. *Camouflage, A History of Concealment and Deception in War,* New York: Charles Scribner's Sons, 1980.

Heikal, Mohamed. *The Road to Ramadan,* New York: New York Times Book Co., 1975.

Herzog, Chaim. *The Arab-Israeli Wars,* New York: Random House, 1982.

Historical Research and Evaluation Organization. *The Development of Soviet Air Defense Doctrine and Research,* Dunn Loring, Va, 1981.

Hinsley, F. H., E. E. Thomas, C. F. G. Ransom, and R. C. Knight, *British Intelligence in the Second World War,* New York: Cambridge University Press, 1979–1984, 3 volumes.

Hogg, Ian V. *Anti-Aircraft, A History of Air Defense,* London: MacDonald and Jane's, 1978.

Horne, Alistair. *To Lose a Battle, France 1940,* Boston: Little, Brown and Company, 1966.

Hough, Frank O., Verle E. Ludwig, and Henry I. Shaw, Jr. *Pearl Harbor to Guadalcanal* [History of U.S. Marine Corps Operations in World War II]. Washington: Historical Branch, U.S. Marine Corps, 1958.

Howe, George F. *Northwest Africa: Seizing the Initiative in the West* [U.S. Army in World War II] Washington: Office of the Chief of Military History, 1957.

Hurley, Alfred F. *Billy Mitchell, Crusader for Air Power*, New York: Franklin Watts, Inc., 1964.

Infield, Glenn B. *The Poltava Affair. A Russian Warning: An American Tragedy,* New York: Macmillan Publishing Co., 1973.

*Insight on the Middle East War.* London: The Sunday Times, 1974.

Jackson, A. J. *Avro Aircraft Since 1908.* London: Putnam and Co., 1965.

Jackson, Robert. *Air War Over France, May–June 1940,* London: Ian Allen, Ltd., 1974.

*Jane's All The World's Aircraft,* London: Jane's Publishing Co., Ltd., 1930 —.

Jones, H. A., and Walter Raleigh. *The War in the Air,* Oxford: The Clarendon Press, 1922–1934. 6 volumes.

Jureidini, Paul A., Alice A. Adanalian, Willian E. Hazen, William C. Key, Ursula Paolozzi, and Sanford R. Silverburg. *The Middle East: A Study of Conflict,* Washington: Center for Research in Social Problems,1969.

Kahn, David. *The Codebreakers, The Story of Secret Writing,* New York: The Macmillan Co., 1967.

Kennan, George F. *Russia and the West Under Lenin and Stalin,* Boston: Little, Brown and Co., 1961.

——————— . *Soviet-American Relations, 1917–1920,* Princeton: Princeton University Press, 1956. 2 volumes.

Kenney, George C. *General Kenney Reports,* New York: Duell, Sloan and Pearce, 1949.

Kesselring, Albert. *Kesselring: A Soldier's Record,* New York: William Morrow and Co., 1954.

Killen, John. *A History of the Luftwaffe,* New York: Doubleday and Co., 1968.

Kilmarx, Robert A. *A History of Soviet Air Power,* New York: Frederick A. Praeger, 1962.

Kirby, S. Woodburn, C. T. Addis, J. F. Miekeljohn, G. T. Wards, and N. L. Desoer. *The War Against Japan,* London: HMSO, 1957.

Kirkpatrick, Charles Edward, *Archie in the A. E. F., The Creation of the Antiaircraft Service of the United States Army, 1917–1918,* Fort Bliss, Texas: U. S. Army Air Defense Artillery School, 1984.

Kohn, Richard H., and Patrick J. Harahan, editors. *Air Superiority in World War II and Korea,* Washington, DC: Office of Air Force History, 1983.

Kozhevnikov, M. N. *The Command and Staff of the Soviet Army Air Force in the Great Patriotic War 1941–1945* [Soviet Military Thought], Washington, D.C.: United States Air Force, 1977.

Knorr, Klaus, and Patrick Morgan, editors. *Strategic Military Surprise, Incentives and Opportunities.* New Brunswick, N.J.: Transaction Books, 1983.

Leasor, James. *Singapore, The Battle That Changed the World,* Garden City: Doubleday and Co., 1968.

Leighton, Richard M., and Robert W. Coakley. *Global Logistics and Strategy 1940–1943* [United States Army in World War II], Washington, D.C.: Office of the Chief of Military History, 1955.

Lloyd, Hugh P. *Briefed to Attack, Malta's Part in African Victory,* London: Hodder and Stoughton, 1949.

MacArthur, Douglas. *Reminiscences,* New York: McGraw-Hill Book Co., 1964.

Manchester, William. *The Arms of Krupp, 1587–1968,* Boston: Little, Brown and Co., 1968.

Manstein, Erich von. *Lost Victories,* translated and edited by Anthony G. Powell, Chicago: Henry Regnery and Co., 1958.

Maurer, Maurer, editor. *The U.S. Air Service in World War I*, Washington, DC: Office of Air Force History, 1978.

McCudden, James T. B. *Flying Fury, Five Years in the Royal Flying Corps,* Garden City: Doubleday, 1968.

Medvedev, Roy A. *Let History Judge, The Origins and Consequences of Stalinism,* translated by Colleen Taylor, New York: Alfred A. Knopf, 1971.

Miller, John Jr. *Cartwheel: The Reduction of Rabaul* [The United States Army in World War II], Washington: Office of the Chief of Military History, 1959.

_____ . *Guadalcanal: The First Offensive* [The United States Army in World War II], Washington: Office of the Chief of Military History, 1949.

Miller, Thomas G., Jr. *The Cactus Air Force,* New York: Harper and Row, 1969.

Milner, Samuel. *Victory in Papua* [The United States Army in World War II], Washington: Office of the Chief of Military History, 1957.

Morison, Samuel Eliot. *The Struggle for Guadalcanal, August 1942–February 1943* [History of United States Naval Operations in World War II], Boston: Little, Brown and Company, 1950.

Morton, Louis. *Strategy and Command: The First Two Years* [The U.S. Army in World War II], Washington: Office of the Chief of Military History, 1962.

Murray, Williamson. *Strategy for Defeat: The Luftwaffe 1933–1945,* Maxwell AFB: Air University, 1983.

O'Ballance, Edgar. *No Victor, No Vanquished,* San Rafael: Presidio Press, 1978.

_____ . *The Third Arab-Israeli War,* Hamden, Ct.: Archon Books, 1972.

Pile, Frederick. *Ack-Ack, Britain's Defence Against Air Attack During the Second World War,* London: George G. Harrap and Co., 1949.

Playfair, Ian S. O., F. C. Flynn, C. J. C. Molony, S. E. Toomer, and T. P. Gleave. *The Mediterranean and Middle East* [History of the Second World War], London: HMSO, 1954–1960. 4 volumes.

Polish Air Force Association. *Destiny Can Wait, The Polish Air Force in the Second World War,* London: William Heineman, Ltd., 1949.

Price, Alfred. *Battle of Britain: The Hardest Day,* New York: Charles Scribner's Sons, 1980.

_____ . *Luftwaffe Handbook, 1939–1945,* New York: Charles Scribner's Sons, 1977.

Quester, George H. *Deterrence before Hiroshima: The Airpower Background of Modern Strategy,* New York: John Wiley and Sons, 1966.

Richards, Denis, and Hilary St. George Saunders. *Royal Air Force 1939–1945,* London: HMSO, 1953.

Rommel, Erwin, *The Rommel Papers,* edited by B. H. Liddel Hart, trans. Paul Findlay, New York, Harcourt Brace and Co., 1953.

Roskill, S. W., editor. *Documents Relating to the Naval Air Service, 1908–1918,* London: Navy Records Society, 1969.

Rudel, Hans Ulrich. *Stuka Pilot,* translated by Lynton Hudson, Dublin: Euphorion Books, 1952.

Sadat, Anwar el-. *In Search of Identity,* New York: Harper and Row, 1978.

Safford, Edward L. *Modern Radar: Theory, Operation and Maintenance,* Blue Ridge Summit, Pa.: TAB Books, 1971.

Sakai, Saburo, with Martin Caidin and Fred Saito. *Samurai,* New York: Ballantine Books, 1957.

Scott, Harriet Fast, and William F. Scott, editors. *The Soviet Art of War: Doctrine, Strategy, and Tactics,* Boulder: Westview Press, 1982.

Sharp, U. S. Grant. *Strategy For Defeat, Vietnam in Retrospect.* London: Presidio Press, 1968.

Sherrod, Robert. *History of Marine Corps Aviation in World War II,* Washington: Combat Forces Press, 1952,

Sherman, William C. *Air Warfare,* New York: The Ronald Press Co., 1926.

Shiner, John F. *Foulois and the U.S. Army Air Corps 1931–1935,* Washington, D.C.: Office of Air Force History, 1983.

Shores, Christopher, and Hans Ring. *Fighters Over the Desert, The Air Battles in the Western Desert, June 1940 – December 1942,* New York: Arco Publishing Co., 1969.

Sidorenko, A. A. *The Offensive (A Soviet View)* [Soviet Military Thought], Washington: U.S. Air Force, 1970.

Simpson, Albert F., editor. *The World War I Diary of Col. Frank P. Lahm, Air Service, AEF,* Maxwell AFB: Air University, 1970.

Solzhenitsyn, Aleksandr I. *The Gulag Archipelago 1918–1956, An Experiment in Literary Investigation,* translated by Thomas P. Whitney, New York: Harper and Row, 1973.

Speer, Albert. *Inside the Third Reich,* translated by Richard and Clara Winston, New York: The Macmillan Co., 1970.

Sutton, Harry Thomas. *Raiders Approach! The Fighting Tradition of Royal Air Force Station Hornchurch and Sutton's Farm,* Aldershot: Gale and Polden, 1956.

Swanborough, Gordon, and Peter M. Bowers. *United States Navy Aircraft Since 1911,* 2nd edition, Annapolis: Naval Institute Press, 1976.

Tedder, The Lord [Arthur William]. *Air Power and War.* London: Hodder and Stoughton, 1948.

——————— . *With Prejudice, The War Memoirs of The Marshal of the Royal Air Force,* Boston: Little, Brown and Co., 1966.

Thorne, Christopher. *The Limits of Foreign Policy, The West, The League and the Far East Crisis of 1931–1933,* New York: G. P. Putnam's Sons, 1973.

Tolstoy, Nikolai. *Stalin's Secret War,* New York: Holt, Rinehart and Winston, 1982.

Townsend, Peter. *Duel of Eagles,* New York: Simon and Schuster, 1970.

Tsuji, Masanobu. *Singapore, The Japanese Version,* translated by Margaret E. Lake, Sidney: Ure Smith, 1960.

Tuchman, Barbara. *Stillwell and the American Experience in China,* New York: Macmillan Co., 1970.

Tucker, Robert C. *The Soviet Political Mind, Stalinism and Post-Stalinist Change,* revised edition, New York: W. W. Norton and Company, 1972.

Updegraph, Charles L. *Special Marine Corps Units of World War II,* Washington: History and Museums Division, Hq. USMC, 1972.

Historical Division, Dept. of the Army. *United States Army in World War I, 1917–1919,* Washington: Government Printing Office, 1948.

Office of the Chief Engineer, GHQ, Army Force, Pacific. *Airfield and Base Development,* Tokyo, 1951.

Wales, Nym, *pseud.* [Helen Foster Snow] and Kim San. *Song of Ariran, A Korean Communist in the Chinese Revolution,* San Francisco: Ramparts Press, 1972.

Wallace, Graham. *R.A.F. Biggin Hill,* London: Putnam and Co., 1957.

Webster, Charles, and Noble Frankland. *The Strategic Air Offensive Against Germany, 1939–1945,* London: Her Majesty's Stationary Office, 1961. 4 volumes.

Weizman, Ezer. *The Battle for Peace,* Toronto: Bantam Books, 1981.

Williams, Louis, editor. *Military Aspects of the Israeli-Arab Conflict,* Tel Aviv: University Publishing Projects, 1975.

Wilkenson, Erik A. *Dive Bombing,* Stockholm: AB Selig and Co., 1947.

Winterbotham, F. W. *The Ultra Secret,* New York: Harper and Row, 1974.

Wood, Derek, and Derek Dempster. *The Narrow Margin, the Battle of Britain and the Rise of Air Power,* New York: McGraw-Hill Book Co., 1961.

Woodbury, David O. *Builders for Battle, How the Pacific Naval Bases were Constructed,* New York: E.P. Dutton, Inc., 1946.

Wuest, William J. *History of Heavy AA and Fire Control,* Fort Bliss: The Air Defense Artillery School, 1951.

## Articles

Boog, Horst H. "The *Luftwaffe* and Technology," *Aerospace Historian* 30, (September 1983): 200–206.

—————— . "Higher Command and Leadership in the German Luftwaffe, 1939–1945," in *Air Power and Warfare,* Proceedings of the Eight Military History Symposium, USAF Academy, 1978, Washington: Office of Air Force History, 1979, pp 128–158.

Cairns, John C. "Great Britain and the Fall of France: A Study in Allied Disunity," *The Journal of Modern History* XXVII (December 1955): 365–408.

Cooper, Malcolm. "The Development of Air Policy and Doctrine on the Western Front, 1914–1918," *Aerospace Historian* 28 (Spring 1981): 39–51

Dobbie, William G. S. "The Siege of Malta." *Royal Engineers Journal* (Jan–Mar 1943): 1–8.

Emme, Eugene M. "The American Dimension," *Air Power and Warfare,* pp.56–82.

Erickson, John. "Radio-location and the Air defence problem: The design and development of Soviet radar, 1934–40," *Science Studies* 2 (1972): 241–263.

—————— . "The Soviet Response to Surprise Attack: Three Directives, 22 June 1941," *Soviet Studies* 23 (April 1972): 519–553

Graeme, Ian. "Singapore, 1939–1942," *Journal of the Royal Artillery* CIII (March 1976): 20–26.

Greenwood, John T. "The Great Patriotic War, 1941–1945," *Soviet Aviation and Air Power,* edited by Robin Higham and Jacob Kipp, Boulder: Westview Press, 1978, pp 69–136.

Griffin, David E. "The Role of the French Air Force, The Battle of France, 1940," *Aerospace Historian* 21 (Fall 1974): 144–153.

Gropman, Alan L. "The Battle of Britain and the Principles of War," *Aerospace Historian* 18 (Fall 1971): 138–144.

Kirkland, Faris R. "The French Air Force in 1940," *Air University Review,* vol XXXVI, no 6 (Sept–Oct 1985): 101–118.

Mets, David R. "Dive-Bombing Between the Wars," *Airpower Historian* (July 1965): 85–89.

—————— . "The Origins of Soviet Air Theory and Doctrine," *Military Review* (August 1975): 36–48.

Murray, Williamson. "The Luftwaffe Against Poland and the West." Draft study for the Office of Air Force History, Washington, D.C., 1985.

Peszke, Michael A. "The Operational Doctrine of the Polish Air Force in World War II. A Thirty Year Perspective," *Aerospace Historian* 23 (Fall 1976): 140–147.

—————— . "Poland's Preparation for World War Two," *Military Affairs* (February 1979): 18–24.

—————— . "Pre-War Polish Air Force: Budget, Personnel Policies, and Doctrine," *Aerospace Historian* 28 (Fall 1981): 186–189.

Stein, Janice Gross. " 'Intelligence' and Stupidity' Reconsidered: Estimation and Decision in Israel, 1973," in *Journal of Strategic Studies,* Sept 1980: 147–177.

—————— . "Military Deception, A Political Analysis of Egypt and Israel, 1971–1973," *Journal of Strategic Studies,* March 1982: 94–118.

Sturm, Thomas A. "Henry Conger Pratt: First Air Corps Permanent General Officer," *Aerospace Historian* 22 (June, 1975): 70–82.

Weldon, H. E. C. "The Artillery Defence of Malta," *Journal of the Royal Artillery* LXXIX (January 1952): 15–27.

# Index

Advanced Air Striking Force, RAF: 70–71, 76, 347
Aerodrome Command, *Luftwaffe*: 192
*Aeronautique Militaire*: 3
African campaigns: 110, 130, 132, 137–76
Air base defense. *See also* Aircraft use in air base defense; Base Defense Battalions
    air defense areas: 167–69
    Allied failure to consider before TORCH: 163
    American: 17–19, 221, 231–34, 242–43, 246–48
    American planning for: 15, 19–20, 27, 48, 346
    British: 43, 82–83, 85, 88–91, 174
    British in Malaya: 95, 97, 100–1, 106–10
    Chinese-North Korean: 272, 277
    dedicated units: 89, 137, 143–44, 165–67
    Dutch: 67–68
    Egyptian: 315, 330, 339
    German: 34, 156, 159, 169–70, 175
    German, in Russia: 181, 189, 192–93, 195, 198–99, 202, 214–15
    German, in World War I: 6–7, 21
    inherent resilience of bases: 344
    Israeli: 317, 323, 327
    Japanese: 38, 101, 106, 108, 235, 249, 251–52, 254–56, 260
    *Luftwaffe* responsibilities in: 33–34, 36, 48, 189
    at Malta: 123, 125, 127–28, 131, 133–35, 344
    North Vietnamese: 285, 287, 294–95
    Polish: 57–59
    Soviet: 42, 187–88, 205–6, 213–14
    Syrian: 330, 339
    in World War II: 343–344, 346

Air Bases immune from attack. *See* Sanctuaries
Air Base Construction Board (USN): 27
Airfields, Soviet
    in World War II: 201, 214
    construction of: 185
    dispersal: 185
Air Component, BEF (RAF): 70–71
Air Corps, U.S. Army (AAC): 25, 31, 82
Air Corps Tactical School (ACTS), AAC: 24–28
Aircraft destroyed on the ground
    Allied, in SWPA: 248–49
    Allied and American, in France: 11–12, 17–18
    American, in Russia: 208
    Belgian: 69, 76
    British, in Britain: 88–90
    British, in Egypt: 144
    British, in Malaya: 101, 109
    British and French, in France: 71, 75–76
    Egyptian: 302, 306, 316, 319, 334, 341, 350
    German, by the Dutch: 67
    German, in France: 11–13, 18
    German, in Russia: 198, 201
    German, in Sicily: 124
    German-Italian, in North Africa: 144, 150–51, 169–70, 175
    Israeli: 316
    Japanese: 108, 110, 219, 234–35, 249, 252–53, 256–57
    Jordanian and Iraqi: 317, 319, 341
    North Vietnamese: 288, 291
    Polish: 54
    Soviet: 177, 179–81, 183, 189
    Syrian: 317, 319, 334, 341
Aircraft types
    A–1 fighter, Douglas Skyraider: 279

A–4 attack bomber (USN), Douglas
Skyhawk: 322

A–7 jet fighter (USN),
Ling-Temco-Vought Corsair II: 294

A–20 fighter, Douglas Havoc: 244,
255–56

A–24 dive bomber, Douglas Dauntless:
244

A–29 bomber, Lockheed: 108

Albatros D fighter: 11

B–10 bomber, Martin: 108–9

B–17 bomber, Boeing Flying Fortress:
97, 204, 206, 208, 219–20, 234

B–24 bomber, Consolidated Liberator:
150, 204, 255

B–25 bomber, North American
Mitchell: 244, 255

B–26 bomber, Martin Marauder:
235–236, 271

B–29 bomber, Boeing Superfortress:
271–73

B–52 jet bomber, Boeing Stratofortress:
287, 293–95

B–339 fighter-bomber, Brewster: 107–8

Battle light bomber (Fairey): 70–71, 76

Beaufighter fighter (Bristol): 129–30

Betty medium bomber (Mitsubishi
G4M): 221–22

Blenheim bomber (Bristol): 70–71, 76,
101, 107–8, 123–24, 147

Blenheim fighter (Bristol): 47

Buffalo fighter-bomber (Brewster):
107–8

C–47 transport, Douglas Skytrain: 208

Defiant fighter (Boulton Paul): 47

Dewoitine 520 fighter: 66, 76

Dornier 17 medium bomber: 59, 71,
75, 77, 181

Dornier 17Z/215 bomber: 77, 88, 90

F2A fighter-bomber, Brewster. *See*
Buffalo

F–4 jet fighter-bomber, McDonnell
Phantom II: 287, 293–95, 322–23,
327, 330, 334

F4F–4 fighter, Grumman Wildcat:
221–22, 229, 231

F–51 fighter-bomber, North American
Mustang: 302

F–84F jet fighter-bomber, Republic
Thunderstreak: 306

F–86 jet fighter, North American
Sabre: 272–73

F–102 jet fighter, Convair Delta
Dagger: 279

F–105 jet fighter-bomber, Republic
Thunderchief: 280

F–111 jet fighter-bomber, General
Dynamics: 294–95, 297

Flying boats (RN): 112

Focke-Wulf FW–190 fighter: 167

Fokker G1-A fighter: 67

Fouga Magister trainers: 307

Fulmar fighter (RN) (Fairey): 124

Halberstadt fighter: 11

Heinkel 111 medium bomber: 77, 88,
197

Hudson III bomber (Lockheed): 108

Hunter jet fighter (Hawker): 307, 317

Hurricane fighter (Hawker): 45, 47, 70,
77, 82–85, 89, 92, 108–10, 112,
123–25, 129, 141, 144, 151, 153,
343

IL–2 bomber, Ilyushin Sturmovik: 184,
198, 201

IL–10 bomber: 269

IL–28 jet bomber: 301, 306–7, 323

IL–14 transport: 301, 306

Junkers 52 transport: 67, 70, 132, 173,
197–98

Junkers 86 transport: 197

Junkers 87 Stuka fighter-bomber: 55,
77, 130, 171, 181

Junkers 88 bomber: 77, 88, 123, 130,
181, 211

La–5 fighter, Lavochkin: 134

LaGG–3 fighter, Lavochkin-
Gurbunov-Gudkov: 184

LaGG–5 fighter-bomber: 180

Martinsyde G100/G102 fighter-bomber:
11–12

Maryland reconnaissance bomber
(Martin): 112

Messerschmitt 109 fighter: 55, 66–67,
77, 88, 123, 195, 343

Messerschmitt 110 fighter: 62, 77, 88,
155

Messerschmitt 323 transport: 173

Messerschmitts: 90

MiG–1 fighter (Mikoyan-Gurevich): 184

MiG–3 fighter: 180

MiG–15 jet fighter: 270–73, 275, 277,
289, 291, 301

MiG–17 jet fighter: 289, 291, 301, 307,
327

MiG–19 jet fighter: 307

MiG–21 jet fighter: 289, 291, 307, 315,
320, 327, 334

MiGs: 279–80, 285, 288, 291, 293, 295,
297, 309, 311, 315

Mirage jet fighter (Dassault): 307, 330

Moraine-Saulnier 406 fighter: 66

Mystére B2 jet fighter (Dassault): 307

Nate fighter (Nakajima Ki27): 107

Noratlas transport: 316
Ouragon fighter: 307
P–38 fighter-bomber, Lockheed
    Lightning: 241
P–39 fighter-bomber, Bell Airacobra:
    220–21, 234, 241
P–40 fighter, Curtiss Tomahawk: 150,
    160, 173, 239, 241. *See also* P–400
P–47 fighter, Republic Thunderbolt:
    255
P–51 fighter, North American Mustang:
    206–7
P–400 fighter-bomber, Bell Airacobra:
    221
PO–2 trainer, Polikarpov: 274
PZL 11 (P11) fighter: 55, 62
Sea Gladiator fighter (RN) (Gloster):
    112
Spitfire fighter (Supermarine): 45, 47,
    77, 82, 84–85, 88–89, 92, 110,
    129–33, 343
SU–7 jet fighter, Sukhoi: 327
SU–20 jet fighter: 324
TU–2 medium bomber, Tupolev: 273–74
TU–16 jet bomber: 307, 334
Vautour SO4050 jet fighter-bomber
    (Sud Aviation): 307
Wellington bomber (Vickers-
    Armstrong): 123–24, 140
Yak–1 fighter, Yakovlev: 184
Yak–3 fighter: 180
Yak–9 fighter: 206
Yaks: 267
Zeppelins: 6–7
Zero/Zeke fighter-bomber (Mitsubishi
    A6M2 Reisen): 39, 107, 221–22
Aircraft use in air base defense *See also*
    Royal Air Force units
    Allied commanders' views on: 163–64
    by Americans: 25, 27, 31–32, 162–63,
        229–34, 243, 247–48
    by British: 43–44, 48, 144, 147, 163
    by Egyptians: 311, 313, 315, 330
    by Germans: 155, 202
    by Germans and Italians in North
        Africa: 170
    by Japanese: 256
    at Malta: 123, 125, 131–32, 135
    by North Vietnamese: 291
    by Soviets: 188, 211
Aircraft Warning battalions, U.S. Army
    Signal Corps: 161–62, 242, 247
Air Defense Command (ADC), U.S. Army:
    29
Air Defense Command (EAF/Egyptian
    Army): 320
Air Headquarters Far East (British): 96, 107

Air Service, U.S. Army: 15–21, 24
Air Staff, USAF: 272
Air Technical Academy (German): 92
Alexander, Harold: 150
Air warning deficiencies
    U. S. in New Guinea: 242
    U. S. in North Africa: 174, 348
Algeria: 159–62, 165–67, 169, 174
Alksnis, Yakov Ivanovich: 40
Allied Air Forces, Southwest Pacific Area
    (SWPA): 219, 239, 242–43, 245,
    247, 261
Allied Force Headquarters (AFHQ),
    Northwest Africa: 161, 163,
    167–68
Allied 18th Army Group: 163
Amer, Abdel Hakim: 315–16
American Expeditionary Force (AEF): 4,
    13–16
American Legion: 29
Antiaircraft Command, British Army: 82–83
Antiaircraft Command, U.S. Army: 348
Antiaircraft units. *See* British Army units;
    Canadian Army; Japanese units;
    *Luftwaffe* units; United States
    Army units
Antiaircraft weapons. *See* Cannon/guns,
    antiaircraft; Machine guns;
    Missiles; Rifle fire
Antiradiation weapons: 288–89, 330–31,
    334. *See also* Missiles
Antrup, Wilhelm: 207–8, 211, 214
Area defense: 10, 12, 24, 345
Arnold, Henry Harley: 175
Assad, Hafez al-: 324–325
Atcherly, D.E.W.: 161
Attacks on enemy air bases
        *See also* Air base defense; Aircraft
        destroyed on the ground
    British-French planning for: 63, 70, 302
    Churchill an early proponent of: 7
    force enemy aircraft to the rear: 19
    German planning for: 33–34, 48, 54
    Israeli planning for: 301–2, 306,
        310–11, 313, 339, 350
    Japanese planning for: 48
    Soviet planning for: 48
    Zeppelin bases: 6–7
Auchinleck, Claude: 142, 148, 150
Australian units
    Air Force aerial reconnaissance units:
        97, 109
    Air Force 453 (fighter) Squadron: 107
    Air Force P–40 fighter squadron: 239
    Army 7th Infantry Division: 239

Baker, Chauncey B.: 21
Balloon Wing, U.S. Army Air Service: 16
BARBAROSSA: 177, 181
Barrage balloons: 28
Barratt, Arthur: 70
Base Defense Battalions, USMC: 27, 220–21, 223, 225, 228–33
Battle of Britain: 53, 71, 76–92, 97, 109–11, 117, 123, 131, 135, 175, 343–44, 347, 351
Beckett, C.T.: 135
Belgium: 66–67, 69
Bomber Command, RAF: 45, 70, 77–78
Borner, Werner: 71
Bradley, Omar Nelson: 271
Brereton, Lewis Hyde: 149–50
British Army units
    Dorset Regiment: 84
    Eighth Army: 137, 140, 142, 147–49, 153, 173
    First Army: 160
    Long Range Desert Group: 151
    Queen's Own Royal West Regiment: 84
    Royal Malta Artillery: 128
    Special Air Service (SAS): 151
    7th Armoured Division: 174
    12th AA Brigade: 142–43, 148–49
    16th Heavy AA Regiment: 109
    34th AA Battalion: 84–85
    90th AA Regiment: 84
British Expeditionary Force (BEF): 3, 9, 66. *See also* Advanced Air Striking Force; Air Component, BEF
British forces fighting the Egyptians: 301–2, 306, 338, 350
Brooke-Popham, Robert: 96–97, 100–1, 111
Budenny, Semeon: 182–83
Buffa, Ernst: 199

Cable rockets: 144
Cambodia: 290
Camouflage of airfields
    American: 15, 17, 21, 28
    British: 84, 89, 91, 149, 167
    Egyptian: 321
    German: 156, 193
    Israeli: 317, 322
    Japanese: 234, 251
    North Korean: 269, 277
    North Vietnamese: 288
    Polish: 57, 91
    Soviet: 42, 180, 185–87, 201–2, 214
    in the World War: 11, 15, 17, 21, 344
Camouflage painting of aircraft bodies: 13, 83–84, 156, 193, 211
Canadian Army 109th Light AA Battery: 89

Cannon/guns, antiaircraft
    3-inch, American: 31–32
    3-inch, British: 7–9, 12, 43, 97, 101, 107–8, 133
    3.7-inch, British: 44, 82, 107, 109, 133, 142
    4.5-inch, British: 44, 82, 89, 133
    5-inch coast defense, USN: 27, 220
    6.5 mm, Japanese: 36
    7.7 mm, Japanese: 36
    12.5 mm, Soviet: 311
    14.7 mm, Soviet: 311
    20 mm, American: 31, 220
    20 mm, British: 48, 83, 163, 166–67
    20 mm, German: 34, 62, 192, 195, 198
    20 mm, Japanese: 36, 38, 251–52
    23 mm, Soviet: 294, 296, 303
    25 mm, French: 66
    25 mm, Japanese: 36, 38, 251
    37 mm, American, U.S. Army: 27, 31–32, 243
    37 mm, British: 41
    37 mm, British, pom-pom, Royal Navy: 7–8
    37 mm, German: 7, 34, 41, 62, 156, 195
    37 mm, Japanese: 252
    37 mm, Soviet: 205, 211, 269, 285, 296, 311, 322, 327
    37 mm, Swedish: 41
    40 mm, American (Bofors): 32, 162, 165, 220, 243
    40 mm, British (Bofors): 36, 43–44, 82–83, 85, 88–89, 97, 107, 109, 125, 131, 133–34, 143, 163, 174
    40 mm, Canadian (Bofors): 89
    40 mm, Dutch: 36
    40 mm, Israeli (Bofors): 322, 327
    40 mm, Japanese: 251
    40 mm, Swedish (Bofors): 43–44, 54
    50 mm, German: 7, 195
    57 mm, American: 31
    57 mm, Soviet: 281, 285, 290, 294, 296, 311, 322, 327
    65 mm, German: 7
    75 mm, French: 9–10, 12
    75 mm, Japanese: 36, 38, 252
    75 mm, Polish: 54
    76 mm, Soviet: 41
    77 mm, German: 9
    85 mm, Soviet: 41, 198, 205, 269, 281, 290
    88 mm, German (Flak 18): 34, 62, 156, 159, 170, 183, 192, 195, 202
    88 mm, Japanese, mobile: 36
    90 mm, American: 32, 220, 231, 243
    100 mm, Soviet: 281, 285

105 mm, German: 62
Putilov M1903 field guns (Russian): 9
Casey, Hugh J.: 245
Chain Home (CH): 44–45, 85, 92
Chain Home Low (CHL): 44
Chapman, Carleton V.: 15
Chennault, Claire L.: 24–25, 345
Chiang Kai-shek: 25
Churchill, Winston Spencer
    aware of *Lufwaffe* losses: 82
    endorses attacks on air bases: 7
    halts advance in Libya: 138
    opposes 1942 invasion of Europe: 159
    orders offensive into Libya: 144
    orders raids on Berlin: 90
    supports Tedder's control of tactical air forces: 142
CITADEL: 199, 202
Coastal Command, RAF: 45, 77, 78
Coast Artillery Corps (CAC), U.S. Army: 26, 31–32. *See also* United States Army units
Coastwatchers: 219, 222–23, 225, 231, 234–35
Commander-in-Chief, Pacific (CINCPAC), USN: 234, 293
Computers: 48
Concrete dibber bomb: 316, 350
Coningham, Arthur
    as commander of the Western Desert Air Force: 142, 176, 346
    loses aircraft transferred to Far East: 156
    on seizure and use of air bases: 163–64, 174
    uses information from radio intercepts: 150
    uses Landing Ground 125 in Libya: 151, 153
Conran, E.L.: 5
CRUSADER: 144, 148, 175

Dawson, G.G.: 141
Dayan, Moshe: 309–10, 313, 316, 325
Deane, John R.: 204, 206, 211
Decoy aircraft and airfields. *See* Dummy aircraft; Dummy airfields
Defence Teleprinter Network: 45
Deflection meters: 10
Desert Air Force. *See* Western Desert Air Force
Diem, Ngo Dinh: 278
Direction finding. *See* Radio direction finding
Dispersal of aircraft
    American: 207–8, 231, 241

British: 85, 89, 101, 109, 113, 117, 133, 147, 344
German: 156, 193
Japanese: 249, 251
North Korean: 269
North Vietnamese: 287–88, 291
Polish: 56
Soviet: 180, 185–86, 188, 203, 214–15
in the World War: 15
Dobbie, William G.S.: 95
Doolittle, James H.: 160, 163
Douhet, Giulio: 25
Doumenc, Joseph: 66
Dowding, Hugh C.T.: 43–44, 47, 77–78, 81–83, 91–92
Drone aircraft: 330
Dummy aircraft: 91, 187, 269, 311, 315, 345
Dummy airfields
    American: 15, 19, 21
    British: 84, 91, 128–29
    German: 13, 21
    Soviet: 187, 201, 348
    in World War II: 345
Dutch East Indies. *See* Netherlands East Indies

Eaker, Ira C.: 205
Eastern Air Command, RAF: 160–61, 167
Eastern Command, Strategic Air Forces, AAF: 206, 212
Eastern Front. *See* Soviet Union
Egyptian Armies: 324, 327
Egypt in the Middle East wars: 300–34, 337–42
Egypt in World War II: 112, 131, 138, 140–41, 144, 148–51, 154–55, 159, 165, 173–74, 346
Eisenhower, Dwight David: 163
Electronic countermeasure (ECM) pods: 323, 327, 330, 334
Electronic jamming: 288, 295, 297
Electronic warfare (EW) sites: 281, 283, 290
Endo, Saburo: 100, 108
Enigma: 81, 131, 170, 173, 175, 199
*Escadrilles Legeres de Defense*: 75
Eshkol, Levi: 309

Fahmi, Mohammed Ali: 320
Far East Air Forces, USAF: 267, 277
Far East Command (British): 96
Far East Command (U.S.): 267, 269
Far East Fleet, Royal Navy: 107
Fighter Command, AAF: 174
Fighter Command, RAF

airfield defense: 45, 82–85, 88–91
creation of: 44, 77
fighter squadrons: 45, 47, 76, 343–44
Filter Center: 78
ground command centers: 76, 78
HQ connected to Chain Home Sites:
45, 85, 92
Operational Research Section: 81
sector commands: 78, 81, 85
*Flakartillerie*: 33, 34, 62. *See also Luftwaffe*
units
FLAX: 173, 175
Fleet Air Arm, Royal Navy: 117, 124, 302.
*See also* Royal Naval Air Service
*Fliegerführer Afrika:* 154
Foulois, Benjamin D.: 16, 25
Fowler, Harold: 15
France in World War II: 62–63, 66, 70–76,
91–92, 346–47
FRANTIC: 204–5
French Armies: 66
French forces in Egypt and Israel: 301–2,
306, 338, 350
French forces in North Africa: 159–60
Froelich, Stefan: 150, 154
Fuze design: 9, 11, 47–48, 344

Gamelin, Maurice G.: 70
Gayler, Noel: 293
Geiger, Roy S.: 230–31, 233
General Headquarters Far East (British): 96
German Air Force. *See Luftwaffe*
German Air Service: 11–12
German Army units
Ninth Army: 185
Second Army: 189
Sixth Army: 189, 193, 195, 198
15th Panzer Division: 113
21st Panzer Division: 153
Goering, Hermann
attacks RAF fighter bases: 78
conserves paratroops: 132
disbelief of initial Soviet losses: 179
drops radar from target list: 85
switches targets: 82, 90, 92
Gorrell, Edgar S.: 15
Graziani, Rodolpho: 138
Greece: 132, 135, 138, 140–41, 166
Grice, Richard: 84, 89
Ground Control Intercept (GCI)
British: 44, 130, 143
Chinese: 281
German lack of: 170
Israeli: 334
Japanese: 38
North Vietnamese: 281, 290–91

Ground observers. *See also* Coastwatchers
in American air defense: 17, 21, 26, 29
in British AA Command: 83
British visual observation system: 12,
25, 45, 78, 96–97
civilian observer corps in Malaya: 97,
108
Eighth Army observer units: 143
in French air defense: 63
German observers: 12, 202
of the Japanese Army: 235, 261
in Netherlands India: 97
Soviet VVS observation system: 42,
197, 201
U.S.-Australian in Papua: 241
in USMC: 225
in V Fighter Command: 242, 247
Guadalcanal: 217, 219–23, 225, 228–35,
261, 347
Gun-laying radar
British: 38, 83, 125–27, 133, 140, 211
German Navy: 36
Gun Dish used by North Vietnam: 291
Japanese: 38, 252
Soviet: 42
used by North Korea: 275

Halder, Franz: 180
Halsey, William F.: 235
Harlinghausen, Martin: 169
Harriman, W. Averell: 204
Hartney, Harold E.: 19
Headquarters Middle East (British): 151
Height and range finding equipment: 58,
97, 109, 134
Henderson, Lofton: 220
Hepburn, A.J.: 27
Hickey, Doyle O.: 267
High level detection: 44. *See also* Chain
Home
Hitler, Adolf
attacks in western Europe: 53, 67
attacks Poland: 54
attacks the USSR: 177
creates independent *Luftwaffe*: 32
emphasizes close air support: 154
establishes *Luftwaffe* doctrine: 34
fails to take Malta: 170, 344
invades Greece: 138
orders offensive against Kursk salient:
199, 202
preempted from occupying Algeria and
Morocco: 160
reacts to raids on Berlin: 90
sends troops to Libya: 111
Hod, Mordechai: 309–311, 313, 316

Home Guard (British): 88
Horii, Tomitaro: 239
Hussein, King of Jordan: 309
Husseini el-, Haj Amin: 299

Identification Friend or Foe (IFF): 38, 81, 154, 243, 345
Independent Air Force, RFC: 21
Indian Army: 95, 106–7
Indian States Forces: 97
Infrared (thermal) detection: 42
Interwar period: 23–49, 344–47
Iron Hand: 288, 293
Itabana, Giichi: 257
Italian forces
    attacking Malta: 93, 111–13, 117, 122, 125, 129, 132, 134
    in Libya and Egypt: 137–38, 151, 153–56
    ship convoys: 131–32, 170, 173
    in Tunisia: 169–71, 173–75

Jackson, H.C.: 5
Jackson, William M.: 208
Jaehne, Heinz Joachim: 181
Japanese Air Forces
    air strength in New Guinea: 241
    failure of defense at Munda: 235
    losses at Guadalcanal: 233
Japanese units
    airfield battalion, defense operations: 233
    Fourth Air Army: 257
    Special Naval Landing Force: 219, 239
    Twenty-fifth Air Fleet (Navy): 219
    3rd Air Corps: 100
    3rd Air Group: 100, 108, 135
    7th Air Group: 135
    12th Air Group: 101
    18th Army: 256
    22nd Naval Air Flotilla: 100, 135
    47th Field AAA Battalion: 252
Jeschonnek, Hans: 33–34, 59, 202
Johnson, Lyndon Baines: 280

Kennedy, D.G.: 222
Kenney, George C.
    advocates low level attacks: 243–44
    airlifts troops to New Guinea: 239, 243, 348
    attacks Hollandia: 253, 256
    attacks Rabaul: 219

attacks Wewak: 252–53, 256–57
    constructs air bases: 346–47
    enlarges Port Moresby bases: 239, 241
    forced by weather to limit attacks: 252
    gets needed air defense: 246–47
    seizure and air support of bases: 245
    strategy of: 243–44, 260, 349
    supported by MacArthur: 245, 247, 346
Kesselring, Albert
    as C-inC, South: 122–23
    attacks Malta: 125, 132
    commander of German forces: 169
    fails to understand radar: 130
    relations with Rommel: 153–54
Kessler, Alfred A.: 206, 211
Khripin, Vasili V.: 40
King, Ernest J.: 219
Kirby, Maxwell: 18
Korean War: 265–78, 296, 349
Kursk battle: 199, 201–3, 212–13, 215
Kuter, Laurence S.: 175–76

Laos: 290
Laser guided bomb: 289–90, 292–93
Laskov, Haim: 300–1
Lavelle, John D.: 290
Lemnitzer, Lyman L.: 165, 348
Lepawsky, Albert: 206
Libya: 93, 111, 131–32, 138, 140–41, 144, 147–48, 151, 153–56, 174, 217, 346
Likes, David H.: 149
LINEBACKER: 290–91, 294–96, 350
Lloyd, Hugh P.: 113, 117, 123, 126, 131, 135
Local Defence Volunteers: 88
Loktionov, Alexandr: 40
Longmore, Arthur: 141
Long Range Bomber Force (Soviet DBA): 41, 204
Long Range Desert Group (British): 151
Long Range Navigation (LORAN): 245
Low Countries: 66–69, 91–92
Low level detection: 44–45. See also Chain Home Low
Lucknor, Georgy: 208
Luftwaffe
    organization: 33
    lack of experience among senior officers: 33
    doctrine: 33
    concept of base defense: 189
Luftwaffe units
    Fliegerkorps: II (2nd Flying Corps): 122, 132
    Fliegerkorps: VIII: 202
    Fliegerkorps X: 112, 122, 140

*Kampfgeschwader*: 55 (55th Bomber Wing): 207
*Kampfgeschwader*: 76: 169
*Kampfgruppe* 2 (2nd Bomber Group): 71
*Kampfgruppe* 4: 58
*Luftflotte* II (2nd Air Fleet): 70, 153
*Luftflotte* IV: 198
*Luftflotte* VI: 199
I/First Flak Corps: 198–99
1st Air Division (Parachute infantry): 202
7th Air Division: 67
9th Flak Division (Antiaircraft artillery): 195, 198
10th Flak Brigade: 199
12th Flak Division: 199
18th Flak Division: 199
19th Flak Division: 156, 159, 170
20th Flak Division: 170
129th Air Signal Battalion: 198

MacArthur, Douglas
    approves coordinated air defense: 247, 349
    attacked by Chinese: 270
    claims control of air in New Guinea: 257
    directs construction of air bases: 239, 346–47
    lands forces at Inchon: 269
    plans offensive to relieve Australia: 219, 255
    prohibits use of ground forces in Korea: 267
    refuses transfer of Engineers to Fifth Air Force: 245
    supports Kenney: 219, 245, 247, 346
MacDonnell, Dermott H.: 225, 228–29, 232–33
Machine guns, antiaircraft employment by troops: 9, 38, 54–55, 192, 269, 278
Machine guns, antiaircraft types
    Hotchkiss: 16
    Vickers: 71
    .30 caliber American: 221
    .30 caliber Lewis: 12, 83, 88
    .303 caliber Browning: 167
    .50 caliber American: 31–32, 162–63, 220–21, 243, 246
    6.5 mm Japanese: 36, 38
    7.62 mm Soviet: 41
    7.7 mm Japanese: 36, 38
    7.92 mm German: 34
    12.7 mm Soviet: 41
Machine guns in air base defense

American: 16–17, 21, 27, 31, 162–63
British: 12, 16, 71, 83–84, 88–89, 143–44, 163, 165, 167
German: 11, 34, 48, 192
Indian: 106
North Vietnamese: 291
Polish: 59
Soviet: 41, 187
MacKenzie, Hugh: 223
Mahmoud, Sidqi: 311, 315
Malaya: 93–111, 133–35, 217
Malta: 93, 110–35, 137, 156, 170, 174, 344, 348, 351
Malta Air Command, RAF: 163
Maltby, Paul: 110
Manchuria: 269–75, 278, 296–97
Marine Corps, U.S. (USMC) units
    Fighting Squadron 223 (VMF–223): 220
    Scout Bomber Squadron 232 (VMSB–232): 220
    1st Marine Air Wing: 220, 223, 228
    1st Marine Division: 219–20, 223
    3rd Defense Battalion: 220–21, 223, 225, 228–33
Marquat, William F.: 247
Marshall, George Catlett: 219
Mason, Paul: 222
Matador: 100
Mattison, Lewis C.: 228, 230, 232–33
Mediterranean Air Command (Allied): 163–64, 347
Medvedev, Roy A.: 182
Meir, Golda: 326, 339
Middle East Air Command (Allied): 163
Middle East Air Force (British): 141
Middle East wars: 299–342
Military Assistance Advisory Group (MAAG), Vietnam: 278
Minh, Ho Chi: 278–79
Missiles
    AGM–78 anti-radiation missile (ARM): 288–89
    AIM–9J (Sidewinder) air-to-air missile: 291–92
    anti-radar missiles: 291
    Egyptian surface-to-air missile (SAM) siting and deployment: 311, 321–25, 327–28, 330–31, 337, 342, 351
    FROG–7 ground-to-ground missile (Soviet): 334–35
    Hawk ground-to-air missile: 279, 317, 334
    Kelt air-to-ground missile (Soviet): 334
    missile hunter-killer groups (USAF/USN): 288, 293, 331

SA–2 SAM in Egypt: 311, 315, 321, 323–24, 339
SA–2 SAM in North Vietnam: 281, 283, 285–88, 290–91, 293–97
SA–2 SAM in Syria: 328, 330–31
SA–3 SAM in Egypt: 321–24
SA–6 SAM in Egypt and Syria: 324, 327–28, 330–31
SA–7 SAM in Egypt: 324
SAMs controlled by the Egyptian Air Defense Command: 320
Shrike air-to-ground ARM: 288, 330–31
Soviet Army missile units in Egypt: 322–23, 325
Mitchell, William: 24
Model, Walter: 185
Molotov, Vyacheslav M.: 204
Montgomery, Bernard Law: 153, 163, 175, 346
Morocco: 159–60, 169
Mueller, Hans: 207
Mussolini, Benito: 138
Mysing, August W.: 165

Nasser, Gamal Abdul
    anticipates preemptive Israeli attack: 310–11, 315
    blockades Gulf of Aqaba: 301, 309
    death of: 319
    obtains Soviet aircraft and instructors: 301, 322
    reaction to aircraft losses: 316, 320
    seizes Suez Canal: 301
    sends Air Force units to Yemen: 307
    threatens Israel: 309
Naval Research Laboratory, USN: 25, 223
Netherlands: 66–69
Netherlands East Indies: 97, 108–10, 217, 220. See also Netherlands New Guinea
Netherlands New Guinea: 236, 243, 245, 247–48, 253, 256–57
New Guinea campaign. See Solomon Islands and New Guinea
New Guinea Territory (Australian): 217, 219–20, 222, 231, 234, 236, 241, 245, 248–49, 252–53, 255–57, 261
New York Air Defense Sector (U.S. Army): 26
New Zealand forces: 96
Nikitin, A.V.: 204, 206, 211
Nixon, Richard Milhous: 293
Noll, W.A.: 228, 233
Northwest African Air Forces (NAAF), AAF: 163, 165, 169, 175
Novikov, Alexander A.: 196, 204

Observer Corps (British): 45, 78
Observers. See Coastwatchers; Ground observers
O'Connor, Richard N.: 138, 140
October War: 325–37, 339–42, 350–51
Office of Tactical Air Research and Survey, Fifth AF, USAF: 269
Old, Archie J.: 206, 208, 211
Oldfield, H.R.: 175
Operational Research Section, Fighter Command, RAF: 81

Pabst, Herbert: 181
Pacific Air Forces (PACAF), USAF: 279–80, 285, 287
Pacific Command (PACOM), U.S. Army: 288
Palestine Liberation Army (PLA): 307
Papua: 217, 236, 239, 241–49, 257
Parachute rockets: 144
Pargiter, R.B.: 167
Park, Keith R.: 78, 81, 89, 91
Parsons, C.A.: 88
Partridge, Earle E.: 26, 267–69, 271–72, 349
PAULA: 75
Pavel, Paul: 199
Peled, Binyamin
    ability of Israeli pilots under: 351
    attacks on Egyptian SAM sites: 337
    difficulty in overcoming Arab air defenses: 341–42
    effects of overestimation of AA weapons: 323
    inability to react to Arab attack: 327
    Israeli Air Force commander: 323
    on fear of SAMs: 324
    tactics against Syrian SAMs: 328
    tactics in airfield attack: 330–31
Pepper, Robert H.: 230–31
Perminov, Alexei R.: 206, 212
Pickert, Wolfgang: 195, 198–99
Pile, Frederick: 82–83, 97
Point defense: 24
Poland: 54–59, 62, 91–92, 180–82
Poltava Air Base (USSR): 204–8, 211–12, 214
Portal, Charles: 163, 167
Position finders: 11
Powder composition: 11
Project Red Baron: 286
Pulford, Conway W.: 95–96, 109–10
PVO Strany (Soviet): 213–14

Quartermaster Corps, U.S. Army: 21
Quesada, Elwood R.: 48

Rabin, Yitzhak: 316
Radar
    airborne: 130, 155, 288, 294
    American: 25–27, 29, 38, 161–62, 165,
        174, 225, 228–34, 242–43, 246–47,
        267–68, 288, 345, 348
    Australian: 242, 245–46
    British: 25–27, 38, 44–45, 63, 76, 78,
        81, 83, 85, 90, 345
    British at Malta: 113, 115, 117, 125–31
    British in Malaya and Singapore:
        96–97, 107–8, 111
    British in North Africa: 140–44,
        149–50, 160–62, 165, 167
    Chinese and North Korean: 270, 275,
        278, 281
    code names for radar (RDF and Chain
        Home): 44–45, 85, 92, 174
    Egyptian: 311, 314, 320–23, 325, 339
    experimental: 25–26, 345
    German: 25, 36, 85, 130, 154–55, 170,
        173, 201–2, 214, 345
    Israeli: 302, 327, 334
    Japanese: 25, 223, 249, 252, 255–56,
        261, 345
    *Luftwaffe* commanders
        misunderstanding of: 85, 130, 130n
    mobile: 141, 149, 165, 167, 202, 345
    North Vietnamese: 281, 283, 285, 288,
        290–91, 295
    Soviet: 25, 42, 201–2, 211, 214, 281,
        345
    United Nations: 273–74
Radar operator training
    American: 26–27, 165, 233, 243, 268,
        348–49
    British: 26, 81, 165, 233, 348
    Chinese and North Vietnamese: 281
Radar sets
    AN/TPS–1B (American): 267
    Freya (German): 170
    RUS–2 (Soviet): 42
    SCR–268 gun laying (American): 27,
        32, 221, 229
    SCR–270 search (American): 27, 29,
        221, 223–25, 228–29, 231
Radio, ground to air: 12, 113, 143, 201, 229
Radio direction finding (D/F): 12, 233–34
Radio direction finding (RDF): 44, 174
Radio interception stations
    provide information about air and sea
        transport to Tunisia: 131, 137, 170,
        173, 175
    provide information complementing
        that available from radar: 150

    warn of German and Italian air
        operations: 81–82, 88–89, 143,
        149–50, 161
    warn Soviets of Operation CITADEL: 199
    in the World War: 12, 17, 21
Read, Jack: 222–23
Reiman, Richard: 199
Remez, Aharon: 300
Renner, Joseph N.: 225
Rice, E.B.: 96, 101, 110–11
Ridgway, Matthew B.: 272
Rifle fire as AA defense
    by British troops: 9, 88, 106
    by German troops: 6, 192–93
    by Japanese troops: 38
    by North Vietnamese troops: 294
    by Soviet troops: 188
    in the World War: 6, 9, 11
Robertson, C.C.: 16
ROLLING THUNDER: 280, 289–91
Romanian Royal Air Force AA units: 198
Rommel, Erwin
    arrival in Libya: 138, 156
    captures Tobruk: 93, 148
    denied air support by fuel shortages:
        153
    distrusts Italian commanders: 154, 175
    under Italian command: 169
    *Luftwaffe* in Libya not responsible to:
        153–55, 175, 346
    message traffic intercepted: 175
    notes mobility of RAF: 173
    offensives into Egypt: 131–32, 138–39,
        148, 150, 155, 173
    reenforced through Tunisia: 169–70
    responsible for *Luftwaffe* losses in
        Africa: 175
    supply ships sunk: 117, 132
    tanks attack British air bases: 144
Roosevelt, Franklin Delano: 31
Royal Air Force, Egypt: 138
Royal Air Force (RAF) units
    No. 2 Armoured Car Company: 151
    Radio Field Interception Units: 143
    Royal Air Force Regiment: 137, 143–44,
        163, 166–67
    Searchlight Companies: 43
    Station Defence Force: 89
    Women's Auxiliary Air Force: 88
    Y-Service Teams: 131, 143, 150, 161,
        173, 175
    11 Group: 78, 90
    12 Group: 78
    13 Group: 78
    32 Squadron: 85, 88
    62 Squadron: 101
    79 Squadron: 88

211 Group: 142, 148, 150
242 Group: 165
262 Wing: 148
322 Fighter Wing: 167
610 Squadron: 85, 88
Royal Artillery: 348
Royal Flying Corps (RFC): 3, 5, 11–13
Royal Naval Air Service (RNAS): 6. *See also* Fleet Air Arm
Royal Navy (RN) ships
    HMS *Eagle*: 131
    HMS *Prince of Wales*: 107
    HMS *Repulse*: 107
    HMS *Welshman*: 127, 132
Rudel, Hans-Ulrich: 181
Rychagov, Pavel: 41, 180

Sadat, Anwar el-: 311, 315–16, 319, 324–27, 337
Sanctuaries
    air sorties from Chinese territory: 270–74, 278
    buffer zone in Vietnam along Chinese border: 281
    Chinese AA along the Yalu: 269–70
    Chinese air bases used by North Vietnam: 281, 287, 289–90, 295–96, 350
    for Communist air forces: 265
    Manchuria a base for North Koreans: 269, 274, 296–97
    Saudi bases used by Egypt: 306
    USAF and RAAF operating from bases in Thailand: 279, 292–93
    USAF operating from bases in Japan: 267, 272–73
Saville, Gordon R.: 25
Seabees (Construction Battalions), USN: 200–21
Searchlight Companies, RAF: 43
Searchlights
    American: 17, 21, 31–32, 221
    Belgian and Dutch: 91
    British: 12, 14, 43, 83, 97, 100, 162
    French: 91
    German: 156, 198
    Japanese: 101
    North Korean: 275
    Polish: 91
    Soviet: 42, 211
Shakurin, A.I.: 40
Sharon, Ariel: 302, 337
Sherman, William C.: 20, 24
Shipton, James A.: 14–17
Shrike antiradar missile
    U. S. use in Vietnam: 288

Israeli use in 1973: 330, 331
Signal Corps, U.S. Army
    experimental radar: 26, 345
    radar in the warning system: 29, 31, 161–62, 242, 247
    radar operators: 165
    radios in the warning system: 17
Singapore: 93–97, 100–1, 107–11, 133–35, 156, 217, 236, 348
Six-Day War: 306–19, 339, 350
Snesarev, A.E.: 40
Solomon Islands and New Guinea: 217–61, 346–48
Sound locators. *See* Sound ranging equipment
Sound ranging equipment, acoustic
    American: 21, 27, 32, 345
    French: 63
    Japanese: 38, 101
South African Air Force: 173
Soviet forces outside the USSR
    in Egypt: 322–25, 339
    in the Korean War: 272–74, 297
    in Syria: 328, 330
    in the Vietnam War: 281
Soviet Union: 177–215, 347–48
Spaatz, Carl A.: 164–65
Speidel, Wilhelm: 70
Stalin, Joseph V.
    and aviation: 40
    and Kursk (battle): 199
    approves American shuttle bombing: 204–05
    as military leader: 179–92
    influence on defensive tactics: 212–13
    purges, effects on Red Air Force: 40
    purges, effect on radar development: 42
    stresses offensive: 40
Stalingrad: 193, 195–98, 212
Strategic Air Command, USAF: 293–95, 349
Strategic Air Forces, AAF: 165, 206, 212
Strategic Direction Finder Station (USN): 233
Stratemeyer, George E.: 267, 269, 272, 349

Task Force 77, USN: 293
Tedder, Arthur
    attacks German airlift to Tunisia: 173, 175
    becomes commander of Mediterranean Air Command: 163
    coordinates air and ground operations: 137, 141–42, 149, 153, 155, 346
    favors attacks on air bases over ground support: 163

gains control of tactical air: 141–42
influences organization of U.S. Ninth
  Air Force: 150
locates fighter fields near bomber
  bases: 141
puts repair and maintenance under
  single commander: 141
stresses need for air base security:
  140–41, 144
uses airfield behind German lines: 151
uses intercepts of *Luftwaffe* message
  traffic: 150, 175
Teramoto, Kunachi: 257
Terrain following radar (TFR): 294
Territorial Army (British): 82
Thailand: 93–94, 100–1, 106–7, 265, 279,
  292–94
Thant, U: 309
Timoshenko, Semeon Kostantinovich:
  182–83
Tizard, Henry: 44
Tolkovsky, Dan: 300–1
TORCH: 160, 174–75
Townsend, Peter: 76
Tracking and gun control systems: 48
Trenchard, Hugh M.: 11, 21
Tsuji, Masanobu: 100
Tubisin, Sgt.: 208
Tunisia: 130, 159–60, 162, 165, 167, 169–71,
  173–75, 344

ULTRA
  code name for Enigma decrypts: 81
  information passed to other Allied
    commands: 131, 149–50, 161, 199
  provides strategic and order of battle
    intelligence: 81–82, 149–50
  used in conjunction with other
    intelligence: 131
  used to attack German-Italian sea and
    air convoys: 131, 137, 153, 170,
    173, 175
Underground hangers and shops
  Egyptian: 320–21
  Israeli: 317
  at Malta: 115, 117, 133, 135
  North Korean: 19, 269
  North Vietnamese: 291, 298
  planning for and use of: 19
United Nations Emergency Force (UNEF):
  306, 309
United States Air Force (USAF) units
  Seventh Air Force: 290, 293
  4th Fighter-Interceptor Wing: 272–73
  8th Tactical Fighter Wing: 292
  307th Strategic Wing: 294

474th Tactical Fighter Wing: 293
620th Aircraft Warning and Control
  Squadron: 267
6132nd Tactical Air Control Group:
  267–68
United States Army Air Forces (AAF) units
  Eighth Air Force: 206–8
  Fifteenth Air Force: 205–6
  Fifth Air Force: 242, 245, 255–56, 267,
    269, 271–72, 275, 349
  Ninth Air Force: 149–50
  Twelfth Air Force: 160
  V Bomber Command: 243
  V Fighter Command: 242–43
  IX Fighter Command: 48
  XII Fighter Command: 162
  1st Air Defense Wing: 169
  2nd Air Defense Wing: 169
  3rd Air Defense Wing: 165, 169
  14th Fighter Group: 160
  33rd Fighter Group: 160
  57th Fighter Group: 150
  67th Fighter Squadron: 220–21
  85th Air Defense Wing: 247
United States Army Air Service units
  Balloon Wing: 16
  1st Air Depot: 17
  1st Observation Group: 17
  1st Pursuit Group: 19
  5th Pursuit Group: 18
  17th Aero Squadron: 13–14
  94th Squadron: 18
United States Army units
  Eighth Army: 272
  First Corps: 21
  2nd AA Machinegun Battalion: 16
  10th AA Sector: 16–17
  14th Antiaircraft Command: 247
  34th Coast Artillery Brigade: 165
  101st Coast Artillery Battalion (AW):
    243
  104th Coast Artillery Battalion (AW):
    243
  128th Infantry Regiment: 239
  164th Infantry Regiment: 232
  200th Coast Artillery (AA) Regiment:
    31
  211th Coast Artillery Battalion (AW):
    243
  412th Signal Company: 162
  565th Signal Air Warning Battalion:
    242
  583rd Signal Air Warning Battalion:
    242, 247
  694th Signal Air Warning Company:
    242
  709th AA Machinegun Battery: 243

745th Coast Artillery Battalion (AA): 243
United States Marine Corps. *See* Marine Corps, U.S.
United States Navy (USN) ships
USS *Chenango*: 160
USS *Ranger*: 160
USS *Wasp*: 130–31

Vandegrift, Alexander A.: 219
Vietnam War: 265, 278–98, 349–50
von Paulus, Friedrich: 195
von Waldau, Otto Hoffman: 154–55

Walsh, Robert L.: 212
Warning systems. *See also* Ground observers, Coastwatchers
American: 17, 21, 25, 31, 161–62, 165, 169, 174–75, 349
American, in Korea: 267–68
American, in SWPA: 221–23, 225, 228–34, 241–43, 245–48, 257
American, in Thailand: 293
British: 25, 44–45, 48–49, 76–78, 81–82, 345, 347
British, in Malaya: 96–97, 101, 108, 111
British, in North Africa: 140, 142–43, 149–50, 160–61, 165, 174
Chinese-North Vietnamese: 281, 283, 285–86, 290–91, 297
Egyptian: 311, 320–21
French: 63, 66
German: 34–35, 154–55, 170, 198–99, 201–2
Japanese: 249, 252, 254, 256, 261
at Malta: 117, 126, 129–30
Polish: 55–57
Soviet: 42, 201, 211
War of Attrition: 319–25, 339
Wavell, Archibald: 138
Weizman, Ezer: 309–11, 317, 319–20, 324
Welsh, William A.M.: 160, 163, 176
Western Desert Air Force (RAF): 141–42, 149, 301
Western Desert campaign: 138–53. *See also* Egypt in World War II; Libya; Rommel, Erwin
Western Desert Force: 138
Wheeler, C.B.: 16
Whitehead, Ennis C.: 242, 245–47, 252
Whitney, Orville L.: 16
Wild Weasel: 288
Wilkinson, Norman: 91
Wireless. *See* Radio
Women's Auxiliary Air Force (RAF): 88
Woods: 233
World War I: 3–7, 9–22, 343–44

Yadin, Yigal: 300
Yamashita, Tomoyuki: 100
Yariv, Aharon: 323
Y-Service Teams (RAF): 131, 143, 150, 161, 173, 175

Zakharov, M.V.: 180
Zeppelin, Ferdinand: 7